The Life and Times of
Richard Castro

by Richard Gould

Colorado History
ISSN 1091-7438

Number 14
2007

COLORADO HISTORICAL SOCIETY

Research and Publications Office
Modupe Labode and Steve Grinstead, *directors*

Managing Editor
Steve Grinstead

Editing and Layout
Paul Malkoski

Cover Design
Susan Romansky

This publication is made possible in part by the Volunteers of the
Colorado Historical Society.

The Colorado Historical Society publishes *Colorado History* to provide a flexible scholarly forum for well-written, documented manuscripts on the history of Colorado and the Rocky Mountain West. Its twofold structure is designed to accommodate article-length manuscripts in the traditional journal style and longer, book-length works which appear as monographs within the series. Monographs and special thematic issues are individually indexed; other volumes are indexed every five years. The publications of the Society generally follow the principles and conventions of the *Chicago Manual of Style,* and an author's guide is available on request. Manuscripts and letters should be addressed to: Research and Publications Office, Colorado Historical Society, 1300 Broadway, Denver, CO 80203. The Society disclaims responsibility for statements of fact or opinion made by contributors.

http://www.coloradohistory.org/

contents

Acknowledgments

A good deal of the research for this book stemmed from personal interviews with those whose lives intersected with Rich Castro's. I am indebted to the many people who opened their homes, gave generously of their time, and occasionally provided a beer.

I am indebted especially to Virginia Castro, who spent hours providing me with files, photographs, ideas, and memories. Her help and support were essential to the completion of the book.

I am thankful, too, for the honesty and candor, the openness and willingness of a great many people to share what were sometimes difficult memories.

Waldo Benavidez supplied me with a wealth of material and insight into the development of the West Side Coalition. So, too, did Celina Benavidez and Cecilia Garcia, whose interviews were rich in detail. Adolfo Gomez, Manuel Martinez, Craig Hart, Jerry Garcia, Jack Lang y Marquez, and the Rev. Don Schierling also provided valuable information about that eventful period in Castro's life.

Those who grew up with Castro and spent time with him at Annunciation High School were tremendously helpful in providing background. I am grateful to Ken Maestas, Andy Lovato, Anthony Lopez, Eloy Mares, and Bobby Federico for their vivid descriptions of Castro's youthful years. Levi Beall, Ricardo Veladez, Emmanuel Martinez, Joe Sandoval, Jack Galvin, Dave Smith, and Ed Byorick helped to give me a broader sense of what the East Side was like in the 1950s and early 1960s. Likewise, Lupe Herrera gave me an excellent sketch of the West Side.

Rich's dad, Archie Castro; his aunt, Rose Ann Sanchez; Eileen Bankson; Gaspar Castro; Everett Chavez; and Lena Starr were invaluable in helping me tell the story of Castro's family. Equally valuable were interviews with Normando Pacheco, Roger Medina, Dr. David Sandoval, John and Lori Helms, Dr. Kenneth Phillips, Alberta Liebert, and Alfredo and Juanita Herrera, who shared reminiscences of Castro's college years.

I sat for several fascinating hours with Lyle Kyle, who offered me a nice crash course on the State Legislature. In addition, Rep. Ruben Valdez, Senator Paul Sandoval, Rep. Don Sandoval, Rep. Wayne Knox, and Pete Reyes all shared their inside knowledge of state politics and the workings of the General Assembly. Nonda Paarlberg assisted me with some excellent research on Castro's first election.

Tom Gougeon, Vickie Calvillo, Steve Newman, and Brenda Tolliver provided excellent background on the Peña administration. I am thankful that Mayor Federico Peña took time out of an incredibly busy schedule at the Department of Energy to grant me an interview. I am indebted also to Governor Richard Lamm, who was extremely generous with his time and very open with his answers to my queries.

Paul Malkoski did a wonderful job at the Colorado Historical Society with editing, and Steve Grinstead's supervision of the project is also greatly appreciated. A special thanks must go to José Aguayo, founder of the Museo de las Americas, whose support was instrumental in the publication of the book.

This project started innocently enough in Dr. Tom Noel's "History of the Southwest" class at the University of Colorado at Denver. I have Tom to thank for getting me started on this endeavor as well as for the valuable feedback he provided when he read sections of the manuscript early on. In addition, Professor Michael Ducey at UCD provided some thoughtful guidance concerning the Chicano experience in America.

Most of all, I am grateful to my wife, Susan, and my kids, Sam and Sarah, who tolerated long periods of temporary insanity while I completed the manuscript. Thank you all.

Richard Gould, 2007

prologue

A story from Denver's West Side goes like this. Tony Gutiérrez, ten years old, walks down to the corner grocery store to buy a bottle of milk. His mom had given him a dollar bill and a set of specific instructions: Return home with the milk and exactly 75¢ change. A large man in a white apron takes the wrinkled dollar bill and returns some coins. The boy looks down, counts out 65¢, and hesitates. Then he remembers his mother's words, gathers his courage and speaks up: "You cheated me." Towering over the little boy, the grocer replies gruffly and sends the kid scrambling home.

On the inside young Tony feels good. He stood up for his mom; he tried to do what his mom told him to. To his surprise, Mrs. Gutiérrez sees things differently. Upon hearing his version of the story, she grabs Tony roughly and beats him till he screams for mercy.

It is not the physical pain, however, that Tony Gutiérrez remembers; that is just a fleeting thing. What hurts is on the inside. After all, his only crime was standing up for his mother. From this day on, an invisible canyon takes shape in the depths of Gutiérrez's soul, separating mother from son. He stands on the far side, a lost boy, hurt and alone, unable to reach out to his mother on the other edge of the chasm. For years he remains sullen, uncommunicative. In fact, a whole generation passes before Tony Gutiérrez is ready to cross back over the canyon; he is well into middle age when he looks back on that beating and finally begins to understand. In her own instinctual way, Mrs. Gutiérrez was trying to protect her little boy, to convey to him the most important message of her generation: Young Mexicans don't talk back to white authority figures. In her mind, Tony's act of defiance was the first step on a path leading inexorably to the maximum security wing in Cañon City. In her mind, the only thing that stood between Tony Gutiérrez and a bleak prison cell was a good whipping administered by a loving mother. She was merely doing the best she could to teach her son the realities of America and the realities of Denver's West Side in the 1950s. As he approached his fortieth birthday, Tony Gutiérrez realized this truth; he forgave his mother for what she had done many years before.[1]

FOR DECADES DENVER'S WEST SIDE HAS been the kind of inner-city neighborhood held tightly together by the traditions of large extended families. It was a place where cousins and aunts and grandparents provided a network of support for the children, who radiated great, animated waves of energy. When West Side natives remember their past, they remember first their family.

There has always been poverty here, but not of the suffocating East Coast variety. The sunlight streams down three hundred days a year, unbroken by the looming walls of tenement housing. Even the housing projects near Lincoln Park climbed only three stories above the ground until they were razed in 1996. Residents have tended to live not in congested apartments rising up from the asphalt, but rather in single-family dwellings— small brick or stucco homes, bordered by tiny fenced-in yards, where kids could play.

The poverty here is of the variety that reflects the expansiveness and open space of its western surroundings. Even from behind the barbed-wire fences along the railroad yards, the panoramic view to the west is breathtaking. Mount Evans rises 14,000 feet above the sea, and in the distance— visible from the sandboxes and jungle gyms of the Projects—lay Grays Peak and Engelmann Peak, snowcapped for ten months out of the year.

It was Germans who first came to the West Side, dominating the neighborhood with their breweries and flour mills. Following in turn came the Irish to work on the Union Pacific, and the Jews, who settled below the bridge on West Colfax.

With the coming of the First World War came also the beginnings of a great northward migration, a wave of rural migrants who left their farms and mining camps in southern Colorado. They called themselves "*manitos*," the little brothers—homegrown Americans who inhabited the mountain towns of New Mexico for centuries and then trickled into the San Luis Valley in southern Colorado. The flavor of the neighborhood began to reflect the flavor of the new immigrant mix. The aroma of chili peppers cooked over West Side stoves drifted up and mingled with the scent of German sausage and the pungent smells from nearby breweries.

Today the memories of native Westsiders are torn in conflicting directions. They remember the strength and passion of their families, the spirit of community among neighbors, and the binding presence of the Catholic

Church. Even so, when Westsiders reminisce, their memories, like those of Tony Gutiérrez, often turn to the hard times.

Growing up a generation after Gutiérrez, city planner Lupe Herrera remembers, for example, the lunch line at Baker Junior High, which she attended in the early 1970s. "You learn to be tough," said Herrera. "If you allow kids to crowd in at lunch and cut in line, it shows you're weak. I remember defending that to a T. 'No, you're *not* gonna crowd in. You're *not* gonna pick on me.' You act tough. You have this tough attitude. Your face is tough. Your body has this tough stance—'No, you're *not* gonna crowd me.' But you don't say it; you don't do it with words. It's posture. It's body language. It's stance. Of course I was just bluffing. I mean, I played the tough role, but I was really bluffing.

"I defended a teacher once, a substitute teacher. I was sitting in front of the class and this kid walked in as high as could be. I mean, you could see his eyes were all red. He pulled a knife in front of the teacher and I said to him, 'We don't need this stuff in class.' He came over and put the knife right in front of my face. I didn't pull it away; I didn't do anything. I just stared him down. Everything was eye contact. What I would have done if he had done anything, I don't know. But it worked, and to this day I thank God he walked away. I remember my adrenaline being really high and shaking and running home and telling my mom at a hundred miles an hour about this thing that happened at school. Neighbors who were listening were saying, 'You were really stupid, Lupe. Next time, you let him knife that teacher. Better her on the line than you. She can leave the inner city, but you gotta live here and sleep here and survive here.' It was a cruddy attitude and even then I didn't really buy it, but I did go to bed that night saying, 'Yeah, Lupe, you were really stupid.' And, yes, I was scared. I was scared.

"I remember looking through a yearbook from Fairmont Elementary School with two guys who went to school with me all the way through West High, where we all graduated. I remember saying to them, 'God, very few of us made it.' I mean, it was a handful. I remember girls getting pregnant in the sixth or seventh grade and not hearing about them after that. People would say, 'Well, what happened to Teresa?' or 'What happened to Frankie?' Life was making them very tough, and one of the guys I graduated with wrote in my yearbook, 'You were right, Lupe. Very few of us made it.'"[2]

The Neighborhood

Denver's West Side rises up from "the bottoms" along the banks of the South Platte River, spills over into the old Burnham railroad yards of the Southern Pacific, then stretches eastward through residential avenues to

Broadway. The names of the streets are American Indian names—Acoma, Bannock, and Kalamath.

Divided into two neighborhoods, the West Side embraces Baker on the south, which runs to Alameda Boulevard and Lincoln Park on the north. As late as the 1960s, Baker stood in the shadow of two gigantic factories, Gates Rubber and Samsonite Luggage. Between them they employed an army of five thousand workers tending their molding and extrusion machines and their endlessly churning assembly lines.

Lincoln Park, often referred to as "La Alma" (The Soul). Here, the West Side's northern boundary at Colfax Avenue blends into downtown and the urban college campus at Auraria. Like Baker, Lincoln Park is dotted with industry. Barbed-wire fences separate residential backyards from small plants and warehouses. Viaducts arch over the railroad yards, looming above blocks and blocks of housing.

As more rural families abandoned southern Colorado towns like Walsenburg and Antonito, as migrant workers left the beet fields of Adams County and Weld County to try their luck in the city, the West Side grew increasingly Hispanic. The 1970 census figures showed that Hispanics represented over 60 percent of the neighborhood.[3]

In that same year, the Denver Planning Board ranked seventy neighborhoods in the city according to a variety of indicators designed to determine quality of life. A rank of one indicated that a neighborhood possessed the best set of conditions in the city; a rank of 70 denoted the worst. These were the findings for Lincoln Park:[4]

1970 Lincoln Park Quality-of-Life Indicators

Family Income	68
Housing Value	68
Families Receiving Welfare	68
Years of Schooling	68
Class I Crimes	65
Overcrowding	68
Unemployment	53

These numbers tell their own story of the West Side. They conjure up a picture of inner-city life—tough, impoverished, focused on the struggle for survival.

The statistics, however, hide another story. In the mid-1960s some residents of the West Side self-consciously began to shape the destiny of their neighborhood. They left behind them the role of spectators of history and assumed instead their places as actors on the historical stage. What happened on the West Side, of course, was part of a much larger picture—a cultural and political renaissance that took root in a hundred different forms in a hundred different barrios across the Southwest.

The Chicano Movement

As it came to life on Denver's West Side, the Chicano Movement gave rise to soaring hopes and newfound pride, to dynamic changes in consciousness, and sometimes to jealousies and bitter infighting. In the aftermath of this "Movimiento"—this Chicano Renaissance—children of Westsiders would grow up in a world radically different from that of their parents.

The Movement also gave rise to a new leadership. Among those who emerged from the turbulent activity of the era was Richard Castro, a social worker and youthful reformer destined to gain statewide prominence. The memory of Castro is celebrated today across the city in murals and busts, in museum exhibits, in the names of schools, community centers, and municipal buildings.[5] He was not one of those legendary giants whose actions, with a single stroke, changed the course of history. He was, instead, among a handful of key players each of whom left a more modest, though quite perceptible, mark on the city.

But Castro's journey through three decades of history placed him repeatedly on the frontlines of social change. In the 1960s and early '70s, when the streets were center stage for the Movement, Rich Castro could be found in the midst of the action. He was beaten by police in Curtis Park. He was shot in a political dispute on the sidewalk along Santa Fe Drive. His home was the target of a bombing attempt. He helped form one of the most spirited community organizations in town during the heady days of the War on Poverty.

In later years, when the Movement was busy consolidating its gains, Castro spent ten years in the State Capitol as a representative of several inner-city neighborhoods. When the Movement flexed its muscles in the 1980s and helped elect the first Hispanic mayor of Denver, Castro served under Federico Peña as director of the city's Commission on Human Rights and Community Relations.

In twenty-five years of political turmoil, Castro's politics stayed relatively consistent. He remained—through wild fluctuations in the political climate—a fiercely loyal Democrat, committed to the gradual reform advocated by the left wing of his party. Castro's death at age forty-four in 1991, left a gaping hole in the leadership of the Chicano community. Thus, in illustrating the contours of Castro's life, we also get a clearer vision of the backdrop of those eventful years that reshaped the Mexican-American community in Colorado and changed it forever. Castro's life provides a window through which we can see the unfolding of a remarkable social movement.

Emerging Patterns

In an examination of Castro's life and the Movement that nurtured him, several themes crop up and demand attention with particular insistence.

Reflected in Castro's tale is the story of the extraordinary rise of a Hispanic middle class that is evident today from Arvada in the northwest corner of Denver, to Littleton on the south. We can find at the same time the stubborn persistence of poverty where the ideals of the reform movement collided with the realities of the 1980s and '90s.

There are relevant lessons to be drawn from the internal feuding that held the Movement in its grip for a period during the 1970s. Though layered with multiple causes from funding to personality clashes, the feud manifested itself largely through a heated struggle between reform and revolutionary factions within the Movement. Engulfed in their ideological battles, each side failed to see that the other complemented its respective path. Reformers and revolutionaries proved in the end to be interdependent, each helping to create an environment in which the other thrived.

It was the militants who challenged traditional racist norms with such urgency and unrelenting pressure that a reluctant society yielded and felt ultimately compelled to eliminate the most naked forms of injustice. Without the existence, however, of a more moderate group advocating gradual reform, the swiftly moving wave of militants would have quickly been isolated, left dangling on the political margins and easily cut off. Despite their mutual dependence, the two factions—liberal reformers and militant revolutionaries—focused on their areas of rivalry and turned on each other with a vengeance. Identifying their next-door neighbors as the primary enemy, they expended precious energy on infighting until both factions bogged down in a slippery marsh, lost their vitality, and temporarily came to a halt.

Castro's story illustrates a third prominent theme: the unique nature of the Mexican-American experience in the United States. The existence of an Indo-Hispanic population in the Southwest for four hundred years distinguishes Mexicans from all other ethnic groups in America. Though they were not indigenous themselves, their roots lay intermingled with indigenous cultures and they were native to the American Southwest long before their Anglo rivals happened onto the scene.

Though not an immigrant culture, the long entrenched communities later received a steady immigrant stream from Mexico. Thus, the Mexican-American communities in Texas and California, in New Mexico and Colorado retained a unique character firmly rooted in American soil, yet nurtured by influences from across the border. The Anglo mainstream tended to simplify this complex process and see Mexicans in the United States as just one more immigrant group. It was an attitude that relegated Mexican

Americans to a sort of homelessness: "foreigners in their native land."[6]

Castro's own life story, when combined with the political passions he pursued, stands as a repudiation of this flawed perception. His search for a Chicano identity typifies the search of an entire generation of Mexican Americans trying to find a new place for themselves in the American landscape.

This search set Castro's generation on a nationalist path; and herein lies a fourth theme that surfaced continually in Castro's life: how to navigate a political course encompassing a benign form of nationalism—one that avoids falling into hatred and separatism on the one hand, or total submersion into mainstream culture on the other.

From our vantage point at the beginning of the twenty-first century we find ourselves particularly sensitive to the hazards of this journey. We have seen the Balkans, former territories within the Soviet Union, and regions of the Middle East descend into murderous scenarios of unrestrained nationalism. We have seen simultaneously the rise of a global economy that seems intent on swallowing up the diverse cultures of the world, creating in its wake a homogenized monoculture—a "McWorld"—where every place looks the same. The attempt to blend nationalist sentiment with respect for universal human rights reminds us of Odysseus's dilemma in the Greek legend of Scylla and Charybdis—two sea monsters who guarded the waters on Odysseus's path.

The dog-headed monster, Scylla, lurking on the rocks adjacent to the sea may well represent the worst aspects of extreme nationalism: isolated, distrustful, hateful, xenophobic, and prone to lash out violently. On the other side of the channel is the whirlpool Charybdis, representing the worst of mainstream culture: smug, powerful, bland, intolerant, insisting on uniformity, prone also to lash out in repressive violence. The twenty-first-century dilemma is how to journey through the straits without being destroyed by nationalist hatred on the one hand or by loss of identity on the other. There is much in Castro's life that reflects a search for a benign form of nationalism that retains the richness of a unique culture while simultaneously teaching universal respect for all cultures.

i

urban campus

The foundation of Castro's politics took form in the cauldron of radical campus activism in the 1960s. A small urban college adjoining the West Side barrio, Metropolitan State College of Denver was barely two years old when Castro enrolled in 1967 as a sociology major. In those days Metro rented seven office buildings in downtown Denver and held its classes wherever it could secure a room in one of twenty-seven facilities scattered across town.

Describing this hodgepodge of offices and classrooms, *Denver Post* columnist Olga Curtis labeled Metro the "invisible college." "The only campus Metro has," she wrote, "is the streets and alleys of Denver."[1]

Educators saw in Metro a new trend for higher education: "the urban oriented, extroverted college,"[2] because it actively sought out a relationship with the city, rather than retreating into the seclusion of academia. A major component was to absorb lower-income kids who, in previous generations, would not have dreamed of attending college. A decade before, those same kids had been needed on America's assembly lines; now in the 1960s, the era of well-paying jobs in the industrial sector was ending. The times demanded a new type of college to train students for the rapidly expanding service and white-collar sectors of the economy.

Young people from inner-city neighborhoods, attracted by open-enrollment policies and low tuition costs, began migrating to Metro State in significant numbers. In those early years, 10 percent of Metro's student body was Hispanic.[3] They were working-class kids. Their fathers had worked on construction sites as hod carriers or as meat cutters in the boning rooms on Packinghouse Road. Some of their parents had topped sugar beets in the sun-baked fields of northern Colorado. Some had traveled the complete migrant circuit from southern Texas to orchards in the Midwest. Rich Castro's dad had spent a lifetime at Eaton Metal—an industrial tank fabricating factory—near the Elyria section of East Denver; his mom made cardboard boxes for Russell Stover Candy.[4]

These were the kids who formed the basis for the rapid rise of Denver's Hispanic middle class. They were the first of their family to go to college. Invariably high school counselors had advised them to get a trade or enlist in the military; college was not for them.[5] Invariably, when they arrived at Metro, their path was unfamiliar; they did not quite belong. It was natural that they banded together for comfort and mutual support.

Many of them, including Castro, had grown up barely aware of the swamp of racial discrimination that had gripped the country in the first half of the twentieth century. They had grown up poor and struggling in predominantly Mexican-American neighborhoods, but for many, the links between their family's individual struggles and the long national history of discrimination were all but invisible. Indeed, many had even been unaware of their own poverty. A common refrain heard among Castro's friends was: "We didn't even know we were poor."[6]

Awakenings

In the turbulence of the 1960s, however, they were swiftly beginning to see the bigger picture. Castro had spent his childhood years on the East Side, a poor industrial neighborhood where family and church had, nevertheless, offered a certain degree of stability. A couple of years out of high school, Castro's old buddies began gravitating toward the Metro campus and sharing their stories. More often than not, their recent personal experiences had exposed them to harsher realities.

Anthony Lopez, for example, hadn't given racial prejudice a passing thought during his high school years with Castro on the East Side. Then came military service in the Navy. People there called him "beaner" to his face. A promotion required the recommendation of the chief petty officer; for Lopez it never came. "You knew," said Lopez, "that you were as good as or better than the people being recommended; in fact, you were doing their job most of time. It's funny; the two people recommended for E5 didn't pass the test. Once, while my chief was on leave, I recommended myself to take the next step. I went and took the E5 test and passed it. When the chief petty officer got back, he was really upset and was going to try to keep me from getting the E5 stripe. I just kind of laughed at him and said, 'Don't worry about it; I'm not going take it anyway.'" To accept the promotion, Lopez would have had to extend his service thirty days. "I told him I would not extend a day in the service."[7] By the time Lopez arrived at Metro, his patience for accepting inferior treatment had worn thin.

Andy Lovato, likewise, had grown up with Castro and had never felt firsthand the sting of racial prejudice. A year at Trinidad State Junior College and a semester at Metro changed the whole picture. Lovato, a big man with an athletic bearing, remembers drinking beer at Metro's most popular watering hole, the White Mule, and being called a "fat Santa Ana" by an Anglo student. He recalls the epithet as a turning point in his consciousness of racial attitudes in the United States.[8]

The mood among many Vietnam veterans was more volatile. Normando Pacheco, for instance—another of Castro's boyhood friends—returned from the war acutely aware of the disproportionate numbers of Mexican Americans killed in the jungles of Southeast Asia.[9] One study found that Chicanos represented an astounding 25.9 percent of Colorado's Vietnam casualties from 1961 to 1967.[10] Pacheco came back angry, ready to fight, and open to revolutionary ideas.

As for Castro himself, he had spent a sobering and thoughtful year studying for the priesthood at St. Thomas Seminary in South Denver where, after years of serving as an obedient altar boy, he began to question favoritism—racial and economic—within the Catholic Church.[11] "We're not sheep!" he would later frequently assert to indicate his belief in a more democratic church.[12] It was time, he thought, for the pastor and the "flock" to develop a new relationship.

These sobering experiences provided the framework through which Castro and his friends perceived the tumultuous climate of the '60s. While simultaneously losing their own innocence, they also watched African-American activists seize the attention of the entire nation, and they were profoundly affected. They watched Martin Luther King on television insisting that centuries-old customs be swept away. They watched the Black Panthers calling for global revolution and the largely white Students for a Democratic Society demanding that the power structure of the university be turned upside down. They had seen the senselessness of the Vietnam War up close, and they had watched as the antiwar movement increased its influence in quantum leaps.

The Four Horsemen of Chicano History

Perhaps closer to their hearts, they watched intently as four Chicano leaders—labeled by some historians as "The Four Horsemen"—gained national attention during the late 1960s.[13] Cesar Chavez, gentle and soft-spoken, had organized half the nation in support of the most ill-treated workers in America. His was the voice of the rural poor—the grape pickers and migrant laborers. Reies Tijerina roused villagers in New Mexico to take back the land he claimed was stolen from them in the years after the Mexican War. His Alianza Federal de Mercedes (Federal Alliance of Land Grants) became the voice for radical land reform in the Southwest. José Angel Gutierrez had triumphed over blatant segregation in a small Texas town and in the process created an independent political force: the Raza Unida Party.

In Denver, however, the undisputed leader of discontented young Chicanos was Corky Gonzales. Chávez, Tijerina, and Gutiérrez had built up their bases in the countryside—in small agricultural towns close to the land. But by the 1960s, 80 percent of Mexican Americans were urban, inhabiting the central cores of Los Angeles, Denver, San Antonio, and Phoenix.[14] Corky was a man of the city, a boxer, a former contender for the world featherweight title, and an inspired poet.[15] He grew up on Denver's East Side, a local hero, and in the late 1960s young men and women flocked to his organization, the Crusade for Justice.

These calls for justice and social change by the Four Horsemen proved irresistible to Richard Castro and his peers. Some three hundred Mexican-American students attended Metropolitan State College in Denver during the late 1960s, and nearly all of them joined the group of student activists known as UMAS—the United Mexican American Students.

Beginning at UCLA in 1968, UMAS swept rapidly through the Southwest, springing up overnight on campuses from California to Colorado.[16] A bold statement by the founders of UMAS in Boulder reflects some of the spirit of the times: "In 1968 the University community found itself ill-equipped to psychologically and professionally deal with the social and educational needs of Mexican Americans. From its inception to the present, the University was established as a perpetual profit-making entity to meet the professional needs of the larger society. Therefore, only the sons and daughters of affluent members of the larger society could afford and benefit from higher education."[17]

Thus, in the confrontational atmosphere of the times, UMAS arose to take on the two overriding issues of the new generation of Chicano students. The first was to increase their numbers at the college level. They sought to open doors by setting up recruitment programs, acquiring scholarships, and establishing college admissions policies more open to minority communities.[18] Upon their arrival on campus, however, this new generation searched for avenues to understand their own Mexican-American history and culture; at most universities they found, instead, a dead end or a giant void. Thus arose the second issue: the sometimes bitter struggle to

create Chicano Studies programs designed to draw to the surface historical themes that had long been ignored in the academic world.[19]

UMAS at Metro

Of the three hundred UMAS members at Metro, only about sixty participated actively, and about twenty of these formed a core of leadership within
the organization.[20] Richard Castro was one of the key members within the
leadership core. He was twenty-one years old, a transfer student first from
St. Thomas Seminary, then from Trinidad State Junior College in southern
Colorado.

In appearance, Castro stood out conspicuously from his more flamboyant peers in UMAS.[21] Prevailing fashion tended toward jeans and a T-
shirt. Hair crept down beneath the shoulders, braided or flowing freely in
the '60s style that expressed a certain scorn for restraint or moderation.
Beards and mustaches of all descriptions accentuated the faces of the men.
There were headbands and colorful jewelry, chains and beads dangling
from the neck or the wrist. Men who worked out in the weight room favored open leather vests worn shirtless over bare skin to expose biceps
and pectoral muscles.

By contrast, Castro's dress came right out of the '50s. He wore dark
slacks for all occasions and plain button-down dress shirts. His black hair,
though not meticulously groomed, was close cropped, his light-skinned
face clean-shaven. By appearance alone, he might have been mistaken for
a Young Republican.

His full oval face and dark eyes could reveal intermittently two distinct aspects of his personality. On first impression, he was the life of the
party.[22] He had a great belly laugh. He could mimic like an actor and loved
to tell stories. On a good night—and that was frequent—Castro could keep
a table or a whole room down at the White Mule in stitches. He sang, made
up rhymes, and pinned nicknames on his buddies. But beneath the laughter, another side of his personality frequently shone through. Even at
twenty-one, he had begun to reveal a serious side. Already he was formu-
lating a political vision that became the backbone of his political instincts
for the next twenty-five years.

He saw immediately that education represented the essential ingredient of the Chicano Movement and the primary vehicle for social change.
Education might be simply a ticket out of the barrio for some, but in the
hands of the rising Chicano Movement, education might become a weapon
and a tool for service. The study of sociology and economics could establish blueprints for community action. The study of medicine, education,
and law could build a reservoir of doctors, lawyers, and teachers to serve
the entire Hispanic community.

And so UMAS set about the task of bringing a college education to the Chicano community. UMAS had to inspire, persuade, comfort, and recruit high school students who believed themselves likelier to see the inside of the Buena Vista Correctional Complex than to visit a college campus.

It was not always glamorous work. Book banks were set up so that struggling students could avoid excessive prices for texts. Tutoring had to be done, and new skills taught. How do you fill out an application for financial aid? How do you footnote a term paper? How do you make sure your grammar is up to par for comp class? In its way, this approach mirrored the century-long conflict between the fierce individualism touted by Anglo culture and the more communal values of the Mexican. Just as their ancestors in southern Colorado had grazed livestock on communal land and built irrigation ditches according to communal norms, so did the new generation embrace the idea that Chicano students were responsible for helping each other get an education.[23]

Recruiting for College

In the task of recruiting the Mexican-American community to go to college, Richard Castro had few peers. All over contemporary Denver are college-educated individuals who swear they owe their degrees to Castro's persistence.[24]

Roger Medina, for example. Medina, a Gang Unit detective for the Denver Police Department, remembers sitting at the bar at the Old Corner Inn on Thirty-eighth and Walnut one evening when Castro walked in. The two had been buddies at Annunciation, the parochial school in the heart of Denver's East Side, but since graduation they had taken distinctly different paths.

"Hey, he was goin' to school," recalls Medina, "and I'm drinkin'. He was tryin' to better himself and I'm in the bars; that was my life."

Castro sat down that night and started a conversation that began to transform Medina's life: "You know, Rog, I've helped some people get into school and you're one of my best friends. I can get you in school."

Medina shot back: "'What are you talkin' about? You're drunk; have another beer.' You know, that kinda talk," remembers Medina.

"No, seriously, Rog. You oughta think about going to school."

"'What the hell am I gonna do in school, Rich? What are you, crazy?' You see," continues Medina, "those nuns used to tell me that I'd end up in prison some day. I'd heard a lotta bad things about me. But Rich kept it up and kept it up. 'Come on, Rog, let's go down to school.' To the point where I finally said, 'OK, Rich, come on, let's go.'"

The next day Castro personally escorted Medina to registration. "Back in them days at Metro's registration all you had was lines. And you could imagine—me, standin' in lines? I'm tellin' him, 'Rich, let's get the hell out of here. Let's go get us a beer. I mean the hell with this shit.' That was my attitude, see? But Rich never gave up."

Eventually the two old friends wended their way together through the maze of paperwork. "So I got all my classes and that's how I got into school. Then we left and had a beer. I never woulda done it without Rich. I was walkin' away a couple of times. I mean, this guy literally went and grabbed me. He said, 'Come on, Rog. Just try it. We're almost there. We're this. We're that. His persistence is what did it, and that's the truth."[25]

While recruitment in the East Denver taverns was not exactly the norm, Medina's story does present Castro in a role he frequently performed. Trained as a social worker, Rich Castro often found himself between bureaucracy and the street, often occupying the tenuous position between the anger and frustration of those with little power and the rigidity of those who wielded it.

Campus Militancy

Conscious of their status on the margins of American society, the core members of UMAS embraced a climate of confrontation. Metro students knew they were breaking norms. They sensed they would have to fight for their education and they engaged themselves in an all-out assault on every form of discrimination in campus life.

Normando Pacheco, who knew Castro as far back as nursery school, spent three years and eight months in the Marines—one of those years in Vietnam—before reuniting with Castro on the Metro campus. Pacheco, one of the early presidents of UMAS, recalled Castro's role in the organization in a 1993 interview:

"Rich was the kinda guy that could deal rationally with a college administration. The rest of us were not interested in any kind of interaction with the administration other than making demands and saying, 'You're gonna fulfill 'em.'

"To understand the genre of the times, we were all very close, very very close. Because it was sink or swim, basically; it was an 'us against the world' attitude. Richard was not a militant. He was the person out of us that you could talk to to get the negotiations done. Everybody had a part to play. That was his part.

"UMAS was kind of like an atom. It had subparts to it. Everybody had the right idea. They just had a different way of doing it. There was no leader. We made sure there was no leader. Richard was a force in UMAS. He was not *the* driving force. There was no *one* driving force. It was broad-based."[26]

Castro's role in UMAS foreshadowed his later role in other organizations. During his college years he was not a public spokesman; his name never got into the papers. What power he held stemmed from his activities behind the scenes. He could get things down in writing. He wrote proposals and position papers. He wrote letters. He did prodigious amounts of research. He investigated the numbers of scholarships available and tried to unravel the bureaucratic maze that surrounded financial aid. He kept phone numbers and membership lists. And when the time came to prioritize demands, to determine which ones to back off from and which ones to pursue, his voice was a respected one.[27]

The contentious issues were often the gritty details that make few headlines. Mexican-American students demanded a budget from the college to help in recruiting efforts. They complained that readmission procedures for students suspended for low grades were arbitrary. They said that too much of their student fees ($30 a quarter) was used for "beach parties." They contended that their $7-a-term health-care fees were superfluous, since so many could get care at the West Side Health Center.[28]

They sometimes squandered valuable political capital on what appear, in retrospect, to be insignificant matters. One demonstration concerned a dispute over double standards in grading. Organizing a rally of seventy-five students at the corner of Fourteenth and Bannock, UMAS accused Dr. Jean Fair, head of the foreign language department, of unfair grading toward Hispanic students in her Spanish classes. Richard Montaño, then president of UMAS, and Sam Abeyta, a student from Commerce City, contended that Fair graded Hispanics on a stricter standard than Anglos because Spanish was some Hispanics' native language.[29] But familiarity with the Spanish spoken in the homes or on the streets of Denver, they argued, did not necessarily prepare a student for classroom Spanish. It was one thing to talk street talk. It was altogether different to know the preterit or past participle or conditional tense of an irregular verb.

Dr. Fair denied the UMAS allegation, saying, "If I had done it, I would never have given an A or a B to a Hispano student, and I have done it many times. These particular students just didn't get good grades."[30] College administrator Sherman Spear told *The Denver Post* he didn't believe these types of problems should be taken to the "sidewalk."[31]

But the "sidewalk" is where these disputes inevitably ended up. Said Pacheco, "You'd be shocked. I mean, some of the most passive people in the whole wide world you'd see show up on pickets for a political demonstration."[32] UMAS activists were convinced that without public pressure, without a mass presence on the street, moderates like Castro could bring back nothing from the table. Castro himself agreed. He, too, did his share of picket duty.

Some disputes tended to end up in the tenth-story office of Metro's first president, Dr. Kenneth Phillips. "It was stormy," recalls Phillips of those meetings in the Forum Building, "but usually pretty civil. Contentious groups would come in and kind of yell at you. I always thought it was part of the process and that the best thing I could do was live through it. I always thought it was better to take it than dish it out, that by giving them the opportunity to talk to the president, we were in better shape than if we pushed them away. I think we came through that period of turmoil in pretty good shape, but it's true I left because my doctor told me my blood pressure was high and advised me to move to a less stressful position."[33]

The "Mau Maus" did nothing to lower Dr. Phillips's blood pressure. Among the members of UMAS and the Black Student Alliance was a small core of activists who sardonically referred to themselves as the "Mau Mau Terrorists," after Jomo Kenyatta's band of anti-colonial revolutionaries in Kenya. "There were some of us," says Normando Pacheco, "that were just known as the heavy radicals."[34] It was these "heavies" whose language and posture introduced a level of intimidation into the dialogue between UMAS and Metro.

Though Castro employed a far different style, the radical environment provided the political soil from which he grew. His formative years were years of struggle. The political atmosphere that surrounded him was rough, confrontational, and angry. It was the politics of a long-marginalized people who had begun to believe that courtesy and good manners had gotten them little respect in the game of American politics.

During the early years, few open conflicts arose between the militants and moderates like Castro. "Everybody had a tremendous amount of respect for Richard," recalls Pacheco, whose politics gravitated more toward those of the Mau Maus.[35] It would be years before tensions between Castro and more militant members of the Movement would explode.

An Early Mentor

The same man who planted seeds for Metro's UMAS chapter also stood at the center of an intellectual controversy that rippled through the organization's ranks. Dr. Daniel T. Valdes, professor of sociology, headed the Division of Behavioral Sciences at Metro State.

The academic world was embarking on a new journey in the late 1960s. For nearly twenty-five years, only one overview of Mexican-American history had been published: Carey McWilliams' *North from Mexico*.[36] Only a tiny number of scholars were addressing neglected corners of history. In 1969, fewer than one hundred Hispanic scholars held doctorates nationwide.[37] Little wonder that titles such as *Forgotten People* and *A Minority Nobody Knows* emphasized the idea that America had turned its back on the hidden story of the Mexican-American people.[38] Daniel Valdes stood at the forefront of those few who launched the movement to dig up the buried roots of the past. The bespectacled professor represented something of a one-man ethnic studies department in the days before "Chicano Studies" became watchwords on campuses in the Southwest.

Valdes traced his family back to the colonizers of New Mexico in the seventeenth century. As a child, he had listened to the stories his mother, father, and grandparents passed down. He discovered an unpublished history of New Mexico written by his grandfather, Gabriel Valdes.[39] The stories filled him with sympathy and respect for his fellow manitos—the settlers of northern New Mexico who forged a unique culture in the remote mountain country along the Rio Grande.

His analysis made him something of a political maverick in the early '60s. Though Republican politicians had consulted with him, Valdes concluded early on that Hispanics needed a third party to give them leverage in the political system. With Tom Pino he formed the New Hispano Party— a development that caused more than a little consternation among Democrats, who, since the Depression, had held a monopoly on the Hispanic vote.

Nevertheless, Richard Castro and his fellow UMAS students—most of them also descendents of the New Mexican settlers—devoured Valdes's courses. For Castro, studying under Valdes represented the first step in a life-long search for the roots of his people. It was here that he became a voracious reader. "If he was sitting in the car waiting for someone," said his wife, Virginia, "he had a book. If you went to the grocery store, he'd say, 'I'll be over here,' and he'd be sitting by the door reading."[40]

The books he read at Metro transformed his entire worldview as, indeed, they transformed the worldview of his whole generation. In Carey McWilliams's *North from Mexico,* for instance, Castro learned that Mexican Americans had formed the backbone of the southwestern economy. In the industries that provided the foundation for modern prosperity in the Southwest—in the coal mines, copper pits, beet fields, and fruit orchards; on the railroads, the far-flung Texas ranches, and the irrigated valleys of California—the backbreaking labor that built the country was performed by Mexican Americans and their cousins from across the border. Yet, as Castro and his friends surveyed the fruit of a half-dozen previous generations of labor, they found that their fathers and grandfathers had gained almost nothing for their sacrifice. In 1967, as Castro started his college career at Metro, one journalist concluded that Mexican Americans were "worse off in every respect than the non-whites (Negroes, Indians, and Orientals), not to mention the dominant Anglos. They are poorer, their housing is more crowded and dilapidated, their unemployment rate is higher, and their average educational level is lower [two years below non-whites, four below Anglo]."[41] All the hard labor had gained Mexicans neither solace from economic hardship nor protection from the mocking condescension of white society.

During his college years, Castro once snipped out a cartoon from the daily newspaper and inserted it into one of his scrapbooks. There were two frames. The first displayed a hackneyed caricature of a Mexican peasant seated against a saguaro cactus, hunched over, hiding his face under his hat from the hot desert sun. The second frame was marked "Siesta Time." Here the man had slid down the cactus and lay prone on the ground with only the top of his hat touching the saguaro. The image conveyed the two states of "Mexican consciousness": sloth and laziness on the one hand, deep sleep on the other. The cartoon symbolized for Castro the racial myths that had long dwelt in the American consciousness and that his generation felt bound to confront.

On the pages of George Sanchez's *Forgotten People* and Stan Steiner's *La Raza,* Castro learned about the New Mexico and Colorado land grants. He learned that the landless workers who formed the base of population in the barrios on Denver's East and West Sides had been dispossessed by the new economic system the Americans brought with them into newly conquered territory. True enough, impoverishment had long permeated the New Mexican economy. But the final nails in the economic casket had been driven by fraud perpetrated by Santa Fe lawyers, by property taxes imposed on cash-poor farmers, and by expropriation of communally shared land—all this imported by the new Anglo masters.[42]

To a generation nurtured from childhood on stories from TV's "Wagon Train" and the unceasing westward progress of Anglo society, these revelations created a new framework through which Castro and his companions began to understand the social status of their own families.

Did the invasion of the manitos' land in nineteenth-century New Mexico bear any relation to the poverty of their present-day descendants? Did the subsequent exploitation of migrant labor bear any relation to the contemporary level of Mexican-American educational attainment? Were unfortunate conditions in the barrio the result of some character defect among the residents, some unlucky genetic structure? Was the barrio simply a warehouse for 50,000 individual failures? Or could one trace the roots of poverty to the injustices that occurred during the five generations since the Mexican War? In Castro's mind, the answer was self-evident. Under the tutelage of Dr. Valdes, Castro concluded that the problems he saw on the streets of Denver were, in large part, rooted in historical forces—in conquest, in systematic exploitation, in racial and ethnic discrimination—that had long been in the making.

Daniel Valdes had taken on the issue of ethnic discrimination in the early '60s, when the subject had barely begun to enter the public consciousness. At Metro he formed the Hispanic Youth Congress as a pressure group to fight for the rights of Hispanic students. "He fought a battle," says Professor David Sandoval, a colleague of Valdes, "when a lot of people weren't around to fight a battle.[43]

On one issue, however, Dan Valdes ran far afield from the sentiments of most of his students. "If he had a blind spot," says Sandoval, "it was this fascination and love he had for Spaniards as opposed to anyone else. There was a quantum leap in his history. It was as if from 1598 (when Juan de Oñate conquered New Mexico for Spain) to 1998, we were all Spaniards."[44]

The Battle of the Names

For rebel students in the '60s, this approach to history elicited a passionate response. Their parents and grandparents before them had called themselves "Spanish" or "Spanish American." These were words laden with emotional connotation. The Spanish identification served to root previous generations in Europe. It permitted an undiluted psychological identification with powerful conquistadors and with a "white" and "civilized" heritage. In American society, "Spanish" was far more polite, far more acceptable than the term "Mexican." In *North from Mexico,* McWilliams had written that "one who achieves success (in the Southwest) is 'Spanish'; one who doesn't is 'Mexican.'"[45]

Interpretations of regional history complicated this "battle of the names." Before the American conquest of the Southwest in 1848, residents of northern New Mexico had been geographically isolated from the rest of Mexico. The vast Sonoran Desert separated the Mexican interior from its northern frontier area. Some, including Valdes, argued that a distinctive autonomous style and a self-reliant pioneer mentality emerged from this isolation.[46] What is more, Mexican independence came late. Not until 1821 did Mexico gain its independence from Spain. The Americans came only twenty-five years later. Although New Mexicans had lived under Spanish rule for centuries, they lived under the Mexican flag for only a generation. Many residents of the mountains of northern New Mexico have therefore rejected identification as Mexicans and taken on the title "Hispano." This was the term favored by Dr. Valdes; hence, the name of his student organization, Hispanic Youth Conference.

Radical students at Metro (most of whom, like Valdes, had roots in northern New Mexico) were rapidly rejecting this terminology. The word *Hispanic* derived from the Latin *Hispania*, which is what the Romans called Spain (or *España* in Spanish).[47] "Hispanic" simply means relating to Spain or to Spanish culture. Using the word *Hispanic* was to UMAS students no different from saying "Spanish."

David Sandoval asserts that Daniel Valdes recognized the problems of racism in America but maintains that "His way of fighting racism was to say, 'Hey, we're part of the white guys.'"[48] In fact, that was explicit in Valdes' writings. "To infer that the Hispano is non-white," he wrote in 1968, "is fallacious, malicious sometimes, and always unjustified. . . ."[49] "The great bulk [of Spanish surnamed individuals in the United States], are anthropologically and biologically white [Caucasians]."[50]

For the rising generation of students in the 1960s, for those Professor Carlos Muñoz had labeled "The Chicano Generation," Valdes' words bordered on heresy. The notion of offering themselves up for assimilation into American society as white "Spaniards" was simply not acceptable.

For them, the crucial missing ingredient in their 500-year-old lineage was Indian blood. The new literature, the new artwork expressed in murals on the walls of housing projects and inner-city recreation centers, the new consciousness stressed a dual heritage. Their ancestry was mestizo; it was the mingling of Spaniard and Indian. To omit the Indian legacy constituted to them the most shameful form of self-denial and self-loathing.

In California Luis Valdez, the founder of El Teatro Campesino, had written that: "Most of us know we are not European simply by looking in the mirror . . . the shape of the eyes, the curve of the nose, the color of skin, the texture of hair; these things belong to another time, another people. Together with a million little stubborn mannerisms, beliefs, myths, superstitions, words, thoughts . . . they fill our Spanish life with Indian contradictions."[51]

Coloradans were drawing the same conclusions. Whether their ancestors came from New Mexico or from Guanajato in the interior of Mexico, their heritage, they claimed, remained mestizo. For one, many of the original colonizers of New Mexico, including the family of its founder, Juan de Oñate, were born of mixed blood.[52] Once established on the northern frontier, the tribal mix may have been different from other regions of Mexico. Perhaps the Apaches and Navajos who intermingled with Spaniards in New Mexico differed from the Nahuas or the Tarahumaras of the Mexican interior.[53] Nevertheless, the children who sprang from the innumerable marriages, illicit romances, liaisons with slaves, or simply brutal rapes that occurred between two peoples in the wake of Spanish conquest—these children shared the heritage of two cultures, not one.

For the new generation, then, the term *Hispanic* did not fit. It implied acceptance of a racial hierarchy students preferred not to embrace. Not only were Indians excluded from the Hispano identity, but Mexican nationals, who had immigrated to Colorado in small waves for half a century, were left out as well.

Richard Castro's old friend Andy Lovato recalls the condescending sentiments of some of his neighbors on the East Side: "The reality was it was better to be called a 'Spanish American' because it showed you were acculturated or assimilated more into the American culture. In the 20s, they brought a bunch of 'uneducated, illiterate Mexicans' up from Mexico and you certainly [if you were born in the United States] didn't want to be associated with them."[54] The native-born manitos often looked down on the "Surumatos"—the Mexican-born newcomers—and labeled them just as the Anglos did: *mojados* or wetbacks.[55]

To be sure, the condescension had always been filled with ambiguous sentiments. On the one hand, manitos often respected Mexican nationals for their language and their hard work. They sympathized with them for their status as outcasts in American society because they themselves were also outcast. They intermarried with them. On the other hand, manitos competed with Mexican immigrants for jobs, and they feared that a close association with them might bring them further disdain from the Anglo community.[56] Sometimes in the Curtis Park area mutual suspicions broke down into fierce gang rivalries.[57] The conflict among intimate neighbors was all the more heartbreaking because the groups were so much alike. The whole thing represented an oft-repeated phenomenon in American history: an oppressed people seeking a group lower in status on whose backs they could leapfrog into American respectability.

UMAS students at Metro were rejecting this approach on several grounds. For one, it had rarely worked historically. For all the psychological distance manitos placed between themselves and their immigrant neighbors, their treatment by the Anglo majority remained the same. Whites made no distinctions: A Mexican was Mexican whether he could trace his Colorado roots back 150 years or had just arrived on the Greyhound from Juarez the night before.

Second, a separate identity for New Mexican Hispanos failed to reflect the reality of barrio life in Denver. Over several generations, the lives of manitos and Mexican immigrants had become too integrally intertwined to engage in these distinctions. Castro's wife, for instance, the former Virginia Lucero, traced her mother's family back not to northern New Mexico but to Zacatecas. Her brother, Richard Montaño (who once served as president of UMAS), shared her family roots, and yet the two of them were as thoroughly Westsiders as any family that had immigrated from the ancestral villages of New Mexico. Trying to distinguish New Mexican Hispanos from those whose roots extended back to Mexico proper would have shattered the organizational unity for any civil rights group on the Metro campus.

Searching for a New Identity

In addition, many of those '60s students took a hard look at mainstream Anglo society and decided they wanted no part of it. Or at the very least, they wanted to dictate the terms of their assimilation.

Thus, the new generation looked for a new vocabulary that would more accurately define their identity: mestizo, not white. They were proud of the Indian side of their heritage and unwilling to subject their naming to approval by the Anglo majority.

A number of names came up for consideration: *Latino, Raza, Indo-Hispano,* and *Mexican.* Many students favored the more militant term, *Chicano.* Although its origins are hazy, this word may have derived from a shortened form of the term *Mejicano* (sometimes pronounced "may-chicano")—the Spanish word for Mexican. *Chicano* had long been used in certain subcultures on the street, but in the 1960s the word took on a self-consciously political connotation. To call oneself *Chicano* meant to call one-self an activist, a militant, one who disdained acceptance by white culture.[58] "A Chicano," wrote *Los Angeles Times* journalist Ruben Salazar, "is a Mexican American with a non-Anglo image of himself. . . . Mexican American activists flaunt the barrio word 'Chicano' as an act of defiance and a badge of honor."[59]

Rich Castro listened intently to these debates and came down firmly in opposition to the term Hispanic. He was equally comfortable identifying himself with the word *Chicano,* as with the less abrasive, sometimes hyphenated term *Mexican American.* During his years at Metro, it was this latter term, more moderate than "Chicano," that won out, at least in regard to naming the student organization.

By 1971, Professor Valdes's Hispanic Youth Congress, in conjunction with the Congress of Hispanic Educators, had merged and consolidated with UMAS. The newly unified organization kept the name of its largest component, the United Mexican American Students.[60] At least for the day, the Battle of the Names had been resolved. A few years after Castro's graduation, the term *MECHA*—Movimiento Estudiantil de Chicanos de Aztlán (The Chicano Student Movement of Aztlán)—replaced UMAS. The generation that rose up in the late '60s had rejected the "Hispanic" identity in favor of terminology that better caught the spirit of the times.

As a young man, Castro fully supported this transformation from the Spanish- and European-centered identity to one that recognized the more complex nature of his heritage. When examining his writings in later years, however, one finds him using the terms *Hispanic, Chicano,* and *Mexican American* almost interchangeably.[61]

A number of factors might explain this change. For one, some people tired of the Battle of the Names. Roger Medina, Castro's East Side buddy, stated facetiously, "They used to argue over whether Montezuma had a beard or not."[62] The confrontational rhetoric alienated him and turned him away from political activity. If the term *Hispanic* or *Spanish* proved exclusionary and divisive, so too did the continuing battle over the use of the new terms. Given the sensitivities of an intricate mixture of cultures from California to south Texas, settling on a precise terminology to fit all sizes proved an elusive task. Moderate by nature, Castro preferred not to add fuel to the fire by pushing one name too aggressively.

Moreover, Denver's demographics underwent a rapid change in the 1980s. More and more, one could find Salvadorans, having fled death squads and poverty in their native country, playing soccer east of the lake at City Park. One could find Peruvian immigrants gathering at salsa clubs on the West Side. These newcomers shared many characteristics with more established residents, but Mexican heritage was not among them. A more inclusive term was needed and many leaders began accepting *Hispanic* as a way to embrace everyone in this new Latin American mixture. Thus, by the 1980s Castro had quietly backed away from the Battle of the Names. Typically he sought out a middle ground. Nevertheless, his early years at Metro exposed him to an earnest collective search for a national identity, a search vital to the formation of his own psychological and political identity. In these years he began to feel the pulse of the nationalist sentiment that was shaping his generation.

ii
looking outward

Well before his graduation from Metro, Rich Castro's interests had expanded to areas beyond the borders of the campus. Several factors drove him relentlessly to participate in activities increasingly distant from Metropolitan State College.

One factor was surely the relationship he struck up in 1967 with a tall, long-haired young woman named Virginia Lucero. The two married in 1970. Castro came from an East Denver family of modest means. While struggling economically, his parents provided him with an ample measure of security and stability. In contrast, Lucero's experience had put her in touch with the harder edges of American life.

She was born Virginia Montaño in the tiny town of Silt on Colorado's Western Slope, about thirteen miles west of Glenwood Springs. Her father was a native of New Mexico; her mother came from one of those families from which some American-born Hispanics tried to keep their distance. They came from the plateau country of the Mexican province of Zacatecas, where the rich soil is copper-colored and the population grows relatively tall. (It's a regional trait that runs in the family. When Virginia attended junior high in Pueblo, her friends, who hovered around five feet tall, nicknamed her "Treetops.")

In 1925, Virginia's grandfather and his adventurous brother made their way from the village of San Pablo to the abundant fruit orchards around Grand Junction. According to family legend, they transported their families in horse-drawn carts over rural dirt roads.

Virginia Castro still retains childhood memories of Western Slope migrant camps where her mom and dad worked the harvests. During the winters, her mom cleaned houses for as little as 50¢ a day. Her father eventually found a job as a section hand for the Denver & Rio Grande Railroad repairing track on isolated mountain stretches. Thus, the family roamed the Western Slope and found homes in places like Minturn, De Beque, Glenwood Springs, and Silt. Unheard of were benefits, pensions, insurance, or vacations. When offered a job at the giant Colorado Fuel & Iron steel mill in Pueblo, her father jumped at the chance.

The new job, however, could not save the Montaño family. Shortly after moving to Pueblo, Virginia's parents separated, and then divorced. She was a ninth grader then, headstrong, determined, and outspoken by the time her mother remarried. She had little patience for the clash that developed between her and her new stepfather. At fourteen, she made the decision to return to Glenwood and move in with her *abuela*, her grandmother. She never returned to Pueblo.

Virginia had already spent some time in Glenwood as a child. Once while she was walking home from school in the second grade, a ten-year-old boy followed her, carefully aimed a rock he carried in his hand, and then called her "dirty Mexican" as she cried in pain from the welt rising on the back of her head. Her grandmother had been philosophical. "Are you dirty?" she asked her sobbing granddaughter. "No." "Are you Mexican?" she asked again. "Yes." "So what's the problem?" said Grandma, and she left it at that.

Only two Hispanic families lived in Glenwood, and Virginia insists she tried hard to fit in. "In a small town," she says, "school is real important. It's where you have your friends and your fun. Glenwood had a nice sports curriculum; the sports teams were always good teams. We were rivals with Rifle. It was your average school situation and I really wanted to be part of it. Our cooking classes used to make candied apples and popcorn to sell at football games. My two cousins and I used to work real hard—after school or any time we could—to make money for the home ec department. I remember one time we were accused of stealing the money. We didn't take one penny. The other kids went to the teachers and the teachers tended to believe them.

"There were the cheerleaders who were the elite group and then there was the Pep Club who was everybody else, except us. When it came time for us to become part of the Pep Club, they used this alleged theft against us. We never got in the Pep Club. Discrimination was there. It was there and it sometimes came out very blatantly in ways that still stay with me."

She almost finished high school. "I needed three classes to graduate from school," she says. "That was it. But I had met this young man from

Rifle, Richard Lucero, a big guy who was on the football team. At that time, his grades had gone down too far and he got kicked off the team. They gave him chances and chances and chances and he just didn't get his school work done, so they kicked him off. To him, getting kicked off the team was like getting kicked out of school; it was one and the same.

"I wasn't happy at school. My grandmother had gotten very ill and I started feeling like I was a burden. Richard and I were just like two little lost souls out there. It seemed getting married was the easiest way out of the whole situation, and that's exactly what I did. I was sixteen years old. It seemed perfectly normal and natural to do such a thing at the age of sixteen. By the time I was twenty-one, I had four children."

Richard got a job in her uncle Manual's body shop and the young couple settled in Glenwood. There they stayed until his older brother, Ben, got back from the Army. He was thirty, a career man in the service, when he was diagnosed with Hodgkins Disease.

The Luceros' parents had long been dead; the kids had raised themselves. Though terminally ill, Ben Lucero assessed the situation and realized it was time to take responsibility for the whole family. He also realized that places like Rifle and Glenwood were not going to lead the family anywhere. In 1961 he packed up everyone and brought them to Denver.

Coming to the City

Virginia, then twenty years old and the mother of three children, followed in the footsteps of thousands who made the classic migration from countryside to city. "We all moved into this little house on Elati Street, 351 Elati. [It's now part of the Fairmont Elementary School playground.] There were seventeen of us. We ended up cleaning out the attic, and that was our piece of the house. My husband and I and three babies. The hardest part was living with all those people.

"My babies weren't old enough to go to school, so I [stayed] at home with them. Everybody else was at school at West High or at Baker [Junior High] and the rest were at work. So I was left there to clean up after all these people. I had three babies and there I was picking up after everybody and doing dishes. In my grandmother's house and my mom's house, you picked up after yourself. There wasn't gonna be anybody around to pick up after you, and why should they? That was the attitude. It was unheard of to walk out a door and leave your wet towels and dirty clothes in the bathroom and your bed unmade. Those were the most criminal things you could do in my family. So this was just a nightmare.

"But I think the worst nightmare of all was [the change in] this young man, who before had been so busy working to help the family. All of a sudden, we're in this big city, and it's just endless what you can do in a big city. The parties and everything.

"So Richard just started not being around. He'd leave early in the morning to go job hunting and I wouldn't see him again till who knows when. [Richard] would get a job, and he'd work for a little while and then he'd be out of a job. So I began to feel very dependent on these people who really weren't making it either. But I was totally helpless because I had all these little kids. I couldn't go to work. I couldn't go to school. I couldn't go anywhere. All I could do was hope there was something to feed them that day.

"If it wouldn't have been for Ben—everybody else was so busy looking out for their own survival—me and my kids would have been in bad shape. Ben was a stable person. He became manager of the Goodwill store on Ninth and Santa Fe and when all the stuff would come in, he would set aside things for everybody. My kids always had plenty of clothes. Shoes. Coats. He made sure they always had really nice things. But foodwise—that sometimes was really critical.

"Then, in 1961, my two-month-old son got sick. It was really cold and I was at home with all these kids and he didn't look right. I had already hooked into a well-baby clinic that Health and Hospitals had set up in the neighborhood. The doctor there said, 'There's something wrong with this baby. I want you to take him over to Denver General.'

"So I walked the baby over to Denver General and they sent us up to Pediatrics. I sat there with that baby in my arms from early morning until about two o'clock in the afternoon before he was seen.

"By the time they took us in, his head was starting to swell. There was this Japanese doctor and she came back and said, 'This baby has pneumococcyul meningitis. They shaved his head and took him right away. They put these needles in his head and started draining out all his fluid. Then they identified a blood clot between the tissues of his brain and began surgery on his head. They told me he probably was not gonna make it and if we wanted to, we should call in the priest and give him last rites. He wasn't even baptized yet.

"They got the priest down to baptize him. And for the next month that little baby was in this crib with oxygen going and massive doses of antibiotics and needles everywhere. He was a teensy little thing and finally his little veins broke and they started putting needles in his feet and ankles. He would lay there and just shake. I could cover the torso of his body with my two hands together and it would warm him up and he would stop shivering and trembling. I would lay there and sleep with him for hours and hours. After a month, he came out of it. He made it. I will always remember the nurses and the doctors at Pediatrics. It was like their own child.

"We finally got out of Ben's house. Richard was working as a house painter. We sort of got ourselves readjusted in our own place and I got pregnant again with my daughter, Brenda. But our marriage was deteriorating the whole time. He went from job to job; we could barely pay the rent and I'd have to worry about how we were gonna come up with the rent the next time. We moved from Elati to Delaware to Lowell Boulevard. We got kicked out of that house on Christmas Eve. I had my tree up and we got kicked out, Christmas tree and all. It was a miracle—I have guardian angels you wouldn't believe—that we were never really on the street. But for me, never ever ever in the history of what I had been through did anybody ever get kicked out of a house.

"I don't think he worried about it. He used to say, 'What are you worried about? The rent's gonna get paid. There's food in the refrigerator.' Somehow, he was usually able to work enough to keep us going with rent and groceries. But it was very sporadic and it was very stressful for me.

"I didn't want to let him go no matter what. There had to be a way to keep the family together and I was gonna do it all by myself. We were living on Newton Street when he got a phone call. Richard had an older brother who was kind of a flamboyant playboy type who was a dance instructor for the Fred Astaire School downtown. He got this job in California and he invited my husband to come there to get a good job. I never saw him for five years. We'd get a fifty-dollar money order here and there."[1]

With Richard Lucero's departure, Virginia realized at long last she was on her own. She signed up for Aid for Dependant Children, and then got her General Educational Development certificate. On the same day she passed her high school equivalency test, she signed up for nursing courses at Emily Griffith Opportunity School. It was 1964, three years after she had arrived in the city. She was beginning to leave the nightmare behind but not before her experience had reshaped her entire orientation toward life.

By the time she met Rich Castro three years later at an UMAS meeting at Metropolitan State College, she had proven to herself—and everyone else—that she could take care of herself. She had four kids, a certificate as a Licensed Practical Nurse, a job at a nursing home, and a lifetime of harsh lessons. She was tough, motivated, focused, but not without compassion for those still struggling on the edge, where she had so recently resided. Her story reflected the paths of a great many like her—migrants from the rural countryside who came to the city, faced the hardships offered them on the West Side, and then, as America slowly began to open up in the '60s, began to take advantage of the new opportunities.

Protected as he was by his own tight-knit family, Rich Castro's awareness expanded immensely when Virginia came into his life. His relationship with her steered him away from campus politics and thrust him into the wider world of grassroots organizing.

"Virg was the perfect partner for Rich," claims Normando Pacheco. "She was much tougher and she had a tremendous influence on him. Virg inspired him to go into politics."[2]

Broader Horizons: Farm Worker Boycott

In 1968, Castro crossed paths with another woman from the countryside who, like Virginia, pushed him to deepen his commitment and extend his political horizons beyond the Metro campus. Juanita Herrera and her husband, Alfredo, arrived in Denver after a lifetime of working the fields from Texas to California. They came to Denver as disciples of César Chávez to organize the grape boycott for the fast-rising United Farm Workers' Union. They occupied a house at 361 Elati, next door to the West Side home Virginia had moved into seven years before.

Both Herreras had begun working at age twelve. Both had chopped cotton from dawn to dusk for $2.50 a day. Both had thinned sugar beets in Montana with the infamous short-handled hoe, and picked potatoes on the Western Slope for four cents per hundred-pound sack.[3] As *campesinos*, landless agricultural field workers, they performed the most essential work in the country: providing food for American dinner tables. In return, they received the lowest wages of any segment of labor in the nation. To boot, the indiscriminate use of chemical pesticides had made farm work the most dangerous job in the country.[4]

As an organizer Juanita Herrera proved to be a ball of fire. She told her story at churches, union meetings, and schools all over the city. "The first time I met Rich," she said, "was the day I went to speak at Metro State. He came over to me and said he would like to be more involved in helping us. I said, 'Well, if you want to be more involved, why don't you send me a committee from here in the college? Number one, I'm gonna tell you I want to speak more times here so I can get more people aware of this problem.'

"Rich and one or two other students came over to the place where we were living," continues Herrera. "He took some buttons and some *Malcriados* [the union newspaper] and some literature. He came over to the picket line and he set up meetings so I could go and speak to people. Richard also started collecting money and giving me envelopes full of cash. He came over to the house often and gave me names and contacts. That's how I got contacts for students at MECHA (Movimiento Estudiantil Chicano de Aztlán) and UMAS. He was fresh then, very fresh." By that she meant not rude, but a very young kid.[5]

To Cecelia Garcia, fifteen at the time, Castro was no kid; he was her teacher. She remembers going to the Safeway picket line with Castro and his then girlfriend, Virginia.

"We as kids," she recalls, "used to have to get up at 6:30 in the morning to get ready to go boycott. This was no easy task. You might be there all day long. I can remember being scared. There were truck drivers, for instance, that didn't want us to boycott Safeway. On the first morning of the boycott I can remember telling Richard and Virginia, 'I'm scared.' And they'd say, 'Don't worry; we'll be there with you.'

"And we went. There were other children there, and there were farm workers and migrants who were there with their children. . . . Richard and Virginia said you had to do it; you couldn't be afraid. It was instilled in you by adults—by my mother and Richard and Virginia—that it was the right thing to do. . . . Here were people who were suffering more than we were. It was a responsibility because you needed to help others.

"They didn't say, 'Oh, poor little babies, you're not responsible.' No. You *were* responsible. It was 'even though you're a child, we're gonna teach you how to do this, and you can help and you're supposed to be here by seven in the morning and don't be late.' Not only were you responsible that way. They'd say, 'OK, what other kids can you bring with you? How many of your friends can you call? What are you young people gonna do about going to other schools and talking to other kids?' It was truly a movement of responsibility."[6]

Cesar Chavez, the national leader of the UFW, was a powerful role model for Rich Castro. Virginia Castro remembers that she and her husband were very moved when they met Chavez on several occasions in Denver. "He was soft-spoken, very calm, very humble. He made you feel comfortable. He made you feel important. He was totally and completely involved with the union; he never wavered from his cause. If Rich had any heroes at all, it would have been Cesar Chavez."[7]

Castro's feelings reflected the outpouring of sentiment for the farm workers that spread through Chicano neighborhoods in many cities in the Southwest. Some residents were one generation removed from the fields, while others still had relatives working the migrant circuit. The intersection of the urban and rural Chicano, the spiritual link between youthful radicals and weather-beaten campesinos, frequently turned out to be the parking lots at Safeway stores where the boycott hit full force.

iii

the west side

Magdalena Gallegos brought her old neighborhood back to life in a 1985 *Colorado Heritage* article entitled "The Forgotten Community."[1] She grew up in Auraria, that part of West Denver that lies on the west bank of Cherry Creek as it approaches the South Platte River. Denver history books never fail to mention Auraria; it was the birthplace of the city. What is forgotten, according to Gallegos, is the Hispanic nature of the neighborhood from the late 1920s until its destruction in 1972. The controversy over what to do with Auraria propelled Richard Castro's life in a new direction, which would immerse him in a life of politics.

Dispersed throughout downtown Denver, Metropolitan State College began its search for a permanent site in 1967, the same year Castro arrived on campus.[2] Touted as an "urban college," Metro naturally cast its eyes toward the Auraria site just west of downtown. By the time survey crews began scoping the neighborhood, a plan emerged that grew far beyond Metro's search for a home. The new vision encompassed a giant mega-campus where three educational institutions—Metro State, the Community College of Denver, and the University of Colorado at Denver—would share the same piece of land under the umbrella of the Auraria Higher Education Commission. From the perspective of the greater community, the concept embodied a number of advantages: The urban nature of the three institutions would remain intact; shared facilities would increase efficiency; and a blighted area of town would be beautified.

The main obstacle was the 155 Hispanic families within the "forgotten community" who had resided there for generations.[3] Homes on the 169 acres of land were earmarked for destruction; the families, in the words of one Westsider, "would need to be uprooted and shipped out."[4]

"The student government at Metro was going around to classes telling everyone how great it would be to have a campus [at Auraria]," recalls Virginia Castro. "All *we* could think of was the people we knew in the community. We found that a lot of UMAS students knew these people through their network of extended families. We found out too, that there were groups of West Side residents that were opposed [to the expansion] and we began to go to meetings all over the West Side."[5]

Two organizations led the resistance. One was the Auraria Residents Organization headed by Father Pete Garcia, the respected pastor of St. Cajetan's Church.[6] The other, El Centro Cultural, was located on Sante Fe Drive in the heart of the West Side.

Waldo

In 1968 one of the West Side's most renowned and colorful characters appeared on the Metro campus representing El Centro Cultural. Everyone in the neighborhood knew him by his first name, Waldo. His purpose in visiting Metro was to recruit the membership of UMAS to the campaign against the Auraria mega-campus.

The appearance of Waldo Benavidez on the Metro campus had a profound impact on Castro. Benavidez was a savvy operator, the acknowledged political genius of the West Side. For the next six years he would become Castro's mentor and closest political cohort.

Benavidez found little difficulty winning UMAS over to his side. Soon UMAS members including Castro and his future wife, Virginia Lucero, were visiting him regularly at the Auraria Community Center on Twelfth and Mariposa where Benavidez worked. "We learned more from Waldo," says Virginia Castro, "than from school. It was a much better classroom than anything we had down at Metro."[7]

Some understanding of the Benavidez family is required in order to grasp the dynamics of power on the West Side. Waldo Benavidez came from Albuquerque in 1956 to marry a young woman from the West Side he had met in San Francisco.[8] His wife, Betty, was a Quintana—a striking woman—whose family was deeply rooted in the community.

Twenty years old and newly married, Waldo hired on with City Sanitation shortly after his arrival in Denver. It was Betty's first cousin, Frankie Anaya, who introduced him to local politics. Nurtured by Anaya and inspired by the charismatic young senator from Massachusetts, Benavidez hooked up in 1960 with the Viva Kennedy campaign headed in Denver by Corky Gonzales.[9] Hungry for young blood on the politically apathetic West Side, the Democratic Party gobbled him up. At twenty-one, he began to make a niche for himself in the party infrastructure, starting as a precinct committeeman.

Paralleling his early political training, his education in city government ran the gamut of jobs, from sanitation, to the paving department of Public Works, to Stapleton Airport, to the City Engineer's Office, where he worked as an assistant engineer. Those years proved an excellent training ground for the young man who would become one of the city's best neighborhood organizers.

Benavidez was an aloof man, a self-described loner. He had developed an eye condition that forced him to wear sunglasses most of the time. "He wore those thick dark sun glasses everywhere, day or night," recalls one observer. "The guy looked like a hood straight out of the fifties. Like those guys with the shades, walking with a strut and talking street talk. The projected appearance was intimidation and militance."[10]

Waldo's avocation as a photographer aptly characterizes an important aspect of his personality. The hobby allowed him to remove himself from social interaction and set himself up as the outsider, as the coldly analytical observer. The walls of his current residence inside the Auraria Community Center underneath the Sixth Avenue viaduct are lined with his own photographs. He loved the old buildings on the West Side as well as those of his native New Mexico. He revered the old churches and the Spanish colonial architecture. "Castro was a born social worker," says Benavidez, laughingly, in comparing their two personalities. "He was gonna be a priest at one time. A humanitarian. I'm not and never was. I like buildings better than people."[11]

In 1964, President Lyndon Johnson declared an "unconditional" war on poverty in America. "We shall not rest," he announced "until that war is won."[12] Even now, politicians and scholars hotly debate the aftereffects of the "war." No one doubts, however, that the flow of ideas and money into the inner cities reshaped the political environment.

Federal rhetoric—some genuine, some diversionary—espoused the unheard-of notion that the poor should have a voice in governing their own affairs. Only by exercising some degree of local control, went the argument, could poor neighborhoods pull themselves up out of poverty. Federal dollars consequently began to trickle into the community centers of low-income neighborhoods. Corky Gonzales's political influence originated with his appointment as director of Denver's War on Poverty program. Likewise, Waldo Benavidez's power can be traced to these same roots: Johnson's War on Poverty provided the national context for inner-city politics in the 1960s.

In the late '60s, Waldo, drawing on years of experience working for both the City and the Democrats, gained a position as community organizer at the Auraria Community Center across from the Lincoln Park

Projects on Mariposa Street. Since 1922, the community center had quietly dispensed social services under the rubric of the nationally famous Association of Settlement Houses founded by Jane Addams.[13] Waldo took that basic structure and built Auraria Community Center into a base of political power.

A knock on Waldo's Mariposa Street door in 1968 brought another character into the picture. His name was Dean Punké, a tall University of Colorado grad student in his thirties, who Benavidez described as a "brilliant Anglo dude, brainy and eccentric, a big blond German-looking guy, but not big in an aggressive kind of way. He was a Saul Alinsky type."[14]

Alinsky had been a radical social worker nationally recognized as the man who wrote the book on neighborhood organizing. In the 1930s he had organized the tough "Back of the Yards" neighborhood in Chicago's packinghouse district, and then spread his ideas nationwide while organizing poor urban neighborhoods throughout the country. His two books *Reveille for Radicals* and *Rules for Radicals* served as textbooks for the neighborhood organizers who knocked on doors for numerous campaigns in the 1960s and '70s.[15]

In Alinsky's view, power should originate from the "grassroots"; it should rise from the bottom up. He loved to shake up traditional city power structures with his unorthodox tactics and irreverent style. Empower the dispossessed; empower the disenfranchised. He loved to take the salt of the earth—people who had spent a lifetime struggling for daily survival—and train them to taste small doses of power they had never before experienced. César Chávez was such a man. His first exposure to the tactics and strategies of organizing occurred within the Community Service Organization, one of Alinsky's networks in California. Through the CSO, Alinsky's ideas exerted considerable influence on the Chicano community.[16]

Dean Punké, though not formally connected with Alinsky's organization, was clearly a man cut in the Alinsky mold. He had combed the West Side looking for someone to pick up on his message about the mega-campus at Auraria. A chance acquaintance told him a visit to Waldo Benavidez's house would be worth the effort.[17]

Neighborhood Preservation

Benavidez and Punké hit it off from the start. "We started talkin' about buildings," says Benavidez. "He was really into historical buildings. We started talkin' about neighborhood preservation. That's what drew him and me together. We had a common interest. We talked about streets and one-ways and saving churches. . . . He said he always had a feeling for Hispanic communities and he's always thought that they've gotten a raw deal in terms of their neighborhood. He'd talk about [Chávez Ravine] in California where they . . . drove thousands of people out to build this big stadium.[18] And Chicago—they did the same thing there and he didn't want it to happen here. He's the one that told me, 'Hey, it's the same deal downtown [in Auraria]. This is gonna happen.' He was lookin' for somebody to pick up on his message and at that time I picked up on it. He was lookin' for someone to pick up the ball and start dealin' with the situation. I jumped on it. He was strictly background, but I would attribute a lot of the neighborhood development to his guidance."[19]

In Waldo's mind, the first task was to stop the invasion of the Auraria Higher Education Center into the West Side. "Every time the powers-that-be want to expand," he said, "they poke around to find the softest spot and it's always the Chicano community."[20]

The struggle against the Auraria project eventually brought the energies of Benavidez, Punké, and Castro together. In a fit of hyperbole, Benavidez later reminisced, "When Dean came into my life and Rich Castro came into my life, it was something that would never be repeated again in a thousand years. All the right pieces came together. Just like in World War II. You had Stalin, Roosevelt, and Churchill," he says with a laugh. "I mean you never get those kinds of minds comin' together. It's just that kind of thing. Just like when Federico Peña got elected mayor. I mean who woulda thought? All the right things came together and it will never happen again. That's the way I see it."[21]

Hyperbole and exaggeration aside, the three of them clicked. Even his later enemies call Waldo the spark plug for the engine that started turning on the West Side in the late '60s. Adolfo Gomez, who would later clash with Benavidez, stated that Waldo was the man who "created a conscience in the neighborhood," a man who "built an interest in meeting neighborhood needs whether it meant dealing with the police department, housing, or employment."[22]

As it turned out, the Auraria expansion project moved forward inexorably, a giant political bulldozer. Just as Dean Punké feared, the grand plans of the majority community easily overpowered the desires of a poor inner-city neighborhood. A 1969 citywide bond election sealed the fate of the beleaguered Auraria neighborhood and gave the final go-ahead for the Auraria Higher Education Commission to move on to the land along Cherry Creek.

As the dust cleared from the bond election, considerable fear lingered that what remained of the West Side would be devoured by the giant campus. Would the rise in property values force low-income renters out of the area? Would landlords begin to favor students over Hispanic families in their rental policies? Would retail stores and food outlets gear up to serve the student population rather than the traditional community?[23] These fears

galvanized the West Side and brought community activists together to preserve what they had left.

What they had left was little enough. Adolfo Gomez recalls the two
decades of economic decline prior to the 1960s. "Normal daily services,"
he says, "were nonexistent. They all moved away. We had in the '50s a
Safeway on the corner of Eighth and Inca which is now the Boys' Club. The
DeLuxe Auto Body on the corner of Eighth and Galapago used to be a
Piggly Wiggly. And then we had another supermarket on the corner of
Eighth and Kalamath. These were major chain stores. We had everything.
We had a Woolworth on the corner of Eighth and Santa Fe. We had a J.C.
Penney's between Eighth and Ninth on Santa Fe. We had three theaters on
Santa Fe. We had two drugstores. In the mid '50s and early '60s they all
moved away. They left because of the lack of buying power in the commu-
nity and the competition from the downtown stores.

"As the stores moved away . . . and all the old buildings were being
torn down, they were replaced by auto parts suppliers and auto body shops.
They didn't employ local people and they provided not much of anything
for the neighborhood. Santa Fe was an easy access street and they were
getting lots of that type of auto business. In the late '50s Santa Fe and
Kalamath changed from two-way streets of slow-moving traffic to fast-
moving one-way streets extending from three to four to five lanes and elimi-
nating parking from both sides of the street in some cases. In the '50s Sixth
Avenue [eastbound] was a dead-end on Kalamath! You can picture Sixth
Avenue today, 50,000 cars a day! Lack of consideration for the neighborhood on the part of the traffic movers destroyed the business activity of the
community."[24]

Aside from the major arteries, other problems faced neighborhood residents. "In those days," continues Gomez, "the zoning laws were weak and
variances were given frequently and without much reason. Businesses
would come in. They would knock down a house or two, construct their
buildings . . . begin to expand, and then just simply eat up the whole block.
That happened a lot."[25]

The West Side Coalition

As the bulldozers moved in 1969 to clear the ground for the new mega-
campus, the West Side began to mobilize in self-defense. Under the leadership of Benavidez, disparate groups tucked quietly away in the neighborhood began to intersect and weave themselves into a pressure group capable of making its voice heard at City Hall. From the alliance of these
groups emerged the West Side Coalition, the umbrella under which the
smaller groups could unify. It started in a tiny hole-in-the-wall office in the
back of the Inner City Parish, behind West High School.

Twenty-three years old and still studying sociology as an undergraduate at Metro, Castro emerged as the Coalition's executive director. The rise of the West Side Coalition paralleled the flowering of the Chicano Movement in Denver. 1969 was the year the "renaissance" came into its own. The explosion derived its energy from many sources.

The Crusade for Justice was climbing confidently toward a pinnacle of national influence and recognition. Artists were bringing life to the drab walls of housing projects with bold and colorful murals in the spirit of Diego Rivera, the revolutionary muralist from Mexico. Students at West High School, in the most dramatic event of the year, shut the school down over charges of racism. Musicians improvised fusions of Latino music with rock and roll.

But in West Denver, the primary engine of change was the West Side Coalition. "We had it down," claims Jerry Garcia, who served a sort of community organizing apprenticeship with the Coalition. "We had plans put together for development corporations. We were looking at employing people. We were talking with the Catholic Church to invest some of their capital into chain super markets. We were talking about how we were going to revitalize Santa Fe Street as a retail strip and how the nonprofit organizations in the Coalition could become self-sustaining. These are the types of things that we were talking about in the early '70s that [in other communities] are just being talked about today. We were ahead of our time. Waldo was ahead of his time."[26]

The Coalition attempted to fuse the energy of a score of organizations. Older civil rights groups, such as the GI Forum, joined hands with the "fix-up, clean up, remove junk car types" of the West Side Improvement Association. Neighborhood Anglos who, according to Waldo, "cared about their little gardens and stuff like that" became part of the fold.[27] The neighborhood churches exerted a powerful presence and brought with them an additional aura of respectability. Community-based organizations nurtured during the heydays of the War on Poverty—the Auraria Community Center and the West Side Action Center— joined forces as did El Centro Cultural. "We were legit," says Waldo. "We were really legit."[28]

It was the microcosmic approach to social change: You took your own little piece of the world and you fixed it up; you made it livable. From the community organizer's perspective, it was the formula for healing the world.

In a 1972 talk at the University of Denver, Waldo Benavidez stated, "I'd been in this whole thing a number of years. There was a Chicano Movement, and I asked, 'What is my concern; how do I help contribute to this movement? After lookin' it all over—the war and kids gettin' into college and education and the whole trip—I thought where I could best contribute was in my own neighborhood. The concept that I've operated on, which I thought has always been a good concept is 'community control.'"[29]

"I thought there had to be neighborhoods," said Benavidez in a much later interview, "for people that could afford a thirty or forty thousand dollar home and live happily ever after. So after [the Auraria struggle] we were talkin' neighborhood development; we're talkin' maps; we're tryin' to preserve the neighborhood." [30]

Some revolutionary groups had already begun to criticize this Alinsky-style approach to social change. The limited goals—opposition to one-way streets or to zoning variances—failed to confront the major causes of economic injustice, they argued. Labeling Alinsky forces "conservative wine in radical bottles," one scholar wrote, "When organizing around concrete, self-interest oriented issues within neighborhoods, Alinsky groups usually fight not for anything resembling radical goals, but rather tend to advance ideas about preservation that smack of Burkean conservatism."[31]

One version of Castro's response to this critique can be found in an article he co-authored shortly after the Coalition's demise in the early '70s. Characterizing the West Side as an "internal colony," controlled by outside forces (as were all barrios of the Southwest), Castro and his colleagues Aileen Lucero and George Rivera identified "socioeconomic powerlessness," "external control," and "intraethnic conflict" as the overriding sources of Chicano oppression. "It was evident," they wrote, "that Chicanos in the West Side did not own the economic base of their community—the land."[32] Absentee landlords, Anglo politicians, Anglo cops, Anglo directors of social agencies sapped the community of any sense of ownership or control over its destiny. "The West Side Coalition," they explained, "was created to limit outside encroachment and to decrease external control in order to preserve the neighborhood as a residential area."[33]

Castro was painfully aware of the Coalition's limited goals as well as the limitations of neighborhood organizing. "The Coalition's efforts to decolonize the barrio were greatly limited," he wrote with his fellow authors. "Since Chicanos in the United States are a numerical minority, the possibility of social change through revolution can be seriously questioned. The West Side Coalition sought change through the only means available—the democratic process."[34]

The tension between the Coalition and more radical organizations can be traced back to the Coalition's beginnings. However, the differences were kept in check early on; they would simmer for a few years before boiling over into open hostility.

Nuts and Bolts

Ideologies aside, the West Side Coalition examined the details of daily life in West Denver and dealt with nuts-and-bolts issues. Housing problems, for instance, cropped up repeatedly. Homes on the West Side were invariably old, frequently decrepit and deteriorating, generally unpainted, and oftentimes overcrowded. One study by the Denver Planning Office concluded that 25 percent of neighborhood homes suffered from major exterior structural defects—cracked walls, deteriorating foundations, damaged roofs. Ten percent of housing units lacked plumbing facilities; 70 percent had sufficient exterior damage to place them in the "deteriorating" category. A bare five percent of West Side homes met the criteria for standard housing.[35]

To counteract the declining condition of the neighborhood, the West Side Coalition sought funding wherever it could, scouring federal, state, and local agencies for finances. It negotiated with the Denver Urban Renewal Authority to purchase vacant sites on which to build low-cost housing. Until the Nixon administration froze the project in 1972, the Coalition worked on plans to build these homes in adobe with Mexican-style architecture in order to reflect the ethnic make-up of the community. Architects and construction firms, likewise, were to be drawn from the community.[36] The Coalition negotiated with the Colorado Economic Development Association (CEDA) to acquire money for loans and subsidies for individual homebuyers.[37] The Coalition received a grant from Model Cities for building a high-rise for the elderly and for providing small home maintenance grants for resident homeowners.[38] It worked with Brothers Redevelopment Incorporated, a nonprofit agency that helped rehabilitate deteriorating homes.[39]

Health issues provided another opportunity for neighborhood organizing. Across the street from the Auraria Community Center was a small house inhabited in the daytime by physicians from Denver General Hospital. Realizing this provided the seeds for a neighborhood health clinic, the Coalition set about the task of gathering funds from the City and County through the Community Development Agency and from the federal government through DURA. Once the Mariposa Health Clinic came to fruition, Castro began researching the health needs of the neighborhood.

Startlingly, one conclusion the research revealed was that the number-one killer of children on the West Side was strep throat. Celina Benavidez, who became a state representative and who was at one time Waldo's daughter-in-law, worked with Castro as a secretary for the Coalition in the early '70s. "In 1972," she asserts, "strep throat was killing our babies in our community at a higher rate than the rate of infant mortality in Vietnam."[40]

One day Castro approached Ms. Benavidez and informed her: "You're gonna become the Strep Throat Lady."

"I said, 'What are you talking about?' To me, strep throat was just a cold. But he and Waldo got John Flores, the artist, to design a coloring book of the Strep Throat Aztec god, the god that fights strep throat. You come and get a throat culture at the Mariposa Health Clinic and you get a coloring book. We started knocking on doors and we'd say, 'Want a coloring book? Come to the clinic.' [In this way] we drastically reduced the epidemic of strep throat on the West Side."[41]

The newly emerging environmental movement in the 1970s, led as it was by a core of white middle-class activists, developed a reputation for clashing with the perceived interests of the working class and of the inner-city poor. However, the industrial nature of West Denver shaped the contours of the Coalition's vision and brought environmental issues to the fore.

Again, Celina Benavidez recalls Castro's role. "In small meetings around the community, Richard was saying, 'It is not acceptable to have overweight trucks traveling down Kalamath Street and down West Eighth Avenue and down Galapago. They are releasing pollutants. They are creating noise. They are a danger to our children.' Richard talked about the dangers of the Komac Paint Company emitting fumes next to the park. [He brought up] the whole issue of open barrels at chemical companies in the neighborhood. It was Richard and Waldo that talked about changing one-way streets into two-ways so that the neighborhood would not be impacted by thoroughfares that [were crowded and polluted]."[42]

On one level, then, the Coalition represented the intersection of neighborhood preservation with the ideals of the budding environmental movement.

Down-zoning on the West Side

For all the deteriorated housing bordering railroad yards, for all the body shops on West Eight Avenue, the area remained, nevertheless, a neighborhood of predominantly single-family dwellings with yards and porches. Faced with the choice, the vast majority of Westsiders favored these homes, in whatever condition, over another Auraria-style invasion from downtown.[43] Better a modest house than a looming high-rise, a commercial office building or one more warehouse emitting diesel fumes from forklifts operating on the loading docks.

In 1971, therefore, members of the Coalition challenged the city's vision of the future. Submitted by the Denver Planning Office, "The 1985 Comprehensive Plan" for the West Side emphasized high-density housing and commercial development. Most of the West Side—at least that part which was not zoned for industrial use—was already zoned R-3 or R-4 for high-density residential use. That meant that the land occupied by single-family dwellings and duplexes was ripe for profitable investments in apartment buildings and commercial establishments; the zoning ordinances were already in place. Residents of single-family dwellings—most of them renters—lived in a zoning netherworld. Their small homes—built before the current zoning laws were implemented—did not conform to the regulations in place in the 1970s. The precarious legal status of their homes imposed significant obstacles to securing home improvement loans and set limits on the extent of improvements that could be made.[44] What was worse, according to one study, was that "there is a constant temptation for a landlord to neglect a small residence . . . with the idea of future redevelopment."[45]

Sizing up the precarious existence of the neighborhood home dweller, the West Side Coalition set out on an ambitious campaign to rezone twenty-six blocks in the area. Down-zoning to R-2 or low-density residential would redefine the nature of future development and lend a greater voice to residents of modest homes. It would provide stability for single-family homes and encourage investment in home improvement.

Response to the proposal was predictably fierce. Castro's own analysis cited Ed Horton, vice president of the Midland Federal Savings board of directors and a West Side landowner. Horton wrote that "property owners stand to lose the $100,000 an acre potential value instead of the $28,000 an acre present value."[46] Fearing a loss of property values and a hemorrhage of future investment returns, a group of property owners formed a new organization, the United Westsiders for Improvement and Progress, to battle the Coalition's rezoning effort.

Their vision of the West Side occupied the opposite end of the spectrum from that of Waldo and the Coalition. The way to improve the neighborhood would be to raze the old structures and erect new high-density apartments. Many people, they argued, had bought land with the expectation that profits could be made from investing in a high-density zoning area.[47] With financial stakes running high, the tension soared by the time the issue reached the City Council in April 1972. Each side accused the other of vandalism, intimidation, and malicious mischief. The final result of the Council's action was particularly disheartening to the West Side Coalition and to most of the neighborhood's residents. By a vote of 10-2, all three sections of the rezoning package went down in defeat. It was a victory, said the Coalition, for the absentee landlord.[48]

Castro attributed the loss to two causes: one economic, one political. First, Westsiders who testified before the Council were predominantly renters, not homeowners. This came out in hearings in which Council members asked pointed questions as to the residential status of the witnesses. Castro and his colleagues Lucero and Rivera claimed that "their status as non-owners greatly influenced the City Council's decision."[49]

Second, no Chicanos sat on the City Council. Even the West Side's representative, Eugene DiManna, an Italian tavern owner from North Denver (the councilman's district overlapped both neighborhoods), abstained without apparent remorse on the rezoning resolution. DiManna's disregard for Chicanos on the West Side and in North Denver so infuriated the Chicano community that two separate recall efforts eventually materialized to force him out of office.[50] Both of these factors—the economic and political forces that led to the Coalition's defeat—underscored Castro's contention that power held by outsiders tended to strangle the aspirations of the Chicano community to exercise some control in its own neighborhoods.

Coalition Politics

In vying for power, the Coalition made conscious efforts to reach out to organizations across the political spectrum. Cecelia Garcia recalls, for instance, a story about the cultural gap between youth who related to the "Movement," and the members of some of the more traditional organizations.

"I was in the Chicano Movement as a girl," she says. "I wore no make-up because I boycotted the make-up industry. I didn't wear nylons; I didn't wear what you would call traditional girls' dress. I wore coveralls—*picheras*—with just a blouse or a shirt and then I had a brown beret. I had a green army fatigue poncho that my mom fixed for me so I could wear it over my head. The reason I had the poncho was because sometimes we would be on marches or in meetings. It would get cold at night and I never knew if we were gonna be outside in the parks or at Safeway. . . . All the kids in the Chicano Movement were dressed like me. [People] in the more traditional organizations became very angry at things like that.

"The GI Forum used to have this big event every year where they would crown the GI Forum Princess. The princess sold the most tickets in her community in order to start scholarships. Of course, the GI Forum princesses were the most beautiful girls with these big gowns and all of that. I'll never forget; Richard and Waldo and Virginia and Betty said one day, 'You have to come to the American GI Forum's crowning of the princess because you're president of the Latin American Clubs in the Denver Public Schools. I said to them, 'I don't wanna go. That is not what we're all about.' I didn't know, of course, that the American GI Forum was a very activist civil rights organization of veterans." Her objection was to the pomp and ceremony, the formal dress and the emphasis on style.

The Castros and Benavidezes insisted. "'It's a traditional Hispanic group,' they said. 'They need to see you there; you need to be there.' Well . . . I went," continues Garcia. "It was an unbelievable event. Everybody was dressed up in ball gowns and suits. It was at a nice hotel just like the Miss America Pageant. And there I came all dressed up—not in a ball gown, not in a dress—but in my coveralls, and my brown beret and with my poncho hanging over my shoulders. My mom wouldn't allow us to cut our hair, so I had hair down to my side. Betty and Waldo and Richard and Virginia looked at me and didn't say a word. They didn't put me down, didn't say, 'Why are you dressed that way?' . . . Most adults nowadays would say, 'No way are you coming in dressed like that.' But Richard and Virginia didn't say a word. . . . What was more important to them was that I was there and I did my job and I gave my speech about the Chicano Movement in front of the GI Forum. They said I did a good job, that I spoke very clearly and I had a [nicely prepared] little speech. They were surprised that I showed up because I didn't wanna go.

"Other kids told me, 'Did you show up in your jeans?' And I said, 'Yeah, what's wrong with that?' 'We knew you would,' they said. I just didn't believe . . . in that traditional role. But Richard and Virginia and Waldo and Betty were visionaries because they knew it was all one Movement. They went to the dances; they went to GI Forum. I never heard Richard use the word 'sell-out.' They could bridge all this gap and at the same time be part of the Movement."[51]

Thus, while other Movement groups jumped ahead and spurned the older, more conservative organizations in the community, the West Side Coalition, at least in the early years, tried to live up to its name. They tried to piece together an organization that transcended the differences of culture, age, appearances, and politics.

Through the endless meetings and ceaseless details of organizing the West Side, Richard Castro was a young man in perpetual motion. He was, say observers, the technical wizard of the West Side. A magic marker seemed to be affixed permanently to his left hand like an extra appendage, ready to jot down ideas on large rolls of white paper. As in the days of UMAS, his writing was prolific: He was the grant writer, the researcher, the recorder of correspondence.

"If you can play the paper game," says Waldo, "you're one up on everybody else. If there's a weakness in grassroots organizations, it's their inability to shuffle the paper, to get it to the right place at the right time to the right person. That was his asset. Research and writing. He was very good and that's what put us ahead of everybody else. That put us ahead of every other Hispanic organization in Denver."[52]

A Difference in Personalities

Technical expertise aside, Castro never claimed status as commander in chief of the West Side Coalition. That role belonged to Waldo. It was Waldo who mapped out strategies, laid down theoretical foundations, and marshaled troops. Waldo was the mentor, Castro the apprentice.

Their personalities differed like night and day.[53] Benavidez was overbearing, his demeanor brusque. He bullied and cajoled. He drove hard and stepped on people's toes. "No one ever said Rich was an asshole," says Waldo Benavidez. "Even the Crusade for Justice said Rich was a nice guy. But me, I was an asshole all the way."[54]

Castro seemed his polar opposite. He could be a good old boy and drink beer with the guys. He was jovial; he had a light touch and a joke for every occasion. If he gathered a single signature for a petition drive, his optimistic follow-up was always: "Well, just 9,999 names to go." If Waldo was the hard-driving general, Castro was the diplomat. He could smooth things over and coax people to his side.

Together they composed a formidable team. In time, things began to unravel but during the heady days of the '60s and early '70s the Coalition forged an effective grassroots organization. Victories were small, to be sure. They prevented an additional one-way street from running through the neighborhood; they stopped a Greyhound Bus terminal—another industrial encroachment—from being built near West Colfax. They closed down an X-rated theatre on Santa Fe, and they helped get a new health center and a new recreation center for the neighborhood.[55]

Even Castro confessed, however, that the Coalition's successes came only in areas that did not represent a threat to the economic and political structure. In the rezoning battle and in some of its struggles for better housing, the West Side Coalition slammed head first into the limitations of community organizing. In the absence of real power at the top or at least in the absence of an administration sympathetic to the needs of the poor, the options for neighborhood organizers remained quite narrow. Nevertheless, as a training ground and as an experiment in grassroots democracy, the Coalition represented a significant step in combating the powerlessness endemic to poor Chicano communities.

Grad School

Castro's energies focused primarily on the West Side Coalition during this period. But through most of his tenure as director of the Coalition, Castro was enrolled in the graduate School of Social Work at the University of Denver.

DU's campus stood a world apart from the busy streets of the West Side. Nestled in a quiet South Denver neighborhood, the lush university grounds sloped gently westward creating a terraced effect, accentuated by gentle waterfalls that bubbled into tranquil fountains and ponds. In spring and summer the place was verdant with the foliage of elms and birch trees interspersed among spruce and Douglas firs. The student population was white and prosperous. Thus, Castro's daily life in the early seventies straddled these two worlds. One foot firmly anchored in the streets and neighborhoods of the inner city, the other planted in this oasis of the academic world.

Cecilia Garcia visited DU at age sixteen and thought she may as well have been on the moon. She went with a theater group from the Auraria Community Center, which had been invited to present a play—*Jose Martinez*—to the School of Social Work. It was a drama about the troubles of a young Mexican boy trying to succeed in an elementary school. When the West Side kids saw Richard Castro seated in the audience, they were stunned.

They quickly cornered him and demanded to know: "What are you doing here? Why are you here at this school?"

"I'm getting my master's degree in social work," he replied.

"We couldn't believe it," remembers Garcia. "We considered him on the other side. We thought, 'Oh my God, he's part of the system; he's part of the institution.' We were very upset with him."

"No," explained Castro. "This is where we belong. You have to get educated. Master's degrees are very important for the movement. This is where we all need to be."

"It was so far removed from reality," says Garcia, "because it was so expensive. To go to DU? You might as well have been saying that you belonged in Mars. It was a whole other world because of the money, because of the people."[56] Garcia, like others who made the successful journey into the American middle class, would come to see Castro as "a living bridge" between the West Side and the opportunities for professional success that opened up with a college education. The tension between the assimilationist option and one that rejected success in Anglo society always hovered in the background. What Castro sought was to serve simultaneously as a bridge to the middle class as well as a role model for service to the Chicano community.

Following the traditions he learned at Metropolitan State, Castro worked to pry open the university and make it available to Chicano students. Lori and John Helms, DU students at the time, described Castro as instrumental in forming a Chicano social group designed to provide a "comfort zone."[57] The eight Hispanic social work students out of a class of 120 tended to gather in private apartments or at the Stadium Inn for relaxation after classes.

Equally important was the challenge to DU's admission policies brought before the Colorado Civil Rights Commission by Castro and his friend Ambrose Rodriguez. The two gained a concession from the university to provide stipends for ten new minority grad students in the School of Social Work.

The victory ended in a challenge because the university maintained it could not find ten Chicanos who could qualify for the master's program in social work. According to Virginia Castro, "They said to Rich and Ambrose, 'if you can go out and find ten students, then we'll reserve the stipends.' Well, they did find ten students and I was one of them. Every one of us graduated and we ended up with a good solid organization at DU for years."[58]

Castro's thesis, written with a team of other students, reflected both of the worlds he inhabited in the early '70s. It was alternately a cry for social justice and a scholarly study. In its pages Corky Gonzales's searing poetry about the soul of the barrio is interspersed with demographic statistics gathered from *Business Week*.

Carrying the cumbersome title, "A Survey of Social Welfare Utilization Patterns in the Auraria Community," the thesis represents a search for a new model with which to deliver social services in the barrio. Castro postulated that there existed "aspects of the Mexican American which might adversely affect his ability to utilize available social services."[59]

He explored other models of social service delivery that had developed during the Johnson years of the War on Poverty, and he suggested that the basis for social work should be the "community multi-service center." This should be "governed by a board of directors, the majority of which would be consumers [of the services] and community residents."[60]

The people of the inner city, he insisted, should have a voice in determining the distribution of government services. The thesis' content paralleled the ideas of community control he had attempted to put into practice for the previous five years at the Auraria Community Center and at the West Side Coalition. Castro, thus, used his time at DU to try to establish a theoretical framework for his ongoing work in West Denver.

East Side Social Work

Despite this emphasis on experimental forms of community control, Castro took a more orthodox social worker's job while working on his undergraduate degree at Metro. His original roots lay not in the West Side but in the East Side barrio, and that is where he returned to serve an apprenticeship in traditional social work. In 1968 he joined the Youth Services Bureau of the Denver Police Department, which had started up a "Street Workers Program" operating out of Curtis Park.

Back home on the East Side, Castro reconnected with two old friends from his high school days. Eloy Mares, a lifelong East Side resident who had been Castro's football coach, was working for Juvenile Court. Just as he had mentored him in athletics, Mares took Castro under his wing as a social worker.[61]

Andy Lovato, who had played fullback on Castro's football team, hired on to the Street Workers Program at the same time. The two of them moved in next door to each other in an old terrace apartment on Thirty-sixth and Humboldt between Angel's Food Store and the Annunciation Parochial School from which Castro had graduated five years before.

The place was the heart of the East Side. Lovato smiles when he remembers their $35-a-month apartments. There was a hole in the roof next to the vent in his bathroom. In the wintertime, when he sat on the toilet, he would look up and watch the snow coming down as it fell softly on his face.[62]

The two young social workers set up shop at the Curtis Park rec center in an area roiling with conflict. The old rivalry between manitos (native Colorado Chicanos) and Mexican Nationals (immigrant families from Mexico) added an additional layer of friction and violence to an already strained neighborhood. Some kids carried two-by-fours sawed off and curved at the edges to look something like a baseball bat. Glue sniffing was a drug of choice for the younger set. Mares recalls searching one morning for a couple of twelve-year-olds notorious for cutting school. He found them in an ash pit by La Hacienda restaurant sucking down the fumes from an open bottle.

"I lived in this community," says Mares. "I worked with families who lived in this community and, with Juvenile Justice, I got to know a lot of other families from a different perspective. Some of the families were terribly—if I can use the word—dysfunctional and some were very violent. Rich used to work with some of these same families."[63]

In this environment, Castro's brand of social work displayed a traditional approach. The idea was to wean kids away from the street and help them overcome their difficulties at home by providing healthy alternatives. It was old-fashioned social work, whose goal was to rescue as many individual kids as possible.

"It wasn't real complicated," says Castro's coworker, Lovato. "It wasn't anything psychological. We just wanted to give kids constructive things to do in the community."[64] The Street Workers Program brought in kids to paint murals, do crafts, or play basketball at the rec center. They would show sci-fi movies on a cinderblock wall on Saturday mornings, charging a nickel or a dime for popcorn or Coke. For older kids, there were field trips to Yellowstone or Mesa Verde, or to mountain streams for river rafting.

It was here, amidst this somewhat innocent rescue attempt, that Castro's rivalry with the growing revolutionary movement began. Like Castro, the revolution saw the street devouring these East Side kids in a swamp of self-destructive behavior. The revolution's response, however, diverged broadly on ideological grounds. Revolutionaries viewed the anger that filled the hearts of these kids as a sign of life, as a healthy response to a society that had abandoned them. Without political direction, however, that raw uncontrolled anger would inevitably turn inward. Frantz Fanon, the psychologist who had put the Algerian revolution under the microscope, had written in *The Wretched of the Earth* that "the colonized man will first manifest this aggressiveness which has been deposited in his bones against his own people."[65] The task of the revolution, then, was to re-channel the anger that ran so rampant on the barrio streets. Barrio residents must direct their anger not toward neighbors or the youth down the block who shared their desperation, but towards the system that had created their environment.

In East Los Angeles, David Sanchez had organized the Brown Berets, a paramilitary organization begun in 1968 to defend barrio youth against police violence.[66] One study described the Berets as a "reconstitution of all the old gangs commonly prevalent in the urban ghetto environment, but with political content and strong emphasis on Mexican-American identity."[67] "One important function of the Berets was to channel the aimless violence of '*vatos locos*' (crazy dudes) into meaningful efforts for the Chicano group."[68] The Berets quickly spread to twenty-seven southwestern cities and, by the fall of 1969, had emerged with roughly two hundred members in the Curtis Park area of East Denver.[69]

The young man who laid the foundation for the East Side Brown Berets was also much sought-after by Eloy Mares, Rich Castro, and the Youth Services Bureau. The revolution and the reform movements fought for the soul of Roddy Miera, a stout, husky amateur boxer who lived across the street from Curtis Park.

"He had a lot of good qualities," remembers Mares. "He was the type of kid who got other kids involved. Whether it was due to charisma or being a strong arm or a combination of both, I don't know, but he would do it. He had a following at Curtis Park and he was a guy we relied on a lot to help organize things. He'd get people to do things from the standpoint of getting word around or selling tickets [to dances] or getting them to meetings. At the same time, Roddy was still trying to get his thing together as far as being a young man growing up."[70]

Miera presided over a small group Youth Services had organized while simultaneously playing a crucial role with the Berets. As the previous leader of a gang called the Curtis Park Boys, Miera had persuaded most of its members to disband the gang and join the East Side Brown Berets.[71] This cessation of gang activity is exactly the scenario laid out by the revolution: Politicize the kids, and the gangs will disappear.

Castro, however, mistrusted this approach because he feared the kids would be too easily manipulated and driven to political violence. "To stir up those kids to become a mob," said Andy Lovato, "was not what we wanted. . . . We wanted to do things within the system."[72] Lovato has vivid memories of Castro telling Brown Berets they could not bring billy clubs to the dances sponsored by Youth Services and they couldn't use the proceeds to buy additional clubs. The kids argued that they needed their weapons to "protect the neighborhood." "We got police to protect the neighborhood," Castro would respond.[73]

Incident at Curtis Park

Unfortunately, Castro was to find his moderate position undermined by the behavior of the Denver police on the East Side. What happened at Curtis Park on April 14, 1970, thrust his name for the first time onto the pages of the *Rocky Mountain News*. It would become a defining moment in his political career.

Shortly after four on that spring afternoon, four Brown Berets were arrested during a disturbance near Thirty-second and Curtis Streets at the northwest corner of the park. It was one of those minor incidents that got out of hand. One of the kids, Leonard Treviño, had allegedly driven a car up on the park lawn, and patrolman Michael Davin testified later that he had to subdue the youth in order to make the arrest. Treviño's arrest apparently triggered resistance among the other youth. Patrolman Davin claimed that one kid picked up a jagged headlight rim and threw it at him while another picked up a tree branch and threatened to kill him. Patrolman Harold MacMillen stated that he was struck in the abdomen, and patrolman Lloyd Summers said he was struck in the chest by a chunk of concrete hurled from the park as he was making out the report.[74]

As the action unfolded, Castro, returning from classes at Metro, pulled up to the scene in his yellow Volkswagen Bug. Having had firsthand experience with the kids from Curtis Park, he felt he could help calm the situation. That approach proved naïve in the extreme. As he exited his car, Castro witnessed a Denver cop relentlessly hammering away at one of the neighborhood kids with a baton. "Nobody had the right to beat someone the way this kid was being beaten," stated Castro, testifying later at a hearing in front of police chief George Seaton and safety manager William Koch.[75]

The kid broke loose, ran up to Castro and pleaded, "Help me, Brother." Castro's hopes of staying out of Denver County Jail that night ended with the utterance of the word "Brother." When he tried to break up a second scuffle, a policeman grabbed him by the shirt and said, "Where's your brother?"[76]

"I pushed his hands off me," Castro stated later, "and said I had no brother here. . . . He said I was under arrest and began hitting me on the side with the nightstick. I didn't hit him, but I grabbed him to keep him from hitting me anymore."[77]

Before the afternoon was over, Castro, Treviño, Carlos Chávez, Tony "Fat Tony" Ornelas, and Miguel "Masa" Renteria found themselves in police custody, charged with assaulting a police officer and resisting arrest. In the privacy of the squad car, and in the darkness of the Denver County Jail, with the suspects handcuffed and vulnerable, the police apparently administered their own justice.

In testimony at a dialogue conducted at the Auraria Community Center, Castro captivated an emotional crowd with his story. The *News* reported that the crowd was momentarily hushed as he delivered his eyewitness account.

Castro and Ornelas shared the back seat of the same squad car on the way to police headquarters. "On the way to the station," Castro said, "Officer (Buckley T.) Stewart mumbled something about my rights and said something like, 'I don't care if you understand them or not, you stupid sons of bitches." The officer then went on, Castro testified, to call the suspects "dirty, slimy scum." When Castro responded in kind with an obscenity, the second patrolman "then turned around in his seat and sprayed Mace directly in my eyes while I sat handcuffed in the back seat."[78]

At the station, the situation deteriorated further. The two officers walked Castro into a wall before taking him through the door. A third officer, said Castro, "without any provocation, gave Tony Ornelas a karate kick to the chest. Tony was still handcuffed." With Ornelas collapsed on the floor, the same officer "kicked him hard four or five times in the back and sides. Then he grabbed Tony by the arms and handcuffs, lifted him off the floor, and dropped him on his face three or four times. . . . Four or five cops were standing in the door, just watching it all." Ornelas was still recovering from four bullet wounds he had received the month before. "When I went in the other room to fill out papers," said Castro, "the cops were all joking about the fat Mexican with four holes in him."[79] Within two weeks Castro corroborated his testimony by passing a lie detector test.[80]

Police beatings were nothing new in Denver's inner city. In 1963, police brutality stood at the top of Corky Gonzales's grievances when he started Los Voluntarios, a civil rights organization that was the forerunner of the Crusade for Justice.[81] In his master's thesis, "Young and Latino in a Cold War Barrio," James Patrick Walsh documents the strained and continually violent relations between Denver police and Chicano youth in the 1940s and '50s.[82]

Beginning in the mid-1960s, the Crusade for Justice had battled over the issue so persistently that by 1970 its tactics had diverged from Castro's. According to author and former Crusade member Ernesto Vigil, "[Corky] Gonzales, who had long experience in these matters, felt that continuous meetings with government officials and bureaucrats would entangle the community and dissipate energy with no positive results."[83]

Castro's associates at the West Side Coalition, however, came forward precisely to confront those government officials. Forty supporters camped out in sleeping bags in front of the police building on a cold April night.[84] A new citizens' group including the Religious Council on Human Relations, the GI Forum, the NAACP, and the Human Relations Commission of the Catholic Archdiocese came together to call for reforms in the Denver Police Department. They made two major demands: that police chief George Seaton resign and that the city create an independent Citizens' Police Review Board. If ever a time existed when the Chicano community trusted the DPD to handle its own investigations through the Internal Affairs Bureau, that time was long gone.

An emotionally charged atmosphere of mistrust, anger, and suspicion permeated every meeting between the new citizens' group and the city. City Council members Elvin Caldwell and Ernest Marranzino were repeatedly shouted down. Chief Seaton and Safety Manager Koch were "harangued."[85] *The Denver Post* described one instance when two conservative speakers were shouted down at a City Council meeting as they stood to oppose the crowd's demands for police reform. The Reverend James Miller, a leader of the John Birch Society, began his speech with "The history of the human race is the history of man's inhumanity to man. All men are by nature sinful men." His words were greeted with boos. "The Hispano crowd and its Anglo supporters," wrote the *Post*, "wouldn't buy Miller's viewpoints. The meeting was theirs."[86]

Chief Seaton did nothing to placate the raw emotions surrounding the case when he told *The Denver Post* that "persons concerned over brutality charges might be influenced by left wing radicalism."[87]

Seaton's statement particularly stuck in Castro's craw. "I'd been told to work within the system and I always have," he said.[88] Others protested that "Every time we go to city council to complain about injustice, we are called Communists, radicals and unpatriotic."[89] Castro's lawyer, Bal Chávez, stated, "We who have been involved on the part of the community, in attempting to present the truth of Mr. Castro's observations expected the city to dodge and bury the reality of police brutality in Denver. But the extent and viciousness of their attack on the character of members of the Chicano community was far beyond that which we expected."[90]

Though the protesters were determined to present the issue within every conceivable forum, an air of futility or at least low expectations seemed to hover over the campaign from the beginning. "We are trying to go through the established channels—the police bureau, the city administration and the courts," said Waldo Benavidez. "And we will continue to try to do so even though they haven't been effective in the past."[91] Spokespersons for the citizens' group predicted a "whitewash" at every level of the investigation.[92]

Among the layers of investigators was Denver's Commission on Community Relations, an agency Castro was destined to inherit under the administration of Mayor Federico Peña. Despite Castro's riveting testimony, despite the fact that he was praised by many for his "integrity,"[93] and despite the fact that Castro had passed a polygraph test, the commission, under the directorship of Minoru Yasui, failed to confirm charges of police brutality.

"The weight of the evidence does not sustain any disciplinary action against the police officers involved," said Yasui. "We can't prove brutality, although there is a doubt in the back of my mind."[94] Not everyone on the Commission for Community Relations agreed with the findings. Staff consultant George Garcia fired off a memo to Yasui calling the entire investigation "garbage."[95]

For his participation in the "whitewash," Castro's supporters called for Min Yasui's resignation alongside that of police chief Seaton. The whole episode was a strange introduction to the complex relationship that developed between Rich Castro and Min Yasui.

Ultimately, Mayor Bill McNichols requested that a grand jury investigate the Curtis Park incident. The proposal met with little enthusiasm among Castro supporters, especially since it diverted the leadership of the investigation to conservative district attorney Mike McKevitt. Waldo Benavidez summed up the general sentiment: "Grand jury investigations usually end up whitewashing the police department," he said, "but at least it's a little breakthrough. I think a grand jury investigation is needed, but as in the past, it probably won't be much help."[96] No one expressed much surprise, then, when the grand jury brought in its verdict on June 6: It found no evidence of police brutality.[97]

It would be many years before even the mildest Civilian Review Board would materialize. Its creation remained a lifelong goal for Castro, but in 1970 that goal seemed a long way off. Chief Seaton accentuated the mistrust between the police and the Chicano community at a stormy meeting at the Auraria Community Center. Following a heated exchange over the community's demand for an independent review board, the chief stalked off. "You're not going to get a Citizens' Review Board," he snapped. "We are capable of handling our own investigations."[98] Of all the contentious issues brought to the surface by the Chicano Movement in its early days, it is this one—police community relations—that has survived most tenaciously through the decades.

Castro's experiences on the street at Curtis Park and behind bars at the

Denver City Jail connected his life to a long line of historical grievances and tapped him into the huge reservoir of simmering resentments that marked Chicano relations toward police all over the Southwest. At Curtis Park he personalized those historical events, and the experience would strengthen his commitment to political activism.

Richard Castro's education during his youthful years carried him on a swiftly moving ride over wildly varied terrain. He came of age during the fiery and confrontational student movement of the 1960s. He walked picket lines at Safeway and at Metro. He sharpened his political skills on the West Side under the tutelage of a natural community organizer—one of the shrewdest in the business. He sought out the big picture in the academic world at DU, and he experienced the terrible clang of the heavy iron door slammed shut in the basement of the Denver City Jail. Alongside these visceral experiences came his first contact with recurrent social dynamics that would continue to shape his life and shape the path of his generation.

Having graduated with a master's degree from the University of Denver, Castro was prepared to enter the rising Chicano middle class that emerged vigorously in the 1970s and '80s. In West Denver, in Curtis Park, and on the campus at Metro, he had already made his first uneasy contact with the revolutionary left. In debates and fervent dialogue at UMAS he had already been exposed to the nationalist sentiment that gripped his generation and compelled it to search out a new identity. Such a breadth of experience imprinted his political consciousness and set him apart from a great many of his contemporaries both inside and outside the Chicano Movement.

iv

la familia

Memories of violence loomed like a dark cloud over the foothills of Huerfano County. In the county seat of Walsenburg, Ramon Castro and Dolores Vigil exchanged wedding vows in the chapel of St. Mary's Church. They made a particularly handsome couple. It was said that women in Walsenburg always whispered about Ramon's good looks when he walked by. A picture hanging in their son's home today shows Dolores to be equally attractive. They were both kids.[1] As the wedding bells tolled out a celebration for the young couple, the situation in the rest of Huerfano County on that September day in 1914 left little else to celebrate.

Richard Castro's paternal grandparents began their new life in the shadow of what came to be called the Great Coalfield War. Much later, when Castro began an earnest search for the roots of his family, he came across a book written by the son of a doctor who cared for many of the wounded during that conflict. Castro was so moved by Barron Beshoar's *Out of the Depths* that he made sure to give a copy to his father, Archie, who grew up in Walsenburg in the decade following the Coalfield War.[2] In devouring Beshoar's account, Castro tried to come to grips with life in the southern Colorado coalfields where his family had its roots.

Like most other families in the Walsenburg area, the Castros would learn well the harsh realities of the coal industry. Not long after his marriage in 1914, Rich's grandfather, Ramon, or "Ray" as some called him, hired on as a digger at the Barber division of the Alamo Coal Mine.[3] Located a few miles northwest of Walsenburg at the end of a spur line for the Colorado & Southern Railroad, the mine was the property of the Colorado Fuel & Iron Company, otherwise known as CF&I. His labor made Ray

Castro a tiny cog in the great imperial machine of one John D. Rockefeller, Jr.

It was an empire that changed the face of southern Colorado and permanently altered the lives of the largely Chicano populace. With the arrival of Rockefeller and his coal mines came the turbulent uprooting of Chicano farmers, ranchers, and sheepherders from their small plots of land and their highland villages.

The story of Rich Castro's family followed the general flow of Chicano history from land, to mining camps, to cities where Chicanos formed the core of a great industrial workforce.

The forces that reshaped the southern part of the state had been in the making since the first train rolled into Santa Fe in 1880. From that moment on, demand for steel in the Southwest was insatiable. Pueblo, with an open-hearth mill run by CF&I, became the center for the manufacture of endless miles of steel rails and fencing wire. Just to the south, Huerfano and Las Animas Counties sat atop a gigantic coal shelf—the Trinidad Field—which proved the perfect source for the mountains of soft coal necessary to feed the giant furnaces at Pueblo.[4] With the heat of molten metal radiating from the furnaces, and smoke roiling out of the smokestacks, CF&I's operation resembled a fiery ritual sacrifice to the gods of the railroad.

When Ray Castro entered Rockefeller's workforce, the soldiers of the Great Coalfield War—miners, militiamen and a private army of company guards—had just packed up their guns and gone home. An uneasy peace had settled in over the foothills and plains of Huerfano and Las Animas Counties. We can only speculate as to Castro's thoughts about Rockefeller or the United Mine Workers union that had dared to challenge his power. We do know that Chicanos played leading roles on both sides of the bloody conflict.

In her book, *No Separate Refuge*, Sarah Deutsch estimates that some 11,000 Chicanos migrated permanently from New Mexico to these coalfields between 1900 and 1910.[5] Additional thousands of ranch hands and farm boys found their way into the mines for seasonal labor in the winter time.

When workers of thirty-one other nationalities streamed into the coalfields from Greece and Italy, from Poland and the Balkans, they found a Mexican-American population with deep roots in the area. Everett Chávez, a southern Colorado native who conducted a demographic study of the period, maintains that so many of the European immigrants were single men—lonely, restless, and transient—that the predominant culture remained Hispanic even in localities where the European population outnumbered the Mexican.[6]

This diverse mix of cultures suffered under heart-breaking conditions. They worked perpetually in the dark. They might spend half a day setting up timbers to keep a roof from caving in, or hauling rock out of a blocked-off pathway, only to be told that their morning's labor was not for pay. According to company regulations, that labor constituted "dead work." Miners received pay only for the coal they dug, which the company weighed on scales rigged to register a lesser weight, so the miners were constantly short-changed. What wages they got were distributed in scrip, redeemable only for over-priced goods offered at company stores.[7] And they lived always close to death: The casualties from mine explosions had touched the lives of every family in the area.[8]

Years of pain and anger came to a head in September 1913 when a strike of 10,000 miners erupted into the Great Coalfield War. In an era of violent labor relations, the conflict in southern Colorado stood out as the most brutal in the nation. There was the incident, for instance, at Seventh and Main Streets in Walsenburg in which fifteen Huerfano County deputies opened fire without warning on a crowd of unarmed miners. In a split second three lay dead on the streets. The union retaliated when 160 miners, armed to the teeth, took over the Hogback north of town and rained fire on the McNally mine below.[9]

One effect of the violence was to bring to the limelight those who wielded local power in Walsenburg. At the center of attention was Sheriff Jefferson Farr. He was one of the biggest cattle dealers in the state, the holder of vast expanses of real estate, the owner of forty-five saloons in the county and every one of its brothels. Farr parlayed his economic clout into a powerful political machine for the Republican Party and in so doing turned the Walsenburg Court House into a "branch office of the CF&I."[10]

Testifying at a hearing shortly after the strike, one prominent southern Colorado attorney said of Farr: "His word was a command to voters. In criminal cases where he took an interest, I have never known [one] where the verdict was not in accordance with his wishes. If he desired a man convicted, there was no lawyer powerful enough to acquit. I have never known or read of any man who had such complete and absolute control over the destinies of the people where their rights and liberties were involved as had Sheriff Jefferson Farr of Huerfano County."[11]

Such was the "democracy" where Ray Castro grew up, a highly personalized police state that resembled a cross between Somoza's Nicaragua and the political machine at Tammany Hall. The gloved fist was fully revealed only in times of crisis. Under these conditions southern Colorado's Mexican-American community split apart when the strike hit.

The county's undersheriff was Shorty Martinez: six foot six inches tall and a longtime Jeff Farr loyalist. At any given time during the strike, 16 to 43 percent of Sheriff Farr's deputies were Hispanic.[12] The rugged backcountry farmers and the sheepmen in the foothills provided fertile recruiting ground for Farr's personal little army. Similarly, many local Hispanics signed up for National Guard units that would later face the striking miners in combat.

Hispanic miners and their families joined the union in far greater numbers, however, settled into the bleak and transient tent colonies, and hung on tenaciously during the long strike. Mineworker records reveal an abundance of Chicano committeemen and delegates to union conventions.[13] When the war broke out in earnest, when the blood began to flow in those tent colonies, the Chicano community was hardest hit.

Such was the case on April 20, 1914, when National Guard troops under the command of Lieutenant Karl Linderfelt opened fire on the tent colony at Ludlow, a few miles south of Walsenburg. They had borrowed a machine gun from CF&I. Linderfelt had told Lieutenant Gerry Lawrence to "put the baby in buggy and bring it along,"[14] and they had fashioned several bombs out of dynamite sticks lashed together. As the miners retreated from the onslaught hoping to regroup into a defensive unit in the Black Hills, their families fled to pits and cellars they had dug for protection under the tent floors.

The advancing guardsmen wasted no time setting the colony ablaze, systematically spreading flames from tent to tent. Huddled together for comfort beneath the battleground, twelve women and children lay trapped in their subterranean hiding places. There they died a miner's death, suffocating in the smoke and fumes, like so many of their menfolk in the past. Among the bodies was Cedilano Costa, 27, along with her four children. She was in the latter stages of pregnancy. Patricia Valdez was nursing her three-month-old daughter and trying to shelter her three other children, Eulala, 8, Mary, 7, and Rudolph, 9. Alcarita Pedregon managed to survive, but not before losing her daughter Gloria, 4, and her six-year-old son, Roderlo.[15] All told, eighteen souls were massacred on that dusty day in the tent colony at Ludlow. State histories frequently document the tragedy, but few of them point out that nearly two-thirds of the casualties were Hispanic.

In 1914, when Ray Castro left his farm in North Veta to go down into the Alamo mine, the coalfields around Walsenburg were just returning to normal. Rockefeller made a few small concessions to satisfy public opinion, but the union's hopes for organizing southern Colorado's European immigrants and Hispanic natives had been ground to dust. The scars from the Great Coalfield War would remain for decades on the region's landscape.

Quest for the Past

The nature of Rich Castro's times made his search for the past political as well as intensely personal. Mayor Wellington Webb caught the politics of this search in a 1993 address to a crowd assembled in the Old Supreme Court Chamber of the State Capitol. They had gathered for a tribute to Castro with an unveiling ceremony. Castro's sculpture, cast in bronze and sitting atop a marble stand, was to be placed in one of the niches of the building reserved for citizens honored by the General Assembly.

"Rich Castro," said Webb, "used to stand on the first floor of this building and say, 'Right here is Colorado history.' With a sweep of his hand, he would point to the surrounding statues of men designated by the state's lawmakers as movers and shakers. 'And right here,' he would say, pointing to an empty stairwell, 'is the Hispanic contribution to Colorado history.'"[16]

When House Joint Resolution 91-1031 created a niche in the capitol building in his honor, Castro became the first Chicano leader officially recognized as a maker of Colorado history. Castro would have been acutely aware of the irony of this situation, for he often wrote of the omissions from standard history books that left the rich Hispanic participation in American history largely forgotten.

In the last years of his life, Castro had quickened the pace of the search for his own personal past. He had begun writing articles for *Nuestras Raices* (Our Roots), the quarterly journal of the Genealogical Society of Hispanic America. He made several visits to the San Luis Valley, home to numerous aunts and uncles, and traveled with his father to Walsenburg and La Veta to look further into family documents.[17]

Virginia Castro tells of an episode at Stapleton International Airport just weeks after her husband's death. At a chance meeting in front of a customs booth for exchanging foreign currencies and selling insurance, the woman at the booth looked into her face and said, "Excuse me, are you Virginia Castro?" When she answered "Yes, I am," the woman said, "You know, your husband was just in the San Luis Valley taping an interview with my aunt and I have to tell you he had such a sense of urgency about him, as if he had to get all this down as fast as possible."[18]

The family journey, which would lead to the State Capitol, passed through the heart of what geographer Robert Nostrand has termed "the Hispano Homeland."[19] This homeland, encompassing the dry sierra of northern New Mexico and the rugged valleys and plains of southern Colorado, forms a portion of the territory known historically as the "Borderlands."[20] This area formed the far northern border of Mexico until 1846, when American troops marched in and took the land over for the United

States. Texas, New Mexico, Arizona, California, and southern Colorado are traditionally included in this frontier area.[21]

It was here that a dramatic clash of four cultures—Indian, Spanish, Mexican, and American—shaped the human landscape of the contemporary Southwest. Indeed, it was this collision that created Rich Castro's world. The barrios surrounding downtown Denver, where Castro grew up and left his political imprint, exist very much as a result of the head-on collision of these cultures.

Before events in the 1940s shifted the drama to the cities, scenes from this conflict were being played out in places like Mora County in the remote high country of New Mexico and Huerfano County on the northern periphery of the Borderlands. It was to these places that Castro traveled to seek the story of his family. His search for a national identity began at Metropolitan State College in Dr. Daniel Valdes's classes, and encompassed the Battle of the Names that swept through campus in the late '60s. Now, in turning to his own family, he had entered a more intimate realm. The unraveling of his family's past, however, was so intricately woven with his political outlook that the two realms—psychological and political—seemed barely separable. The Castro family history represents a microcosm of the story of a whole people—a people whose unique language, culture, and relationship to America had finally come to the forefront of American politics.

In 1991, Castro drove to La Veta, seventeen miles up the Cuchara Valley from Walsenburg, to meet with a diminutive, energetic woman named Eileen Bankson. A native of southern Colorado who stems from a line of Castros, Bankson spent every spare moment in the libraries, hospitals, and churches of Pueblo, Walsenburg, and Conejos searching out baptismal certificates, marriage records, or any documentation she could find to trace the roots of the people in her community.[22]

What drove her were names; she loved the sound of them. She pronounced multisyllabic names like Francisco Rodriguez Calero as if reading poetry; they flowed off her lips like song lyrics. History without names, she said, was history without life.[23] After Castro approached her with a request for help in tracing his own ancestry, Bankson buried herself once again in county and church archives between Santa Fe and Pueblo and returned with a very long list of names. That list, she claimed, traced the Castro family lineage over the course of three centuries.

When Castro studied with Dr. Valdes at Metro State, he absorbed the basic contours of that history and learned of four broad eras, each one represented by a different power structure, holding sway over the Southwest. First, there was the pre-Columbian era. Then came the Spanish colonial period of 1519 to 1821. It was followed by the period of Mexican Independence, when the Mexican people drove out their Spanish rulers and flew the flag of the eagle and the serpent from 1821 to 1846. Finally came the American conquest, which brought Anglo rule and the Stars and Stripes to the Southwest.

The Spaniards Return to New Mexico, 1693

If Eileen Bankson's research holds true, Rich Castro's ancestors witnessed the entire historical sweep from Spanish conquest to American rule. According to her version of events, the story began in the year 1693 in the days of the Spanish Empire.

In that year Governor Diego de Vargas returned to the village of La Toma in the heart of northern New Mexico after thirteen years in exile. The Spaniards had first entered the valley of the Rio Grande a century earlier when silver magnate Juan de Oñate established a colony in 1598 at the confluence of the Rio Grande and Chama Rivers. In 1680, however, an extraordinary revolt by the Pueblo Indians wiped the villages of the Spanish Crown in northern New Mexico off the map. The Taos Rebellion—the most successful Indian rebellion ever to occur on the North American continent— expelled the Spanish colonists en masse, and sent them fleeing to what later became the Mexican city of Juárez.[24]

There, for more than a decade, the Spaniards waited—demoralized and leaderless—until 1693, when Governor de Vargas retraced the steps of Juan de Oñate and led what Spanish historians labeled *"la reconquista"* (the reconquest) back into the mountainous area above Santa Fe. Father Angelico Chávez, most poetic of the chroniclers of New Mexico, called it the "return from Babylon."[25]

Among the men who accompanied Diego de Vargas was José Rodriguez, forty-three years old and a native of the Spanish province of Segovia. He was described as "of medium height, with a round face, a broad nose and a large number of moles on his face." Sometime before the reconquest, he emigrated to Mexico City and there married an Indian woman, Maria de Samano, a native of the capital who was "dark with big eyes and a small sharp nose."[26] Rodriguez and his wife migrated to the village of Santa Cruz in 1696 and later to Santa Fe in 1718.[27]

According to Bankson, José Rodriguez and his wife Maria de Samano were the first of a long line of Richard Castro's ancestors who can be traced to his New Mexico, and later southern Colorado homeland. One of Rodriguez's descendents had a baby girl in the village of San Lorenzo de Picurí in 1791, who was named Maria Ignacia Rodriguez. She would become mother to the five children who established the Castro name in New Mexico.[28]

For many years, there had been talk in the Castro family of a priest somewhere in the hazy past, who slipped away from holy vows and became a father to more than just his congregation. Some controversy exists over the identity of that priest. Lena Starr, a cousin to Richard's father, Archie, recalled that her grandfather was often teased for his "gypsy" heritage. She heard the story that "great grandpa was on the way to California to become a missionary in the early part of the nineteenth century. He had come from Valencia in eastern Spain where so many other gypsies had their origin. Before he even got close to the mission, he met a Chippewa Indian girl in Florida, married her, and later settled down in New Mexico. He never did become a missionary."[29]

Bankson's version places the date of immigration from Spain at about the same period, but differs considerably in other details. The priest in her account was a Franciscan friar, Fray Juan José de Castro, raised in the northwest Spanish province of Galicia.

Sometime around 1802, a brown-robed Father Castro appeared in the village of San Juan, New Mexico, eager to bring the blessings of the church to those same Pueblo Indians who had driven the Spaniards out more than a century before. Father Castro appears, by all records, to have been conscientious in fulfilling his priestly duties under the harsh conditions on the northern frontier.[30] But in between the baptisms, confessions, and last rites, in between the wanderings from one mission to the next, Father Castro apparently found his way into the arms of Maria Ignacia Rodriguez, descendent of the same José Rodriguez who had accompanied Vargas during the reconquest. She was only fifteen when the thirty-nine-year-old Father appeared in Picurí. Together, the two of them had five sons, who formed the foundation of the Castro family in New Mexico.[31]

This makes for a juicy chapter in any family history, but such things were not uncommon. In 1818, a representative from the bishop of Durango, Mexico, traveled northward to inspect the missions of New Mexico and charged "that the Franciscans lived scandalous lives, 'satisfying their passions' while their churches and their communicants suffered neglect."[32] Antonio Barreiro, writing in 1832, added, "Charity demands a veil be thrown over many things which would, if they were narrated, create a scandal."[33]

Perhaps Father Castro remained much loved by his congregation despite the human frailty that drove him to seek the companionship of Maria Ignacia. The evidence shows that he abandoned neither his parishioners nor his family, although he clearly abandoned his vow of celibacy.[34]

In his riveting first novel, *Bless Me, Ultima*, New Mexican author Rudolfo Anaya writes of childhood discoveries, which guide the journey of his protagonist, Antonio, into adulthood. One of those events is the discovery that the patriarch of his mother's family, the Luna family, the family that so carefully cultivated the valley of El Puerto, was, in fact, a priest. "It was true," writes Anaya. "The priest that came with the first colonizers to the valley of El Puerto had raised a family, and it was the branches of this family that now ruled the valley." Antonio's father revealed this family secret with a grin and said to the boy, "They do not talk about that, they are very sensitive about that."[35]

Though he was on the trail of Fray Juan José de Castro in the search for his family roots, Richard Castro never caught up with the elusive friar. Eileen Bankson did not complete her search until after Castro's death. Had he met up with the specter of Father Castro, it is likely he would have reacted, like Antonio's father, with a mischievous grin and a twinkle in his eye rather than with hushed embarrassment. Castro's sense of humor was far too prominent, his sense of irony too keenly developed for him not to enjoy the ancestral prank that history had played on his family.

In the late 1970s, Castro participated in a play, a spoof written by state senator Don Sandoval called *A Just Punishment*. Castro played the role of "Padre Perdido" (the Lost Father) and delighted in portraying this comical character who may well have represented the lost founding father of the Castro family.[36]

Southern Colorado, the 1860s

The man who moved the Castro family farther up the frontier and north-ward into Colorado was Isais Castro, grandson of the Spanish priest.[37] Born in 1854, Isais was raised in a village not far from Taos called Arroyo Hondo, a place where the river bed remained dry for years at a time, until for a brief moment here and there it transformed itself into a raging torrent.[38]

Geographer Richard Nostrand describes the general process of this northward trek as a "stockman's frontier." From northern New Mexico, he writes, "stockmen in quest of suitable pasture would venture across a divide to the next valley, where they would build adobe shelters, irrigate patches of land, and eventually attract others."[39] Thus, many of the first pioneers into Colorado were Mexicans headed north with their herds and flocks, rather than Anglos in covered wagons moving westward.

By 1859 these herdsmen had crossed the San Luis Valley, over the towering Sangre de Cristo Range, and on to the flood plain of the Arkansas River and its tributaries. Here on the Cuchara River they built a tiny agricultural and trading community called the Plaza de los Leones, a village with a central plaza surrounded by adobe homes.[40] It was this Hispanic plaza, situated in the heart of the Trinidad Coalfield, that would become the town of Walsenburg, battlefield in the Great Coalfield War and home to Rich Castro's father, Archie. Rich's great grandfather Isais settled on higher ground up from Walsenburg in the smaller village of North Veta, eight miles north of the current resort town of La Veta.[41]

Two geological formations mark the area around Walsenburg and the two La Vetas. To the northeast is a small black butte—a tower sitting on the prairie several miles away from the foothills, jutting out unexpectedly from the flat land. Formed from volcanic rock, the butte looks so out of place and alone on the prairie that the Spanish called it "El Huerfano," or the Orphan. Hence the origin of Huerfano County.[42]

To the southwest is a more spectacular sight: two massive peaks, 13,000 feet in height, towering over the Cuchara and Huerfano Valleys like a couple of gigantic ceremonial mounds. The Indians called them the *Huajatollah*—the breasts of the earth—and shrouded them with a collection of mysterious legends. Even today, Route 12, which winds its way around the peaks, is known as the Highway of Legends. The Spaniards called these massive twin mountaintops the *Cumbres Españoles* or Spanish Peaks. It was here in the shadow of these Spanish Peaks that Isais Castro settled in the tiny hamlet of North Veta and raised his family.

Born into the Archuleta family, Gaspar Castro was adopted and raised by Isais and his wife, Agapita (Pita for short). Gaspar recalls his years on the ranch as years of hard work and struggle, but not without their pleasant side. It was a small piece of land, about five acres, but the public land nearby was used for grazing and "nobody said anything." There were only four or five milk cows on the place, a half-dozen horses, a dozen or so chickens. A couple of sows and a couple of pigs rounded out the livestock. "One of them," states Gaspar, "would get the axe every Christmas."[43]

The village of Norte Veta presents a classic picture of rural life in the Hispanic Homeland. Fifteen or twenty families congregated loosely around an area of about three or four square miles. The hamlet itself consisted of a small grocery store, a two-room schoolhouse, and a church a couple of blocks down from the road leading into town. Isais Castro's ranch straddled the road with a dwelling on either side of it. They were simple adobe structures, rectangular in shape, made from the brown earth of the surrounding mountains. It was the size of the extended family that caused the spillover into two houses. Isais's and Pita's sisters lived on one side of the road; Isais, Pita, and their eight children lived on the other.

For all the thrift, self-reliance, and cooperative effort, these small farms fell short of providing a living for a family of ten. "Everyone had to go get a job off the farm," says Gaspar.[44] Like other families engaged in the daily struggle for existence, the Castro family had to hustle a temporary job here, a seasonal one there. They had to string together the resources and meager incomes of everyone in the family just to hang on tight to that five-acre farm.

Thus, Isais Castro, "a strong little man and a pretty tough one" according to Gaspar, had to hire himself out as a sheep-shearer and spend months at a time away from his family. Despite their poverty and calloused hands, ranchers and sheepmen had always been called gentlemen or *caballeros* by their compatriots. So, too, Isais Castro was addressed by his family and neighbors as Don Isais, a sign of respect.

Don Isais followed the ways of many Hispanics before him on the "stockman's frontier." Every spring he would pack up and head for the remote back pastures in Green Horn, northwest of Walsenburg or cross over La Veta Pass into the San Luis Valley in search of wages. They were lonely jobs in deserted meadows, but the splendor of the Spanish Peaks or the distant beauty of the Sangre de Cristos always hovered in the background and perhaps made life a bit more satisfying, a bit more meaningful. Perhaps, too, the beauty of the surroundings lent a spiritual air to the wanderings of Isais Castro, just as they had done for the shepherds and horsemen who had preceded him centuries ago.

Los Abuelos, 1914

Finding any sense of spirituality down in the black hole of a coal mine is quite a different matter, but the times were changing. Given the grinding struggle for existence, it was natural that Don Isais's son, Ray, would end up in a Rockefeller mine. Perhaps the farms and pastures in the shadow of the Spanish Peaks were beautiful, but they could scarcely feed an extended family. Agricultural wages paid about a dollar a day in 1913. Ray Castro found he could double that shoveling coal at the Alamo mine.[45]

The Great Coalfield War made little dent in working conditions. Castro still worked by the light of a candle atop his miner's helmet. Every morning, he carried with him down into the pit a ring of brass tags with his number etched into the surface. He left one of the tags on each cart he filled with coal, so that he could be paid according to the weight. Then again, if the mine walls collapsed he could be more easily identified as one of the men buried in the debris. Whoever failed to return his brass ring at the end of the day was among those still down in the pit.[46]

Ray Castro's personal life appears to have been a struggle all along as was that of his wife, Dolores. Dolores, or Lola as she was called, grew up as a Valdez, a family of sharecroppers who were so poor they could not afford to raise their own daughter. Sometime around Lola's teenage years, her family allowed her to be informally adopted by Don Ricardo and Doña Monica Vigil, who at least owned a little land up by Baldie Mountain.[47] Located above Walsenburg on the Huerfano River, the farm was much like the one owned by Don Isais Castro in North Veta. Lola had already taken on the Vigil name when she met Ray Castro.

Despite their striking beauty, Ray and Lola's marriage in 1914 did not bring happiness to either of them. They had three children and lost a fourth to a tragic accident. Three-year-old Allowishus was playing with an empty shoebox on a bridge that crossed the irrigation ditch flowing through the farm. The box fell into the current and little Allowishus tried to save his cardboard toy. They found the child's body a mile or so downstream.

Richard's Father: Walsenburg, 1923

Archie Castro, Richard's father, the youngest of the Castro children, was born in 1923. By that time, Ray and Lola were quarreling bitterly and, shortly after Archie's birth, the couple separated.[48] Lola took Archie and moved into Walsenburg, settling there into the difficult life of the single mother. Lola was not alone in her struggle. Historian Sarah Deutsch points out that even before the 1920s more than a third of Hispanic households in Trinidad, some thirty-six miles down the road from Walsenburg, were headed by women. Half those numbers were widows, a testimony to the precarious nature of life in the mining camps.[49]

A quiet, retiring man, Archie recalled his early childhood during a conversation in his southwest Denver home. "My mom made nothin' in those days," he remembered. "Maybe seven dollars a week. Enough to pay rent and eat." With the money Lola made as a housekeeper, the family lived in a small, one-bedroom, cinderblock house with a kerosene lamp for light and a tiny stove for heating and cooking. "We had nothin'," said Archie, "but she raised me to be respectful."[50]

The sons and daughters of Walsenburg's miners seemed to get along, whether they were Hispanic, Slav, or Italian. Archie Castro remembers no incidents of racial tension in his hometown. It was traveling about with the baseball team that made him aware of what the outside world thought of Mexicans. During the Roaring Twenties, Mexican labor from across the border had taken root in the flatland farming communities of southern Colorado, especially in the beet fields of the Arkansas River Valley. In the conservative racial climate of the times, everyone of Mexican descent— native or Mexican born—was relegated in most communities to the lowest rung on the ladder. Archie Castro could not help but see the signs that read "No Mexicans Allowed" as he traveled with the ball team to La Junta or Colorado Springs. "You knew what discrimination was," said Archie, "as part of growing up. You just had that feeling that you weren't liked."[51]

Archie's life was partially shielded from the coming Depression when Lola married a dump truck operator who hauled wood and coal wherever he could pick up a job around town. Combining this thin thread of security with the thirty dollars a month he received working summers for the Civilian Conservation Corps, Archie achieved a rare feat for Chicanos in southern Colorado: As the Depression drew its last breath in the spring of 1940,

Castro finished his studies at St. Mary's Parochial School and received his high school diploma.

The following day, his stepfather asked him straight out: "What are your intentions?" "The very next day," said Archie, "I was on my way to Denver."[52]

At seventeen, Archie Castro had instinctually sized up his future in Walsenburg and found nothing. The mines that had provided steady work for his father were no longer hiring. The Age of Coal was giving way to the wave of the future; petroleum was king now. In 1928, when a massive natural gas pipeline connected the West Texas oil fields to Denver to heat homes and businesses on the Front Range, the economic fortunes of Walsenburg and southern Colorado began a gradual descent from which they never recovered.

And so a new wave of Chicano migration began. Just as his father's generation had trekked out of the mountain villages to claim their places in Rockefeller's coalmines, so did Archie's generation ride the Greyhound, hitchhike, and motor their way into the northern cities of Pueblo and Denver. There they found work in the factories and packinghouses and began to set down roots just as countless other urban immigrants had before them.

Archie spent barely a year in Denver before going off to the Navy at the beginning of World War II. During that year, he moved in with his aunt, who ran the North Hotel on the northern edge of downtown at Nineteenth and Champa Streets. He found work as a busboy at the Oxford Hotel, a block away from the railroad station.

That was also the year he walked over the Sixteenth Street viaduct with a group of friends to the roller-skating rink at the top of the hill on Tejon Street. "I wasn't much of a skater," says Archie, "but we used to enjoy it." Also at the rink that evening was Josephine McGrath, a shy, diminutive teenager who had grown up on the East Side. "She claims," said Archie, "that I fell down right at her feet."[53] A world war and an overseas correspondence would intervene before this skating-rink romance culminated in marriage, but in 1945, while Archie was still finishing his tour of duty in the Navy, he and Josephine married on an October day in East Denver. Their son, Rich Castro, would be born the following year.

Mora, New Mexico, 1850

Like the Castros, the McGrath family was rooted in the arid, piñon-covered front range of northern New Mexico.

The name McGrath tells a story in itself. It is a "coyote" family—a mixture of white and Mexican that reflects the mingling of cultures in the Southwest after the American conquest of 1848. Castro's aunt, Rose Ann

Sanchez, traces the McGrath family origin to the 1845 potato famine in Ireland. Fleeing with a million and a half of his countrymen, Rich Castro's great-great-grandfather left Tipperary for Philadelphia in the late 1840s.[54]

Thomas McGrath landed on the East Coast just as history exploded in the Southwest. Hungry for land and intoxicated with the idea of Manifest Destiny—of ruling the continent from "sea to shining sea"—the United States had just crushed the Mexican army and signed the Treaty of Guadalupe Hidalgo in 1848. A humiliated Mexican government ceded a third of its land for a pittance.

New Mexico, with 60,000 new Hispanic citizens, was the most populous of the new territories. Some welcomed the new government; others seethed with discontent. It seemed wise, in these volatile circumstances, to fill the political vacuum with the blue-coated troops who constructed half a dozen new forts in the floodplain of the Rio Grande. The first of these was Fort Union not far from the little town of Mora,where Hispanics had staged a violent uprising the previous year.[55]

It was to this center of Hispanic discontent that the first McGrath, then a red-headed sergeant in the U.S. Army, was assigned in the 1850s. The soldiers at the fort mingled freely with the local populace, and in no time McGrath—half a world away from the lush meadows of Tipperary—married into the Lucero family.

The Battle of Glorieta Pass, 1862

Family lore places this same McGrath in the midst of the Civil War battle of Glorieta Pass, sometimes known as the Gettysburg of the West. Over a century later, Rich Castro became fascinated by this crucial battle for the western frontier, and his interest would result in a presentation to the Genealogical Society of Hispanic America, as well as an article in the newspaper *La Voz*.

The battle at Glorieta Pass was pivotal despite its isolation because the Confederacy hungered for control of the Southwest. Southern strategists eyed the goldfields of Colorado and California and saw in them a storehouse of wealth by which they could finance the war. They looked westward to the ports of California and envisioned them as a way to relieve pressure from the Union blockade on the East Coast. They imagined a swift annexation of such vast proportions—from Texas to the Pacific—that Europe would be forced to take notice and offer diplomatic recognition to the rebel states.[56]

With this blueprint in mind, General Henry H. Sibley set out in the winter of 1862 to conquer New Mexico Territory. As his troops rode northward, however, they encountered unforeseen problems. For one, the

Hispanic population in the mountains above Santa Fe refused to cooperate. They had long harbored resentment toward Texans who viewed New Mexico as their own colony. These Mexican Americans refused to supply Sibley's army, and many of them offered their services as volunteers to the Union forces.[57]

"The vast majority of New Mexico volunteer soldiers were Hispanics," wrote Castro in his 1990 article. "These civilians were unschooled laborers and farmers who spoke little English and were unfamiliar with standards and attitudes of the American military establishment in which they were serving. They made excellent soldiers, however, particularly suited for the rugged service they saw. For generations their families had lived in the Southwest and these men had acquired a vast store of practical knowledge. . . . This combined with their familiarity with the harsh and formidable terrain of the mountains and deserts of the area gave them an advantage over Anglo soldiers who had arrived from other parts of the country."[58]

The North gathered its forces at Fort Union, where McGrath had been stationed for a decade. When the dust settled at Glorieta Pass in late March 1862, the southerners' grand scheme of westward expansion lay in ruins. New Mexico Hispanics had carved out a significant, though largely unsung, role in Civil War history. But Rich Castro's great-great-grandfather lay dead atop Glorieta Pass.[58]

Despite his Irish lineage, Rich Castro's grandfather, Trinidad McGrath, was raised in a thoroughly Hispanic environment. He spoke little English, married a Trujillo, and worked the ranches of small New Mexican villages before ending up in the heart of East Denver on Lawrence Street.[59]

During the '50s, as his parents worked long hours outside the home, Rich Castro spent much of his childhood in the McGrath household, where he absorbed some of his most fundamental political values. Through years of ranching and herding, through the Great Depression and a couple of years of government relief, the McGraths maintained a sense of pride, generosity, and community. They were the working poor; they understood that their poverty was no sin, and they embraced the New Deal. They were Roosevelt Democrats.

Castro especially watched his grandfather, who was a delight to neighbors and family alike. Here was a man who had educated himself, who devoured the newspaper, who kept up with the politics of the times. He was an ordinary man who carried himself at all times with dignity.

If Castro absorbed the broad sweep of his people's history in Dr. Valdes's classes in the 1960s, he began to fill in the more personal pieces of the puzzle in the '80s and '90s. He began to find that his own family's past read like a textbook of Chicano history. The Castro family's centuries-long journey from Mexico's northern frontier to the barrios of Denver fit into a continuous flow. His ancestors had borne witness to the whole stream of events—invasions, intermarriages, the comingling of cultures—that would culminate in the urbanization of the Chicano people.

Tapping into this flow served a dual purpose for Rich Castro, as it did for many others of his generation. It offered him insight into the underlying roots of the difficulties that plagued the barrios of Denver. George Sanchez named Castro's ancestors "The Forgotten People"—Los Olvidados—in a book by the same name published in 1940. They had been cast aside, he implied, when the expanding Anglo culture clashed with the long-standing Hispanic one. Investigating this process put Rich Castro in touch with the soul of his fellow manitos and with the losses—psychic and material—they had suffered. At the same time, it offered him a heritage he could be proud of. For him, finding the story of his ancestral roots was a healing process. He believed the discovery of this past could help heal the wounds of others who had been similarly cast aside, and thus he was always passing the stories down. In a typical introduction to one of his many columns for La Voz, he wrote, "Most of the United States' history lessons given to Hispanic children take on an east-to-west orientation, with little mention of the fact that the Southwest was originally settled north from Mexico. Similarly, as the United States expanded into this region following the Mexican War . . . our children are led to believe that Hispanics played little or no role in the settlement and development of the West. We need to record history as it happened, and share with our children the cultural pride they deserve."[60]

Castro's heart and soul stood with his Manito ancestors in New Mexico, in the San Luis Valley, and on the front range of the Sangre de Cristos. His role as a cultural nationalist, however gentle and non-abrasive, followed naturally from that emotional tie. In the search for a national and psychological identity, he believed ethnic pride to be an essential element.

V

the east side

The South Platte River loops westward around downtown Denver, forming an arc in the prairie as if drawn by a compass. As the arc curves gently northeast on its journey to the Missouri, the muddy river marks the boundary of the city's East Side—the vibrant working class district where Richard Castro spent his childhood.

Anthony Lopez, a lifelong poker-playing friend of Castro's, grew up on the banks of the South Platte. His house was a block down from the Burlington Northern Railroad yard where his grandfather worked. Twenty-three kids grew up on that block between the tracks and the river. The river was their backyard; it was their park and their play area. Their parents forbade them to go down there, but who could stay away?

"We were there all the time," says Lopez. "When it rained in the afternoon, the first thing we did was run down to the Platte River. There was this one place at the end of a sewer line where all the balls in the city would come through. You'd have basketballs, tennis balls, hula-hoops, anything. They'd be stinky and dirty 'cause they'd been through the sewer line. But you'd take 'em home and wash 'em and to us it was like a brand-new ball."[1]

Lopez's memories of growing up in the '50s paint a vivid picture of life on the East Side in that era. "Underneath the bridges," he says, "we used go after the pigeons. The bridges weren't concrete back then; they were arched, steel bridges, maybe fifteen feet high, and we'd climb along the beams looking for pigeon eggs in the nests up there. We were always looking for a white pigeon or a spotted pigeon; sometimes we'd try to tame them. But mostly we'd take our BB guns. The companies along the railroad yard, the Goodyear warehouse, for instance, used to pay us ten cents for every pigeon we killed. The birds would ruin their property by coming in and building nests inside the buildings. Goodyear would even leave the window open for us so we could get in there at night to kill the pigeons. We'd clean the nests out for 'em and show 'em the next day and say 'these are all the pigeons we killed,' and they'd pay us ten cents for each one. Today I'm sure there'd be a lawsuit, but none of us ever fell. And none of us were ever scared. Today I'd be scared to death to go up there but back then it was different.

"We'd play tag at the warehouse all the time 'cause they used to have those big tractor tires. We'd jump from tire to tire and get so filthy from the black tar that your mom knew exactly where you had been."

Down on Wynkoop Street where the Lopez family lived, the kids played tackle football on the hard pavement. In a display of freedom unheard of for children in later times, they used to hop freight cars along the Burlington Northern track just to get a ride downtown. In the summer they'd hang around the docks at Denargo Market waiting to load delivery trucks in return for a couple of watermelons they would eat on the spot. The whole Lopez family collected pop bottles; they could get two cents each if they returned them in Denver, but if they filled their pickup and waited for a trip to the homeland in Trinidad, the bottles would net them an extra penny apiece. On Saturdays Grandpa would herd up the kids and go to the "Segundas," the second-hand stores along Larimer Street. "We'd all fight to go to the Segundas," says Lopez. "That's where the toys were."

Lopez's description of the '50s illustrates the struggle of those who lived on the East Side and the thrift required for survival in one of Denver's poorest neighborhoods. Yet there is something of a Huckleberry Finn quality here, a refreshing breath of freedom in the experiences of these young kids. From the reminiscences of those who grew up in the neighborhood, one is struck with the notion that the East Side—despite the struggle, despite the grinding poverty—was full of life; for kids, the East Side could be downright fun.

Residing down by the river, the Lopez family lived on the fringe of the East Side; its heart was up the hill, up from the Pepsi warehouse where Thirty-eighth Street curves into the southbound thoroughfares that lead downtown. That is where Rich Castro spent his earliest years.

From practically any vantage point on the East Side today, one can see the towering skyscrapers of downtown: the Republic Building with its fifty-seven stories and the United Bank Building rising like a giant cash register. In the late 1940s, however, Denver was a smaller town. The D&F Tower, downtown's most imposing structure at the time, was only twelve stories high. When Eastsiders in the '50s cast glances to the south, they were likely to see the familiar outlines of their own small, tight-knit community rather than the towering spires of Seventeenth Street that later came to dominate the skyline.

Archie and Josephine Castro came home to the East Side shortly after the war's end. They rented a small apartment at Thirty-fourth and Lawrence two doors down from the house Trinidad McGrath had restored a few years before.[2]

They were part of a new generation of Hispanics, a generation that had seen the world from Munich to Okinawa. They had increasingly left the villages, ranches, and small towns behind to join the swollen ranks of city dwellers. They had shed a disproportionate amount of blood during the war. Even the *Rocky Mountain News* referred respectfully to the "brown faces lying silent in the white snows of Belgium."[3]

Archie Castro served four years on a Navy submarine in the Pacific, and then traveled to the East Coast, to New London, Connecticut, and Charleston, South Carolina, for assignments decommissioning ships. Upon his return, he heard how his brother, still reeling from malaria, had barely escaped with his life during the Bataan Death March in the Philippines.[4]

This was not a generation of militants, nor was it one prone to confrontation. But having sacrificed so profusely for America's victory, they were less willing to accept the raw forms of discrimination that their parents had endured.

Hispanics in the "American Century"

Time magazine publisher Henry Luce had already proclaimed the years after World War II the "American Century."[5] America was Number One in everything imaginable, from military hardware to production of tennis shoes. Within this bountiful setting, the Castro family was determined to work hard and to stake out its own modest claim to American success.

For Hispanics, this was no simple matter in the postwar years. The mayor's Committee on Human Relations found in 1947 that eighty of 189 businesses surveyed—nearly 45 percent—did not employ Spanish Americans. One employer said, "Negroes and Spanish have a slight mental inferiority," while an employment agency admitted, "Spanish and Negro applicants are hired only for domestic work."[6] The Denver Area Welfare Council reported in 1950 that the average Spanish-American family earned only $1,840 a year compared to $1,930 for black families and over $3,000 for whites. Fully 60 percent of Hispanics, read the council's report, lived in substandard housing.[7]

The East Side, however, lay in an industrial corridor along the river and the railroad tracks, and there in the industrial sector, jobs for minorities began to open up.

Zoned for Industry

The East Side was the kind of neighborhood where the barbed-wire fences of factories crept up to the edges of residents' backyards. Gardner Denver's massive plant at Thirty-eighth and Williams, for example, turned out hard-rock mining equipment—percussion drills and tempered steel bits—as their neighbors peered at operations from porches across the street.[8] The Burlington Northern's tracks linked innumerable warehouses and small manufacturing plants bordering the river. The Denargo Market, where Anthony Lopez spent many a summer morning, hummed with pre-dawn activity in its quest to distribute fruits and vegetables to every corner of the city.

And always there was the presence of the packinghouses to the north. The Big Four—Armour, Swift, Cudahy, and Wilson—employed a veritable army of workers in the vicinity of the stockyard pens back of the Coliseum. A dozen or so smaller houses added hundreds more to the payrolls. The smell of the slaughter drifted up from Packinghouse Road and, when the wind was right, permeated all of East Denver on a warm summer's night.

For years, a janitor's job in these basic industries was the most a Mexican American could hope for. In 1941 Paul Shriver, director of Colorado's Works Progress Administration, told blacks seeking construction jobs at the Denver Ordnance Plant that "Negroes and Mexicans have one chance out of a thousand [to be employed]."[9]

Alfonso Gonzalez, who later became a high ranking union leader, tells of getting a job in 1942 cleaning up the Capitol Packing Company's boning room after everyone had gone for the day. Late one night, three white employees, smelling heavily of alcohol, caught him alone in the boning room and threatened him with his life if he didn't quit. When he refused, the three stalked him into the parking lot, and then pursued him as he fled in his father's car. Driving the company truck, his attackers chased him to the turn at Forty-ninth and Washington, where their vehicle rolled over, thus unavoidably exposing the night's incident to the plant owner. "The following afternoon," relates Gonzalez, "he took me aside and told me, 'with you in this plant, there'll be nothing but trouble. I'm gonna have to let you go.' He never asked for my explanation or anything. He just said that's the way it is."

Gonzalez talks further about the hiring hall for temporary work. "The hiring boss," says Gonzalez, "would stand up on a high platform and look out at the crowd and say, 'You, you, and you. The rest of you come back tomorrow.' They hired mostly according to the color of your skin unless they needed someone for the hide cellar. If it was the hide cellar, then it was the blacks and us. Primo Carnera, the heavyweight boxer, used to go down there. He was six-foot-three and an animal and they never hired him. So you know they didn't hire by size or strength."[10]

The war, however, slowly changed America, and by the time the veterans began drifting back from overseas, momentum had shifted. Blacks and Chicanos who stayed home during the war got a toehold in industrial jobs simply because of the labor shortage. When the white men in uniform came back and applied for work, men like Gonzalez had already hurdled the initial taboos in basic industry. By the early '50s, many of the workplaces on the East Side harbored more black and brown faces than white.

There was work on the East Side, yes. It was dirty, gritty, low-paying work, to be sure, but if you were frugal, you could raise a family, and if you could get a Veterans Administration loan you had a shot at owning your own house.

A Job at Eaton Metal

Archie and Josephine Castro each landed one of these low-wage jobs shortly after they arrived back from the East Coast. Archie found a job with one of the small East Side manufacturers that surrounded the neighborhood. Eaton Metal Products Company, at Forty-seventh and York, operated a booming steel fabrication business in the late '40s and '50s. Their primary product, underground gas tanks for service stations, placed the company in a position to ride the powerful wave of the automobile industry. Amidst the smoke from welders and acetylene torches, forty to fifty men sheared off sections of quarter-inch steel plate, and then constructed reinforced metal tanks as big as a house. When business slowed, they performed specialized fabrication: hoppers, support structures for dams, steel chutes for mines, and later on, even tunnel liners for missile silos.[11]

Archie Castro hired on in the warehouse in 1946 and dug in. "It wasn't far from the house," he said. "I was walking in the area around Swift and Company, looking for work and I just dropped off an application there. I didn't know an elbow from a nut, but they hired me to work the counter. When someone from the shop needed welding rod or elbows or joints, I'd go chase it down. When someone from a service station would come in needing a part, I'd do the same thing."[12]

They hired him for eighty-two and a half cents an hour, six dollars and sixty cents a day. Archie hoped to get a higher-paying government job, but with little Richie on the way, he opted to hang on to what he already had. Eaton Metal, for better or worse, became his vehicle for gaining the American Dream and he embraced the opportunity. He learned the components of every part in the shop. If something broke, he'd tear it apart to see what made it work. After fifteen years behind the counter, Archie became an expert on propane tank assembly and moved across the street to the sales department.

Meanwhile, Josephine hired on downtown at the Deline Box Company. For minimum wages, she made boxes for Russell Stover Candies. Years later, in a column for *La Voz*, Castro thanked his mother for her sacrifice in helping him get a parochial school education. Having just read Vickie Ruiz's book *Western Women: Their Land, Their Lives*, Castro viewed his mother's work at Deline as another chapter in the historical exploitation of Mexican-American women. "She took pride in her work," he wrote, "but she was not paid the salary she was due."[13]

Richard was born September 29, 1946, at the height of the baby boom. In this first year of the "American Century," the neighborhood he grew up in was the quintessential American neighborhood. The East Side's very soul was blue collar. Its residential pockets—laced between the river and the railroad tracks, between the factories and the packinghouses—embodied the entire ethnic mixture of the American Southwest. There were blacks concentrated in Five Points, Mexicans, Poles, Slovenians, and Asians in Curtis Park, and just to the northeast in Elyria lay another neighborhood of Eastern Europeans.

Eloy Mares, who grew up on the East Side and would later become Castro's high school football coach, recalled, "there were people around whose last name was Castro or Lopez or Gonzalez, but there were also people named McCarthy, Kreitzer, Chloberdanz, or Preslach."[14]

These people worked together in the same plants and attended the same schools. Manual, the public high school, was known as a little United Nations. Annunciation, the parochial school where Castro got his education, was, likewise, rich in ethnic diversity.

What defined the neighborhood, what bound it together, was not race, but the struggle for economic survival. As late as the 1950s, Ricardo Valadez recalls rolling a little red wagon from his house on Lawrence Street down to the railroad tracks to look for broken skids and pallets. The railroad workers, aware of the poverty of the surrounding neighborhood, would often leave pallets in places easily accessible to the kids. Valadez would load the pallets atop his wagon, then drag them up the hill and chop them up for fuel for the wood stove his mother cooked on.[15]

Valadez's experience represents that of the poorer segment on the East Side, but it marks the '50s as a transitional period in terms of technological change. His chores at the time included carrying in a bucket of coal a couple of times a week from the coal shed out by the alleyway. If he stoked the coal at night before he went to bed, the heat would usually last till early morning. Twice a week, he'd go down to the gas station to get kerosene so that stoking the wood fire and the coal furnace would go a little easier. Valadez recalls how wonderful it was in the mid-1950s to get gas heat. "We'd get fifteen below zero sometimes," he said, "but I'd still have to go out and take care of business while the wind was whipping out there by the coal shed."[16]

The iceman would come a couple of times a week from the ice factory at Twenty-eighth and Wazee. He would have hundred-pound blocks of ice in his truck, which he quartered into twenty-five-pound chunks and sold to households for use in their iceboxes. Sometimes the iceman would shave off a few little slivers of ice from the blocks, wrap them in paper and hand them out—without flavoring—as a treat for the kids.

The Flavor of the East Side

After working hours, the bars on the East Side were a magnet for the energy and passion of the neighborhood. The memory of a stinking hide down in the cellar at Swift's, or the jar of a rivet gun at Timpte Trailers slowly melted away after a few beers.

Around Twenty-first and Larimer, taverns like the Juarez and the Mexico City already formed the core of a downtown nightlife district for Mexican Americans. A few blocks away in Five Points, jazz horns at the Rossonian Hotel blew till the early hours of the morning. At the Cowboy Bar on Thirty-third and Downing, young men looking for action could roll up to a drive-in stall and order a pitcher of 3.2 beer to be served curbside as they huddled in their aging American cars. The times were indeed different.

Just across the river was the Slovenian Hall with its old-country polkas. And in the late '50s, Corky Gonzales, the East Side's shining hero from the professional boxing ring, opened up Corky's Corner near the bend at Thirty-eighth and Walnut Streets. Here, some of Rich Castro's closest friends would hang out in the back alley like the knothole gang at a ball game. On warm evenings, when they opened the door for ventilation, the younger kids could catch the intoxicating sound of Mambo and the Chili Peppers, who played a strange new musical mixture reflecting the new climate of the neighborhood: Mexican *corridos* mingling side by side with rock and roll.[17]

The churches, too, overflowed with the faithful. There was Sacred Heart on upper Larimer and Annunciation further north in the Cole district. There were the Baptist congregations in Five Points, and the Eastern Europeans held their services across the viaduct in Globeville. Holy Rosary for the Yugoslavians, St. Joseph's for the Poles, a Russian Orthodox church on Logan Street—there was practically one on every block.[18]

Quarter Night on Tuesdays directed the flow of humanity toward the Uptown Theater on Thirty-third and Williams. For twenty-five cents you could see two movies on the same evening.[19] Westerns and horror movies, King Kong and Dracula. There was always a throng of kids at the Uptown, and Castro with his whole crew of young Catholic Eastsiders devoured the offerings of 1950s American culture.

A mile north of downtown, Curtis Park served as another nerve center for the energy flow on the East Side. The place was awash in activity: day camps, swim meets, talent shows, and family picnics. Some of Castro's buddies said later that they practically lived at the park.[20]

The East Side in the post-war era pulsated to the sounds of jackhammers in the railroad yard, polkas at the *quincenarias*, and gospel melodies floating above the black churches on Ogden Street.

In this first decade of the American Century, Denver's East Side was the quintessential American neighborhood. Residents worked hard, played hard, struggled for each dollar, and reveled in the full mix of southwestern culture. The young Richard Castro drank in the whole bottle of magic potion. He absorbed it all; he breathed in the climate of the East Side.

Reconstructing the East Side

Years later some of Castro's friends tried to reconstruct a picture of life on the East Side in the '50s and early '60s. Among them was Andy Lovato, tall and athletic, perhaps the best all-around athlete at Castro's high school. Like Castro, he would later become a social worker. Bobby Federico became a successful accountant and manager for Castro's legislative campaigns. Ken Maestas, who became a letter carrier with the Postal Service, played saxophone as a young man with the Dual Tones and the Playboys. Normando Pacheco would become a criminal defense lawyer. Roger Medina cruised the East Side with the gang unit of the Denver Police Department. Anthony Lopez, who tutored Castro in algebra, taught math at Skinner Middle School. And there were the cousins Sandoval—Don, Joe, and Paul—two of whom served in the State Legislature and one who became a principal in the Denver Public School system. Their accounts share the same fundamentals as Rich Castro's East Side story.

A glance at the newspapers of the '50s reveals a tone of innocence, which might lead one to idealize the community of times past. The *Rocky Mountain News*, for instance, expressed shock over two incidents that occurred in March 1954. The first was the arrest of the "Tiger Tots," a group of seven youngsters ranging in age from eleven to fifteen and led by a thirteen-year-old girl. The kids, described as a "pint-sized burglary gang," carried out a string of burglaries in the neighborhood of Twenty-sixth and York. They frequently employed the eleven-year-old to enter homes by slipping in through the milk chute. The lurid details of the story revealed that the gang's leader was in love with an eighteen-year old in the Denver County Jail; she used some of the proceeds to win his approval. The rest she gave away to friends, asking "nothing in return but their admiration."

When a neighbor caught them in the midst of a burglary, the youthful thieves turned on him, scratching him and biting his arm. In a follow-up article, the *News* noted that there was no food in the home of the gang leader and her eleven-year-old brother, and "there was no love which they wanted and needed just as badly."[21]

The second incident was the arrest of three girls ages twelve, thirteen, and fourteen, for having "innumerable intimacies" with junior and senior high school boys at an apartment house on Twenty-fourth Street. "They were reported to the police," says the *News*, by a landlady "who first pleaded with them to mend their ways."[22]

What makes these incidents particularly noteworthy is the fact that they made the commentary page under the headline, "14 Kids Out of Control."[23] Compared to the slaying of teenagers in the 1990s due to the color of a jacket or the insignia on a baseball cap, the 1950s examples of juvenile delinquency suggest a rather touching wholesomeness present on the East Side.

Life on the Street

A search beneath the surface of the news accounts, however, reveals a far more complex reality. Conversations with Castro's childhood friends uncover disparities, disagreements, and ambiguities about the nature of the streets on the East Side.

From his sixth-floor office on Grant Street, lawyer Normando Pacheco can look out his window at the whole panorama of East Denver. As he reminisced about his childhood, gunshots rang out from some unknown corner of his old neighborhood. Pacheco attended the same nursery as Castro—the Margery Reed Day Care Center at Twenty-second and Larimer—and later he attended elementary school with him at Sacred Heart.

"We're talkin' about a very poor neighborhood," says Pacheco of the 1950s East Side, "where one-half of the guys that Rich and I went to grade school with are either dead or in jail. I'm not just talkin' about the guys who grew up hard and went to the joint and dropped dead. I'm talkin' about the girls, too. It was a tough neighborhood. I don't see any difference between now and then. It was tough then and it's tough now. The only difference is that then you had a zip gun that fired one round and today you have a Mac 10 that fires many rounds. But people were still armed and people were still running in gangs."[24]

In the back of every school kid's mind was the image of the young rebels who hung out in the parks at night. It is what awaited you if you dropped out of school or fell off the tightrope. Diagonally across the street from Corky's Corner was St. Charles Park. It was here that the "38ers" staked out turf near the bend at Thirty-eighth Street. In the Curtis Park area were two other gangs, the "Heads" and the "Dukes," and towards town around Twenty-third Street were the "Hoods."[25]

As Emmanuel Martinez recalled the streets in the '50s and '60s, he flipped through an album of photographs of himself and his friends. "Here's Joe [Gallegos]," says Martinez. "Joe went to prison. Probably spent most of his life in prison. A couple of decades anyway. Dave Sanchez, who was our leader; he's still in prison now. He got addicted to drugs. Here's Bruce Dimotta. He's the mayor of a small town in Colorado; I think it's LaSalle."[26]

Martinez had two cousins and a sister who ran with the Heads. "The cousins were big shots in the Heads," says Martinez. "They used to call them Big Fish and Little Fish. They both ended up in prison. I can remember as a kid going to the meeting places of the Heads and it would be right there in Curtis Park. As kids [in the '50s], we looked up to 'em, and I was startin' to do things that they did. This tattoo right here was inspired by them. They'd usually put a cross with little rays coming out [between the thumb and the forefinger]. One reason I didn't pursue that path is because it hurt."[27]

Martinez maintains that the style made famous in the '70s by the TV character "The Fonz" was actually an imitation of these Chicano gang members. A tight T-shirt rolled up at the sleeve so as to cradle a pack of cigarettes clinging to a tattooed arm, a duck-tailed haircut, angling to a conspicuous peak in the middle of the forehead—the look originated with the Mexican-American gangs from L.A., and it worked its way from the West Coast to the streets of East Denver.[28]

The weapons of choice in those days were fists, clubs, tire irons, and switchblades, but some gang members packed zip guns. These were homemade devices, fashioned from car antennas wide enough to hold a .22-caliber bullet. The hammer came from toy cowboy guns, the handle was made of wood, and the firepower was unleashed from the dozens of rubber bands that connected the hammer to the antenna. Crude and simple, it would be a mistake to underestimate the zip gun. It was a lethal weapon.[29]

Yet many Eastsiders look back to the '50s as a time of relative tranquility. Ricardo Veladez remembers, "Yes, we did have gangs in those days. The Dukes and the Heads—they would clash every now and then. They'd come and do a little smalltime extortion on you for a quarter or a nickel. But you always knew who they were and most of the time they wouldn't mess with you unless you were causing problems. I knew a gang member they called Sluggo. When I was first learning to ride a bike, I remember falling off and being upset until Sluggo came along, picked me up, and put me back on my bike. I also remember walking many nights from Twenty-seventh and California to my girlfriend's house at Thirty-seventh and Adams. Crime? There was none at all."[30]

As is the case today, the gangs played only a minor role in creating the general level of violence on the East Side. Roger Medina lived on the second floor of the Sunshine Inn at Twenty-eighth and Larimer, where his father tended bar. He maintains that on Saturday nights, he and his brother would play a game to see who would be closest to the bullets coming up through the ceiling from the bar down below. "I'd say there was a shooting there twice a month," says Medina, "usually on a Friday or Saturday night when it was busy. I'd stick my head out the window on a Friday night and I didn't see good things. Upper Larimer was a mess then. A lot of ruffians hung out at my dad's place. They'd start arguin' and sometimes they'd pull switchblades or straight razors. We seen one guy pull an ax out from the trunk of a car. Times like that, my mom would yank us back in because we'd have our heads hanging out the window."[31]

Ken Maestas, another longtime friend of Castro's, likewise remembers the difficulties of growing up in the neighborhood just north of Manual High School. "The neighborhood wasn't really secure," says Maestas. "There were burglaries and thefts and muggings. We didn't call it gang activity; we just called it being raised in a rough neighborhood. My mom and dad often used to pick us up at school even though we lived at Thirty-first and Franklin, only about six blocks from where Rich and I went to school. I played in the band and there were times when I had to run home with my saxophone in hand, running from a group of six to ten kids who were hot on my heels. I feared they'd take my saxophone and I feared, too, I'd be looking at a spanking from Mom and Dad like I'd never had before. I had to do this all the way through high school. When Rich and I did travel through the neighborhood, we went two, three, four strong wherever we went."[32]

A rough consensus emerges from these memories of Eastsiders looking back to their formative years in the '50s and '60s. The East Side was, indeed, tough. The streets claimed heavy casualties; they devoured no small number of youthful warriors and hapless victims. Indeed, when Castro was called upon in the 1980s to mediate a dispute in Cañon City's maximum-security wing, he recognized several inmates as old friends and acquaintances from the East Side.[33]

But there were influences that ameliorated the harshness of conditions on the East Side.

For one, the firepower was not there. Disputes that escalate today into lethal exchanges, more likely resulted in knife wounds or broken bones in the '50s. "There used to be gangs back then, too, says Medina from the DPD's Gang Unit. But it's not like now. Now they got drive-by shootings without you knowing anything. That's the chicken-shit way of doin' things today. It's not like years ago when you'd fight somebody one on one. You shook hands, went out and had a beer. But now they'd just as soon kill you as look at you."[34]

Paul Sandoval, a schoolmate of Castro's who became a State Senator, expressed sentiments common to many who grew up on the East Side. "You had your '38ers,'" says Sandoval in recalling the '50s. "You had your different little cliques. You got in fights. You got in brawls. But there was never a gun. If you were picked up with one joint of marijuana, you did ten or fifteen years in jail. You knew who the gang members were; you grew up with them. They had names like Snooky and Spunky and Stinky. They were just regular guys, but they'd dropped out. They got as far as Cole [Junior High] and you knew for them it was all over. They never even got into Manual [High School]. You'd go over to their house. Their mom and dad, they didn't give a shit. I mean our mom and dad, they'd kill us if we didn't get in by eight o'clock."[35]

Thus, the hard-living kids lived side by side with the kids who studied rigorously. They mingled together and shared the same parks and street corners. Everyone knew the gang members, but the magnetic pull toward the street life was not insurmountable.

Family discipline, at least in the memories of Castro's young companions, carried far greater clout.

"My parents," remembers Roger Medina, "they were the boss. No matter what your mom and dad did, you had respect for them. In them days, they'd knock you out, man; it's not like today. Parents ruled then."[36]

Castro's friends all remember Archie Castro as a strict no-nonsense parent. "He was a nice man," recalled Andy Lovato, who would room with Rich later on, "level-headed but firm. You didn't want to push him."[37]

Archie Castro himself stated, "The kids grew up knowing I meant business. I only said it once and that was it. There was no sass, no nothin'. What I said was to be done. And they grew up to mind me."[38]

For all the strictness of the fathers, many of them were present for their sons on an everyday basis. Author Luis Rodriguez, in his powerful autobiography, *Always Running*, described his early flirtations with gang activity in a tough L.A. suburb in the '70s. He wrote this about the formation of his first gang, Thee Impersonations: "It was something to belong to—something that was ours. We weren't in boy scouts, in sports teams or camping groups. Thee Impersonations is how we wove something out of the threads of nothing."[39]

This desperate existence of lost souls on the fringe of society bears no relationship to the upbringing of Rich Castro and most of his circle of East Side friends. Archie Castro was one of those fathers who made himself available to his kids. Bobby Federico's dad was co-scoutmaster with Archie of the local Boy Scout troop. Ken Maestas's dad, Jack, was also a scoutmaster. Together, fathers and sons would head up to mountain campgrounds—to Waterton, Deckers, and Boulder Canyon. They'd travel to Adams County farms for fishing trips and hay rides. Relationships were cemented around blazing campfires, ghost stories, and roasted hot dogs.

Back in the city, relationships were also tightly knit. Commonplace among the old Eastsiders are memories of a rich sense of community, where extended families and networks of friends wove a net of security around the children. Josephine Castro is remembered particularly by Castro's friends for her warmth, kindness, and good humor. Roger Medina remembers especially the glass cake tray she kept in the kitchen. She would say, "You go right in there and get yourself something to eat. You know whenever you come over I'll have a cake for you every time."[40]

"We'd always hear critical statements about the area," says Bobby Federico, "because it was a poor neighborhood and a blighted neighborhood. But I remember mostly good things. I remember swimming in Curtis Park and how close the families were."[41]

Economic Transformation

Perhaps the most profound change to haunt the East Side was the slow, almost imperceptible transformation of the economy. Richard Castro and his friends were the children of the industrial working class. Archie Castro, chasing parts at the counter of Eaton Metal, worked with the din of clanging steel ringing in the background. Everyone had an uncle or a cousin working on the kill floor or the boning room of one of the neighboring packinghouses. Bobby Federico's dad welded for Thompson Pipe and Steel and Ken Maestas's father, Jerry, worked with pick and shovel as a drain layer. Anthony Lopez remembers his father continually burning himself as he heated and bent rubber hoses as a vulcanizer for Gates Rubber.

They were, by and large, wrenching, even dangerous jobs, but many of them came with union contracts, cost of living adjustments, holiday benefits, and the hope of a steadily rising standard of living. They were jobs at the core of the American economic system and thus could provide, despite their grinding nature, a shred of dignity and a sense of pride.

Most of those jobs disappeared in the '60s and '70s. Gardner Denver shifted its operations first to Henderson in Adams County and later to Roanoke, Virginia.[42] The packinghouses moved out closer to the feedlots in the rural areas of Nebraska and Iowa, where nonunion labor held down costs. Railroads computerized their operations and drastically cut their labor force. Gates Rubber shut down its Denver production of radiator hoses and V-belts.

With the closures, a cloud of decay gradually descended on the landscape of East Denver. In the '50s those without a high school education or even a skilled trade could still look forward to a job in the economic mainstream. In the '70s and '80s, increasing numbers of East Side mothers and fathers strung together temporary jobs mopping the floors of high-rise office buildings on Seventeenth Street.

Moving from the Core City

However one assesses the changes, however one evaluates the relative rates of poverty and crime, by the mid-1950s Archie Castro had had enough of East Denver. He was a man of few vices; he saved money carefully and held on to his wartime dream of claiming a stake of American life.

In the mid-'50s, he was able to move his family to the northern suburb of Thornton. There was no mall or eight-lane highway. Thornton was no more than a tiny patch on the windblown prairie. Josephine Castro nearly died of loneliness. She missed the closeness of her family. She missed the tightly knit community on the East Side and all of the landmarks of the place where she had grown up. And she hated the long commute to the Deline Box Company, which had moved to South Santa Fe Drive across the street from Gates Rubber. The Castro family's stay in Thornton lasted barely two years.[43]

Archie, however, still hungered for a better life and so when they moved back to East Denver he refused to return to its bustling, high-density core area. Instead, they found a small rental on Thirty-fourth and Cook, in a quiet area on the fringe of the East Side called the Clayton Skyland neighborhood, where the yards were larger and the homes newer and more likely to be of brick construction. It was a step up from the inner-city neighborhood where Josephine Castro's folks still lived about a mile and a half away.[44]

As Archie looked for a home to buy, conditions in the mid-1950s conspired to present him the opportunity he was searching for.

Through most of Denver's history, the black community had been kept tightly bottled up in the East Denver neighborhood of Five Points. When Archie Castro left the Army in 1946, the unyielding dividing line between black and white stood at the ironically named Race Street, some fifteen blocks east of Five Points. As early as 1920, a black fireman named Claude DePriest challenged this line by moving his family two blocks to the "wrong" side. An angry crowd of 250 whites greeted him at his new home at Twenty-sixth and Gaylord with cries for his removal. Members of the neighborhood improvement association told him, "if you continue to reside at your current address, you do so at your own peril."[45] DePriest took the hint; he sold his new home shortly thereafter. Another black home was bombed in 1921 when Walter Chapman tried to move into the previously all-white block at Twenty-first and Gilpin.[46]

Enforcing the Color Line

By the end of World War II, enforcement of racial segregation had become subtler, but the implacable eastern dividing line remained at Race Street. A variety of instruments were designed to enforce this ghetto policy without resorting to such boorish tactics as mob violence or terrorist bombs.

Among the tools used in this battle was the "restrictive covenant clause" written into the title deeds of homes in many Denver neighborhoods. Here is a sample: "Only person(s) of a Caucasian race shall own, use or occupy any dwelling or residence erected upon any lot, tract or building site; provided, however, that occupancy by persons of another race who are employed as domestic servants by the occupying owner or occupying tenant shall not constitute a violation of this protective covenant."[47] The consequence of selling a house to a black family was an immediate lawsuit and the loss of revenue.

Struck down by the Supreme Court as unconstitutional in the late 1940s, the legacy of the restrictive covenant clauses persisted well into the next decade. Real estate agents had long been sensitive to the nuances of invisible boundaries that minorities were forbidden to cross.

Stirling Kahn, who worked for the real estate firm of Foster and Barnard, got his apprenticeship in the real estate business during the 1950s. He described his early training in this way: "There were certain 'gentleman's agreements,'" says Kahn. "There were certain understandings that you just didn't sell a home to any minority over a certain boundary line. There was nothing in writing. . . . You just became aware of it."[48]

Banks added their own brand of discrimination to the equation. Dave Smith, a black realtor in the '50s, maintains that downtown banks erected fortress walls practically insurmountable to black families attempting to get loans. His mother, who cleaned houses for a living, was able to buy a house on Franklin Street, within the acceptable boundaries, only by relying on a small real estate company called Bollinger and Robinson to finance her purchase. Under the terms of the deal, payments on the principal were never permitted; only payments on the interest were allowed.[46]

Smith recalls showing an elderly white woman's house at Twenty-eighth and Gaylord to a black couple. The couple had a savings account at the downtown office of Empire Savings and Loan, so Smith felt confident they could secure a loan through that institution. "We don't make loans in that area," a loan officer told Smith. "I went down to the president of Empire and I said, 'Do you accept deposits from black people?' And he said, 'Oh yeah, we accept deposits from anybody.' I said, 'So you accept this black money, but you don't loan it out, is that it?' But he just said that was the policy and he was going to follow it."[49]

In the realm of discrimination, Chicanos occupied a sort of shadowy netherworld. Were they considered "Caucasian enough" to circumvent the barriers placed by restrictive covenant clauses, by real estate agents, and by bank loan officers? Well, it all depended. It depended on the darkness of skin complexion, the intonations and accents of the English language, the degree of cultural assimilation, the whims and inclinations of the particular Anglos empowered to make financial decisions. By and large, Chicanos fared poorly. Added to the pot of racial discrimination was the simple economics of poverty on the East Side. Very few blacks were prosperous enough to even consider the jump across Race Street. Financial conditions for Chicanos were even worse. Of all the minorities in Denver, Chicanos occupied the bottom rung of the economic ladder. Along with blacks, the huge mass of Chicanos remained bottled up behind the Race Street boundary line.

Breaking the Color Line

In 1949, Dr. Edmund Noel, a black physician and husband of Rachel Noel, Denver's first black School Board member, purchased a two-story house on the 2200 block of Race Street. With this purchase, the dam began to crack. Elsewhere on the East Side, other minorities began to leap over the forbidden boundary lines.[50]

The invisible color line quickly moved two blocks east to York Street, but now the environment had changed radically. Covenant clauses were no longer legally enforceable; black real estate agents began appearing on the scene; and a small group of entrepreneurs in the heart of Five Points challenged the downtown banks and mortgage companies.

Half a dozen black businessmen came together to devise a scheme to outflank the financial discrimination practiced on Seventeenth Street. They established Equity Savings and Loan as a way of funding housing for blacks on the East Side. The plan was simple: Divert the savings of black railroad employees, dining car waiters, federal workers, domestics, and chauffeurs away from the conventional banks and into the hands of a black-owned bank, then use those funds to invest in home ownership for the black community.[51]

At the core of the conspiracy were Roy West, a dining car waiter for Union Pacific who sold insurance on the side; Dave Smith, a liquor store owner turned real estate agent; Chris Ashley, a barber who ran a shop out of his Five Points home; Lester Nelson, an auditor for the city; Tom Bean, a well-heeled property manager who had started a Five Points cab company; Elvin Caldwell, who for years dominated East Side politics as a city councilman; and the block-busting Dr. Edmund Noel.

Says Smith, "We had a lot of doubters in the neighborhood. There were those who said, 'These people don't know anything about how to handle money and have no experience in real estate lending.' But we had been refused loans for years and it was time to put an end to it."[52] Equity Savings and Loan began to finance the relentless move eastward by the black community. Once the momentum changed, the downtown banks, now pressured by white homeowners trying to flee, rapidly switched their policy on loans to blacks. The trickle of minorities that crossed over Race Street and later York Street in the early 1950s became a torrent by mid-decade.

Former state senator Paul Sandoval remembers, even as a kid, the impact this had on the Chicano community. "There was an unwritten rule that past York they would not sell you a house. I can remember when I was young going out to Stapleton Airport to sell newspapers. York Street, you knew. That was the dividing line then. You just knew. Nothing but white past York. Later I can remember people saying, 'Christ, they passed York. But they're not gonna cross Colorado Boulevard.' Then they crossed Colorado and you heard, 'Oh, they're not gonna go to Dahlia. That's too beautiful an area.' I can remember those conversations, yeah.

"I remember my folks saying, 'Uncle Dave bought a house on York Street.'

"'No! He did?'

"'Oh yeah, he got a nice house right there on York. Two bedrooms upstairs, a kitchen and a full basement.'

"Then my cousins bought east of York Street. People said, 'Jesus, you got a house *there*?'"[53]

Struggle Hill

The area just east of York became known as "Struggle Hill" as more and more middle-income blacks crossed over the color line and spent their life savings to stake out a claim in a formerly forbidden neighborhood. Between 1950 and 1960, the percentage of minorities residing in the Clayton Skyland neighborhood rose from less than one percent to over 50 percent. White folks fled like a herd of frightened buffalo. In the wake of their stampede, housing prices in the contested area spiraled downward.

The Castro family purchased their brick two-bedroom home at Twenty-ninth and Cook in the midst of this quiet social upheaval. They bought it because it was affordable—less than $10,000 in 1957—and yet, being nine blocks east of York, it symbolized a step up from the family's inner-city origins. "I wanted my kids to grow up without circulatin' with bullies," says Archie. "The old neighborhood was startin' to get rough about that time, and I wanted to better the family."[54]

From age ten, Richard Castro spent his formative years in what Americans politely called a "changing neighborhood." It was still working class: Wives worked; husbands worked; kids worked. It was comfortable and respectable, lined with neat, tidy yards replete with barbecue grills in the back lawn. But as blacks moved in block by block, whites moved out. It was an integrated neighborhood but simmering beneath the surface with racial tension. Because the migration pattern ran overwhelmingly black, Struggle Hill was physically cut off from the East Side Chicano community, which still clung to the core area closer to downtown.

Castro's youthful experience was cut, therefore, from a unique pattern. His physical surroundings were a bit less harsh than the barrio a few blocks to the west. His world remained working class but it was the upwardly mobile segment of that class. His neighbors on Cook Street were black and white. Few Hispanics lived in Clayton Skyland, yet he maintained intimate ties with the Chicano community particularly through his close relationship with his grandparents, the McGraths, who continued to live in the midst of the barrio on Thirty-third and Marion. Then, too, the Castros' new home was just a five-minute drive to Annunciation, the inner-city parochial school that would leave a tremendous imprint on the youthful Castro.

vi

school years

"We were all 1950s Catholic kids," said Joe Sandoval from his principal's office at North High School. "We said, 'Yes, Father; no Father.' We obeyed the nuns. We went to school every day. We went to confession on Saturdays. We went to Mass on Sundays. We played by the rules and regs. What can I say; that's all we were."[1]

For many who attended school at Thirty-sixth and Humbolt, Annunciation provided a refuge from the more turbulent life that surrounded them on the streets of East Denver. Some refer to it as a cloister, a sheltered community, a cocoon. Indeed, a visit today to Annunciation Church across the street from the old school induces a striking sense of tranquility and peacefulness in the midst of the poorest neighborhood in the city.

It was a small town. "We were all pretty close knit," says Anthony Lopez. "You knew almost everybody in the school. It was really like one big family."[2]

Some three to four hundred students populated the place, their colors reflecting the racial composition of the immediate neighborhood. It was perhaps the most integrated school in Denver. Glancing at a yearbook for Castro's graduating class, the breakdown appears to be about 60 percent Hispanic, perhaps 15 percent black, and 25 percent white.

Alumni invariably remember the atmosphere as one of racial harmony. Such was the nurturing climate of the school, that some alumni confess to having been unaware that racism in the larger society even existed.

Some were unaware, too, of their own poverty, but the school, itself, was quite conscious of its place in Denver's socio-economic structure. Its tuition rates were rock bottom. A family with three schoolchildren might send its kids to Annunciation for as little as sixty dollars a year.[3] A private school located in that neighborhood had to be accessible to the poor.

It was the nuns who kept the school together. Clad in their old-style black-and-white habits, they came from Leavenworth, Kansas, members of the Sisters of Charity.[4] Their tradition was service to the poor; their style stern and demanding.

"The sisters ran the school with an iron hand," says Ken Maestas, "with very little opposition from the student body."[5] As an observant student, he remembers the whole spectrum of techniques the nuns employed to deal with unruly students.

For one, there was the ever-handy presence of rulers. "They used rulers and pointer sticks all the time," says Maestas, "for a quick little slap to the hand. I remember in the fourth or fifth grade, I would always be struck by the nuns for hitting a wrong note on the piano. Father Woody's favorite thing to do was to 'knuckle' guys' heads. He got me one time when I made a bad mistake serving Mass. He took me to the back and said, 'Kenny, if I told you once, I told you a hundred times. I don't want you to do that again.' BOOM! It hurt! He knuckled Richard's head so many times I can't even remember. I think Woody kind of picked on Rich in a friendly way.

"Myself, coming from a strict family, I didn't see anything really wrong with how they handled themselves. They were just doing what they had to do to get done what had to get done. But I know for a fact there were a lot of students—usually the ones who didn't do so well in school—who feared the nuns on a daily basis. The nuns would holler at the top their voices for not turning in homework. They'd prevent students from going to pep rallies on Fridays and make them stay in class and work."

I Shall Not Be Late to Class

Maestas recalls, "They'd make you write on the blackboard several hundred times, 'I shall not do this' or 'I shall not do that.' 'I shall not talk in class' or 'I shall not be late.' You'd fill up the board, erase it, and have to fill it up again. I remember one girl, Trinidad Benavidez, who was always catching the ire of the nuns. They'd catch her wearing lipstick and talking in class and she was always in the doghouse. For some people it was an intimidating atmosphere."[6]

"There were some *big* nuns," remembers Andy Lovato, "some six-footers, and they could get mean. Sister Lawrence, now there was a tough nun. I'd be in her class and I'd look up like this at the clock, and she'd say, 'A half-hour after school.' A half-hour after school for looking at the clock! Now that's tough."[7]

Eloy Mares, who taught civics and history, loved the atmosphere. "There was no messing around," he says. "You didn't walk into class late. You didn't throw paper wads at anybody. You didn't chew gum. Very seldom did I have to deal with these things. Those things just didn't happen."[8]

Despite the strictness and rigorous enforcement of the rules, Annunciation could still be a physically tough school. Eastsiders in the public schools did not consider Annunciation boys soft just because theirs was a private school. Boxing was a favorite sport at Annunciation and so its student body had a reputation for holding its own in a street fight. Thirty-fourth Avenue was an informal boundary line between those who went to Manual, the largely black public high school, and those who attended Annunciation. When a dozen or so students from each school would happen to meet around that line, the fists would sometimes fly and a few of the incidents got pretty bloody.

One block north of the Annunciation schoolbuilding was Hagus Hall, a gymnasium, which was abandoned and boarded up in the early '60s because it was unsafe. "Whenever there was a score to settle in the neighborhood," says Maestas, "the fistfight would take place inside Hagus Hall. We'd get in there and—I'm not lying to you—it was just like the Friday night fights. You'd have the spectators and sometimes even a referee to make sure there was nothin' dirty going on. It was our own little world. Back in those days a fistfight was a fistfight. There wasn't any kicking or anything like that.

"I remember Richard fought it out with the block bully one time and Rich held his own. He wouldn't back down from anything."[9] Castro could hold his own because of the long hours he had spent in the ring on the boxing team. Friends often remember the anguished evenings he spent dieting, trying to keep his weight down to his standard classification. After the matches, they'd celebrate by gulping down batches of cheeseburgers at Sam's No. Three on Fifteenth Street.

The Weeding Out Process

As with all private schools, Annunciation tried to keep the lid on serious disciplinary problems through expulsion—swift and unceremonious. "Step out of line and you're gone," was the rule of thumb.

"There were a lot things that went on in that school," says Maestas. "There were locker searches carried out by the priests to confiscate weapons. They were looking for guns, knives, brass knuckles. I believe Father Barry once found three small firearms and a sawed-off shotgun. Those guys were gone immediately. Sometimes, when there were shootings in the neighborhood, especially around the Cowboy Drive-in, there would be locker searches once a week. I can also remember a fight in the school right in the middle of the hall when somebody used brass knuckles. It turned my stomach just to see the results of the blows this guy took. It was one of those things when somebody had taken out somebody else's girlfriend. It was a big deal; a lot of people got kicked out of school for that one."[10]

Anthony Lopez had two brothers kicked out of Annunciation. One was expelled for a "poor attitude: he told a Sister 'No, you can't make me do anything.'" The other was struck by a nun's ruler and responded, according to Lopez, by jumping out of his chair and hurling the Sister over his desk. "You don't ever hit me," he shouted as she escorted him down the hall. Both brothers were shown the door immediately.[11]

In this manner most of the kids who refused to cooperate were quickly weeded out. Perhaps this is why many felt the school to be such a safe haven despite its rough edges. Those who felt cloistered or sheltered did so because they had made the cut. In effect, they chose to cut themselves off from the tougher street life. The kids who were attracted to the street life did not last long at Annunciation.

For all the firmness of the nuns and the ease with which some of the students came to blows, these things do not begin to tell the whole Annunciation story. As Normando Pacheco stated, "This was no Charles Dickens story."[12] Behind their tough veneer, the Sisters of Charity carried on their duties lovingly and with an inspiring dedication to service. Said Roger Medina, "The nuns must have been great. They tolerated *us*."[13] And, indeed, for most students, the nuns' firmness was not so oppressive and stifling as to prevent a good deal of adolescent mischief.

Andy Lovato recalls the time he had a water fight in the hall with Kenny Gonzales. When they were sent to the office of the principal, Sister Ann de Sales, they still carried a mouthful of liquid ammo. "Aren't you ashamed of yourselves?" said the principal sternly, at which point they each spewed forth a stream of water expertly directed at the other's face. "She got really mad then," says Lovato, "but I think in some sense she was trying to hold back her laughter. I'm sure she was laughing after we left the office. They were strict, but not that strict. Especially when they started to get to know you in your junior and senior year."[14]

Angel's corner grocery store, owned by the parents of an Annunciation student, was on the corner of Thirty-seventh and Humbolt. Since attendance at Mass was mandatory every morning, Angel's became a popular spot for avoiding the morning service. Each day, about a half-dozen kids could be found hanging out, waiting for the bell to ring signifying that Mass was over and eight-o'clock classes would soon begin. Once a month or so, a squad of priests or nuns would pay a visit to Angel's, and then the kids could be seen scurrying behind the counters to hide.[15]

And there was a game around confession. Every Friday was confession day at parochial schools, and the nuns and priests drummed in its importance. Necking after a dance, it was thought, might lead to a one-way trip to the Inferno unless the sin was cleared through confession. The lines snaked around the confessional booths every Friday.

After each confession, the Father meted out the penance: repetitions of prayers—perhaps three Our Fathers, three Hail Mary's, or three Glory Be's, depending on the severity of the offense. Among the priests at Annunciation, however, were a couple of hanging judges. Monsignor Barry, for example, tended to hand out full rosaries instead of a couple of Our Fathers. Father Woodrich would do the same. A rosary consists of a series of prayers involving fifty Hail Mary's, five Our Fathers, and five Glory Be's. A kid didn't want this under any circumstances. It might take twenty minutes to complete a rosary.

On the other end of the spectrum was Father Morgan, fresh out of the seminary, and looking more or less like a high school kid when he donned civilian clothes. Father Morgan would fraternize with the students, cruising Sixteenth Street, hanging out at the Rockybilt hamburger stand, and even buying beer occasionally for his youthful flock. From his confessional Father Morgan tended to dole out much lighter sentences than the elder priests.

Thus on Friday afternoons, word regarding which priest was manning which confessional quickly spread through the throngs of students. Long lines formed behind the booth occupied by the suddenly popular Father Morgan, whereas the lines for Monsignor Barry or Father Woody's booth were virtually nonexistent. Then the nuns came in riding herd. "There's no one over here," they would say. "You five, get over in this other line." The big sinners, especially, would try to position themselves away from the nuns so as to avoid at any cost the fate of a meeting with Monsignor Barry.[16]

One Friday afternoon, Castro entered Father Barry's booth hoping to gain forgiveness for a drinking incident that had occurred the previous week. "Bless me, Father, and forgive my sins," concluded Castro. "Is that you, Castro?" yelled the gruff monsignor from the behind the curtain. "Get the hell outta here!"[17]

On another Friday, a particularly brazen student—a football player and prankster—noticed that one of the confessional booths was momentarily vacant. Seizing the opportunity, he jumped into the priest's side of the booth and waited for a victim. Within moments another student entered the other side and knelt down on the kneeler. "Go ahead, my son," echoed a deep authoritative voice from the priest's side, and the hapless victim began the recitation of his week of sin. Not half an hour later, the entire student body had heard exactly what sins had been committed. It became an incident endlessly repeated at class reunions—the classic Catholic school prank. People say Rich Castro laughed at that one till the day he died.[18]

In fact, people say that Rich Castro laughed at everything, including and especially himself. Even as a state legislator, he was notorious for bringing humor into the political fray. His companions at Annunciation trace this streak of craziness all the way back to his childhood.

One time, as a second-string guard, Castro was watching a closely matched basketball game from the sidelines. Coach Bob Moore turned to put him into the game but, as he glanced around, was stunned and angered by what he saw. There was Castro, in full uniform, sitting on the bench eating a box of popcorn. Moore knocked the box out of his hands and refused to let him in the game. For a day Castro suffered in embarrassed silence, but by the next evening he was mimicking himself once again to an audience of friends, replaying the scene with an imaginary box of popcorn.[19]

The Sports Scene

Annunciation was the social center of the Hispanic East Side and at its heart was its athletic program. The source for this emphasis was an eccentric, shabbily dressed assistant pastor named Father Monihan. In later years, Father Monihan distinguished himself by being the only man in Denver allowed to play on the City Park Golf Course without shoes or shirt. You could find him there every day shooting eighteen holes and dressed only in shorts. But in the 1940s the Father was busy organizing a junior parochial sports league in order to fight the influence of poverty and gangs in the Chicano community. He was seen as a sort of Father Flanigan, the miracle worker at the Boys' Town orphanage in Nebraska. He believed that athletics provided the discipline and character necessary for low-income kids to work their way out of the ghetto.

Monsignor Barry, the pastor at Annunciation, shared similar views. Besides, he fancied himself something of a Moose Krause, the one-time athletic director at Notre Dame. He liked to sit down with the coaches and talk strategy. Barry was a gray-haired, bespectacled priest with an authoritarian demeanor. He was hard driving and disciplined and he expected a lot from students and staff alike. He liked to stay in control; he referred to "my gym," for instance, and "my school." He could rant and rave and stomp around with the best of them.[20]

Some students remember him for the full-fledged ritualized funeral he held in the rectory backyard for his cocker spaniel, Paddy-Fu. He drafted several altar boys including Castro, Bob Federico, and Early Thomas to come in formalized garb to perform the services. Later that night some-one—one of the school pranksters—dug up the dog's corpse and buried it somewhere outside the rectory.[21] Father Barry had his idiosyncrasies, but he was well respected and influential with the kids.

One of the coaches he hired was Eloy Mares, a local East Side athletic hero who grew up in a house on the same block as Annunciation High School. One of the kids singled out by Father Monihan for special atten-tion, Mares had been a high school All-American in both football and bas-ketball, and gone on to play halfback for the University of Denver.

Andy Lovato maintains that he and his friends were subconsciously hungry for a Chicano role model to admire. "If I asked you to name a His-panic in sports," says Lovato, "who would you think of? Joe Kapp? He wasn't really Hispanic to us until we found out later. Lee Trevino maybe. My role models were Superman, Roy Rogers, and Hopalong Cassidy. I didn't have any Hispanic role models; they were all Anglo. They certainly didn't look like me. When we came across Eloy, it was really something. Eloy in his day looked to me like a cross between Jim Thorpe and Burt Lancaster. I was an athlete then, and I needed an athletic role model."[22]

Mares's memories of Annunciation football give rise to the notion of the classic underdog, perpetually undersized, perpetually outmanned, but always scrappy, always feisty, always full of spirit. The middle- and up-per-class parochial schools—Regis, Mullen, and Machebeuf—towered over Annunciation in sheer numbers and muscle. Says Mares, "We were a small school. We'd play Regis or Mullen, for example, and they'd suit up seventy or seventy-five players. On our side of the field we were our own little motley crew: I'd generally suit up twenty or twenty-one kids. Almost im-mediately, the sheer numbers could have been demoralizing.

"Rich and Art Tapia were two people I relied on a lot as far as leader-ship, and as far as morale. They were two individuals I could really count on and in turn they were the types of individuals who would keep other players going on the field when the temptation was to just give up. Rich was a linebacker. He wasn't very big—maybe 140 pounds—but he was a pretty aggressive young man on the football field, the kinda guy who never gave up. Both he and Tapia were elected team captain and they could both take care of business on the field.

"I remember having a center named Bobby Montez who typified the kind of player we had on the team. He was very courageous, very gutty, and at five foot five he weighed all of 135 pounds. [Notre Dame coach] Frank Leahy's son was attending Machebeuf, and when we faced them they decided to put him head up over our center. Now Frank Leahy's son weighed 210 pounds. That was their strategy; he outweighed Montez by almost 100 pounds. Bobby Montez's reaction was typical. He stayed in there, played four quarters and gave all he had, but I think he strained every muscle in his body trying to keep Leahy out of there. And did a good job of it. But that's usually what we were up against. Mullen and Regis always outweighed us.

"We always tried, and we were recognized as a testy group and a group of players who would stick in there. The parochial coaches—Julius Carbello and Lou Kellog, Guy Gibbs and Frank Evans—used to meet at places like Pomponio's DX [a tavern at Forty-eighth and Pecos in North Denver] maybe once a month. They were always telling me, 'Look, we knock your guys down but before you know it they're back up on their feet.' I remember they made comments like that more than once about Rich Castro. Our guys stood out because they were so damn small and so skinny that they couldn't figure us out. They'd have a hell of a time knocking us down, but once they did, we'd be right back up harassing them. It was like trying to swat a fly. Or like a flea on an elephant."[23]

The athletic experience was central to Rich Castro's development at Annunciation. His friends by and large survived that cultural cut that divided the kids who stayed on the East Side streets from those who stayed in school. An essential thread, which bound Castro's circle together, was sports. Together they dieted on Thursday nights to make sure their boxing weights remained beneath their designated limits. They jogged daily the eight tenths of a mile from the locker room to the practice football field at Thirty-seventh and Clayton, the clatter of their cleats alerting the whole East Side to their youthful presence. They learned not to give up, even when the odds dictated that surrender might be the easy way out. It was sports that cast this crew together and nurtured the perseverance and social skills for the later success that many of them achieved. It was sports, too, that offered a degree of shelter from the storm many other East Side kids had to contend with.

Preparing for the Priesthood

Like many good Catholic kids, Rich Castro aspired early on to the priesthood. His environment deliberately encouraged his entrance into the spiritual life.

There was the church building itself. It stands today—an imposing red brick structure encircled by a wrought iron fence designed as symbolic protection for the saintly relics stored within. Inside the arched doors, the sanctuary abounds with ornamentation reminiscent of a past era: flowery wood carvings, a marble baptismal fountain, elaborate religious murals bathed in light flooding in from the ubiquitous stained-glass windows.

People speak in soft voices, which reverberate about the sanctuary, creating a hushed, mysterious atmosphere. Parishioners say that in the morning hours when the sun rises in the east, the dawn light slipping in through the stained glass produces a feeling of the utmost tranquility. The place radiates an aura of sacredness contrasting with the urban bleakness of the surrounding neighborhood. In staking out a small corner of peace, the sanctuary at Annunciation Church literally barricades out the turbulence of the streets.

Father Woodrich cast the original spell over Castro.[24] In later days Father Woody would be revered by Denver's homeless as the builder of the Samaritan Shelter, but as a religious instructor at Annunciation he carried a reputation as a sort of gruff old bear who alternately inspired and intimidated his students. He frightened his young flock with warnings of an eternal afterlife straight out of the pages of Dante's *Inferno*. In exquisite detail, he dramatized the agonizing pain of the burning soul, searing endlessly without respite or relief. The number of souls descending into Hell, he used to say, was like the number of leaves falling from the trees in the autumn.[25]

Andy Lovato remembers the lore that surrounded this conception of the afterlife and the exaggerated stories that circulated among the students. "If you got a hamburger at McDonald's on a Friday night," he believed, "then got in an accident and died before you could confess and say 'Bless me, Father for I have sinned,' you could spend eternity in Hell. Oh, man! In high school, Hell was right there and you better be good. I prayed every night. I prayed in Church; I prayed at home; I prayed for my salvation."[26]

The outwardly happy-go-lucky Castro seemed to accept this theological view.

In addition to the Castro in the boxing ring and on the football field is the image of Castro at the church in the altar boy's robes. Says Lovato, "I remember him taking communion. Understand, to take communion without having gone through confession was a sacrilege. You had to have a clear mind. When you went to get Holy Communion, you were clean. It was a sacred act, and Richard would go on a regular basis."[27]

Serving Mass required meticulous training under the watchful eyes of the priest. The hands had to be just so, perfectly upright, chest-high. Improper movements were commonly reprimanded—for bows or genuflections, for the unfolding of hands or the fidgeting of fingers. Altar boys had to know what they were doing. Of course, there were perks for the righteous. Serving Mass at a funeral meant a half a day off from school. Everyone volunteered for funeral service.[28]

Like most other young men at Annunciation, Castro feared God's wrath and the fires of Hell but not enough to drive him into the eight years of solitary life the seminary had to offer. What drew Castro like a magnet to the priesthood was the vision of a life of service. Here was Father Woody, living in the rectory next door to the church. He was full of vigor and vitality and symbolized a life of commitment to the young and the needy on the East Side. The Sisters of Charity, residing in a convent on the school grounds, carried with them their century-long tradition of serving the poor. By the end of his senior year, Castro, with considerable nudging from Father Woody, had decided to enter training as a diocesan priest.

Seeds of Nationalism

A certain innocence or naiveté accompanied Rich Castro's upbringing. In the neighborhood around Annunciation, seeds of a conscious movement to organize the Mexican-American community had begun sprouting as early as the 1940s. Sheltered in the cocoon at Annunciation and out of touch with the Spanish language, Castro, as a youth, remained oblivious to it all.

He was largely unaware, for instance, of the cultural glue provided by Paco Sanchez. Sanchez arrived from Guadalajara in 1948, an entrepreneur looking to promote Mexican bands touring the "Borderlands" with their ranchera sounds, their mariachi music, their polkas, and their *musica tropical*. Bands hitting the circuit from Texas, Arizona, and California—Lalo Guerrera, Beto Villa, and Pete Bugarin—would storm into Denver to play at the Rainbow Dance Hall on Fifth Avenue between Broadway and Lincoln.

When Sanchez learned that there was no Spanish-language station to advertise these events, he sensed an untapped gold mine. The "manitos"—the ex-farmers and miners coming up from the San Luis Valley to settle in East Denver—still spoke Spanish in large numbers. From his own house at Thirty-third and Lafayette, three blocks away from Annunciation, Sanchez began broadcasting the first of the Spanish stations, KFSC, in 1954.[29]

That was the same year a minor upheaval hit the East Side—a small wave of nationalistic sentiment, which foreshadowed the turbulence of the 1960s. In that year, the *Rocky Mountain News* assigned Robert Perkin to write a seven-part series on Denver's largest minority, the Hispanic community. It was not an entirely unsympathetic portrayal. Many of the articles were fair-minded and accurate, but the tone of the first piece left the East Side reeling. Many Eastsiders picked up the front page of the *News* on January 31 to see themselves portrayed as a race of aliens invading Denver like the Martians in H. G. Wells's *War of the Worlds*.

"Study of a Critical Denver Problem," read the headline on page one. "The hush-hush subject is Denver's so called 'Spanish American' problem," continued the story. "If you want to be informed about this problem, be sure to read this series."[30] The first article detailed the presence of Hispanic criminals at the downtown police station and ended with the words "Denver has a 'Spanish American problem.'"[31]

Incensed and hurt at the condescending tone, some young Eastsiders erupted in anger. They overturned *News* trucks and destroyed or vandalized newspaper vending machines.[32]

Pillars of the community called a meeting at Cole Junior High to consider the situation. Councilman Jimmy Fresquez stood at the podium with Bernie Valdez, the highest city official among Denver's Hispanics. A youthful Corky Gonzales was present. Father Monihan, the youth worker from the parish, was there, and so was Paco Sanchez with his impeccable mastery of the Spanish language. Sanchez's partner at KFSC, Levi Beall, claims that the school auditorium overflowed by a thousand people and that scores of police lingered on the fringe to monitor the tense crowd.[33]

A modest organization sprang from that initial assembly. Beall recalls that the people's sentiment was, "Hell, we're as good a bunch of citizens as anyone else. We'll form an organization and we'll call it the 'Good Citizens Organization.' Then Father Monihan stepped up on the dais and said, 'Look, we're all Americans. Let's call it the Good Americans Organization.'" And so it remained.[34]

As one of those grassroots affiliations that represent a quiet germination of consciousness, the Good Americans Organization took its place alongside other civil rights groups. The Latin American Education Fund had already formed to help Mexican-American students progress in school.[35] LULAC—the League of United Latin American Citizens—had expanded into Denver in the 1940s, as had the GI Forum.[36] All these organizations grew quietly in the shadow of the McCarthy hysteria of the 1950s. And they were assimilationist; they all yearned for acceptance by white society, yet often simultaneously expressed feelings of ethnic pride.[37] In tune with the times, they made few waves and drew little media attention. They did, however, plant seeds. And they helped set the stage for the more dramatic expressions of militancy and nationalism that would explode all over the Southwest in the 1960s.

The Backdrop of Discrimination

It appears that none of this touched Castro in his youth. He was busy living the all-American life as one of the 1950s Catholic kids. No wonder Castro could reminisce about Walt Disney fantasy legends in a 1990 article for *La Voz*, when he wrote: "During the 1950s, when I was about ten years old, I can remember cheering for Fess Parker, who played the role of Davy Crockett in one of the first film versions of the fall of the Alamo. The film ended with Parker beating back Mexican hordes as they climbed the walls of the battle-torn mission. Imagine a Mexican-American youth identifying more with Crockett than his own roots. It's like a Sioux Indian cheering Errol Flynn playing General George Armstrong Custer in the film *They Died with Their Boots On. . . ."*[38]

In his school days, American pop culture appears to have seized Castro's imagination far more than any dream of a Chicano awakening. For gang members and those closer to the street, police nightsticks in Curtis Park were teaching the lessons of race in America in a markedly unsubtle manner. But for others, the general culture of the '50s, in tandem with the cloistered atmosphere of Annunciation, tended to discourage awareness of racial inequities. Nevertheless, the reality of racial discrimination occupied the subconscious minds of many Hispanics on the East Side, including some of the kids at Annunciation.

When Senator Paul Sandoval was questioned about discriminatory practices during his childhood in Denver, he hesitated to respond at first because of the subtlety of many of his experiences. "You know when you're being looked at differently," he finally said. "You just know it. I mean we would go to Elitch's [the more upscale amusement park] when we were kids and the cops would look at us and say, 'Hey what are *you* doin' here? You're s'posed to be at Lakeside.'" Chicano kids, he said, were discouraged from going to Elitch's, and when they did, the slightest infraction of the rules would be grounds for removal. "Go to Lakeside where you belong" was the implication.

"After a while," continues Sandoval, "[someone would say] 'Let's go to Elitch's,' and you'd say, 'Aw, what the hell you want to go to Elitch's for? They're gonna kick us out anyway; let's go to Lakeside.' You knew, and I hate to put it this way, but you knew your place. You knew where you were welcome and you knew where you weren't welcome. You'd go to the movie houses and the ushers would watch you constantly. You knew if you'd ever go to North Denver, [which was largely Italian] especially around Columbus Park, you were going to get into a fight. You go into Globeville which had Polish, German, etc.—you go into Globeville Park to swim, you knew you're gonna get in a fight. That's why we went to Curtis Park."[39]

Ricardo Veladez corroborates this memory. He recalls going to the roller rink at Mammoth Gardens on Colfax and Clarkson on the periphery of the East Side. These trips went smoothly, but a visit to a predominantly white rink on South Broadway produced different results. "Like dummies," he says, "we went down to South Broadway. We got run out of there; it was either that or get our butts kicked. So we decided it was wiser to stay in our own neighborhood."[40]

The public high school that served the East Side was in itself a palpable symbol of racial as well as class discrimination. Manual Training High School on East Twenty-sixth Avenue was designed, as the name implies, to give vocational training to the children of the East Side. Its role in the school system and its expectations for students were revealed in the school song, still prevalent in the 1950s: "We are bricklayers one and all."[41]

Ricardo Veladez recalls a pattern that appears repeatedly in the Hispanic experience. Like most other Mexican Americans at Manual, he had been directed towards shop classes at the school. Teachers expected little from black and Chicano kids in the way of academic achievement. One day his speech teacher pulled him aside and suggested gently that he join the Armed Services. It was an invitation to drop out. Veladez took the hint and did. He enlisted.

Annunciation was not immune to this pattern. Andy Lovato, the premier athlete at Annunciation in 1965, remembers walking into the counselor's office in his senior year. Sitting in front of the counselor, a sixty-five-year-old nun, he brought with him letters from Colorado State University, Trinidad State Junior College, the University of Kansas, and Georgia Tech, each with an offer of a football scholarship. "What do you think I should do?" asked Lovato. "Well," she said, "you should also consider the military."[42]

While the rigorous Jesuits at Regis High School enforced the highest academic standards on its affluent student body, more modest expectations permeated its sister school at Annunciation. It was part of American culture; it was unconscious and well-intentioned, but nevertheless debilitating.

In 1964, however, as he walked through graduation ceremonies, most of these things had not occurred to Richard Castro. A political education was one thing he did not receive from the nuns and priests at Annunciation.

Despite its shortcomings, he did obtain the fundamentals he would later need. The school had done a remarkable job of educating the forty or fifty seniors who survived the cut to get their diplomas. Till his last days, Castro expressed gratitude for the instruction and preparation he had received there.

In a 1985 article for the *Denver Catholic Register*, Castro lamented the loss of eighteen inner-city Catholic schools over a twenty-year period. He wrote that Annunciation had built the foundation for his later success. "I flashbacked several times," he wrote, "to my teachers and coaches at Annunciation that dedicated so much of their lives to me and my other classmates. There was my coach Eloy Mares who became a role model for all of us growing up in the lower East Side. Mr. Mares was the first Chicano any of us knew who went to college. There was Sister Ann Margaret, my tenth grade biology teacher, who ran her class with an iron fist. She had to; we were a rough bunch of kids who didn't begin to appreciate her strict discipline until many years later."

When Annunciation closed, he continued, "many of the young people who would have gone there dropped out of school. They couldn't make it at Manual. There wasn't the small classroom atmosphere. There wasn't the opportunity to participate in all aspects of school life. The public school was not the center of their life that Annunciation was to me."[43]

Castro and his classmates graduated as the cream of the East Side. They had steeled themselves against the chaotic living that coursed through much of the neighborhood, and they had come out winners. In those years, Annunciation produced some of the most extraordinary graduates in the city. Three of their number—Rich Castro, Don Sandoval, and Paul Sandoval—went on to the Colorado General Assembly. Paul Meek became a first-class cardiologist. Early Thomas, cut, incredibly, from the football squad at Trinidad State Junior College, went on to become a first-round draft pick for the New York Jets. Don Chávez became a prominent golfer in the Denver area. Michael Simmons ran Denver's Commission of Youth, and Tupy Davis worked with troubled youth at Denver Juvenile Hall.

"This little school on the East Side," wrote Castro, "has turned out more than its share of first class citizens. These were individuals who grew up in poverty, but who were never poor. They had the benefit of teachers and parents who really cared and society is better today for that concern."[44]

The Seminary

St. Thomas Theological Seminary was located in a quiet South Denver neighborhood at the intersection of East Arizona Avenue and Steele. It was here that Castro enrolled for an arduous eight-year program and it was here, within the contemplative confines of the seminary, that Castro underwent a major life transformation. By the end of his first year, Castro's vision of himself as a priest would shatter, and he would take his first tentative steps in a new, more political direction.

The Catholic Church was braced for change as Castro entered the seminary. The Ecumenical Council known as Vatican II—the first such council in a century—had astounded the Catholic world with reforms drawn up two years earlier under the energetic leadership of Pope John XXIII.

Latin would be dropped from the liturgy!

A document entitled "On Priestly Training" outlined changes in educational programs for priests. No longer would philosophy be the only major available to seminarians. The Church was lurching toward a new era.

But changes came slowly; at St. Thomas Seminary life continued much as it had in the past. Each day began at 6:00 A.M. with Mass and a half-hour of silent meditation. Meals were silent, although a reader would deliver passages covering a wide array of topics. Studies were rigorous: eighteen hours a week in classes taught by the Vincentian Order, and often six hours a day of study outside the classroom.[45]

The sober climate did not transform Castro's personality. He was quick to laugh in this all-male society and remained, as always, the practical joker. One night, for instance, he and a conspirator removed the bolts from the hinges of another student's door. When the door subsequently crashed to the floor and the unsuspecting student caught holy hell from the floor director, Castro and his partner in crime covered their sides in the next room trying to conceal their laughter. On another Saturday night, Castro's creative energy was directed to one of the statues that decorated the halls of the dormitory. Imagine the surprise of one of his companions that evening who peeled back his bed covers and found himself sharing his bed with a life-size statue of one of the holy saints.[46]

In between the comic episodes, the dorms at St. Thomas were abuzz. Students wondered aloud if this austere life, resembling in some ways the life of a soldier, was the life for them. In truth the Fathers did not discourage these evening dialogues. They wanted only those young men whose commitment to the call was beyond question. But in 1965, the casualty rate was particularly high. Some students estimate that only 10 to 15 percent of Castro's class was ultimately ordained.[47]

Castro studied diligently, but he was not immune to the climate of questioning. He would walk the grounds at night, inside the gated walls, and hear the voices of neighborhood boys on the other side chasing after the girls. There he was inside the compound, eighteen years old and facing a lifetime of chastity. Sometimes the boys on the outside, knowing the vulnerability of the seminary students, would chide them with adolescent cruelty. His humor never left him; he could laugh at his own predicament as well as at the victims of his practical jokes. But it was a lonely time.[48]

Then there was Latin. Its mastery was still required, despite the Vatican II revolution. Castro had not the slightest knack for the ancient language. Father Yallary would walk into class without a greeting or a hello, turn on the overhead projector, and begin conjugating verbs.[49] Learning the prayers in high school was one thing, but fully understanding Cicero was an entirely different matter. Latin was Castro's curse.

For two consecutive semesters Castro got Ds in Father Yallary's class. While every other student was packing his bags for a summer break in June 1965, Castro was informed he had to stay behind, alone, for a Latin tutorial program.[50] He felt guilty and terribly discouraged.

Chicano students at St. Thomas were rare as pearls. Why this was so is a question that begs further research but some scholars hold that the Church discriminated against Hispanic clerics as far back as the Mexican War. The eloquent Father Angelico Chávez, whose pride in New Mexican Hispanic culture radiates from all his literature, sets down one such theory. In a short biography of Father Antonio Jose Martinez of Taos, Father Chávez asserts that the much-revered pioneer, Vicar Joseph Machebeuf, set out to purge the Church of its Hispanic priests as early as the 1850s. According to Chávez, Machebeuf, as a French immigrant, disdained the culture and customs of these mixed-blood priests, who for centuries had offered the sacraments on the Mexican frontier.[51] Calculated or not, the new diocese was largely rid of these Mexican priests by the end of Machebeuf's career.

Some former students at St. Thomas assert that the racial climate when Castro enrolled at the seminary reflected a state of uneasy transition. "When I went to St. Thomas in 1959," says Craig Hart, "Hispanics were not accepted as students for the priesthood in the Archdiocese of Denver. It was an unwritten policy." Hart, who became known as something of a rebel priest before leaving the fold in the 1970s, argues that Archbishop Urban J. Vehr adhered to a policy of de facto segregation.[52]

Until the mid-1940s, Hart explains, the Diocese of Denver governed the Church for the entire state of Colorado. When the population grew, the Church divided the state in two: the Denver Diocese in the north, the Pueblo Diocese in the south. "They started over in Grand Junction," says Hart, "which became part of the Diocese of Pueblo. They get to Colorado Springs with its Penrose money and its Broadmoor and find it's about fourteen miles south of the dividing line. So they dipped down, took in Colorado Springs [for the Denver Diocese] and then went straight across. You can see how that's divided racially and economically."[53] The whole southern half of Colorado was Hispanic and poor; the northern diocese was whiter and more affluent.

Although a few Hispanics broke the color line at St. Thomas, those students came from other dioceses. They would return to their parishes in the Pueblo Diocese, or New Mexico or Texas. There was, says Hart, not one Hispanic priest from Denver attending St. Thomas in the late 1950s.[54]

Barely a mile from St. Thomas, on the other side of Colorado Boulevard lay another smaller seminary, St. Andrew's Avelino, run by the Theatines, a Spanish order. It was there that Hispanic priests trained to serve the Mexican-American flock of the Denver Diocese.[55]

So, when Castro enrolled at St. Thomas Seminary in 1964, he was among those breaking new ground. Adaptable though he was, it was not a perfect fit; it was not the most comfortable place for a Chicano kid from the East Side. By springtime a sense of demoralization had begun to creep in.

In April of 1965, Castro called his old friend Andy Lovato, who was still a senior at Annunciation. Lovato was facing an important boxing match and said to Castro, "Pray for me; I gotta fight this big brute," after which he added, "How's it going at St. Thomas?"

Lovato remembers the disillusioned tone in Castro's voice for the first time. "He said things like, 'I have to go to confession every week and I don't have anything to confess.' It's the first recollection I have of Richard starting to think of what he really wanted to do."[56]

Later in the spring, Castro visited Lovato and over a couple of beers began to express more fully his unhappiness at the seminary. By the end of the evening, he was downright drunk and tears welled in his eyes. He complained especially about the inequity of a policy whereby the wealthier churches provided financial aid to seminary students from their own parishes, while students from poorer parishes were left out in the cold.

"You know," he said to Lovato, "I really worked hard all last summer to save money to go to St. Thomas. My parents saved money so I could go. But there's a whole bunch of guys there that are getting free rides from the Church. It doesn't seem right that poor people are the ones that have to pay. I don't understand it," he continued. "We live in a poor parish so we're expected to sacrifice; our families are expected to sacrifice; our community is expected to sacrifice. Yet here's people from Regis and Machebeuf who really could afford to pay for their education and yet they get a free ride from their parish."

"I think at that point," says Lovato, "he was starting to see some inconsistencies. He was starting to say, 'Yes, I want to help people, but maybe not in the religious sense. We had kind of lived in a sheltered community. He was starting to identify that the real world was not quite the way we thought."[57]

With doubts and uncertainties plagueing his consciousness, Castro quit the seminary in the summer of 1965, one year after leaving home. It marked a turning point in his life. He was slowly exchanging his vision of a life in the priesthood for a new one: The notion of social work was beginning to plant itself in his mind. He was also beginning to develop a sense of class and racial justice, which would endure throughout his life.

That fall, Castro set out for Trinidad State Junior College, following in the footsteps of his Annunciation mentor, Eloy Mares. A new chapter in his life would begin, ironically, in the old Hispanic Homeland in southern Colorado. Within two years he would be back in Denver, and a year after that he would be taking his first political steps with the formation of the West Side Coalition.

vii

meltdown

After five years of hard work, after half a decade of establishing a presence in the neighborhood, the West Side Coalition began to unravel in 1973. As it spun out of control, Denver's Chicano Movement began to fracture, splintering like large fragments of broken glass. The disintegration of the coalition, so promising in its infancy, marked the low point in Richard Castro's political career. Indeed, it marked a tragic period for the entire Chicano Movement in Denver.

Even today, the community discusses those events only in hushed tones and with great reluctance. After all, there were crimes committed still unsolved and no one wants to stir things up again.

In retrospect, some refer to West Denver during those years of 1973-74 as a "little Beirut" or a "Northern Ireland."[1] Waldo and Betty Benavidez's house on Lipan Street was called a "little Alamo."[2] One would-be peacemaker recalls walking into the Inner City Parish one evening, glancing around the room, and thinking, "Shit! This looks like an ammunition dump!" Proceeding then to the "enemy camp" a couple of blocks away, he knocked on Waldo's door, looked around the living room, and thought to himself: "This place looks like an ammunition dump, too!"[3]

If the Beirut analogy falls into the realm of hyperbole, it is no exaggeration to say that terror reigned in the hearts of a good many Westsiders during that brief period. A tiny civil war had erupted and the stakes were very real. It was the era of the bombings—firebombings, Molotov cocktails, pipe bombs. They were planted on front porches and building entrances or hurled through windows. Drive-by shootings and sniper attacks shattered the silence of the night. There were slashed tires, broken glass, angry words, and unrestrained fistfights. The young warriors had taken over. Gandhi, personified in the southwest by César Chávez, was nowhere to be found in West Denver.

The press played up the events for all they were worth. It was a time of intense embarrassment for many Westsiders as all the inevitable warts of an ugly family squabble were held up to public exposure.

But the outlines, at least, of the story must be told here, because Richard Castro, characteristically, found himself in the thick of things. Any attempt at sorting out the events runs the risk of oversimplification since a multitude of personalities played off of each other, adding layer upon layer of personal nuance to the political mix. But one can put a few pieces of the puzzle together. There were at least three political configurations operating on the West Side and vying for power.

There was the Benavidez family—Waldo and Betty. With their primary supporters, Richard and Virginia Castro, they had built up a base of power centered on the community organizations they had nurtured: the West Side Coalition and the Auraria Community Center. Within the Democratic Party, too, they wielded clout. Betty made history in 1970 by becoming the first Hispanic woman elected to the state House of Representatives.

The Crusade for Justice, likewise, had established a presence—though a more tenuous one—on the West Side. Their's was the politics of revolution. Their leader, Corky Gonzales, had ascended to national prominence through his poetic appeals to revolutionary nationalism and uncompromising attacks on established powers. The youth he appealed to so passionately called his brand of ideology "Chicanismo."[4]

By late 1973, a third force had emerged. Its members danced all around the political spectrum from leftists spun off from the Crusade to practical-minded community activists. At its core were the ministers in the churches adjacent to West High School: the Inner City Parish and the First Mennonite Church. The one thing they all had in common was their discomfort with Corky on the one hand and Waldo on the other; they wished to place their allegiance with neither of the two.

Each of the three factions had its share of young warriors, armed and sufficiently prepared to get down to business in the street.

The Crusade for Justice

In the early days, in the 1960s, the brightest and most talented Chicano youth were drawn to the Crusade like iron filings to an irresistible magnet. Many who later became mainstream leaders served apprenticeships with the Crusade for Justice. Ruben Valdez, destined to become Speaker of the

House in the Colorado General Assembly, traces a portion of his political roots to the Crusade. Sal Carpio, later a highly respected City Council member, served a stint with the Crusade. Emmanuel Martinez, destined to national fame as a sculptor, painter, and muralist, counted himself a Crusade member. Waldo was an early member of the inner circle and Rich Castro used to visit the Wednesday night "Fishermen's Meetings" at the Crusade building.[5] They were a determined group and attracted those with inner strength and resolute character.

Whatever human failures the organization later revealed, it was the Crusade for Justice that banged down the doors of discrimination. It was the Crusade that altered the consciousness of the entire Chicano community and put the urban Chicano Movement on the map. Even moderate politicians like Don Sandoval still say, "They allowed us to be heard."[6]

Key to the Crusade's popularity was the presence of Rodolfo "Corky" Gonzales. Corky's life embodied the spirit of the Movement. He was a man who grew up poor in the heart of the East Side barrio; his rise to prominence touched the hearts of everyone around him.

"Yes, I am a city man," he once said, "but I did a lot of farm work. I have relatives in the villages in San Luis Valley. Every spring and summer, as a boy, I worked in the fields. Every fall and winter I lived in the city slums."[7]

Corky's ticket out of those East Denver slums came via the boxing ring. "I became a fighter," he said, "because it was the fastest way to get out of the slaughterhouse,"[8] where he—along with half the East Side—had worked for a time after completing high school. In the ring, he was quick and exciting. As a featherweight, he piled up victories, winning first the National Amateur Championship, then the International Championship. Turning professional in the early '50s, he hammered his way to a top ten ranking in the featherweight division.[9] His fighting spirit would work its way into the Crusade philosophy. Whatever you won, you had to fight for. No wonder the organization's newspaper would be called *El Gallo*— the feisty, truculent fighting cock, the rooster baring its talons.

Stardom gave Gonzales the usual access to rungs on the ladder, which could pull a poor boy up into the American mainstream. Retiring from the ring, he attained financial success with a bail-bond business, a bar called Corky's Corner at Thirty-eighth and Walnut near St. Charles Park, an automobile insurance business, and later as general agent for the Summit Fidelity and Surety Company of Colorado.[10] Corky Gonzales was riding high. He wore fine clothes and drove shiny new cars through the streets of East Denver. All the kids at the Twentieth Street Gym dreamed of living like Corky as they pounded away at frayed punching bags.

He went into politics as well: straightforward, conventional Democratic politics the way it was played in the 1950s on the East Side. At twenty-nine, he became a district captain for the Denver Democratic Party, the first Mexican American to attain such a position. At thirty-two, he was tapped as the Colorado coordinator for the highly successful Viva Kennedy campaign in the 1960 presidential election.[11] In business and politics alike, Corky Gonzales was a rising star.

Yet with all the external success, something still tugged at his soul. To the outside world he revealed the face of the up-and-coming politician; on the inside he was seething and searching. The poet in him anguished at the thought of the poverty he had left behind, raged at the arrogance of Denver police in their treatment of Chicano kids, and fumed especially at his memories of the public school system, which he said had merely taught him "how to forget Spanish, to forget my heritage, to forget who I was."[12]

In his oft-quoted poem "I Am Joaquin," Corky wrote:

> And Now!
> I must choose
> Between
> the paradox of
> Victory of the spirit
> despite physical hunger
> or to exist in the grasp
> of American social neurosis,
> sterilization of the soul
> and a full stomach.[13]

Faced with this dilemma—material success versus spiritual poverty—Corky made his choice very clear. In the mid-1960s, the American Dream firmly within his grasp, he turned his back on the whole system.

Embroiled in a controversy over his job as Denver's chairman of the War on Poverty, he abruptly quit in 1966.[14] He chose, instead, to devote his career to building an independent Chicano civil rights organization, the Crusade for Justice. No longer would he be beholden to the mayor's office, to the business world, to LBJ, or to the Democratic Party. When he left the mayor's employ, he burned his bridges.

At the time, Corky's break with the Establishment gave him an almost saintlike aura. He had been to the wilderness and had overcome temptation. He had been offered the American Dream; he could have had it all. When he walked away from it instead, his new moral stature was irresistible to the revolutionary youth of the 1960s. The ingredients of his life—the boxing, the struggle to the top, the poetry, the uncompromising rejection of Anglo society—seized the imagination of Denver's youth and, indeed

Chicano youth all over the southwest.

1966 was the same year Bobby Seale and Huey Newton began selling Mao's "Little Red Book" on the streets of Berkeley and using the money to start the Black Panther Party. Martin Luther King's nonviolent leadership of the civil rights movement was besieged, coming under attack from all directions. It was a time when revolutionary ideas—embraced by some, feared by many—were, nevertheless, taken seriously. Corky's embrace of revolutionary nationalism catapulted him and the Crusade into the national limelight.

Dramatic as it was, Corky's unique path to the Revolution had its downside. In breaking so cleanly with the established powers, he wrapped himself easily in a mantle of moral purity.

Take, for example, the style of his letter of resignation from the War on Poverty program, written to Dale Tooley, liberal chairman of Denver's Democratic Party.

"The individual who makes his way through the political muck of today's world, and more so the minority representatives, suffers such an immense loss of soul and dignity that the end results are as rewarding as a heart attack, castration or cancer. . . . I can only visualize your goal as the complete emasculation of manhood, sterilization of human dignity, and that you are purposely creating a world of lackeys and political bootlickers."[15]

His style of rhetoric drew large numbers of enthusiastic converts at the beginning, but in the long run tended to separate the Crusade from thousands of ordinary Chicanos struggling to get a better job, to scrape up money for a house, to finish college and get a degree. It represented a puritanical strain that, in a few short years, left the Crusade vulnerable to the isolation more characteristic of a sectarian group than a mass organization.

The word *vendido* (sell-out) rolled easily and indiscriminately off the lips of Crusade members. For women, the epithet was *Malinche,* a reference to the Indian mistress of Hernan Cortez—the woman who helped white man conquer the Aztecs. As the Revolution stormed forward, polarization began to settle in: You stood either with the Crusade or with the enemy; there was little in-between. Surely real vendidos existed but not in the numbers Crusaders imagined. The harsh judgments, the indiscriminate labeling, the fierce name-calling ultimately assured the Crusade's marginalization.

The Revolution Comes to Curtis Park

Rich Castro's coach and mentor at Annunciation, a lifetime resident of the East Side, remembers the times vividly. Eloy Mares worked as a probation officer with Juvenile Justice and because of his employment with the system was quickly labeled one of the vendidos.

"If you worked for the court at that time," he says, "you were an authority figure and you were considered—there was a common phrase—a 'pig.' I went to the Crusade . . . because there were some good things there. They were right about the police brutality, education, the Vietnam War. These things at the time were sort of above my head; that's when my politicization was evolving.

"I admired [Crusade members like] Ernesto Vigil. The Crusade attracted people like Ernesto. That was part of *my* attraction. He was the kind of guy who would not get involved with drugs or not get involved with the Denver Juvenile Court. In that sense I felt he was a good role model for the kids I was working with. I liked that. I liked his strength, the inner strength. In a lot of senses they were talking the same tune that I was talking.

"But I just didn't get into it, I guess, the way they wanted me to get into it. I mean joining and being a 100 percent Crusader. The criticism came when I didn't jump on the bandwagon totally. I didn't classify certain individuals as 'political prisoners.' In the Crusade's mind, all prisoners were political prisoners. I disagreed with that a lot. But you couldn't have any disagreement. And that was the bad part."[16]

There was a revolutionary presence on the East Side. The revolution crept into conversation at bars and dinner tables. Eloy Mares used to like to hang out at Louie's, the neighborhood tavern on Thirty-seventh and High Street near the Gardner Denver plant. Inevitably, however, someone from the Crusade or close to the Crusade would pepper him with questions: "Why aren't you behind the Revolution, Eloy?" Or, "Why are you against the Revolution?" "It was a situation," says Mares, "where you were sure to be uncomfortable if for some reason you didn't understand them or for some reason you disagreed with the concepts or the principles of the Revolution."[17]

Mares remembers that era as the time of "the Poison," because, he says, an atmosphere of intimidation seemed to hover in the air. "It was just a terrible time to live here and raise a family in this community. . . . I was worried about my kids all the time. There was a lot of rumor and character assassination . . . and you could be physically intimidated."[18]

Undoubtedly, a policy of fierce government repression took its toll on the Crusade's reputation. It is clear that a covert FBI operation known as COINTELPRO (Counter-Intelligence Program) was active in Denver during the Johnson and Nixon administrations. The idea behind COINTELPRO was to disrupt the operations of radical organizations, such as the Crusade, and render them ineffective. There were spies and agents provocateurs. A COINTELPRO agent who had infiltrated a group and could inspire some mindless act of violence could easily discredit the whole group. Perhaps a score of sundry agents, some of them heavily into drugs and in need of ready cash, were turned loose in the Denver area.[19] It is also known that the Denver police infiltrated leftist groups and were quick to implicate Crusade members in a variety of crimes, often on flimsy evidence.[20] Ernesto's Vigil's impressive work, *Crusade for Justice*, examines the full extent of the repression and the degree of its impact on the Crusade. The police and the FBI placed the Crusade for Justice under intense pressure and certainly played a provocative role.

It is clear, too, that an element of monumental hypocrisy entered into the government's stormy relationship with the Crusade and the militant nationalists. In 1973, as it preached nonviolence to its homegrown dissenters, the U.S. government busied itself in putting the finishing touches on the deaths of one, two, perhaps even three million people in Southeast Asia. Simultaneously, it was orchestrating the killing of thousands more in the military coup that overpowered Chile.

Taking all this into account—the provocation, the repression, the government hypocrisy—it must be said, nevertheless, that the Crusade for Justice cultivated an aura of intimidation and violence that proved counterproductive in the end.

Eloy Mares recalls the atmosphere on the East Side in the early '70s when he was working with Rich Castro among youth at Curtis Park. The Brown Berets who had established a presence in the park included loose and sometimes overlapping associations with the Crusade. The Crusade clearly worked effectively to minimize intra-gang violence, but the level of rhetoric oftentimes was overblown.[21]

At meetings organized by Castro and Mares, kids would show up sporting their berets as part of a quasi-military uniform. "At one meeting," says Mares, "they were talking about 'liberating' the police building downtown. Rich and I were in the back of the room when all of a sudden they all pulled out their clubs. Jeez! We didn't even know they had 'em. That's how they spent the money they had raised from a dance. They were gonna march down the street with clubs to liberate all the political prisoners!

"Well, there wasn't much we could do," Mares continues. "Rich was a little more vocal than I was: 'You're not gonna go liberate anything. That's crazy!' I'd be more forceful today than I was then. From the standpoint of knowing the so-called power structure, they [the police] are the ones who had been trained to kill. They're the ones with sophisticated weapons and all that good stuff. But that was sort of above us; the whole thing was hard to comprehend. And someone had gotten to those kids. The [militant segment of the] movement was very appealing. It was tough talk and that's what those kids liked to hear. And it was an overwhelming thing, you know, like an idea whose time has come."[22]

Like the Left nationwide, the Revolution in Denver showed little patience. If its analysis of social problems sometimes hit the mark, its sense of timing was far off target. When Father Craig Hart left his classroom at St. Joseph's High School, for instance, to join the strikers and demonstrators gathering at Sunken Gardens to protest racism at West High School, he caught the spirit of many in the revolutionary movement. "I thought the Revolution was gonna happen on the weekend," he said, "and it was already Friday. It was like 'seize the time; seize the moment.'"[23]

Perhaps it was this impatience or the miscalculation of revolutionary timing that contributed to the atmosphere of intimidation. With the Revolution so near, was there any need to patiently cultivate seeds that might take twenty years to bear fruit?

Seeds of Confrontation

In the early '70s, Richard Castro and Waldo Benavidez began to openly criticize the Crusade and the militants who stood closely along the organization's margins. Politics was not the only issue, but a quick survey reveals plenty of political differences: Rich Castro remained a loyal Democrat; Corky disdained the Democrats and turned, instead, to an independent third party, La Raza Unida. Castro believed in coalition building — carefully pulling disparate groups together under one umbrella; Gonzales saw the Crusade as a cutting edge and did not wish to be slowed down by alliances with moderates. Castro's nationalism was muted and restrained; Corky flirted with separatism. Rich Castro publicly denounced violence as a means to political progress and looked to César Chávez for inspiration, although he did not share the union leader's religious devotion to nonviolence. Corky believed that violence was sometimes necessary. Castro was a reformer; he espoused gradual change from the inside in the style of Franklin Roosevelt. Gonzales was a revolutionary; he wanted a clean break with the system. Richard Castro admired the Kennedys; Corky Gonzales looked to Mexican revolutionary Emiliano Zapata for inspiration.

Electoral politics quickly came to the fore as a litmus test. Waldo had become a Crusade member in the late '60s when he started walking the few short blocks from the City and County Building to the first Crusade headquarters at Twelfth and Cherokee during his lunch hour. He took his family to New Mexico in support of Reies Tijerina and flew to Washington to participate in the Poor People's Campaign. All the while, he remained fiercely loyal to the Democrats. "My civil rights heart is over here; my Democratic Party affiliation's over there," he explained while pointing in two different directions.[24] In those early years a fragile coexistence survived within the Crusade between Democrats and those who spurned the two-party system.

The gap rapidly widened as Corky moved farther beyond the Democratic pale and Waldo burrowed more deeply inside the party. While Corky called Democrats and Republicans "two pigs feeding out of the same trough," Democratic state chairman Dan Lynch hired Waldo to recruit Hispanics into the party.

La Raza Unida

As Waldo tried to open up the Democratic Party for Chicano participation, Corky's vision moved in an entirely different direction. It was 1968 when José Ángel Gutiérrez turned Crystal City, Texas, upside down with a third-party victory. It was the year La Raza Unida Party was born.[25] Ultimately Corky and Gutiérrez would travel their separate ways, but in '68, La Raza Unida Party was unified and on fire.

Crystal City, a town in the Rio Grande Valley in South Texas, had been an old-fashioned segregated town until Gutiérrez's organizing broke it wide open. It had been a closed society—a town with a majority Mexican-American population but where, until the early '60s, Anglos held every political office. When La Raza Unida swept the 1968 elections for school board and city council, it represented a complete overhaul of the town's power structure, a virtual revolution in political power.

La Raza Unida Party, in Gutiérrez's view, would provide the vehicle for self-determination for Chicanos. If Chicanos wanted the type of community control that both Waldo Benavidez and Rich Castro were advocating, they would need also to control their own political party.

The events in Crystal City turned heads all over the southwest. From Texas to California, Chicanos mulled over the startling concept of a new party and considered the possibilities in their own surroundings. Corky immediately embraced the idea. Virginia Castro visited Crystal City in the early 1970s and returned with considerable admiration for La Raza Unida.[26] Richard, too, expressed admiration, but drew conclusions different from Corky's.

He presented his own perspective at a conference in 1972 before an audience of University of Denver Chicano graduate students largely receptive to La Raza Unida. Castro delivered his appeal for the Democrats in a soft, even self-demeaning tone. He had done, as usual, some thoughtful homework and laid it out carefully and soberly.

"The Republican Party," he said, "doesn't want us. In the Democratic Party we see kind of a two-faced type thing. They say they want us, yet . . . they don't really encourage Chicanos to run for office. They don't really support us financially. They don't go out of their way. Chicanos here have to organize themselves to find candidates and to basically support themselves.

"One of the things Chicanos have done is to try to develop third parties. La Raza Unida has been very successful in Texas. They've shown through bloc voting and through organizing Chicanos that it is possible to get our people elected where we're a majority. They've used the whole Chicano bloc down there to form an independent party and run candidates [against] the traditional two-party system. I think that down there La Raza Unida is very appropriate and I wish we could do the same things up here. But we're a minority up here and even if we had all Chicanos voting together—which they're not—we still wouldn't have the numbers to elect statewide officials. So for the time being—I don't know where this is gonna go in the future—but for the time being I've chosen to work with people who are in the Democratic Party. I've chosen to work with people there because I think the Democratic Party could be a vehicle for us to get people into office. . . . I don't think we'd be successful in running independent candidates. I guess," he added with a combination of irony and defensiveness that reflected the political atmosphere, "this makes me a 'sellout.'

"Gutiérrez talked here in West Denver when he was here for that social welfare conference," continued Castro, "and one of the things that I heard him say was 'what's appropriate in Texas might not be appropriate here.' What he was after there was to win seats and I think that's what we should be about up here. If an independent party can get people in, then, fine, we go that way. But getting more Chicanos into office is what's important. You do that any way you can. . . . I recognize that the independent party can exert political pressure if organized effectively. . . . But it's very important for us to make sure that we get candidates in.

"In 1966, another independent party started; it was called the New Hispano Party," continued Castro, referring to the organization begun by his professor at Metro, Daniel Valdes. "What they were basically addressing themselves to is the same idea that Republicans and Democrats weren't being receptive so they had to develop a [separate] power group. In my researching, I saw that out of 170,000 votes cast for the gubernatorial election in '66, the candidate running for governor on the New Hispano ticket got less than 3,000 votes. This was Levi Martinez and Tom Pino, his Lt. Governor. I wasn't really following things at that time so I based my observations on just researching the newspapers. One of the reasons why I believe that they were ineffective [and why La Raza Unida is ineffective] is that traditionally our people vote Democratic. The third party [idea] was [considered] a radical type of thing. Most of our people just go in and flip that lever for Democrats.

"Another reason was that there was a lot of intimidation. Some of the guys running with the New Hispano Party were intimidated and even dropped out of the race due to phone calls—'I'm gonna kill you' and this type of thing. I don't know if that should be a reason for dropping out 'cause you're always gonna have people do that to you," he said, unaware of the prophetic nature of his comment. "But they publicized this thing in the papers . . . that some of these guys' lives had been threatened and that they were gonna run 'em out of town. So some of the people might have been afraid to align themselves with this party.

"Another reason was that there was a split in the Chicano community. People like Corky—well Corky talks about third party now—but one of the things I read in the newspaper was that he was saying things [in 1966] like, 'Don't be misled by third parties. Don't waste your time and effort.'

"I think," he concluded, "we all have a time to evolve. Some people are at one point; some people at another. And sometimes the people up here really get heavy on the people back there. If Corky at that time didn't believe in a third party, he's evolved to a third party now. Maybe he should allow some other people to work within the Democratic Party, become turned off and maybe they'll go third party. I think we have to allow people to learn. You don't create a radical overnight without him knowing why he's the way he is. I've seen too many times when they grab kids and indoctrinate 'em. You can make 'em hate and hate everybody. If they don't really understand or know what they're really attacking . . . it's a very superficial type of thing.[27]

Though quiet and unassuming, Castro's speech clearly expressed the gaping chasm that had developed between himself and the Crusade. It was not, in this case, so much a matter of goals, but of tactics.

Waldo's Battle

Waldo's speech before the same audience was far less restrained, far less diplomatic. The Coalition had just lost its campaign to downzone the West Side and Waldo was weary, frustrated, and in a bad mood. His tone was already beginning to convey the bitterness that would mark his temperament in later years. His speech was rambling, cynical, and characteristically abrasive, but it brought into vivid relief his numerous differences with the Crusade for Justice and with the militants on its margins. He lashed out in a number of directions, the first of which dealt with the Crusade's alleged tendency to concentrate its critical fire at fellow Chicanos rather than the established power structure. It illustrated how far out of hand things had gotten between Waldo and the Crusade.

Following the downzoning campaign defeat on the West Side, Waldo had attended the Chicano political caucus in San Jose, California. According to Ernesto Vigil, La Raza Unida activists outnumbered Democrats and

Republicans by a two-to-one margin and attempted to have the caucus endorse La Raza Unida in the upcoming election. Tempers between radicals and moderates flared so high that Black Berets twice restored order at the speakers' podium.[28] Waldo espoused his own personal perspective at length: "If nothing else came out of it," he said, "at least I could go over there and have a little vacation for the weekend, and rest and recuperate. Well, we drive out there, me and Rich, for twenty-four hours straight and as soon as I walk into that building and flop myself on a chair to rest, some guy from Denver calls me out to the street to go battle because he didn't agree with some principle or idea I had. And this is [supposed to be] a unity conference. Well, fine, it was one guy and we got past that battle. But the point is that you walk into the convention and here [we start] all over again.

"Well, that's where we were at in San Jose. The young people are waking up, which is beautiful. They're questioning the system, which is beautiful. But the trouble is . . . they attack their own people. . . . They go to a convention to holler the rhetoric, to talk about the Movement and to blast and to scream and to shout and then they leave and they say, 'I really told 'em.' And then they go back to the bar and drink up and talk about it all night and that's gonna be the end of it for many of 'em. Not for all of 'em, because some people do have a commitment to continue. But for many that was their big moment of glory to blast another Chicano at a conference.

"But here's Nixon or here's some other rip-off in his community, probably his own landlord that is rippin' him off and . . . don't even fix the plumbing and don't even fix the toilet—he's not doin' nothin' to that dude. It's easy to fight somebody that's not going to fight back or doesn't want to hassle you back. But you go out and hassle the Man, it's a little bit different story. If [you're] being so exploited, then the place to go is to go after the guy that's exploiting you, man. And many people don't do that. You know . . . there's a lot more involved than just blasting a Chicano brother in front of the cameras. . . .

"I would hope that all Chicanos, all six million or whatever we got, would open their eyes right now so we can get down to takin' care of business. So we don't have to continually go next year to another conference where some . . . seventeen-year-old kid that was out of touch with reality . . . and said, 'All you guys are all full of shit and this is where it's at and I want you to do it this way and this is the Movement.' And that's where I differ with many people who are expounding on the Chicano Movement and *carnalismo* (brotherhood) and then'll turn around and bust me in the mouth 'cuz they don't like what I'm doin'."[29]

Having grieved his own personal persecution at the hands of the militants, Waldo went on to outline further differences with his old *compañero* Corky Gonzales. Particularly fierce were the battles over what constituted a betrayal of the Chicano community. The great question that confronted the Movement, the question that created a gaping chasm between the revolution and the reformers was this: What degree of assimilation into the vast American economic and cultural machine was acceptable to the rapidly changing Chicano populace?

Reconsidering the Melting Pot

It boiled down not simply to a case of Crusade nationalism versus the universalism of Castro and Benavidez. Both Rich Castro and Waldo Benavidez traveled solidly in the nationalist orbit. Neither was prone to surrender his unique Hispanic identity to the mainstream. Castro, especially, emphasized in article after article the role of Chicano history as a psychological healer, as a rebuilder of shattered pride and a source of identity.[30] Waldo conducted sometimes bitter campaigns to replace white employees with brown ones at the West Side agencies where he wielded influence.[31]

Corky, for his part, was no dogmatic separatist. The Crusade's publication, *El Gallo*, reported a 1968 speech in which, "Gonzales called for all the minorities and the Appalachian whites to join together for a common cause."[32] He did, however, believe that Chicanos were a colonized people, and Ernesto Vigil wrote that, "when he spoke of self-determination, he meant it literally."[33]

A remarkable document sprang from the 1969 Chicano Youth Conference and lent a consistently nationalist tone to the Crusade for Justice. Written by the young poet Alurista, *El Plan Espiritual de Aztlán* became the rough framework for the Crusade's political orientation.[34] *Aztlán* refers to the mythical homeland of the Aztecs, which, according to legend, encompassed the entire southwestern region of the United States. Here in Aztlán, wrote Alurista, "With our heart in our hands and our hands in the soil, we declare the independence of our *mestizo* nation."[35]

El Plan was indeed a radical document. It called on Chicanos to "drive the exploiter out of our community. . . . Aztlán belongs to those who plant the seeds, water the fields and gather the crops and not to the foreign Europeans." It called for "Chicano defense units" and proclaimed that "Chicanos must use their nationalism as the key . . . for mass mobilization and organization. . . ."

"We can only conclude," it stated, "that social, economic, cultural and political independence is the only road to total liberation from oppression, exploitation and racism."[36] Forceful and bold, the plan was also ambiguous and subtle in many respects, perhaps inevitable when poets, instead of lawyers, create political declarations.

There was, for example, the question of territorial boundaries. The Youth Conference called on Chicanos to take "control of our barrios, campos, pueblos, lands, our economy, our culture, and our political life." Never do we read, however, that a certain portion of the land between Texas and California should be set aside for possession by a Chicano Nation. The very name of the plan—the *Spiritual* Plan of Aztlán—gives rise to the idea that perhaps the document could refer to a spiritual affinity between communities and barrios separated by miles of terrain. There was even room here for an Aztlán as a state of mind, for a Chicano homeland in the *corazón*, in the individual heart rather than in the physical sand, sage, and sierra of the Southwest. Was this a nationalism of the soul; was it cultural or was it grounded in the possession of territory? The language left all this open to debate and, indeed, writers responded with answers all over the spectrum.[37] Corky clearly advocated self-determination, but the Crusade itself was too busy dealing with arrests, with police repression, and with everyday survival to spend much time worrying about the nuances.

When the rhetorical smoke cleared, a good deal of overlap existed in Waldo's concept of "community control" and the Crusade's more grandiose vision of "social, economic, cultural and political independence." On the day-to-day level, both groups practiced a sort of cultural nationalism in which Chicanos would assert power, nurture their native language, teach their history, and cultivate their traditions within their already established communities.

On a couple of points, however, Waldo and Castro's brand of nationalism differed radically from the Crusade's. The two would cross swords particularly over economics. Neither Waldo nor Castro much questioned the capitalist economic structure of the country. They fought hard for the West Side's right to a place at the economic table, but neither considered the idea of replacing the table with something entirely different. While advocating community control, they also believed in the individual's right to leave the barrio, to ascend the economic ladder, even to move, if he wished, to the treeless, manicured plains of suburbia.

Again Waldo's DU speech brings out some of the flavor of the controversy. "If the end result of organizing," he said, "is not financial benefits or economic gains for your people to where they can live comfortably, feed their families comfortably, send their kids to college without having to beg for grants or whatever the case—if that's not the end result, then what is it?

"Some of the guys . . . are saying that it's all like communal living. You help your brother, your home is wide open, *mi casa es tu casa*, and you all live nice and you just trip around and it's all a friendly atmosphere. Well, I don't think that that is necessarily true. [I don't think] you have to give up your goals as far as bettering your life financially . . . and where you might want to live. If that's not what it is, then I question, what is the Chicano Movement? They say it's not economic betterment, well then what is it?"

"A lot of the guys in the Movement," he continued, "will come up and say, 'Well you're not s'posed to own homes or you're not s'posed to be a businessman because if you're a businessman, then you're a sell-out automatically. Well then, by you owning this business and gettin' ahead with your family financially and servin' the people—is that part of the Chicano Movement or is it not? That's the question I'm askin' you. Is a guy that's a Chicano that struggled and hassled and kicked some of the Establishment somewhere and finally got a small business loan and sets up his business and has a little cleaners—is he a part of Movement or is he not? Or are you s'posed to sell all your worldly goods like Jesus Christ and go out there and just preach? OK, you guys got to answer that one. Is a social worker with a master's degree that goes out and gets $16,000 a year workin' for the Welfare Department—is he part of the Movement or not? By gettin' your education, are you part of the Chicano Movement? In order to be Movement, then, do you have to be poor?"[38]

Clearly Waldo was parodying here the Crusade's economic position and oversimplifying a complex perspective. Nevertheless, his diatribe touched on some major differences.

While never advocating socialism, the underlying tone of Crusade proclamations remained anti-capitalist. In criticizing the Vietnam War, Corky stated that America was run by "the ruthless financial lords of Wall Street" and by "great and powerful corporations."[39] The Crusade's nationalism superceded a Marxist-style class analysis: "Nationalism . . . transcends all religious, political, class and economic factions," stated the Plan de Aztlán. Nevertheless, when the document states that "Aztlán belongs to those who plant the seeds, water the fields and gather the crops and not to the foreign Europeans," it leaves a clear implication: In the southwest, Chicanos are essentially the workers and the present-day economic system was imposed from the outside by white conquerors. This is why Corky had said it's better to be hungry than to be caught up in the American economic system with its "social neurosis and sterilization of the soul."[40] This is why he had said that a bear in the zoo might be satiated and fat, but not free. In integrating an anti-colonial analysis with a nationalist outlook, Corky aligned himself with the left-wing nationalist movements, which wielded so much influence in the '60s and '70s. Ho Chi Minh, the man who most skillfully synthesized the integration of communism and nationalism, was part of this movement. So was the Black Panther Party.

Though not explicitly socialist, the Plan de Aztlán does advocate the defeat of the "gringo dollar value system." It espouses the belief that Chicanos' "cultural background and values which ignore materialism and embrace humanism will contribute to the act of cooperative buying and the distribution of resources and production to sustain an economic base for healthy growth and development."[41]

Thus, for all the strategic overlap between Waldo's forces and the Crusade for Justice, there existed marked differences as well. The two camps lived in the same neighborhood but their view of the metropolitan area—that is, of the white society that surrounded them—led them to divergent paths and styles.

On the cultural level, this meant the Crusade's brand of nationalism was far purer and more doctrinaire than that of Waldo or Castro. The Crusade tolerated far less movement towards assimilation into the white mainstream. The relationship with white society was harsher and more abrasive. At the Crusade, you were far more likely to hear talk about gringos, *gabachos*, and pigs. You were more likely to receive critical glances if you dated a blonde-haired gringa or went out with an Anglo man. Castro and Benavidez gave permission to make compromises and blend, to some degree, into the Great Melting Pot; Corky tended to say Chicanos don't melt.

One of the personalities who came under the fierce fire of Crusade denunciations was Waldo's wife, Betty Benavidez. She made history in 1970 by riding Waldo's political machine to a seat as state representative from the West Side. She was the first Chicana ever to attain such a position. It was this seat that Rich Castro would inherit four years later.

Betty Benavidez was a native Westsider. She had grown up hard, dropping out in the eighth grade, and delivering four children before turning twenty-one. Respecting her toughness and the fact that she was one of them, the Chicano community often cheered her wildly and gave her red-carpet treatment in the early years of her political career.

In the legislature, however, her style did not play well. It was not just the big issues. She fasted in support of César Chávez's grape strike and she opposed the war in Vietnam, actions considered not quite tasteful or elegant by her legislative peers. But it was more than that. Like her husband, she often came off brusque and abrasive. She knew little about slapping backs and playing the intricate chess game necessary to put a bill through the General Assembly. In fact she had little use for the game at all, which is reflected in her shoddy attendance record. Sometimes she would play hooky from the Assembly and with a friend go down to shop at the second-hand stores on South Broadway. She couldn't quite fit in on Capitol Hill.[42]

However unpopular she may have been among lawmakers, she was downright cursed by the Crusade for Justice. Between her Democratic Party affiliation and her marriage to Waldo, they showed no mercy; they called her "Malinche" with a vehemence reserved for no other. Once, at the Crusade school, a teacher had asked this question on a multiple-choice exam:

"Which of the following is a traitor to their people?" The correct answer was Betty Benavidez.[43] By 1972, ideological conflicts had begun to overlap with the personal ones. The sectarian feuds had begun to descend into palpable rancor and bitterness.

Turf Battles

For a variety of reasons, the Crusade had made little headway organizing Denver's West Side. Corky was an Eastsider, born and raised. His network of kinships and friendships only weakly penetrated inside the borders of West Denver.[44] Between East- and Westsiders stood the usual barriers of native mistrust for the outsider and the stranger, even when the "outsider" had lived his whole life in the same city. It was not primal territoriality alone that had fenced off Corky, but that explains some of it.

Jerry Garcia, a native to the West Side, raised on Galapago Street, re-members his own wedding in 1969, when he married Corky's niece, Rebecca Romero, at the Inner City Parish. "You could hear a pin drop; the tension was so thick. The Gonzales family stood on this side, my family and friends stood on that side. Two people walk out the door from that side, two others follow them from this side. Two people look at each other wrong, you gotta be right there to break up the fight." Even as the ceremony broke up and one of the West Side's largest parties ever moved over to the American Legion Hall at Eighth and Santa Fe, the two sides kept their distance. "I mean it was tension," says Garcia.[45]

The Crusade had citywide, regional, and even national followings, but nowhere had they sunk their roots into the rich soil of a single, solidified neighborhood or a natural geographic community. When Corky cast his eyes across Broadway from the Crusade's East Side headquarters, he saw in the West Side a solid and cohesive Chicano neighborhood, poor but on the move and ripe for revolutionary activity. The West Side should have been with the Revolution. He also saw that the strongest grassroots orga-nization around—the West Side Coalition—had been nurtured not by the Crusade, but by his bitter rivals Waldo Benavidez and Rich Castro.

West of Broadway, Waldo Benavidez was having problems of his own. He had operated for some years like an old-time Chicago wardheeler. He had his little machine on the West Side, and he worked it the way a skilled railroad engineer runs a train. He liked to stay in the background and play the role of powerbroker. Not only the militant Left, but his own Demo-cratic constituency as well, began accusing him of old time dirty politics.

For instance: When the time comes for precinct caucuses, it is custom-ary to put up a sign in front of the house where the meeting convenes; everyone is, therefore, informed, and meetings remain open. Waldo would not post those signs, say some of his critics, so he could maintain control.[46]

If only his inner circle of loyalists showed up, they could call all the shots and choose their candidates at will. There was, as well, an accusation of cheating at political conventions. According to these stories, he would bring his own people—non-delegates—to the convention floor and then wait for the roll to be called. If someone failed to respond to roll call—let's say a Mr. Sanchez—one of Waldo's backers would raise his hand and take Mr. Sanchez's place. Classic, underhanded Tammany Hall-type stuff. It was downright embarrassing to some of his former allies.[47]

Through his influence over the West Side Coalition and the Auraria Community Center, he had a few jobs at his disposal. These could provide leverage for rewarding friends and punishing those disloyal to him. He owned some fifteen houses in West Denver and could offer you a home on good terms if he liked you. They weren't much—these jobs and homes— but they could be little footholds to power on the West Side where jobs were scarce and down payments for home ownership were hard to come by.[48]

These stories gained Waldo an unsavory reputation. Perhaps his street appearance, his tough language, and the ever-present sunglasses contributed to the perception. The rumor mill on the street kicked into high gear with charges of his amassing a small fortune through political corruption and of backing up his "dictatorial" rule with armed thugs.

The charge of "ill-begotten wealth" appears to be a bad rap. Waldo had begun buying homes on the West Side as a young man with a $500 loan from his in-laws as start-up money. He was handy; he kept things fixed up and could do some remodeling here and there. He rented out several homes to extended family. He generally had a steady income from the city and, after 1970, Betty brought in an additional $7,500 as state rep. By the standards of the struggling West Side, Waldo and Betty prospered. But the total value of Waldo's property never exceeded $60,000.[49] To the man scraping by on Social Security and living in the apartments above the laundromat on Kalamath or in the yellow projects on Navajo, this sum may have resembled Donald Trump's fortune. In reality, Waldo's wealth was modest; he was part of the struggling middle class. Nor did his stand on downzoning reflect the interests of a wealthy landlord. Absentee landlords out to maximize profits preferred higher, not lower zones, so they could sell their inflated property to high-rise developers or to commercial enterprises. Waldo may have been a sinner, but no evidence supports the charge that he was a thief "ripping off the community."

One venture that further damaged his reputation was an attempt to purchase a building on Santa Fe Drive called Casa del Barrio. As part of his vision for "community control," Waldo organized a half-dozen couples into the "Santa Fe Development Corporation." The project aimed at providing housing for community-based agencies such as West Side Legal Aid. In 1974, when rumors on the street hit a fever pitch, the assets of the Santa Fe Development Corporation totaled $62,000 against liabilities of $54,000. For its twelve stockholders, the investment had netted a total of $8,000 or about $660 each. The weekly alternative newspaper, *Straight Creek Journal,* labeled the project "another well-intentioned, but misunderstood effort at community organization of little financial benefit to its founders."[50]

Nevertheless, rumors of Waldo's financial misdeeds proliferated and added to the tension. In the eyes of the Crusade and other militants, what with his financial dealings and his maneuvering in the Democratic Party, he fit the mold of the classic vendido.[51]

The Face-off

The roots of the initial clash on the West Side are tangled in a complex web. There was ideology to be sure. There was the Revolution versus the Reformers and La Raza Unida versus the Democrats. There was the matter of assimilation and nationalism and how far to compromise and what constituted "selling out."

There was fighting over the distribution of jobs from the money that was filtering down from the federal government, the city coffers, and the United Way. In the '60s, the money came down like rain from the Johnson Administration, but in the early '70s the well began to run dry. "What some of these programs were, in terms of effect," says Jack Lang y Marquez, former director of the Colorado Civil Rights Commission, "was tossing crumbs or bones to a lot of hungry people. . . . You throw a few scraps of meat to a lot of hungry animals and you have the animals fighting among themselves. The animals that are fighting are destroying each other and then there's always that other animal that comes along and snatches it up and then goes off and eats it himself. The same phenomenon—you have East Side competing with the West Side; you have the blacks competing with Hispanics; you have elderly people competing with Head Start; you name it. The dollars were limited and the needs were great and so the competition became very very intense. . . . The reason it wasn't working was the very nature of the program itself. It was inadequate to do the job. And because it was inadequate, it forced people into an intense competition."[52]

Some say the clash boiled down to a contest between two giant personalities with two giant egos. Waldo and Corky faced each other off like a couple of magnificent elk during rutting season. Who would control the West Side? "Dollars had nothing to do with this," says Waldo. "It has to do with ego, it has to do with power, it has to do with influence and with who gets more press coverage. It has to do with personalities."[53] Waldo and

Corky, each intent on building their own empires, were destined to clash. All of the political and personal factors had simmered for years.

And so in the early months of 1973, tensions began to build, layer upon layer, until by the time that summer of record-breaking heat rolled around, the neighborhood was ready to explode. What happened could provide *corrido* material for the balladeers along the Mexican border. This one, however, had a more urban setting with a scene only a few blocks away from downtown Denver.

The clash between Corky and Waldo was largely fought by proxy. The focal point for the initial confrontation was a barrio school at Ninth and Santa Fe, called La Escuela de Aztlán, its very name conjuring up the ideals of revolutionary nationalism. One school leader, a native Westsider, had attended the Crusade's Chicano Youth Conference in 1969 and had been deeply stirred by the energy and spirit. "Corky and Juan Haro were my leaders," said the school official, "And they really did push education."[54]

The school was designed to educate the poorest of the poor—*los pobres*, the kids on the West Side unwanted by the Denver Public Schools—seventh graders with reading scores at the third-grade level, fourteen-year-olds who needed instruction in counting change. Teachers recall taking rags away from the kids after school when they caught them sniffing paint in the alleyways.[55] The idea was to wean them off the street and off the drugs by channeling their rebellion into radical politics and giving them a sense of pride. The idea also was to build a bridge between the Crusade for Justice and the West Side community. The school clearly represented a Crusade presence in the West Side neighborhood, a vehicle for building influence and recruiting youth for the revolution. Though started with federal funding, Corky's group supported the school with modest financial help and by trading materials and curriculum from their own East Side school, Escuela Tlatelolco.[56] The key personnel—Lois Lujan, Willie Montoya, Chuck Kohler, and Juan Archilla—all shared a rough affinity for the Crusade and for the militant wing of the Chicano Movement. Some had worked previously for Waldo and had either been fired or had turned away from him.

Jerry Garcia, who, through marriage and employment, inhabited the Crusade's world as well as the Coalition's, claims he was "hearing rumblings" and began receiving phone calls from Crusade members. "Stay away from Waldo," they said. "There's some stuff comin' down between Waldo and the Crusade . . . and we don't want to see you get hurt."[57] The Crusade, he says, was "flexing its muscles" and making its move on the West Side. It is still difficult to unravel who did what to whom. Few bombings were ever solved, nor were any of the numerous shootings. Someone bombed the Auraria Community Center in June of 1973 and Waldo himself appears to have been a marked man; his house was bombed and shot at repeatedly. For Waldo's part, he freely admits that his family did not hesitate to shoot back.[58]

Building Tension

Any insignificant incident could erupt into a full-blown fight. Such an incident occurred on the afternoon of July 2, when Archilla, Kohler, and Montoya from the Escuela de Aztlán visited Waldo at the Auraria Community Center to demand $300 in payment for a broken display case. There had been a history of antagonism: Waldo had fired Archilla and Montoya from jobs they had held at the community center. A girl from the community center, they said, had broken the glass case, and it was only right that the center or Waldo should compensate them. Waldo responded, true to form, with contempt and sarcasm. It was an indiscretion for which he paid dearly seconds later when one of the three, according to several newspaper reports, buried his fist in Waldo's face and another followed up by swinging a soda bottle.[59]

An enraged Betty Benavidez took things into her own hands that same evening. She marched over to La Escuela to "talk things over,"[60] carrying in her purse a rusty, antique pistol, which she later called "only a toy gun."[61] The question as to whether or not the gun actually worked was academic to Lois Lujan, five months pregnant, as she peered down its long barrel. She called the police to press charges, claiming that Benavidez had threatened to kill her and her students as well.[62] The story of a state representative brandishing a pistol, Wild West fashion, made for extraordinary headlines the next day.

The following day things lurched out of control. In the afternoon came the arrest of Betty Benavidez on a "breach of the peace" charge filed by Escuela de Aztlán. Castro was present at the Benavidez home and was visibly upset from the whirl of events. The community center had been bombed just two weeks before and Waldo had been assaulted the previous day.[63] The previous night someone had shot a hole through the wall of the house at 1165 Lipan Street next door to the Benavidez home.[64] Even more disturbing, that morning Castro had received the terrifying news from his babysitter that an anonymous phone caller had threatened the lives of his children.[65]

Then came Betty's arrest, and Castro lost his composure. "What the hell are you doin' here?" he had shouted to the police. "How dare you come over here and do this to Betty?"

"He just snapped," recalls Cecilia Garcia, who worked in the office of the Coalition. "I'll tell you one thing; that constant battling back and forth . . . had gone on for a long time."[66]

Incident on Santa Fe Drive

With emotions still raw from the day's events Castro, passed by La Escuela de Aztlán on his way to work that afternoon. In front of the school stood Florencio Granado, a militant activist who apparently waved him a greeting with his middle finger.

Castro had generally acquired a peaceful reputation and certainly had never advocated violence as a political strategy. But he was not a passive man, and on that particular day in July he was breathing fire. One friend recalls that "You could differ with Rich, but you didn't confront him. If you said, 'Fuck you,' he'd slap you down."[67]

Cecelia Garcia describes his personality in this way: "If you screamed and cussed at Richard, he wasn't gonna run away. He was gonna come back and say, 'What is goin' on? You're not gonna talk to me like that.' He was a young man. Richard and Waldo—these were Chicano men that had very strong personalities and quick tempers if you ask me. Richard was not a soft-spoken, meek kind of person, no. He was a very forceful person. He was a tough guy. He was not a peacemaker. He was a civil rights activist with all that toughness and forcefulness you have to have. . . . And Richard was a boxer; Richard could punch it out. He could be a conciliatory person, yes, if it was set up . . . that way, but he was not going to be threatened; he was not going to be harassed. Let me put it to you this way . . . he could go to blows.

"In our community politically, you had all these strong personalities. These were people who could fist it out. . . . There was nothing to scruffing it up if you had to. You're not gonna grow up a meek person and make it [in that] neighborhood by being a pansy or being weak. Betty wasn't gonna back down from people who were gonna threaten Waldo. She grew up in Lincoln Park; she was a Quintana. Richard wasn't gonna back down from people who were trying to threaten him. These were very strong people, and threats were threats. If people were threatening, they were going to go *confront* those threats. Maybe that wasn't the best thing to do; maybe they should've called the cops. . . . Maybe [they] should've just moved on with it and gone on to another strategy. . . . But it was their neighborhood. It was their West Denver. *They* weren't gonna back down."[68]

Rich Castro, having just been flipped off, entered the second floor office of the Coalition trembling with anger. "That son of a bitch!" he yelled, slamming the door behind him. Celina Benavidez tried to calm him down. "Please don't go out there," she pleaded.

"It was an explosive atmosphere," she remembers.[69] The heat was oppressive. Just two hours before, the thermometer at Stapleton Airport had registered 103 degrees, the hottest day since 1878. Outside the Coalition office, the street was a furnace permeated with tension and ill feelings.

Celina Benavidez could not contain Castro that evening. He jumped back into his Volkswagen and sped off toward Metropolitan State College, where he was scheduled to teach a Chicano studies course. His route took him once again by La Escuela where a group of parents were meeting with the staff about the dangerous events of the last several days. With several others, Kohler, Archilla, Lujan, and Montoya stood outside the school. And there again was Florencio Granado.

Granado had come up from Texas in the late '60s to enroll at the Boulder campus of the University of Colorado, rooming in a cabin with his wife and child on a hill above Chautauqua Park. The Boulder United Mexican American Students chapter had set up a Migrant Action Program to recruit the children of migrant field workers for a college education. Since the migrant stream ran from Texas to the beet fields of Colorado, a number of Tejano students ended up in Boulder.[70] Granado gravitated quickly toward radical politics, toward the Crusade for Justice and La Raza Unida Party.

He quickly developed into an effective organizer and gained considerable popularity among militants in Boulder and Denver. Running as the Raza Unida candidate in 1972 for Board of Regents at the University of Colorado, he received a remarkable 22,000 votes.[71] In Denver he spearheaded a campaign to recall city councilman Eugene DiManna, who had alienated most of the Chicano community in North Denver as well as the West Side. When the Denver Election Commission rejected the petitions, Granado successfully challenged the decision in the Colorado Supreme Court. A poem, written by Santiago Valdez, honored him as a man of the people who fought hard for their benefit: "With a beer in his hand/With his car which wasn't working well at all/With his torn boots/And his worn out vest . . . he went to the people/he called the students/he raised the signatures/Five thousand in all. . . ."[72]

As an activist, he was good, but he tended to live on the edge. In 1971, on Flagstaff Mountain, he faced off a Boulder policeman who had tried to arrest him for car theft. He had grabbed one of the policeman's two guns and for several seconds they stood shouting at each other and pointing the pistols until two other policemen arrived on the scene. Defended by renowned lawyer Walter Gerash, Granado beat the rap a year later, claiming he took the gun in fear for his life.[73]

The following year, he accompanied Ricardo Falcon, a talented young organizer, to the Raza Unida Convention in El Paso. Falcon had built up a loyal following among youth in his hometown of Fort Lupton, where racial oppression had long been a staple of life in the small town on Colorado's high plains. In a tiny town in New Mexico the two pulled into a gas station because their car was overheating. A dispute between Falcon and the station owner escalated into a fight, and Falcon was shot dead, "an early martyr of the Chicano Movement."[74] Granado watched helplessly as his friend died at the scene.

During the hot summer of 1973, Granado and Castro tangled politically. When the election commission declared Granado's petitions to recall Councilman DiManna invalid, Castro and Benavidez initiated a second petition. Whichever faction—Castro's Democrats or Granado's radicals— succeeded in unseating DiManna might have the inside track on winning the council seat. Castro and Granado were battling over political turf. After Granado's petitions were turned down, Castro and Waldo vowed "to do it right," a statement that must have infuriated Granado especially since it was his work which eventually prevailed in court.[75]

The fury between the two—the radical and the reformer—culminated as Castro, no longer in control of his anger, rounded the corner in front of Escuela de Aztlán. After an exchange of predictable incivilities, Castro, still livid from the previous confrontation, bounded out of his car. Later on he said things happened so fast that he barely remembered what happened.[76] The pregnant Lois Lujan stood in his way and Castro pushed her hard enough to make her fall to the sidewalk. Someone hustled her into the school building to get her out of the way of flying fists. It was an act for which Castro would apologize repeatedly some years later, long after the smoke had cleared.

Freddy Granado was no match for Rich Castro. A fighter at Annunciation, Castro still had quick hands and a powerful punch. He was stocky and solid. Granado hit the ground in seconds just as a random passerby came on the scene. Juan Archuleta, a volunteer coordinator with the Jefferson County Probation Department, and his wife, Joaquina, exited from the Aztlán Theater across the street just as the fight broke out. The well-intentioned Archuleta tried to break the scuffle up without success. The fight reignited and Joaquina Archuleta said Castro was kicking Granado as he fell again to the sidewalk.[77] But this fight would not end like the old schoolyard fights behind Hagus Hall at Annunciation when a couple of guys used to go at it with bare fists until one gave in.

On this day, five pistol shots from a .32-caliber automatic pierced the twilight air. Juan Archuleta, the Good Samaritan, took a bullet in the chest. It nicked his heart, ricocheted into his liver, and then landed in his right kidney. Dr. William Turner, the emergency room physician at Denver General Hospital, said, "It's a miracle he is alive."[78]

As for Castro, he didn't even know he got hit. He ran instinctively to his car when he heard the shots ring out. Only after he slammed the door behind him did he see the blood flowing from his head and neck, gushing like water from an open faucet. Four pints of blood flowed from the wound as he drove the half-dozen blocks to the old police headquarters at Thirteenth and Champa and stumbled in, asking for help.[79] Bill Perry's frontpage picture in the *Rocky Mountain News* next morning caught the image of Castro, pale and anguished, his face contorted in pain and fear as Officer Barbara Barnhill tried to stop the bleeding.[80] His white shirt was soaked through with blood. "Please call a priest," he told a friend, who had rushed to the station.[81]

Arriving on the scene, *Denver Post* reporter Rich Maes called Virginia Castro to let her know her husband was en route to Denver General. She left their baby son, Rich Junior, with his older sister and flew out the door of their West Ellsworth Avenue home. As she hurried by the intersection of Bannock and Irvington, she saw from the corner of her eye Florencio Granado rounding the corner in a blue van.[82] She had no idea at the time that Granado's fight with Castro had led to her husband's near encounter with death.

Rich Castro's wound proved, in the end, more superficial than it appeared in those first harrowing moments. He recovered quickly, but not without scars etched in his memory and perhaps a new resolve. Castro seemed to emerge from the peril a changed man. "Rich was different after the shooting," says Celina Benavidez. "He talked and felt as if he wouldn't have the same longevity as the rest of us and that he only had a short time to accomplish what he wanted. He'd make comments like, 'We don't have a lotta time you know; I'm a pretty old guy.' How could a twenty-seven-year-old man say 'we don't have a lotta time?'"[83]

Within a week, Florencio Granado turned himself in to face charges of first-degree assault. Perhaps the trial, scheduled for a year away in July of 1974, would have cleared up the mysteries that surrounded the incident on Santa Fe. Some witnesses that evening maintain that Florencio Granado could not possibly have shot Castro in the neck with that .32-caliber pistol. Granado was flailing on the ground getting pummeled when the shots went off. It must have been one of the other men in the crowd in front of La Escuela, they say, who pulled the trigger. The action unfolded so rapidly that many left the scene stunned and dizzy with confusion.

The Bombings in Boulder

The long-awaited trial never happened. Two months before the hearing, four men sat in a borrowed 1968 station wagon parked in the lot of a Boulder Burger King on Twenty-eighth Street. Shortly before midnight on May 30, witnesses in the lot reeled in shock as they watched the vehicle explode in a ball of fire that blasted the roof off and left the seats smoking and shredded. Police pulled three bodies out of the wreckage; one of them was Freddy Granado.[84]

Florencio Granado had danced around the edges of death for three years. He had held a gun on a Boulder cop and seen his compañero, Ricardo Falcon, shot dead in New Mexico. He had been present on Ninth and Santa Fe when Rich Castro and Juan Archuleta escaped death by a matter of millimeters. Only two days previous, three of his companions in UMAS— Reyes Martinez, Una Jackola, and Neva Romero—had been blown up in a similar car explosion in Chautauqua Park, near Granado's old home. Now Florencio Granado was dead.

To this day, the deaths of the six Boulder militants remain unsolved; their demise gave rise to bitter controversy. The Boulder Police Department insists they blew themselves up. Like the faction of the Weathermen— the most adventuresome of the white radical underground— who destroyed themselves in a New York apartment, the six militants of Boulder detonated their homemade bombs prematurely in an inept campaign of urban guerrilla warfare.

Others familiar with the UMAS scene in Boulder maintain that sinister forces within the government were responsible for the debacle. The six were murdered, they say, by law enforcement agents trying to break the back of the militant Chicano Movement. Or perhaps, as say some, right-wing civilians or white supremacists did the job. Only further revelations can unravel the mysteries of the shootings and bombings of that era, and those revelations may never be forthcoming.[85]

There is no mystery, however, surrounding the climate in which Rich Castro's shooting took place. The Crusade for Justice might have reacted to the incident in a variety of ways. It might have disavowed the shooting and claimed no formal ties with those involved. It might have labeled the whole affair an unfortunate tragedy, or even called for a cooling-off period for all factions on the West Side. Instead, in a terse but dramatic statement, the Crusade placed a most menacing and politically destructive spin on the events that occurred at La Escuela de Aztlán. In its July edition, *El Gallo* ran the same bloody photograph of Castro that had previously graced the front page of the *Rocky Mountain News*. This time the caption under Castro's tortured face read: "If you can't do anything for the Movement, don't do anything against it . . . because it may cost you your life."[86]

"After the shooting, you couldn't walk the streets," recalls Jerry Garcia. "It was like the tension was ready to blow up any time. I've never had a feeling like that in my entire life; I mean it was deserted. The tension was really high between the Crusade and West Denver. As far as we were concerned, a Crusader had shot Rich Castro."[87]

In the year that followed, the violence mounted. Corky Gonzales beat Waldo to a pulp at Corky's apartment in North Capitol Hill.[88] The Escuela de Aztlán was firebombed. The West Side Action Center, the First Mennonite Church, the Auraria Community Center, and the Inner City Parish all suffered bomb attacks during the years 1973 and 1974, as did Waldo's house on Lipan Street and Castro's home on Ellsworth.

For Denver's Chicano Movement, those years represented a heartbreaking setback, an era marked not by progress but by internal feuds, factional disputes, and sectarian warfare.

viii

waldo's fall from grace

T he months following Rich Castro's shooting provided no respite from civil strife, but some of the faces changed and the number of factions proliferated. The crisis erupted anew in 1974 around the small building at 1212 Mariposa Street that housed the Auraria Community Center. The West Side Coalition—that delicate quilt woven painstakingly in the previous five years from the fabric of a score of independent organizations—ripped apart at the seams.

After Castro's shooting, Waldo Benavidez issued a public statement: "I'm encouraging the disbanding of the Coalition. No organization, no political ambition, nobody's ego is worth someone getting killed."[1]

For their part, the activist churches—the Inner City Parish, the First Mennonite, and the First Spanish Methodist—originally major pillars of the Coalition, recoiled from the umbrella organization and dropped their memberships. The problem, as they saw it, was Waldo Benavidez's leadership.[2]

The churches aligned themselves with a third force, which had arisen on the West Side. There was Waldo. There was the Crusade. And now came a loose conglomeration of allies who wanted nothing to do with either.

The leaders included the Reverend Ramiro Cruz-Aedo of the Inner City Parish and the Reverends Bryce Balmer and Don Schierling of the First Mennonite Church. For years, their liberal parishioners had provided

132

seed money for West Side social activists. The clergy joined forces with secular characters in the rebellion against the Benavidezes' leadership. There was Adolfo Gomez, the director of the Auraria Community Center, and Kelly Lovato, a former Crusade member who would later direct La Alma Recreation Center. There was Craig Hart, the ex-priest, who had previously served as unofficial chaplain of the Crusade for Justice, delighting radicals with unorthodox Masses in which—dressed in a serape and without vestments—he dispersed bits of tortillas for communion. Manny Martinez, director of the nonprofit construction agency Brothers Redevelopment—the man who would later oppose Castro on the electoral level—cast his lot with the new force. It was an eclectic ideological mix: Marxists and progressive Christians, Alinsky-type community organizers, moderate Democrats, and former Crusaders uncomfortable with its inner circle, abrasive rhetoric, or increasing intimidation. Each had his own circle of influence but all coalesced to oppose what they viewed as an over-concentration of power on the West Side.

Thus, the second bitter round of conflict on the West Side pitted this emerging force against the traditional power in the neighborhood, the Benavidez family and their most loyal supporters, Richard and Virginia Castro. The Crusade, though still playing a minor role, had begun to fade into the background, at least as far as the politics of West Denver was concerned.

A New Strategy

In the spring of 1974, Waldo's faction hammered out a two-pronged strategy in an attempt to hang on to its waning political power. The plan, as it had in the past, included an electoral component as well as grassroots community organizing.

On the electoral level, they would run Betty, not for her old seat in the House of Representatives but instead for the State Senate. One of the Castros—either Rich or Virginia—would run for the District 6 seat in the House left vacant by her departure.[3] A victory would double the group's influence in the General Assembly, bringing with it a corresponding influence on the West Side. The decision to run Rich for Betty's House seat was destined to keep Richard Castro in the public eye for the next two decades.

"It was no big conspiracy to run Rich," says Waldo Benavidez in response to criticisms that a backroom machine made the choice. "He had the smarts. He could sit up there and talk that stuff. He was Democratic District Captain. He took a bullet in the neck. He was next in line; that's all. We said, 'Hey, Rich, you're the most logical. You deserve it. You want State Rep? You got it.'"[4]

To Waldo's opponents, of course, this smacked of cronyism. They saw

Waldo, wearing his dark shades, maneuvering and pulling strings in the background like some kind of Wizard of Oz. They recoiled at the idea that the democratizing impulse of the '60s had ended up with one man standing dominant over the political process in their West Side neighborhood. Thus, Manny Martinez stepped forward to oppose Castro in the Democratic primary in August of 1974.

The real head-on collision, however, came in response to the second component of the Benavidez strategy. With the West Side Coalition dismantled, the Benavidezes shifted their focus towards the Auraria Community Center.[5] Here at the building on Mariposa Street across the avenue from Lincoln Park (which the Movement had recently dubbed La Alma Park) the Benavidez faction would dig in to maintain a power base within the neighborhood. It was for control over the governing board of the Auraria Community Center that the most turbulent confrontation would take place.

Some background is necessary. When Waldo began working with the Auraria Community Center in the late 1960s, whites held the key jobs: the leadership positions and the board of directors. Betsy Keester, a social worker and a solid administrator—but a community outsider—held the executive director's job. Driven by the principles of "community control," Waldo and Dean Punké undertook a successful campaign to replace Anglo administrators with Chicanos who lived in the neighborhood.[6]

Filling these positions was one reason Rich Castro moved from the East to the West Side. "I said, 'Rich—you and Virginia—if you're gonna get married, why don't you buy a home over here on the West Side?'" recalls Waldo. "'We got a brain drain over here. There's not one person with a college education in this area.' There was just not a big resource pool of minds that you could say, 'Hey, this guy could fit here and this guy could fit there.' It was really a lonely battle out there. The impression was, yeah, we had troops everywhere. We were very active and it looked like there was a lot of troops. But it was really very small."[7]

What few jobs were available, Waldo tended to keep close to his vest. Someone had to direct the community center. Someone had to run the Head Start program and the neighborhood alcoholism program. They needed to hire a youth counselor and a custodian. In job-starved West Denver, those few jobs translated into power, and Waldo held it.

The few who had gone to school or received training took the more skilled jobs. Willie Montoya, who held a master's degree in English, took the directorship of the community center first. After his falling out with Waldo, Adolfo Gomez got the position.[8] He was a long-term resident of the West Side with a mind of his own. Waldo trained him well in the intricacies of political organizing. When Gomez, too, clashed with Waldo, the battle for control of the board of directors set the stage for the next conflict.

By this time Waldo's personality had alienated half the neighborhood.

"The Coalition could have been saved," claims Jerry Garcia, "if Waldo had not been so controlling. Waldo was a great organizer but he kept things really close to the vest. That made people very suspicious. He needed to let people do stuff on their own. Waldo was the perfect community organizer except for the end. He didn't know how to let go. When you're organizing the community, you don't make it a career. You have to get in and get out. You have to train other people to take over and let them decide what they want to do. Waldo was starting to become the godfather of West Denver. Everything went through him in order to get things done. There were people like myself who were questioning that, who were saying, 'no, that's not what we were working towards.' We were looking to get programs in here with a democratic process. To disagree professionally and not to take it personally."[9]

A Dictatorial Personality

Years later, Waldo tends to concur with some of the criticisms leveled against him. Had he, over the years, become dictatorial and no longer in touch with his constituency? "That's probably a fair assessment," he says. "For my part it evolved into that. Autocratic? Dictatorial? Yeah. The pressures, the dynamics of the neighborhood, the dynamics of what was happening pushed me into making [dictatorial] decisions. Maybe I was dictatorial. Maybe I cussed somebody out I shouldn't have. Maybe I said the wrong thing to the wrong person."[10]

The story he related about a burglary at his residence and the subsequent emotional fallout for a member of his family illustrates Waldo's lack of diplomatic skills. When Waldo was seventeen, having just married his twenty-one-year-old wife, he found himself playing the role of father to seven children ages one to fourteen. There were Betty's four children, her sister, and her niece and nephew. "I got broken into here the other day," said Waldo in beginning the story. "They took my stereo, TV, and all that stuff. Little gang assholes. Well, I had some real valuable paintings up here. They didn't touch them 'cuz they don't know the difference between a piece of turd and a Rembrandt. So one of the girls I raised came over and she took all the paintings to her house. One painting disappeared and I told her later 'there's a painting missing, but that's alright; I don't give a shit.' Anyway I come over to her house one day and say, 'How ya doin'?' and she was in the bathroom cryin' and she says, 'I'm hurt that you accused me of stealing your painting.' Then she sat down and everything comes out. 'You never did show me any love when I was growin' up. You never paid me any attention. Why didn't you help me when I was in school, when I was havin' trouble, like you did other kids?' She was runnin' all these hurts down, you know, man. I said to her, 'I was seventeen years old raisin' seven kids and you want me to give you special treatment, special love? I didn't pat you on the head enough? Why don't you see some counselor you got such a big old problem?"

"'Oh, you think I need counselin'? Why didn't you just do what you were s'posed to do and show me love?'"

"The reason I'm tellin' you this story is cuz there's people all during that time—maybe I stepped on a whole lotta toes. Unintentionally. But it happened. And all these people got these hurts. And they called me 'dictatorial'; call me this, call me that. Maybe that's what happened, ya know? I never realized I neglected any of my family. I didn't give her enough love; I didn't realize it. And I used to get tough. I was hard on people. I pushed people. If I wanted somethin' done, I pushed people. Maybe I was dictatorial."[11]

More and more the terms 'dictator' and 'autocratic' cropped up in association with Waldo's name. According to the Reverend Don Schierling, Waldo took a "Nixon approach to politics. If people aren't for them, they are enemies." Schierling added, "the tactic employed by the Benavidezes has been to gain power within an organization and then not permit dissent."[12]

Many Westsiders, with their appetites for democracy whetted by small doses of empowerment, hungered for more, not less, democracy. The whole thrust of the '60s had created a tidal wave of democratic desire in those pockets of society traditionally devoid of it. The Students for a Democratic Society, the civil rights movement, the War on Poverty, the women's movement, the whole freewheeling and experimental nature of the '60s, in large part represented attempts to broaden democracy, to distribute its fruits beyond the white middle and upperclasses to those who had never before had access. It was no time to stand up and oppose that wave. It was not an era for *padrones* or *caudillos*—for political bosses and hardcore ward heelers.

Yet the whole of Waldo's personality and style tended to flaunt that yearning for democracy and respect. Cecilia Garcia, a close associate of Waldo's, offered a sympathetic but revealing description of his personality. "He's a no-nonsense type of person. He didn't want to fool around. He has very good ideas, but he cannot sit and do the technocratic work. He doesn't see all the work involved. He wants to lay it out and then you do it, but he doesn't see all the steps involved to do it. He was a very, very hard taskmaster. He wasn't about stupidity. If you were there to campaign for a certain politician and you didn't want to do the job, he would throw you out. He would physically throw you out. He wanted to reach a goal and people didn't understand the seriousness of it. How could I put this to you? Some people come for whatever reasons to a campaign or for their own ego. And it's only about one person; that's the person you're trying to elect. Waldo would get very, very angry if you were gonna be an obstructionist. If you weren't gonna do the work, get the hell out. He was not an easygoing person. He wasn't gonna sit there and listen to your problems. You were there to do what you were supposed to do. If not—leave! So that's what was hard about Waldo—the way he would tell you. He would tell you straight out: 'You're screwin' up. Get your silly ass outta here.' Or if somebody said, 'Well, I have to go home 'cuz I have a family,' he'd say, 'OK, well go on. And don't come back.' Because he was driven.

"You know, these were very powerful men that were used to getting what they thought was the right thing to do. So Waldo was very, very hard. Corky was just as hard.

"Waldo was a very strong personality and a political genius. But he was just not the diplomat; he was *not* a diplomat.

"Let's say we were runnin' a politician for office and it would be Easter. A campaign manager . . . would say, 'OK, people will be off Monday and Friday. That gives us four days. That gives us Friday, Saturday, Sunday, and Monday to get this politician to these parts of the city. Do we have thirty-one Catholic churches that we could get this politician to?' And he lays it out. And then maybe somebody would say, 'Well, it's *Easter*. We have to cook dinner and we'll be with our families, and why would you want to make someone go on Easter?' Waldo would just lose it. He'd grab that person and say, 'Is that what you wanna do? Make Easter dinner? We're tryin' to elect a politician here!' And he'd throw that person outta the meeting. Richard was driven the same way but he didn't abuse people personally. He would manipulate it where he would talk people into working day and night, day and night, day and night. But they were both driven people."[13]

Leashing Waldo

Why could no one restrain the destructive side of Waldo's nature? Why didn't Rich Castro take him aside and say, "Look, Waldo, you're driving people away from us in droves. You'll alienate us from the whole neighborhood. You'll lose everything you've built up in the last decade."

"Nobody ever said anything," says Cecelia Garcia. "I think culturally it was unacceptable to tell people about their personal way of dealing with each other. Now we all talk to each other about what is needed, about what the problem is and that type of thing. For some reason in those times, people didn't talk as openly; I don't know why."[14]

Just as likely, Castro was still young, still a student of Waldo's, still the junior partner, and, thus, not ready to challenge him on so touchy an issue.

They were in the heat of battle and perhaps had little time for the personal aspects of the conflict. Then, too, many of the pressures Waldo exerted were on Castro's behalf. Like a pugnacious lawyer who can take the heat on behalf of a nicer guy, Waldo's bulldog style was sometimes directed at helping Castro win office. In choosing to ride Waldo's political machine, Castro left himself little room to criticize his benefactor.

In the final analysis, however, it is clear that Rich Castro still believed in Waldo. For all of Waldo's personal frailties, he was the man on the West Side who most consistently delivered the goods.[15] In the constantly changing political arena where the nuances of democratic process meet head-on with the need for efficiency and productivity, Waldo Benavidez came down on the side of the latter. Ironically, his very weaknesses—his single-mindedness, iron will, and driving ego—had also been his strength. These were the qualities that allowed him to get things done. For his track record on the West Side, he had won Rich Castro's fierce loyalty. In these waning months of Waldo's power, Castro could neither leash him, cage him, nor abandon him.

Violence Visits Again

The hardness in Waldo's personality dovetailed with a growing reputation for settling disputes with gun or bomb. Benavidez adamantly insists that any violence during that time was strictly defensive on his part and bristles at the suggestion that "goons" backed up his power.

"I did *not* have any goons," he says. "Who? Who's my paid goons? Rich? Bobby Federico, our bookkeeper?" he asks, relying on the pair's reputation for not engaging in gunplay. "Who was the goons?"[16] Instead, Benavidez maintains that he and his family began fighting back after repeated attacks on his home by enemies wielding pistols, rifles, and fire-bombs. He points to the conviction in a federal court of Tommy Aragon, who served time for placing a crude but effective bomb in Waldo' back-yard: a beer bottle full of gasoline with a wick, and an M-80 and a .22 caliber cartridge taped to it.[17]

What some called "goons," Waldo insists, were in reality family members who fought back against attack. "My kids would come home from school beat up," he says. "They got Tommy one time—my youngest one—with a *baseball bat*. The Brown Berets had a house right directly across from us. They were shootin' at our house with rifles. My kids, they get beat up. They got friends. They go back and beat somebody up. We fought back; we didn't just take it. We're not just sittin' on our hands cowering. They shot at us; we shot back. Chuck Kohler. We took a few shots at him. It was mostly the family. Rich wasn't doing any of the fighting. My brother-in-law lived around the corner. He was there. . . . But hey, if you're bein' threatened and your home is bein' threatened, your brother's gonna come and help. Family, ya know. But there's no goons."

Some of the retaliation targets, however, appear to be unlikely candidates for the role of combatant in neighborhood warfare. Adolfo Gomez, director of the Auraria Community Center, had the windows of his car shot out, and former priest Craig Hart received similar treatment.[18] Asked about those shootings, Benavidez replied ambiguously: "Adolph? I don't know who coulda' shot at him. Maybe. It's possible."[19]

Self-defense notwithstanding, the Benavidez family was perceived as fueling—if not orchestrating—the tiny civil war that wracked the West Side. Indeed, once the cycle of retaliation began, few really bothered to try to untangle who fired the first shots and when. The beginnings of the war were too murky and complex for most people to decipher. By summer 1974, it had become simply a Hatfield-McCoy affair. One act of violence inspired another and so on down the line. Certainly, the Benavidezes did nothing to try to stem the violence.

The ministers condemned the whole thing, but they laid most of the blame on Waldo, particularly after the firebombing of the First Mennonite Church. "He who lives by the gun, has to fear the gun," Mennonite minister Don Schierling said in a quote in *The Denver Post* clearly aimed at Waldo Benavidez.[20]

Things came to a head in the late spring of 1974, when the two feuding factions met head-on in an election for board of directors at the Auraria Community Center. It culminated in a mini-riot on the afternoon of May 31. Gomez's side had quietly recruited members to the center, with the aim of defeating Waldo's supporters. Membership cost only a buck, and that was all that was needed for eligibility to vote.[21] In early May, one of Gomez's backers got drunk and attended a caucus meeting at Waldo's house. "We're gonna beat you at your own game," she announced brazenly to the Benavidez partisans.[22] It was like throwing down a gauntlet. Waldo's team took the hint, and hastily got busy recruiting new members. As the election approached, membership had swollen to 600 families and the tension was thick.

An accusation of rape against Adolfo Gomez turned bizarrely political and further clouded the atmosphere. Gomez insisted it was a trumped-up charge instigated by Waldo's forces to pressure him to resign.[23] From the other side, Virginia Castro, who had encouraged the young woman to file charges, had been fired from her Head Start position for allegedly "spending too much time on Rich Castro's campaign for State Rep." Mrs. Castro believed the real reason for her dismissal was her encouraging a rape victim to go to the police. In the end, charges were never filed. The police said there was sexual contact but no evidence of rape.[24] The whole incident, however, ratcheted up the tension by one more notch.

Rumors

Rumors, which had exacerbated the tension for years, spread like wildfire. Waldo must have Mafia connections, went one of them.[25] Waldo might bring in Reies Tijerina to wreak vengeance on the West Side, went another.[26] Even Virginia Castro's flight after Richard's shooting the previous July became grist for the mill. Following the shooting, Virginia had taken her children for safekeeping to Glenwood Springs until the storm blew over. On the street this maternal precaution translated to: How could Virginia love Richard when *she* vacations in a resort town while *he* is recovering from his wounds? Few realized that, for Virginia Castro, Glenwood Springs was no vacation wonderland. It was her hometown where the grandmother who raised her had resided for decades.[27]

The *Straight Creek Journal* quoted an anonymous member of the Auraria center with the following ominous statement: "The thing that was said over and over is that this election should never be held. Everybody knew there would be trouble."[28]

"Everybody" was right. Jessica Luna, chairwoman of the board—a rare Chicana feminist who used to do crafts with women at the center and talk to them earnestly about their oppression at home—stood inside the building supervising the election on that spring day.[29] Outside, the place got out of control rapidly. Proponents of Gomez's faction insist that Waldo had placed four or five "thugs" outside the building to intimidate the voters.[30] It was clear, however, that Waldo's opponents were also armed. Five complaints to the Denver police were later filed; the complaints charged that "they were told not to vote under threats of assault."[31] Arguments broke out over who was eligible to vote.[32] Then tensions soared as upwards of seventy-five kids gathered around the area in the park across the street.[33]

Jerry Garcia, who opposed Benavidez, remembers the park scene well. He claims, "Waldo was bringing his people in from all over the city and saying, 'Hey, they paid their dollar to get in.' We told 'em, 'You cannot bring in outside people as Auraria members. It has to be in the neighborhood; that's the by-laws.'

"I was across the street with a group of guys," Garcia continues, "because [Cruz] Ramiro said there might be a hassle here. 'If there's a hassle,' he told me, 'come back and get us.' There was about a dozen of us. We had guns. We were sittin' there smokin' a cigarette. All of a sudden we hear all kinds of screamin' and hollerin,' and we heard someone say, 'She gots it; she gots it; she gots it.'"[34]

The rumor that the ballot box had been stolen spread through the park. "We were going for a democratic process," says Garcia, "and now the ballot box was stolen? . . . That just pushed everybody over the edge. People started physically fighting with each other. . . . Next thing you know Chuck Kohler and a bunch of kids from the Escuela de Aztlán flipped over this car and started breaking all the windows out." The car, a small Opal, turned out to be that of Celina Benavidez, Waldo's daughter-in-law.

Things were not going smoothly inside the building either. Virginia Castro, enraged at the situation outside, charged in to confront Jessie Luna. "I said, 'Jessie, do you see what's going on out there?' There were people outside carrying guns, turning over cars, screaming and hollering. And she's just sitting there signing people up for this election. I blamed her for what was going on outside, maybe wrongly so. What they should have done was close the place and say 'We're out of business today, folks. Somebody's gonna get hurt; let's just do this another day.' I said to Jessie, 'What's going on outside, it's your fault.' When she said something 'smart,' I slapped her. It was kind of a reaction. I didn't plan to do it. It was out of anger and the out-of-controlness of the situation."[35]

Rich Castro stepped in quickly to break up the fight and then called the police. Within moments the election was suspended.[36]

It took a while to calm things down outside. People hit the ground. The police released tear gas. It was a mini-riot at Lincoln Park.

"The whole thing was goofy," explained Adolfo Gomez.[37]

The ensuing days ushered in additional acts of violence. It was the next night when someone shot out the windows of Adolfo Gomez's car, even as policemen stood in his house taking down reports of the previous day's events.[38] On that same night the windows of Craig Hart's truck were shot out. And in that same period, Chuck Kohler took a bullet in the chest, afterwards awakening Jerry Garcia in the middle of the night by pounding on his Galapago Street door. Slumped over, Kohler asked Garcia's assistance in tending to a wound just above the heart.[39]

It was also in that same period that Waldo and Betty Benavidez quietly slipped out of their Lipan Street home and went into hiding in fear of the growing violence directed at their family.[40]

Things had grown so out of control that many Westsiders welcomed the outside mediation the city provided to stem the violence. District Attorney Dale Tooley called two meetings at the community center to discuss a truce. With Waldo and Betty still in hiding, many of those present expressed the belief that peace would prevail only if Waldo stayed away from the neighborhood.[41]

The Benavidezes had come to their own conclusions. "We were sittin' in the living room," Waldo says, "Betty and I with the lights out and her gun on the table, lookin' out the windows. [Beginning] about midnight, every once in a while somebody'd take a shot at the house. We just said,

'What is this all about? Is the West Side worth it?'" Their answer was no. "We just made some arrangements—it took us about three or four days—and we left." With bitterness in their hearts towards the neighborhood that, in their eyes, had turned on them, the couple fled to Albuquerque. Although they returned long enough to run Betty's faltering Senate campaign against the North Side's Paul Sandoval, their stay in Denver was short. With her loss in the August Democratic primary, the two returned, defeated, to Waldo's hometown in New Mexico to spend several years in unofficial exile.[42]

A Change in National Mood

In some ways, the tragic and self-destructive events that played out on the streets of West Denver represent a reflection of a much larger wave of events that took place nationwide. Though Waldo might have contributed to his own downfall, he did so within a particular historical framework which hastened his political demise. The civil rights movement, the student movements, and the War on Poverty combined to heighten the expectations of the nation's disenfranchised. At a time when Westsiders, Eastsiders, and Northsiders, indeed the poor all over the nation, were hungry for democracy, hungry for power long denied them, Waldo's ego, impatience, and dictatorial tendencies placed him out of step with the aspirations of his constituency.

And yet that same hunger for democracy produced its own problems. In its zeal for democratic purity, the left across the nation—whether reformist or revolutionary—tended to chew up its natural leadership and spit it out without a moment's afterthought. Those kept outside the political process for so many years possessed no reservoir of trust for any political leaders. The New Left, whose ideas permeated into other sections of the movement, rejected strong leadership on ideological grounds. Thus, both inside and outside the Chicano community, the rank and file tended to berate, censure, or bad-mouth movement leaders simply because of their leadership qualities.

For all of Waldo's faults, the gossip on the West Side dealt harshly with the man who had dedicated himself so thoroughly to the community's struggles. The delicate balance between respect for leadership and the leaders' respect for the democratic process never seemed to exist.

The demise of the Chicano Movement in Denver reflected the climate of the country in other ways as well. The revolution represented locally by the Crusade for Justice was consuming itself nationwide in the early '70s. The Black Panthers, the Weathermen, and the Brown Berets all self-destructed and suffered from large doses of in-fighting. In the late '60s, with

Rich Castro, 1948, with his father, Archie Castro, and
mother, Josephine McGrath Castro. Born in 1923, Archie
grew up in Walsenburg, his family's roots deep in the
southern coalfields of Colorado. Josephine was born
in Denver to a family with origins in New Mexico and
southern Colorado. (Photo Virginia Castro.)

Rich Castro, four years old, in his grandparents'
backyard at Thirty-fourth and Marion. While his
father worked at Eaton Metals and his mother at
I. A. Deline Box Company, the young Castro spent
many hours with his loving grandparents at their
East Side home. (Photo Virginia Castro.)

Virginia Montaño Lucero Castro, age four, in front of the Grand
Junction, Colorado, house where she lived. Born on the Western
Slope, her father worked on the railroad while her mother cleaned
houses to provide for their family. Virginia would move to Denver
when she was twenty years old and already the mother of three.
(Photo Virginia Castro.)

Above: Inspired by his parish priests and educated in East Side Catholic schools, Rich Castro spent a year at Denver's St. Thomas Seminary. He continued his education at Trinidad State Junior College and Metropolitan State College of Denver. (Photo Virginia Castro.)

Right: After graduating from Metro State, Castro became a social worker while earning his master's degree in sociology from the University of Denver. This photo was taken for his 1974 campaign for the Colorado State House. (Photo Virginia Castro.)

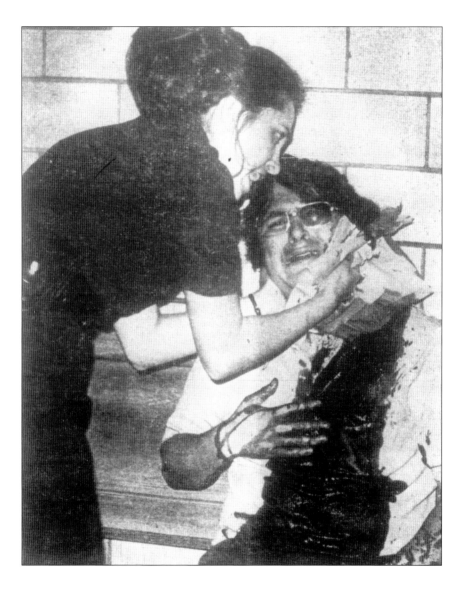

Above: Denver police officer Barbara Barnhill tends to Castro after he was shot during a confrontation with Florencio Granado at La Escuela de Aztlán on Santa Fe Drive. The wound proved to be superficial, but the incident changed Castro forever. (Photo Bill Perry, *Rocky Mountain News*.)

Rodolfo "Corky" Gonzales was the founder of the Crusade for Justice. The charismatic ex-boxer was the most visible and outspoken Chicano leader in the Movement. (Photo Colorado Historical Society.)

Above: In 1970, Castro, then a twenty-three-year-old senior at Metro State College and a social worker with the Denver Youth Service Bureau, charged police brutality after he was beaten and arrested during a minor disturbance at Curtis Park. Days later, city officials met with Castro (lower left) and other Chicano activists at the Auraria Community Center to hear his impassioned testimony. Denver police chief George Seaton is at far right. Waldo Benavidez (left, standing behind Castro), in his ever-present dark glasses, represented the West Side Coalition. Castro later took a lie detector test that corroborated his testimony, but the investigation brought no charges against the police. (Photo Dick Davis, *Rocky Mountain News.*)

Left: After school officials suspended Manuel "Rocky" Hernandez and other Black Beret members for demanding the inclusion of Chicano studies, 600 students protested at Denver North High School. Corky Gonzales addressed the peaceful demonstration. (Photo Denver Public Library Western History Collection.)

Castro shares pizza and a laugh in the State Legislature with then Representative Federico Peña, who would serve as Denver's first Hispanic mayor from 1983 to 1991 before leading the Department of Transportation during the Bill Clinton presidential administration. (Photo Virginia Castro.)

A thoughtful Rich Castro testifies during formal hearings on proposed legislation regarding child prostitution in 1980. (Photo Ann Duckett. Courtesy Virginia Castro.)

While serving in the Colorado State House of Representatives, Castro was a prominent and active member of the Chicano Caucus. From left: Castro, Leo Lucero, Laura DeHerrera, George Chavez, Federico Peña, Polly Baca, Don Sandoval, Paul Sandoval, Bob Martinez. (Photo James Baca.)

Left: Always quick with a laugh and a smile, Castro knew how to have fun. He and Michael Simmons, Federico Peña's director of the Commission on Youth, mimicked the Blues Brothers at a fundraiser for the mayor's reelection campaign (top). At another Peña fundraiser, John Soto, Frank Solis, Simmons, Castro, and Edmundo Gonzales did a take on Motown singing group the Temptations. (Photos Virginia Castro.)

Above: Rich Castro joins U.S. Representative Pat Schroeder at a news conference. (Photo Virginia Castro.)

Virginia Castro with Rich in 1986 when he received the Human Rights
Award from the American Jewish Committee for his community service.
(Photo Virginia Castro.)

Right: Castro in 1986 with his son Richie,
age fourteen, and daughter Brenda, age
twenty-three. (Photo Virginia Castro.)

An official portrait of Richard Castro when he was a representative in the Colorado State Legislature.

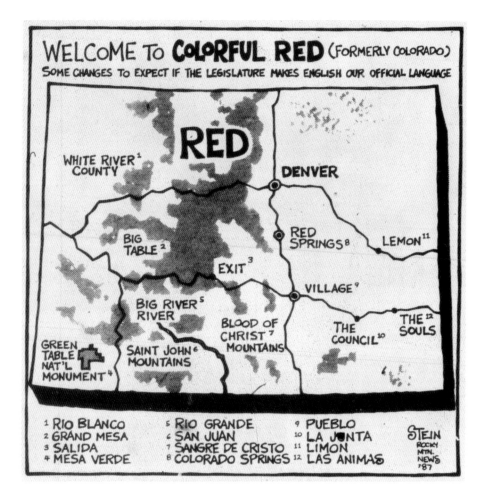

WELCOME TO **COLORFUL RED** (FORMERLY COLORADO)

SOME CHANGES TO EXPECT IF THE LEGISLATURE MAKES ENGLISH OUR OFFICIAL LANGUAGE

RED

WHITE RIVER[1] COUNTY

DENVER

BIG TABLE[2]

RED SPRINGS[8]

LEMON[11]

EXIT[3]

VILLAGE[9]

BIG RIVER[5] RIVER

BLOOD OF CHRIST[7] MOUNTAINS

THE COUNCIL[10]

THE[12] SOULS

GREEN TABLE NAT'L MONUMENT[4]

SAINT JOHN[6] MOUNTAINS

[1] RIO BLANCO
[2] GRAND MESA
[3] SALIDA
[4] MESA VERDE

[5] RIO GRANDE
[6] SAN JUAN
[7] SANGRE DE CRISTO
[8] COLORADO SPRINGS

[9] PUEBLO
[10] LA JUNTA
[11] LIMON
[12] LAS ANIMAS

STEIN
ROCKY
MTN.
NEWS
'87

The late 1980s saw a heated and emotional debate on the proposed English-only state constitution amendment, which Castro strongly opposed. He clipped this biting Ed Stein cartoon from the newspaper and added it to his scrapbook. (*Rocky Mountain News.*)

Castro meets with voters during his unsuccessful 1989 campaign for the Denver School Board. (Photo Virginia Castro.)

Castro spent his adult life committed to civil and human rights issues, regardless of ethnic association. In the late 1980s, he visited the Pine Ridge Indian Reservation in South Dakota, the site of the Wounded Knee incident in which American Indian Movement activists clashed with authorities while protesting poor conditions on the reservation. (Photo Virginia Castro.)

Che Guevara hiding among *campesinos* in Bolivia, with Mexican students laying down their lives at the 1968 Olympics, and with the descendants of ancient Mayans walking the remote ridges of Guatemala cradling submachine guns, it all seemed perfectly realistic to talk about the Revolution at Louie's Tavern on Thirty-eighth and High in East Denver. The Revolution seemed a palpable, breathing entity; it seemed just around the corner.

Likewise, with Lyndon Johnson's declaration of war on poverty, with Congressional support for VISTA (Volunteers in Service to America), Head Start, and the Great Society, with George McGovern (only a little later) campaigning to redistribute the national wealth, it seemed perfectly natural for reformers like Waldo Benavidez and Rich Castro to talk about community control.

By 1974, however, the radical wave hit the rocks. American involvement in Vietnam ended and civil rights legislation was slowly permeating the soil of American culture even as a backlash simultaneously emerged to inhibit its progress. These changes effectively smoothed over the jagged edges of American injustice and diffused the passions previously aroused by the war and the most blatant forms of racial discrimination. Besides, the country had grown exhausted; a new, more cautious era was dawning that tended to blunt any thrust toward rapid social change. As the national mood turned inward, reformers and revolutionaries alike receded into the background, and groups like the Crusade and the West Side Coalition found themselves at a historical dead end, isolated and cut off from the main thoroughfares of political action, cut off, as well, from the vitality provided by the existence of a national movement. Operating in a political vacuum, the movement in Denver imploded. It should come as no great shock that it turned on and devoured itself.

And so, as the Benavidezes fled down Interstate 25 to Albuquerque, peace came to the West Side but at great cost. The movement had been reduced to shambles. With Waldo gone to New Mexico and Corky's influence waning, with the rest exhausted from the struggle, the Chicano Movement in West Denver lost both its dynamism and its bearings; feuding and factionalism had cut out its heart and soul.

Jerry Garcia remembers the period with sadness. "Nothing was going on," he said. "It was dead. We sort of destroyed ourselves. We lost funding [from church groups]. Nobody talked to each other. Rich and I didn't talk to each other for two years. Everything we had built went down the drain. It was horrible."[43]

The Campaign

In one sense, the 1974 election campaign for the State House of Representatives was Rich Castro's personal attempt to pick up the pieces. Even during the campaign, the recently established peace on the West Side was shattered for an instant one July evening in the midst of the primary. Someone placed yet another bomb on the front porch of Castro's next-door neighbor and blew the place up. An anonymous phone call to the Associated Press had made it clear that the Castro home had been the real target.[44]

"Hey, I heard they tried to blow your house up," said Roger Medina, Castro's old school buddy, when they met by chance on the street. "Yeah," replied Castro with a characteristic grin. "But they couldn't even find the right house."[45] The incident remained just one more unsolved act of terror on the West Side.

Castro's loyalty to the Benavidezes had cost him considerable support on the West Side in his campaign for state representative. Manuel "Manny" Martinez, his opponent in the Democratic primary, differed not a whit from Castro on the issues. Both stressed education, housing, crime, and the problems of the elderly.[46] The only real issue was who would wield power. Castro's opponents saw him as Waldo's pawn; they wanted to wipe the slate clean of all traces of the Benavidez dynasty.

It was one of those big-city elections in which the winner is determined solely by the results of the Democratic primary. No Republican was about to take the House seat in District 6. Covering downtown, the West Side, the integrated but largely white area north of Eleventh Avenue in the Capitol Hill neighborhood, and a small piece of the African-American area around Five Points, District 6 was a rock-solid Democratic district in the inner city. It was here that Castro and Martinez slugged it out in the primary.

Martinez claims that had the primary been limited to West Denver, he would have won hands down. He was a native of the West Side, an usher at St. Joseph's Church, and a long-respected citizen of the community. It was only the Anglo Capitol Hill area, says Martinez, that won the election for Castro.[47]

An analysis of precincts in that 1974 primary shows Martinez was largely correct. With the final votes tabulated, Castro scored a resounding victory, winning 56 percent of the vote, 1,261 to 974. In precincts on the West Side, however, Martinez won a narrow victory, 618 to 596—a margin of twenty-two votes. Castro did well in the Baker area, the southern part of West Denver where he resided. But in the heart of the West Side—in Lincoln Park and Sunken Gardens and along the Santa Fe corridor where the West Side Coalition had once reigned supreme—Castro received only 36 percent of the votes. In those core West Side precincts, the vote was 315 to 179 for Martinez.[48]

Thus, in January 1975, as he prepared to enter the General Assembly and begin a new stage in his life, Richard Castro was not the all-conquering hero of the Chicano community. He had won his campaign as most football games are won; he had won imperfectly by making fewer mistakes and by taking advantage of the weaknesses of his opponent. He easily out-organized Manny Martinez and proved himself to be the sharper politician. But the little civil war on Denver's West Side had taken its toll. There were still many fences to mend and many wounds to heal.

ix

the state house

At age twenty-eight, Richard Castro rolled into the State Legislature with a wave of like-minded "young Turks." Enthusiastic reformers, a shade rebellious, they arrived ready to shake things up a bit in the traditionally conservative General Assembly. In 1968, they had flocked to the peace-oriented campaign of Bobby Kennedy, and, in 1972, to the idealistic agenda of George McGovern.

It was Richard Nixon who brought them to the State House in such numbers. His politics of vengeance, secrecy, and dirty tricks, as revealed in the circus surrounding the Watergate scandal, had so turned off the American electorate that they abandoned the Republicans in droves.

In 1975, Democrats broke the Republican hold on the State House of Representatives for the first time in a decade. They came to the table hungry, having spent years in the political wilderness. In the State Senate, however—slower to change—Republicans clung to a slim margin.[1]

As Castro entered the State House, an entirely new set of social conditions was rapidly transforming the Front Range. From half a world away, the effects of the Yom Kippur War in Israel swept into the Denver area like a windstorm. As the Organization of Petroleum Exporting Countries (OPEC) cut off the West's supply of crude oil, American and Canadian oil companies alike scoured every promising geological crevice for new sources of fuel. Their search brought massive quantities of investment capital to Denver, which became the administrative center for operations in the Williston Basin on the Dakota plains, in the Overthrust Belt in the western

Wyoming Rockies, and on the oil shale mesas of the Western Slope. Lyle Kyle, director of research for the Legislative Council and a savvy observer of the political scene, who worked for the legislature from 1958 to 1985, recalls, "You couldn't walk downtown without countin' two dozen cranes up in the air all at once. The money was just flowin' in."[2] Denver was becoming a sleek, sprawling, booming metropolis.

Suburban populations were swelling. The women's movement ignited a revolution in attitudes, which brought increasing numbers of women into positions of political power. And in the Capitol building, minority politicians were becoming more commonplace.

Not since its territorial years before Colorado became a state had so many Chicano legislators occupied the State House.[3] Though the Movement had suffered from disarray, the cumulative struggles of the last decade had provided enough momentum to bring political power to Chicanos more commensurate to their population. Of the 100 members in the General Assembly in 1975, seven were Chicano; that number rose to nine in 1977. This in a state where the Chicano population totaled 15 percent.

The road to Chicano power in the legislature had been paved earlier. Ruben Valdez, undisputed leader and mentor of a whole generation of Chicano lawmakers, entered the House in 1971. He had worked closely in the '60s with the Crusade for Justice but with the turn of the decade opted pragmatically to run on the Democratic ticket rather than La Raza Unida. "I talked it over with some of the folks," he says, "and Corky in particular. The mission of La Raza Unida was not really to elect candidates but was to bring issues to the forefront. Obviously, if we wanted to get elected, we had to participate in one of the two major parties. Those of us who wanted to get elected and serve knew that that's the way we had to go."[4]

In the House district running out to the Lakewood boundary just to the west of Rich Castro's District 6, Valdez defeated Jerry Bohn in the Democratic primary. The Bohn family had gained prominence on the far West Side by virtue of its ownership of Eddie Bohn's Pig and Whistle, a popular and colorful barbecue spot on West Colfax, and through Jerry's position on the State Boxing Commission. Valdez had honed his leadership skills in the United Steelworkers, having built a local base at the Continental Can Company. That Valdez could take on a formidable Anglo opponent and beat him handily signaled a shift in the political wind.

Racial tension perhaps overstates the case, but there was a certain discomfort in the overwhelmingly white legislature with the minority upsurge in the early 1970s. Lyle Kyle illustrates the atmosphere of the times. "If you're an Indian in Fort Lewis College in Durango, you get free tuition," Kyle relates in his Missouri drawl. "We were asked to look into that and we came to the conclusion that there was no real legal obligation on the part of the state to do that. But I'm tellin' you, the Indians came un-glued over that. I walked down to the Capitol one Saturday mornin' for a session and there were probably 200 Indians camped out on the north steps. I knocked on the door and the guard came and he said, 'I checked with my boss and all these people out here—he didn't want them takin' over the Capitol.' So I called the Speaker," continues Kyle, "and . . . we decided we can't lock citizens of the state out of the Capitol Building. . . . He ordered it unlocked. Well, the Indians went into the two chambers. . . . The bill passed in the Senate [although never in the House], which would have prohibited free tuition for anybody other than residents of Colorado. How they did it, I don't know to this day, but the tom-toms started beatin', and the drums started beatin', and they stood up and started chantin'. Now old Don McManus was in the Senate at the time, and I'm tellin' you, he dived under the desk. I mean he thought an arrow was gonna come at him any minute. It scared the crap out of people," he chuckled.[5]

A Chicano Becomes Speaker of the House

Ruben Valdez stepped into the political arena during this time of profound changes in race relations. Within a short period, Valdez won the utmost respect of legislators across the entire political spectrum, but there were some rough moments in the beginning.

"When Ruben first came into the legislature," recalls Kyle, "he had a mustache just like Corky Gonzales. And I swear to God, he almost looked like Corky, at least my stereotype of Corky. I thought, 'Oh boy. We are really going to have somebody that's gonna raise holy terror around here. . . . But he turned completely around—or rather the rest of us turned completely around in our attitude towards Ruben. We have tremendous regards for the man."[6]

The House followed a longstanding tradition that on their birthdays, representatives were required to bring a small gift—a candy bar or a pack of LifeSavers—to place on the desks of all the other House members. As it happened, Valdez's birthday came first, only three weeks into his first session. Pueblo's Tom Farley, the House's leading Democrat, having just been elected minority leader, stepped up to the microphone one January morning in 1971 and said, "Mr. Speaker, I want to announce that Representative Valdez's birthday is tomorrow and I think he should follow the tradition of bringing something for all the members."

Being the greenest of freshmen representatives, Valdez pondered what he should do all that afternoon before a thought crystallized in his mind while at the supermarket. Then, late into the night, he and Mrs. Valdez stayed up tying ribbons onto the long green chili peppers they purchased at the store. Next morning he had the sergeant-at-arms place the gifts on everybody's desks.

"I followed the instructions of the Minority Leader," Valdez announced at the microphone. "I know the tradition and I brought to you green chili, which is a traditional Mexican food. It's the Mexican LifeSaver because if you take one bite, there's no germ that can survive it."

It was the perfect touch. "It was humorous," recalls Valdez, "and it kind of helped to ease the tension in a way. But there was more than one message there. There was also the thing that I am proud to be a Mexican American, that I'm proud of my heritage, that I was sharing something with them of *our* culture and *our* tradition."[7]

When Don Sandoval—elected to the Senate in 1976—heard the story of chili peppers on the House floor, he remembers tears coming to his eyes. "It was like saying, 'the Mexicans are here,'" he said, in an arena where Mexicans had never before had access. "It was like South Africa today," continued Sandoval, referring to the political power blacks obtained for the first time in 1991.[8]

But in fact, there had been others before Valdez. Among them was Rich Castro's abiding hero, Casimiro Barela, the "perpetual senator" from Trinidad, who served forty-three years in the General Assembly between 1876 and 1919. "There is a stained-glass window dedicated to Casimiro Barela at the State Capitol," wrote Castro in an article for the journal *Nuestras Raices* in 1990. "When I served in the Colorado General Assembly, I used to go to that window and ponder what a great man he must have been. He gave me the strength to continue during difficult times. I only hope that some Hispanic young men or women rediscover the stories of Barela and others. For the younger generation of Hispanics will also contribute to our state in the years ahead."[9]

Castro was particularly aware of the historical significance of Chicanos in the legislature. Their power represented an accessibility long denied the community, and their stature made them effective role models for young people looking for adults to emulate. Castro's overriding dream—"El sueño de Rich Castro"—was to chronicle the lives of Hispanic members of the General Assembly, tracing their stories back to the Mexican-American War of 1848.

By the time Castro's post-Watergate generation came into office in 1975, Ruben Valdez had four years in the House under his belt and had set his sights on the role of speaker of the House. The speaker's position was a powerful one. Its secret lay in its appointive powers. All the essential way stations in the intricate process of guiding bills through the House lay in the hands of the speaker. The speaker appointed the chairman of the Rules Committee, who, at that time, could kill a bill before it even reached the floor. Of the guardians of the treasury who served on the all-important

House Appropriations Committee, the speaker appointed the majority. The caucus chair, who acted as a sort of whip to line up party votes for particular bills, was another speaker appointment.

In 1974, the Democrats held only twenty-six of the sixty-five seats in the Colorado House of Representatives. By the time the Watergate fiasco had run its course in January of 1975, the Democrats held thirty-nine seats, fully 60 percent of the House.[10]

"We had, first of all, a heavy influx of women legislators," recalls Valdez. "We had minority legislators. We had Democratic legislators from the suburbs, which was fairly rare. We had folks in the Democratic Caucus in numbers that traditionally hadn't been there."[11]

For a moment, Rich Castro hesitated in backing Valdez. The old shadow of factional fighting on the West Side followed him into the House. In the bitterly fought Senate race between Castro's friend, Betty Benavidez, and her challenger, Paul Sandoval, Valdez had backed the former. For a short time, Castro and Sandoval weren't even talking. They stared across the table at each other in Senator Roger Cisneros's office, the air thick with tension, until Castro realized the absurdity of the situation. After all, Castro and Sandoval had been old friends and classmates on the East Side. Neither had the luxury of continuing a grudge; now that Democrats had taken over the House, there was too much business to take care of. "OK," said Castro after a long pause, "I'll vote for Ruben."[12] The healing process began on that day.

The Role of Ruben Valdez

With new numbers in the House, with new young Democrats hungry, Ruben Valdez cakewalked into the speaker's position. He had studied well. He was unusually astute, and his first four years had given him a thorough understanding of the labyrinth through which each proposal had to be engineered.

Besides taking the reins of the machinery, Valdez took on an unofficial duty. It became his task to orient the new crop of Chicano legislators to the realities of their newfound power.

"One of the things I kept telling all the Hispanic legislators," relates Valdez, "is that we had to be well informed on *all* the issues. It wasn't enough to go in there and talk about civil rights. People expected us to do that. We had an obligation to do that and we *would* do that. But what I advised my colleagues was—if we were gonna be successful—we had to become experts in taxes and water law and other things that really affected a lot of Coloradans, but that were not traditional for us.

"I think that's where I surprised a lot of people. I became real knowledgeable in those areas and was able to articulate those concerns. That did two things. It enhanced my standing with my colleagues, but I also think it helped the other side realize that we had some legitimate points of view on all the issues. As a result, we gained a lot of respect and were able to have more success than most people thought we would.

"It's a lesson I learned early in life," Valdez continues. "I knew I could compete with anybody and I . . . knew the way to do that is to let people know you understand the issues, that you were on top of them and that you were not just a representative for a minority community, but that you were a *state* representative that could deal with anything. Part of [why I was elected originally to union office] was that I was able to demonstrate . . . that I was broad-based and not focused only on one particular issue. . . . The thing you're looking for is respect and if you have respect, people will listen to you even when they may not always agree. But when people don't have respect for you or your position or your knowledge . . . they'll tend to shut you off. . . . You're not going to be able to succeed if you don't have an audience. . . . I was [also] listening to the other side and getting other points of view, so we didn't go in with closed minds. The art of compromise is something you learn in the legislature."[13]

From his position as speaker, Valdez set the standards high for the new breed of legislators and generally won praise across the political spectrum. His philosophy seeped through and often guided the behavior of his newer colleagues. Castro, for instance, sponsored legislation on everything from boxing reform to handicapped parking spaces to mandatory sentencing for possession of a firearm by a juvenile. He served on committees ranging from Education to Health, Environment and Welfare, to Correction Oversight. "Castro has gone to bat," wrote *Denver Post* political columnist Carl Hilliard, "for veterans suffering from the effects of Agent Orange, prisoners at the State Penitentiary, folks who have trouble getting places to rent and then paying the rent when they do find them; and for people [ripped off] by unscrupulous car dealers and loan sharks and utility companies."[14]

The Chicano Caucus
Despite Valdez's emphasis on "broad-based" issues, there was still the Chicano community to protect and the new Hispanic lawmakers gathered together regularly to discuss the impact of laws on their own people. Seat belt laws, for example. Would the cops bear down harder on a young Mexican cruising West Thirty-eighth Avenue with unlatched seat belts than on a businessman on his way home to Cherry Hills? (Of course.) What about the unacceptable dropout rate at West High, or North High, or even Baker Middle School? Could changes in school financing help to stem the tide?[15]

Over beers at the Guadalajara on Larimer Street ("It's a dive but they served up good *caldo de res*"),[16] or at Leo Lucero's apartment house in Capitol Hill, the newly emerging group of Chicano lawmakers threw their ideas out on the table, formulated strategies, and hashed out priorities. The Chicano Caucus met every Thursday for lunch. Through the mid- and late '70s, their numbers grew steadily.

The new numbers signaled the end of a long drought of political power for the Latino community.[17] Beginning in the 1920s when the Ku Klux Klan rode high in Colorado politics, Hispanic representation was reduced to the barest trickle. From the beginning of World War II through the mid-1950s, not a single Mexican American could be found in the State Capitol. Even in the mid-'50s, Chicano legislators were the rare exception. Bert Gallegos took office in 1955.[18] Frankie Anaya, Waldo Benavidez's mentor, entered the House in the early '60s. ("He only got elected because his name started with 'A'," says one observer in commenting on the odds for a Chicano victory at that time.)[19] Gallegos and Anaya were the exceptions that proved the rule.

The real change began in the mid-'60s. Known as the "One Man, One Vote" decision, the Supreme Court in 1964 began throwing out apportionment plans for state legislatures in a number of states including Colorado.[20] In effect, the Court ruled that you could not have one legislator from southeast Colorado representing 25,000 citizens while another from Denver represented 50,000. No longer could rural interests in the legislature overshadow large metropolitan areas. The Supreme Court threw the whole system back to the state General Assembly for a major overhaul. At the same time, another related issue was working its way to the forefront. In those days, all seventeen representatives from Denver were elected "at large," as were its eight senators. District-wide voting—the closer-to-home approach—with lawmakers representing clusters of neighborhoods was nonexistent. "If your name didn't start with A, B, C, or D," said Lyle Kyle, "you didn't have much chance."[21] The whole setup effectively eliminated minority representation. A Garcia or a Sanchez with a 90-percent popularity rating in West Denver stood little chance of defeating a white candidate in a citywide election. The same logic held true for blacks in northeast Denver.

When the State Legislature completed its new apportionment plan in the wake of the One Man, One Vote decision, the rules of the game changed entirely. Ironically, it was the Republicans, not minority discontent, that tipped the scales in favor of district-wide voting. Under the old system, Denver's seventeen representatives were invariably Democrats. Republicans surmised that they could nibble away at the edges of Democratic hegemony in the big city. In the more prosperous southern regions of Denver, they figured they could win three or four or five contests under a district-wide voting system. Perhaps inadvertently, then, Republicans struck a blow for minority representation. Under the new district voting plan, West or North or East Denverites could directly choose their own representatives for the first time.[22]

The change happened about the same time that Chicanos were beginning to awaken to new possibilities of asserting power. It coincided also with the time that Waldo Benavidez was running around town making a nuisance of himself to established Democratic Party officials by encouraging Mexicans to run for office even against long-term Democratic incumbents.[23] It wasn't long before these changes began to pay off.

With his election to the State Senate in 1966, Judge Roger Cisneros was the first to benefit from the switch to district-wide elections. Then came Paco Sanchez, the old radio announcer from the East Side. In 1971, Ruben Valdez and Betty Benavidez took their places in the General Assembly. Polly Baca Barragan came in from the Adams County suburbs in 1974, and then came Castro and Senator Paul Sandoval, swept in with the post-Watergate wave.

By the late 1970s, the Chicano Caucus totaled nine members. Valdez, the "elder" statesman, was still around. Leo "The Flash" Lucero—so named for his style of dress—was commuting up I-25 from Pueblo. Castro remained the representative from the West Side and north Capitol Hill. Polly Baca-Barragan moved over to the Senate and took her place with Paul Sandoval and his cousin Don Sandoval, who arrived in 1976. Laura DeHerrera and George Chávez came aboard in 1978, the same year a slender, boyish-looking young Texan, destined to change Denver's history, entered the House of Representatives. His name was Federico Peña.

Like other legislators, the new crop of Hispanic lawmakers soon realized that the bulk of legislative work rarely consisted of glamorous, dramatic battles pitting the forces of social change against conservative defenders of the status quo. More likely, the daily routine dealt with an infinite array of minute details guaranteed to put the average guy on the street to sleep.

"Friendships and respect in the legislature," says Lyle Kyle, "cross party lines. Most people think the Democrats wear certain colors and the Republicans wear others and you can easily identify them. For the ordinary observer goin' up and watchin' the legislature in action, I doubt very seriously—if no one told you where they sit or what they're doing—that you could tell a Republican from a Democrat. We had a bill one time on gettin' rid of barn and garden manure and regulatin' fertilizer. Now who in the devil would want to make a partisan issue out of that? That's 95 or 98 percent of the legislation the General Assembly considers, things that are not related to partisan politics."[24]

Castro used to joke about paying his dues as a rookie legislator by carrying out a committee obligation to sponsor a "cooling off" period for marriage. Under the law, couples had to wait five days after the issuance of a license before they could get married.[25] Not exactly the stuff of great partisan battles.

Nevertheless, there were times and issues when lines were drawn in the sand. They usually dealt with money, but sometimes they reflected the clash of cultures and distribution of political power. The Chicano Caucus surveyed the field of play and determined to marshal its forces around several issues that were destined to have an unsettling affect on American politics: bilingual education, affirmative action, and reapportionment. These were the things they would fight for. And their struggles set the stage for some of the most explosive controversies of later decades. As an integral team player on the caucus, Castro played key roles in each of them.

The Bilingual/Bicultural Issue

No two issues lay closer to the heart of Chicano lawmakers than education and language. "Without education," says State Senator Paul Sandoval, "you had nothing. With education, the doors were open to you. We were all cognizant of that."[26] They had seen it materialize in their own personal lives. Practically all of the new Chicano legislators had been the first in their family to get college degrees. Since his early days at Metro, Castro had seen education as a cure for social ills.

At the intersection of language and education stood the issue of bilingual education. A searing and emotionally charged topic, it sprang immediately to the forefront.

Language was an issue that touched the inner feelings of each of the Chicano legislators because so many of their childhood memories, their early identities, and their most soulful reminiscences were immersed in the Spanish language. From the cradle, Rich Castro grew up hearing the language of his grandparents, Trinidad and Lucinda McGrath. One of Castro's favorite stories dealt with a toast Trinidad delivered at a party given on the occasion of the couple's anniversary. The dignified old man always struggled with English; you could almost see the internal gears grinding away in his native language before English passed haltingly from his throat. On this particular evening, he wanted deeply to express the romantic feelings he still held for his beloved. He raised his glass and addressed the whole party: "When I think of all the years with my beautiful wife"—he hesitated at this juncture, searching for the words to express his deep feeling, and chanced upon the Spanish word *enfermado*, which in a certain context means "deeply moved." The literal translation, however, doesn't always catch that context. "When I think of all the years with my beautiful wife, it makes me sick," he said, as he translated directly from Spanish to English. Castro would roar upon telling this story without the least bit of condescension towards his grandfather, whom he held in the greatest esteem.[27]

If there was mortification over the matter of language, it was not at his grandfather's inability to master the vagaries of English; it was his own failure to retain the language of his ancestors that caused Rich Castro profound embarrassment. Somewhere in the confusion of the Davy Crockett movies of the '50s, of the Motown sound of the '60s, of the everyday American life at Annunciation, and at his northeast Denver home, Castro had lost the language his grandparents had brought with them from their New Mexico homeland. Castro viewed the loss as tragic.

As were all of his colleagues, Castro was familiar with endless stories of peers for whom language problems represented towering obstacles in school. Senator Paul Sandoval was one of the lucky ones. He grew up just beyond the packinghouses along Fifty-eighth Avenue, an area which today serves as a launching pad for mile after mile of northern suburb. In the '40s and '50s it was pure farmland. Every day, as his father headed for the Cudahy packinghouse, Sandoval and his mom left for the beet fields in Adams County. In the fields, there was but one language, Spanish, and that is what the younger Sandoval spoke until he enrolled at Annunciation. He had only had a smattering of English until Sister Mary O'Nita took him under her wing and tutored him daily after school. "I'll never forget her," says Sandoval. "She did that every day for two years."[28]

Roger Medina, the East Side gang unit police officer and one of Castro's closest buddies at Annunciation, experienced harder times. As a child, Medina had traveled up a well-worn path starting from the little town of San Pablo in the San Luis Valley. His father had hired on as a ranch hand in Platteville some forty miles north of Denver. "I had a lotta problems there," recalls Medina, "because I couldn't speak English. Where I came from *everybody* spoke Spanish. In Platteville, I couldn't understand a lotta stuff. The kids would laugh at you and tease you. They always made fun of me because of my accent. In them days, of course, the teachers labeled you a troublemaker because my answer to everything was right here in my fist. You're gonna get even, you know. You don't care, at least I didn't. I started hittin' people. Instead of goin' to school, I'd get off the bus and I'd walk into town."

By the time the Medina family arrived on the East Side a couple of years later, Roger's school career was fast slipping into oblivion. A lost boy from the country, he enrolled at Sacred Heart, around the corner from the Sunshine Tavern where his dad worked as a bartender. He was embraced by the elderly in the neighborhood for his fluency in Spanish, but he received no such affection from his new school. "It was a Catholic school," says Medina, "and I never been to no Catholic school. You ask about trouble. Yeah, I got in trouble; I didn't know the rules of the game there. First day, some nun comes out there and rings a bell and everybody stands still. I'm still shootin' baskets, dribblin' the ball, and arguin' with some kid. Then they ring the bell again and everybody's s'posed to run up and get in line. I bounced the ball a couple of times—splat, splat, splat—before I realize what's going on. Well this nun, Sister Ruth Marion, had already looked at me anyway, bouncin' the ball. She comes up and she says, 'You boob.' I'll never forget it. I said, 'What?!' Well, you're s'posed to say 'Yes, Sister,' or 'No, Sister.' 'I can see we're gonna have problems with you,' she said. They had already labeled me a smart-ass, I guess."

"The second day they threw me out. There was this guy by the name of James Reier, who apparently was the bully of the school. This guy kept causing problems and antagonizing. I didn't want none of that stuff and I kept tellin' him that, but it seemed to make matters worse. That Friday, the kids were laughin' and teasing as we got in line. On the way up, I got outta line to get some water. That's when this guy hits me on the back of the head and I hit my mouth on the drinking fountain. I went off on him with one of the bells they used to ring on the balcony rails and I tried to throw him off the balcony. They threw me outta school 'cuz they thought I was just problems."[29]

Following a parent conference, Medina eventually did return to Sacred Heart and did graduate. His bouncing ball story would bring spasms of laughter to Rich Castro as well as tears of compassion. It illustrates the complexity of the whole dilemma: the difficulties of rural migration, the cruelties of children, the rigidity of some schoolteachers. But just as surely, it traces a portion of the roots of the brawling and the defiance, the hostile behavior, and the ditching of school back to a central problem: language. How does a bewildered six-year-old kid function in a first-grade class with barely a dozen words of English?

Sandoval and Medina—these were East Denver boys. They had not journeyed from Jalisco or Sonora or some other state south of the Rio Grande. They were fifth-generation Americans. Their families had farmed in the Valley before Denver was a city. And they had required special attention—urgent attention—to complete their education.

Losing the Language

The more assimilated Rich Castro had lost the language of his grandparents, neither through calculation nor conspiracy; it simply slipped away over the years like an ephemeral stream in the late summer prairie. For others, the process was more conscious. "As we were growing up," states

Jack Lang y Marquez, director of the Colorado Civil Rights Commission, "English was the primary language in the home and Spanish was seldom used except around my grandparents. That was done as a very deliberate choice by my parents, who didn't want us to grow up experiencing the discrimination that occurs when you speak with an accent. They insisted that we speak only English, somewhat to my regret. I think it was a common experience around the time that I grew up. Where parents *could* raise their children to speak English, they did. . . . There was enough discrimination based on surnames and based on color of skin without adding to that by speaking strangely, speaking with an accent."[30]

For over a century after the Treaty of Guadalupe Hidalgo, American educational policy toward the Spanish language, at least insofar as Mexican Americans were concerned, consisted of a variation on an old theme: stamp it out; kill it before it multiplies. Every Chicano legislator remembered stories their parents and grandparents told them. Talk Spanish on the schoolyard and end up standing in a corner or leaning against the blackboard wearing a dunce cap. Stan Steiner tells of children forced to kneel in the playground for speaking a Spanish word or having to write 'I will not speak Spanish in school' five hundred times on the blackboard.[31] To children growing up in the San Luis Valley or along the Rio Grande in Texas, this sent a clear message: The Spanish language does not quite measure up. And if this were true, what about the people who spoke it?[32] No wonder Corky Gonzales had written that American schools had taught him only to forget his heritage.

Before 1968, no fewer than twenty-one states legislated that schools teach only in English. In Texas, a teacher risked criminal penalties or revocation of license for teaching in a language other than English.[33] Spanish clearly represented a threat. It was, in the eyes of most American educators, an obstacle to learning English and an obstacle to the assimilation process.

Scholarly research had begun to question those assumptions. In 1965, in his book *Spanish-Speaking Children of the Southwest*, Herschel T. Manuel offered conclusions stemming from three decades of experience. "As the world grows smaller," he wrote, "the ability to communicate in a language which is used by millions of other people becomes a matter of increasing practical importance from the standpoint of international understanding and cooperation. Too, competence in more than one language widens the horizon of an individual and makes significant contribution to his intellectual life. It provides a source of deep personal satisfaction as well. From this point of view, the ability in Spanish, which a child develops in his home, is an asset to be cultivated rather than carelessly cast aside. The chief practical hope for conserving and developing this asset is found in the school." Elaborating on the psychological aspect of this topic, Manuel went on to say, "There is no place for a policy which makes a child ashamed of his mother tongue."[34]

George Sanchez, another respected scholar on the subject, wrote, "We all love to be addressed *'en la lengua que mamamos*—in the language we suckled.' When a child enters a school that appears to reject the only words he can use, 'He is adversely affected in every aspect of his being.'"[35]

This, then, provided the context for Chicano legislators when they took up the torch for bilingual education during Castro's first legislative session in 1975. They had seen their friends or themselves diminished by the mainstream attitude toward the Spanish language. They had all known kids whose self-worth had been devastated by disrespect for a language that, like Navajo or Ute, had been native to American soil when the English speakers arrived. They all understood the necessity of learning English, but they did not accept the necessity of denigrating Spanish in the process.

The debate had invaded the national scene in the previous decade. In the early '60s, the primary strategy for instructing children whose native tongue was not English was to pull them out of regular classes for forty-five or sixty minutes a day and give them intensive instruction in English. The rest of their subjects—math, history, and science—were taught in English in the standard classroom. Typically, as they were learning English, students fell two to three years behind in other subject areas.[36] One writer observed that "the most conspicuous failure group in the American educational system is composed of children whose home language is not English."[37] Surveying the dismal situation in his native Texas, Senator Ralph Yarborough began sponsoring legislation in 1967 to provide an alternative curriculum.[38]

The Federal Program

It was not until the following year, however, that Representative James Scheuer of New York succeeded in passing Title VII of the Elementary and Secondary Education Act to the United States Congress.[39] What Scheuer introduced became known as the Bilingual Education Act, a piece of legislation whose purpose was to provide English-language skills while simultaneously maintaining native language skills and supporting the cultural heritage of the students.

It was backed with scarce resources. In 1973, for instance, Congress authorized only $35 million to support 213 bilingual projects in thirty-two states. In those days, federal money provided merely a token gesture or an initial boost. A comprehensive program would require state commitment as well.

As Castro entered his first session of the General Assembly in January of 1975, the Chicano Caucus had selected bilingual/bicultural education as its number-one priority. It was no radical piece of legislation. It provided for no more than three years of initial instruction in the native tongue for students in any school where fifty children or 10 percent of the student body were identified as linguistically or culturally different.[40] Previous attempts at similar legislation had succeeded in getting only a small amount of seed money. That year, with a Democratic-controlled House, the Chicano Caucus vowed to win. Senator Roger Cisneros sponsored the bill in the Senate and Leo Lucero did likewise in the House.

A far-reaching Supreme Court decision the previous year reinforced their cause. In *Lau vs. Nichols*, 1,800 Chinese-American students in San Francisco challenged school policies that compelled them to take classes only in English, even though they understood hardly a word of it.[41] In upholding the plaintiffs' case, the Court wrote that requiring children to have already acquired basic skills before they can participate in the educational process is "to make a mockery of public education. We know that those who do not understand English are certain to find their classroom experiences wholly incomprehensible and in no way meaningful."[42] The court ruled that the school district had a responsibility to help these students overcome their language barrier. Although it did not specify bilingual education as the only solution, the Court's recommendations lent tremendous impetus to the bilingual movement.

In the Colorado General Assembly, the vote of the House, under the leadership of Ruben Valdez, was a foregone conclusion. The Republican-controlled Senate, led by Majority Leader Dick Plock, was a different story. Littleton Republican Hugh Fowler was outspoken in his opposition. "It was extremely controversial. Oh my, yes!" recalls Paul Sandoval. "I never saw racial tension in the legislature. The only time it reared its head—and that was immediately—was upon the introduction of the Bilingual Bill. . . . I could never say Hugh Fowler's speeches bordered on racism. It was always, 'It's bad education. It's bad for America; it's bad for Colorado. It costs too much money. We have to be united together; we can't be split. I never heard one racist comment from anyone. . . . The whole tone was, 'If you're American you have to speak American. You're in Colorado. Why do you need two different cultures? You're gonna divide the city. You're gonna divide the state. It's gonna be another Quebec. The Crusade for Justice is gonna take it over. We don't need it.'"[43] In a General Assembly, whose style was largely congenial and non-partisan, the Bilingual/Bicultural Act deeply polarized the lawmakers.

"I'm sure [the racism] was there," continues Sandoval. I just never heard it. Part of that was because I was on the Joint Budget Committee and they didn't want to piss me off."[44]

Guiding Bills through the Senate

Therein lies one of the secrets to the bill's passage. The Joint Budget Committee wields tremendous clout, and in the year 1975, party lines on the committee were split right down the middle. Two Democrats held positions in the House, and then there was Sandoval from the Senate. For the Republicans, there were two from the Senate and one from the House. It was a 3-3 tie. "Oh, boy," says Sandoval, "there was a lot of horse trading."[45] Through all the trading, Sandoval was able to win the support of Republican senator Joe Shoemaker, whose position as chairman of the JBC made him one of those crucial leaders no one wanted to cross.[46] Thus, in the rough and tumble deal-making inherent in a split General Assembly, the Bilingual/Bicultural Act slid through the process.

Senator Don Sandoval, Paul's cousin, attributes much credit for the bill's passage to Ruben Valdez. Speaker Valdez and Majority Leader Plock were the two most powerful men in the General Assembly, and they used a mediator—Lyle Kyle—to communicate with one another.[47] Valdez insists the two were "real good friends; we had some tough partisan battles . . . but there was no animosity."[48] Nevertheless, they did not talk to each other about political issues; Kyle did their talking for them. Sandoval maintains that Plock indicated the Bilingual Bill would never make it through the Senate and that no "special legislation for immigrants" was needed. "Ruben got real unhappy," says Sandoval, "and said 'OK, fine. No Senate bills are coming through the House.' So Ruben just shut down all those Senate bills and told Plock he wasn't willing to talk until he'd talk about bilingual education. That's how much power Ruben had. And that's how we got the bill."[49]

The bill's passage in 1975 did nothing to abate the controversy. As the Watergate backlash faded rapidly, Republicans regained control of both chambers within a year. A legislative battle ensued every year thereafter. In 1977, for instance, Carl Showalter, a Republican representative from Greeley, stepped up to the microphone during a debate on bilingual and got so angry that Speaker of the House Ron Strahle (Fort Collins, Republican) had to intervene. "Calm down," Strahle told him, advising him to confine his remarks to the bill. Showalter was claiming that the program was a "divisive force within communities."[50] Confessing that his amendments to the bill were designed to cut back the program, Showalter said, with his voice rising, "Yes, ladies and gentlemen, it's designed to narrow the scope of the programs. If you want to know where [the bill] came from, it came from me and people in my district and people who don't have activist groups going around the state."[51]

The level of emotional intensity indicated that the dispute might include more than just which language to teach in. One of the side issues involved provisions in the original bill, which called for parent participation in the newly established programs. The 1975 legislation called on local school boards to recognize committees made up of parents from the community and to give them some input into the decision-making process.[52] In a sense, this foreshadowed the Collaborative Decision Making committees that have operated in the Denver Public Schools. Thus, committees at elementary schools all over North and West Denver—at Del Pueblo and Valdez, at Remington and Bryant Webster—sprang up to oversee the new bilingual programs, and many Chicano parents for the first time became involved in their children's schools. Nowhere did this have a more explosive effect than in the San Luis Valley, where languages and cultures had clashed for over a century.

Language Struggle in the Valley

In Center, Colorado, an agricultural town in the heart of the valley known for its lettuce and potatoes, 65 percent of the schoolchildren were Chicano, but the school board was overwhelmingly white.[53] A 1973 strike in the lettuce fields bitterly polarized the community, and Hispanics for the first time confronted the local power structure. In a sense, the bilingual fight represented an extension of the economic and political struggle.

Every little concession required a battle. For instance, when elections for the bilingual committee were first set up, the school board refused to allow absentee ballots. This might have appeared reasonable if the election had not been scheduled in the middle of the potato harvest, when most Chicanos could not vote. It produced a bitter parental protest before the board reluctantly gave in.[54] Even then, at every turn, the school board insisted that the bilingual program was ineffective, and that the number of Spanish-speaking students was not sufficient to justify the program in the first place. For two years, Chicano parents made repeated trips to Denver to complain that the school system was in "open and blatant defiance" of the bilingual law. An investigation by the state attorney general's office reached the same conclusion. The Center School Board, said the report, was in violation of the Bilingual/Bicultural Act.[55]

The dispute tapped a much deeper reservoir of resentment. The Center School Board blamed the whole dispute on a "well-funded political activist group" using "activist tactics."[56] Its terms echoed the language of white governors in Mississippi and Alabama who, in earlier decades, used the "outside agitator" label to discredit the Civil Rights Movement.

In his angry outburst on the House floor, Representative Showalter echoed the very words of the Center School Board. The term "activist" had been relegated to the status of a dirty word. Bilingual education represented a threat to the status quo, in part, because it was inciting Chicano parents to confront school administrators about their children's education.

The polarization and the decibel level of the rhetoric caused Senator Paul Sandoval to declare in disgust that bilingual education had become one "big political football" with no opportunity to prove itself as an educational program. "We haven't been given a chance to see if it will work," he argued before the Senate Education Committee.[57] Conservatives sought to destroy bilingual education before it even got off the ground. The dispute made the new crop of lawmakers very conscious of the limits of their power. "Hispano Legislators in for Major Test of Power," read a 1977 headline in *The Denver Post* describing the upcoming battle over the legislation.[58] By that time, Republicans had already regained the majority in both houses of the General Assembly; Democrats were a diminishing minority.

Chicano lawmakers had insufficient power to withstand the increasing opposition. The last-ditch weapons they held were the interpretive powers of the federal courts and the veto power of Democratic governor Dick Lamm. For a few years, Lamm's veto power held the conservatives at bay, but in the end the courts proved a more loyal ally. In 1981, Lamm surveyed the local and national situation, agonized over the consequences, and then cast his fate with the opponents of bilingual education. It was a far-reaching decision that would impact the political climate in Colorado for years to come. Rich Castro found himself deeply entangled in the ensuing controversy.

The fierce debates in Colorado in the late 1970s provided a preview in microcosm of similar discord on a national scale. As the country rallied to Ronald Reagan's conservative politics in the 1980s, the issue of bilingualism in the classroom, as well as in civil society, spawned a nationwide reaction.

The Center for Equal Opportunity, for instance, began in the early 1980s to launch attacks on bilingual education with a wide range of criticisms. Interpreting a maze of confusing and contradictory studies, the center concluded that the use of bilingual education was no more effective in teaching English than other methods, and oftentimes was less effective. It argued that too often the desires of individual parents were disregarded. Kids were placed in bilingual classrooms against the will of the child's parents. Further, bilingual tended to segregate Latino kids, separating them into their own distinct clusters.[59] These represented powerful arguments and tended to undercut the already diminishing support for bilingual education.

On a deeper, sometimes subconscious level, however, there was something fearful in Reagan's America about teaching a "strange" language in an American classroom. With all the increasing prosperity, at least in the upper half of American society, a certain uneasiness settled in, an anxiety about global directions. Bilingualism and bilingual education seemed to increase that anxiety. It was divisive, argued its opponents; it ran counter to the idea of assimilating Spanish speakers into the American mainstream. There was a lot of talk of the need for social glue to keep the disparate elements of American society together. If respect for diversity had been the watchword of the '70s, the electorate in the '80s and '90s wanted a return to uniformity.

For all the potency of their arguments, there remains in the writings of bilingual education's critics a failure to take into account the history of the Southwest. Their historical amnesia erased the memory of the San Luis Valley, the manitos of northern New Mexico, and the generations of Spanish-speaking Texans, who had ridden the migrant circuit since the beginning of the century. Had there never been an American conquest of Mexico, had there never been a Treaty of Guadalupe Hidalgo and a takeover of communal land from Mexican farmers, had Depression-era deportations of Mexicans never occurred, had Chicano students never been forced to kneel on the school ground for speaking Spanish, then there need be no dialogue about the nature of assimilation. Had all these events never occurred, the policy toward Mexican Americans might rightfully be the same as toward other voluntary immigrants from Italy, Germany, or Russia. Learn English, get a job, move to the suburbs, accept the monoculture, and enjoy the American dream. If one wished to carry on the traditions of one's grandparents, do so quietly in the privacy of your own home and don't make a political issue of it.

But all of these events had occurred. Many Mexican Americans came to the United States not through immigration but through conquest, and the doors to American success were closed to them for over a century. The Mexican experience was vastly different from the immigrant experience, and it required different solutions. History argued for a dialogue and for compromises on the ways Mexican Americans should relate to American society, for a give and take, for a healing time. Castro and the Hispanic politicians in the General Assembly should be seen in the context of that dialogue.

There lies within the debate over bilingual education layer upon layer of incredible complexity. What is the purpose of bilingual education? Is it to hasten the transition to English? Is it to make Hispanic kids more comfortable in their classroom settings and thereby lower the dropout rate? Or is it to nurture the heritage of the Spanish language and thus encourage the culture to flourish side by side with English-speaking culture? Is its goal simply to carve out a modicum of respect and dignity for a people long abused by the majority culture? Is it to sow seeds for a more multicultural understanding by encouraging mainstream kids to learn

Spanish? At least in their public posture, Hispanic legislators in the '70s, like Sandoval and Castro, stressed educational efficiency: the transition to English and the lowering of the dropout rate. In choosing this arena, they sometimes fell into a hopeless morass of contradictory educational data. More often than not, particular educational strategies are less important than the individual effectiveness of the teachers who implement them, or of the myriad unique school climates where they are put to the test. Disparities and contradictions discovered by researchers would naturally abound. Nevertheless, the dialogue these Chicano lawmakers unleashed reverberated far beyond the dry data of educational studies; it touched on assimilation, immigration, and multiculturalism and reached deeply into the national psyche.

Affirmative Action

Bilingual education was not the only contentious issue in which Castro, in his quiet and behind-the-scenes manner, participated. There was affirmative action, an abrasive issue today if there ever was one. A study published in 1970 by the Equal Employment Opportunity Commission had come to the not very startling conclusion that "Hispanos are victims of educational and vocational discrimination which keeps them in blue collar jobs."[60] In a sense, Castro's early student career at Metro and at the University of Denver consisted of one big struggle for affirmative action. UMAS, his training ground for political activity, had essentially a single goal: to make college education a reality for as many Chicanos as could fit in the doors. Castro's goals were similar at the DU School of Social Work. If social workers were needed disproportionately on the West Side, or in Curtis Park, or in Northwest Denver, then it only made sense to train more Hispanic social workers. The idea then was to hurdle over barriers that had been generations in the making. Both justice and pragmatism required that universities specifically recruit minorities and provide them with scholarships and remedial training if necessary.

In the 1970s, no apologies seemed necessary for this sort of attitude. The idea behind affirmative action in jobs was rooted in the reality that six or seven generations after the Treaty of Guadalupe Hidalgo, vast segments of middle-class jobs remained inaccessible to the average Chicano. Where calculated discrimination failed, social networks stepped in to preserve jobs for the white middle class. White kids from southeast Denver or Lakewood frequently looked to an uncle who owned a small machine shop, a friend of the family who did subcontracting, or one of Dad's fraternity brothers who worked with an accounting firm to provide the kind of entry-level jobs that served as gateways to middle-class life. When East Side boys looked to their uncles, they were more likely to find men suffering disabilities from fifteen years of backbreaking work at Armour Packing, which had recently shut down its Denver operations and left the city. No intentional discrimination here, but the result was the same. Chicano kids had a tougher time breaking into that circle of middle-class privilege still protected by the social connections built up during the age of blatant discrimination. That protection represented a sort of white man's affirmative action program, that had been operating for a couple of centuries. If Chicanos wanted a piece of the middle class, they needed to break into the circle; they needed to establish a beachhead. Affirmative action was one of the few weapons available.

The political tide, however, was no longer on the rise during Castro's legislative years. No militant movement stood by to back up demands. So Chicano legislators restricted themselves to give-and-take negotiations with a Republican legislature and an increasingly conservative Governor Lamm. In 1977, the General Assembly grudgingly approved a plan offered by the State Personnel Board designed to close the gap between the percentage of minorities in the state population and the proportion that held government jobs. Dubbed the "three-plus-three" policy, the plan called on state agencies in which minorities and women were under-represented to fill vacancies from two lists of three names each. The first list contained the names of the top three finishers on the examination. The second list contained the names of the top three minority or female candidates for the post. Agencies had to select an employee from one of the six. The bill specifically excluded a formal quota system.[61]

Although Chicano legislators lobbied heavily for the measure, the threat of lawsuits against the state for violating anti-discrimination laws probably had a more persuasive effect.[62] Despite the unpopularity of the policy among conservative legislators, three-plus-three helped spur upward mobility in the state's minority population. The State Personnel Board governed some 26,000 employees at that time. During the ten-year period following, about 1,000 minority individuals were hired under the three-plus-three program.[63]

Perhaps equally effective were the informal efforts of the Chicano Caucus in alliance with black leaders, such as Wellington and Wilma Webb, Regis Groff, and Arie Taylor. "We would push to make sure that state agencies made it a priority to hire blacks, Chicanos, American Indians, and Asians on all levels," recalls Senator Paul Sandoval. "A particular issue I remember . . . was the Highway Patrol, which had a very limited number of Hispanics and blacks. We fought very hard to increase those numbers. We'd be with the heads of the departments sayin', 'How many blacks, how many Hispanics, how many American Indians [are there]? When are openings coming? When are you gonna hire more?' Yeah, we pushed very hard.

They knew if you're meeting with six or seven Chicano legislators and three black—you've got a hundred people in the legislature—you're dealing with 10 percent of the legislature! And if that 10 percent of the legislature has power, and I mean the power of the budget, the power of the Speaker, the power of committee chairmanship, you bet they're gonna listen to you.

"You didn't have open resistance. You would have the same old thing of 'Well, we don't have enough qualified applicants.' [Then we'd say,] 'What happened to so and so and so and so,' because we knew they applied. We never went in there making claims that we couldn't back up."[64]

The caucus would go as a group—ten strong—for maximum effect. They would walk into the Highway Patrol office on East Arkansas, for instance, and their numbers would cause the chief to scramble and bring additional captains and lieutenants into the meeting. "We called it 'picking off' if they just talked to one of us," says Sandoval. "Instead, we'd all go in there and say, 'We're all in agreement.' The best time to do it was when they had to face all ten of you."

Did their numbers tend to intimidate? "Sure they did," continues Sandoval. "We'd meet with college presidents—Metro State and CSU. They'd say, 'Am I just gonna meet with you, Rich, or you, Paul?' 'No, all ten of us want to meet with you.' My God, they'd bring in the chancellor, the president, some vice-presidents. I mean they all came. Absolutely we used group dynamics. It was a strategy that we used very effectively."[65]

These early battles helped set the stage for the entrance of increasing numbers of Chicanos into the American middle class in the 1980s. In addition to the thousand minorities hired by the state under the three-plus-three program, Governor Roy Romer appointed 125 Hispanics to state boards and commissions. Clearly, federal and municipal policies added to the momentum. University and college policies, spurred in part by affirmative action, began to increase the numbers of diplomas awarded to Hispanics. Thus, the Chicano middle class began to proliferate in the Denver area, from Littleton in the south to Broomfield in the north. The middle-class Chicano wave cannot be attributed solely to affirmative action programs, but those programs certainly pushed the process along.

Reapportionment

The issue of reapportionment—so crucial to the original creation of the Chicano Caucus—came up again with the new 1980 census, and Castro played a key role. As assistant House minority leader, he was appointed to the Colorado Reapportionment Commission, the eleven-person agency mandated to redraw district lines for legislators for the next decade. In later articles in *La Voz* and the *Colorado Statesman*, Castro argued the importance of the entire process. "Hispanic and other minorities have been denied access to political power by various means in the past," he wrote. "These include at-large election schemes, the carving up of Hispanic neighborhoods by placing them in different legislative districts [i.e., gerrymandering], and by regressive voter registration laws."[66]

"It is critically important," he wrote in *La Voz*, "that the Hispanic community understand this process and play a role in redrawing these districts. Reapportionment means whether or not our community will have a voice in the elective process."[67]

Upon his appointment to the commission, Castro worked closely with Pete Reyes, a lawyer who chaired a group of Democratic Party activists called the Coalition of Democratic Chicano Caucuses.

Reyes put the matter a little more bluntly. "We always got jerked over in reapportionment," he said, "and we were not gonna get jerked over again." They feared, for instance, the chopping up of Senator Don Sandoval's district in West Denver. "Sandoval," said Reyes, "had the West Side—everything from the Highway [Interstate 25] west to the [Jefferson] county line on Sheridan and everything from Twenty-sixth Avenue down to Westwood." A basically Chicano area. If the commission cut that district in half, Sandoval's job was on the line. "They might lump Westwood [a poor Chicano area dotted with projects and Section 8 housing]," continues Reyes, "with a lot of Southwest Denver folks [in the whiter and more affluent Bear Valley area]. Then they'd lump the other half of the district in with the [majority white] Capitol Hill neighborhood."[68] In this way, a demographically unified area in terms of income, ethnic grouping, and community would be chopped up and its voting power diluted.

Castro's strategy was to organize hearings all over the state. "It doesn't do me any good to be out here," he told Reyes, "unless I can have good people to testify. I need people to testify." "We had to have people come to the hearings," says Reyes, "to testify about neighborhoods and natural boundaries and communities of interest and those sort of things. We had to develop a record basically and we had to keep 'em [the commission] honest. We had to have enough support that if something happened, we'd squawk; we'd put political pressure on."[69]

The Reapportionment Commission consisted of six Republicans and five Democrats, including Castro and Ruben Valdez. Predictably, partisan politics entered into the fray and the battle over gerrymandering was fought not only on Don Sandoval's West Side turf, but also on the North Side, where Republicans lumped three incumbent Democratic senators into the same district.[70] Senators Dennis Gallagher, Barbara Holme, and Paul Sandoval suddenly found themselves facing each other in the same district. Chicanos, thus, faced the possibility of losing seats held by both

Sandoval cousins.[71]

From within the Reapportionment Commission, Ruben Valdez and Rich Castro protested vigorously. Hispanic organizations such as the Democratic Chicano Caucuses, the GI Forum, and the Mexican-American Legal Defense Fund rose to support them. The plan "diluted the Hispanic population's voting strength for the next decade," they complained, and "split communities of interest by removing a west Denver section from the main West Denver community."[72] Senator Gallagher brought out supporters of his own; ultimately, the Colorado Supreme Court questioned the way the lines were redrawn.[73]

The combined pressure eventually paid off; the boundary lines were again redrawn. Looking back on the situation in a column in *La Voz* some years later, Castro wrote: "I spent a great deal of time organizing various communities and getting them to testify at hearings around the state. Ruben Valdez was instrumental in using his legislative experience as former Speaker of the House to negotiate the boundary lines. . . . As a result of this effort, the number of Hispanics serving in the Colorado Legislature went from seven in 1981 to ten in 1990."[74] By 1990, 10 percent of the Colorado General Assembly was Hispanic; 15 percent of the state's population was Hispanic.[75] Thus, Chicanos, starting with one senator, Roger Cisneros, in 1966, were edging closer to the proportional representation they had long sought.

The battle over reapportionment fit into a larger strategy. The overall goal was to translate changes in Hispanic demographics into Hispanic political power—a long scarce commodity in the Southwest. In an article for the *Colorado Statesman*, Castro quoted a report by Willie Velasquez of the Southwest Voter Registration Project. The nationally known Velasquez, who had once worked with Castro in registering voters on the West Side, released data that revealed Hispanics as the country's fastest growing group in both population and voter registration. Hispanics, he said, constituted 15 percent of the population under eighteen, and 13 percent of the newly registered vote.[76] The issue of reapportionment, in Castro's mind, fell under the category of how best to organize this promising potential and how, in his words, to best "flex our political muscle."[77]

The Daily Fare

Whenever an issue touched the sensitive nerve of nationalism or ethnic politics, sparks flew. For Castro's career, these were the issues that represented the abrasive and confrontational side of politics in the State House. Yet it would vastly misrepresent the General Assembly's atmosphere—and Castro's role in it—to infer that Castro was constantly embroiled in controversy. Those superheated issues reflected only a small segment of his everyday life in the Colorado General Assembly.

For one, Castro was no fiery speaker; secondly, his demeanor on many issues was conciliatory. Just as he operated quietly behind the scenes during the UMAS and Coalition days, Castro tended to do the same in the legislature. Summarizing his political style, *Denver Post* reporter Carl Hilliard wrote, "He is not flowery at the microphone, is seldom argumentative, never nit-picks and has not made a career of building small items into big ones."[78] He was, after all, a Democrat, not a revolutionary, and was well aware of the endless compromise and defeats inherent in playing the legislative ball game. Except for the post-Watergate years 1975 and 1976, Democrats constituted a perpetual minority in the Colorado General Assembly. They could wield some clout, particularly when they held key positions in crucial committees, but basically, Castro, like his predecessor Betty Benavidez, found that serving as a Hispanic Democrat did not generate prodigious amounts of power.

State Representative Wayne Knox recalls, "Rich was a very strong voice on behalf of Hispanics and poor people and on behalf of the underdog. . . . But being in a minority party day after day, year after year can get pretty discouraging. . . . To a certain extent, you're beating your head against the wall, speaking in opposition to bad bills, sometimes really horrendous bills, and a good deal of the time knowing you're being the loyal minority and you're not gonna prevail. But Rich was always upbeat; I think Rich could always laugh at things."[79]

Even when times were troubled, Castro brought his joy of life to the floor of the legislature. "He kept the House happy," recalled one of his colleagues.[80] He could poke fun at himself: "He used to say he enjoyed being a rep for three reasons," remembered State Representative Nolbert Chávez. "You get to wear a suit and tie every day. People want to take you to lunch. And you make $11,000 a year."[81]

He poked fun at his opponents, especially the most conservative among them, who were known as the "House Crazies." When the time came for the annual rite of the "Hummers"—the traditional event in which the minority party got to mock the majority with outlandish skits, Castro was always in the lead. He portrayed Rep. Ann Gorsuch mercilessly as the wicked witch of the North, and Rep. Ken Kramer picking his nose as he "searched for his roots."

The hard partying that had characterized the legislature in years past was beginning to tone down by the time Castro entered the scene. Nick Frangos, who runs the dimly lit, slightly rundown tavern on East Colfax known as the Congress Lounge, observed from behind his counter huge changes since his place became popular with state politicians around 1960. Frangos remembers that upwards of seventy legislators used to meet at the Congress back in the days when Doc Lamm, who chaired the Rules Committee, began holding informal after-hours legislative sessions right in the bar. This, despite the fact that the fire code limited the building's capacity to forty.

"Years ago," recalls Frangos, "it was a cowboy legislature. Used to be ten, fifteen, twenty cowboys in this bar and now there's only two."[82] When the Congress Lounge opened in 1958, nine women counted themselves as lawmakers; by 1985 the number was twenty-four. As the makeup of the legislature changed, so, too, did the behavior.

The transformation from rural to suburban particularly impacted the social habits of legislators. "When I first came here," remembers Lyle Kyle, "two-thirds of the members of the legislature came to town for the legislative session. Most of 'em rented a hotel room because sessions lasted sixty to ninety days in the odd year, and in the even year, it was over within thirty days at the most. Consequently, they were living away from home. They didn't move their families here with them. The guys came down and they were free to party. The old Shirley Savoy and the Cosmopolitan Hotel were the two key spots at that time. But now probably three-quarters of the members of the General Assembly drive to and from their homes to the Capitol. The ones that come now from out of town rent an apartment and generally bring their families with 'em because the sessions are longer. I'm not so sure it's because the individuals are more serious today than they were then, but it's the circumstances that have changed. If you're a representative from Denver or Jefferson or Arapahoe or Adams or Boulder County, what's your reason for not goin' home from the office the same as you would if you were practicin' law or runnin' a business?"[83]

Add to that the fishbowl atmosphere created by a more probing and less restrained press in the wake of Watergate, and the impact of the Sunshine Law, which prohibited legislative business from being carried out in private. In these new circumstances, the social patterns of the State Legislature transformed drastically by the late '70s.

Nevertheless, the Congress Lounge remained a popular gathering place for congressional insiders, and Castro was counted among the more loyal customers. He loved the backslapping; he loved the beer; he loved the banter; he loved the give-and-take; he loved the whole social scene of the Colorado State Legislature.

When push came to shove, however, when the issues were close to his heart, he could fight hard and at times use his humor as a political weapon. Once, while sparring with Governor Richard Lamm over a disagreement on immigration policy, Castro rose to address the floor during discussion on the Long Bill, the all-important annual proposal for the state budget. Approaching the microphone, Castro offered an amendment to appropriate an additional $140,000 for the governor's office. Its purpose, said Castro, was to extend to Lamm the resources with which he might fortify a wall at the bottom of Raton Pass and purchase enough cannon and artillery so that the besieged state of Colorado might defend itself against the onslaught of illegal immigrants.

X

a feud with the governor

Govevnor Richard Lamm seemed an unlikely candidate to clash implacably with Richard Castro. Lamm's political journey took him over some of the same territory Castro wandered. As a young lawyer, when Castro was still in high school, Lamm worked for the Colorado Anti-Discrimination Commission. While Castro was organizing the West Side with Waldo Benavidez in the '60s, Lamm was working the halls of the Colorado Legislature and becoming the state's leading liberal politician.

Elected in 1966 to the State House of Representatives, Lamm authored, in the days before *Roe vs. Wade*, the most liberal abortion bill in the nation and successfully guided it through a Republican legislature. His efforts on behalf of abused children earned him the title "champion of the battered child." His political savvy won him the position of assistant minority leader (whip) in the House, the same position Castro would occupy a decade later.[1]

Lamm sank his deepest roots, however, into the burgeoning environmental movement. In 1970—in the days when Castro was studying the works of Paulo Freire at DU and getting his head beaten in at Curtis Park—Dick Lamm was leading one of Colorado's most remarkable grassroots political campaigns. In that year every contractor, every developer, every metropolitan mayor, every member of the Colorado Association for Commerce and Industry, every economic booster of the state aspired to bring international attention to Colorado by hosting the 1976 Winter Olympics. In opposition to this vast array of powerful interests stood an unknown quantity of ordinary citizens who mistrusted the rosy financial forecasts and feared the despoliation of their beloved high-country canyons and passes. Lamm, in what the press labeled a "quixotic" campaign, led the drive to organize this latent discontent during a 1972 referendum on the issue. The resulting upset shook Colorado politics. By a 3 to 2 margin, Coloradans rejected a bond issue that would have raised state money for building the Olympic infrastructure. The next day Denver withdrew its bid to host the games.[2]

Riding this unexpected triumph, Lamm emerged as a formidable player in state politics. Youthful, with a trim athletic appearance, articulate and bold, unafraid to challenge conventional wisdom, Lamm possessed a rare blend of idealism and practicality. He could envision a variety of scenarios for the future, but he could also play political hardball.

In 1974, he sought to parlay his newly acquired political capital into a bid for the governor's office. Clad in his "road outfit"—hiking boots, cotton pants, and open-collared western-style shirt—Lamm walked nearly 900 miles through the state in an offbeat campaign that resembled the wanderings of a Biblical prophet. Beware, he warned Coloradans, of the Los Angelization of the Front Range.[3] Coloradans temporarily heeded the message and sent Dick Lamm to the Governor's Mansion. Thus, he and Castro rode the same wave of post-Watergate nausea into political office. He handily beat Republican Johnny Vanderhoof and took office about the same time that Polly Baca, Paul Sandoval, and Rich Castro were installing Ruben Valdez as speaker of the house.

It is startling that Castro and Lamm should ever have been seriously at odds. They were both liberal. They both perpetually battled uphill against Republican-controlled legislatures. They were both committed to civil rights. Lamm even won a civil rights award from the Chicano Caucus, presented at a North Side dinner during the early part of his first term.

Yet, less than a decade later the governor found himself alienated from virtually every Hispanic leader in the state. It was a rift that would have a significant impact on Colorado politics.

A few episodes during Lamm's first term released a trickle of discontent that by the mid-1980s had become a torrent of bitter invective. The early grievances centered on political appointments. Since the Depression, Democratic Party officials had taken for granted black and Hispanic support without the political payback customary in other communities: jobs, political appointments, or infrastructure improvements. Anglo politicians could count on minority votes no matter how they behaved in office. As the urban civil rights movement exploded in the 1960s, this pattern of political behavior became unacceptable to white office holders' minority constituents.

A 1974 dialogue during the gubernatorial campaign captured the change of attitude. Addressing Lamm at a Colorado Springs stop where he appealed for the Hispanic vote, one Chicana told him bluntly: "We're accustomed to the white liberal politician using us as a stepping stone and then once they reach their goal, forgetting about us. . . . I hope you are very sincere."[4] A Chicano leader at the same speech stood up and added: "We're tired of hearing 'we're looking for qualified people.' We don't know what that means anymore."[5]

Lamm responded with no specific promises but spoke in a reassuring manner. According to the *Post*, "he believed his involvement in civil rights . . . beginning in 1963 should be an adequate 'road map' for minorities to know his attitude." "There is no question," Lamm said, "that there are many qualified Chicanos in Colorado in terms of serving the state government. I can see why you're cynical. Be cynical. Hold my feet to the fire if I'm elected. I'm sensitive to these things. But I can understand your frustration, your sense of rage and anger that here's another damn Anglo politician down here making promises."[6]

The First Sign of a Rift

In this context the emotional reaction to some of Lamm's early decisions becomes understandable. By 1974, a symbolic payback had become a necessity. Chicanos considered cabinet appointments the minimal gesture to set the tone for a new administration committed to equality. Perhaps this was a narrow, tokenistic focus, but after years in the political wilderness, minorities wanted a visible symbol. Upon his election (heavily supported by blacks and Chicanos, in some precincts by margins of ten to one),[7] Lamm quickly extended his hand to the Hispanic community by appointing Raul Rodriguez, a young Seventeenth Street lawyer from the firm of Holland and Hart, to head up a key cabinet position in the Department of Regulatory Agencies. However, his failure to appoint an African American to a similarly important post got Lamm off to a rocky start in minority relations. Black leaders Regis Groff, Arie Taylor, and Wellington Webb expressed their anger in no uncertain terms and Senator Paul Sandoval jumped quickly to their defense. Webb found it inconceivable that Lamm couldn't find a single qualified black to serve in high office. "If Lamm should run for re-election," said the future Mayor Webb, "I can tell you how certain districts are going to vote."[8] The whole exchange set an ominous tone for the future.

Lamm fired the first salvo in the bitter feud with Chicano politicians on a fall afternoon in 1977 when he informed the seven members of the Chicano Caucus of an unexpected development in his cabinet. Raul Rodriguez had resigned his position to take a federal job in Washington.

Just hours before a press conference made his selection public, Lamm informed the caucus of the new appointment: Gail Klapper, a white attorney from a rather privileged Denver family, a graduate of Wellesley College, and a former aide to President Carter's secretary of interior Cecil Andrus. Lamm's announcement came without warning or consultation.[9] It was a done deal. The seven members of the Chicano Caucus sat dumbfounded for a second as they heard the news; then they got angry.

Ruben Valdez fired off some feisty comments to the press.

"The decision was reached behind closed doors with a selected elite," complained the caucus's patriarch. "The speed with which it was made indicates a desire to preclude input from the Chicano community and any other community group."[10] "The appointment of Mrs. Klapper," he added, "differed from past instances in which Lamm has informed the legislators of openings in the administration so they could suggest possible candidates."[11] Valdez, who later made his peace with Lamm and became the governor's closest Chicano ally, was hoping for a more "open and competitive" process. "Consultation with Chicano groups," he stated, "could have resulted in the emergence of a similarly qualified Chicano for this position. Instead the Chicano community was closed out before the competition began. . . . We must conclude that Governor Lamm seeks only our support but not our input."[12]

An angry Valdez then upped the ante and threatened to abandon Lamm altogether. "If Chicanos continue to be excluded," he said, "then it will become necessary for us to take a broader look at the future and perhaps consider other candidates."[13]

For his part Lamm refused to back down, at least in the beginning. Declaring his sympathy with the "frustration of the Chicano population, often forgotten and still tragically discriminated against," he then defended vigorously his record on minority appointments. He had, he claimed, "appointed more than 125 Spanish-surnamed persons to state posts ranging from Rodriguez and Dan Luna [a top Lamm advisor from the Office of Human Resources] to county commissioners, state boards and advisory boards."

But he added, "I can't run a government by race. I must try to find the right people to fill the right jobs. . . . Every time I appoint a minority to a position, I do not want to have that [position] labeled a minority position and tie my hands in the future forever making that a 'minority position.'"[14]

John Lay, Lamm's top aide, tried to smooth things over. He referred to "unusual circumstances" that prevented Lamm from seeking Chicano advice. He said the governor had been impressed early on with Klapper and that her work as an aide for Interior Secretary Cecil Andrus had made her the top choice for the regulatory job. "It would have been hypocritical," he asserted, "to ask for fifteen names and then say we were going to select Gail Klapper."[15] Later, Lamm offered a conciliatory statement revealing that he intended to appoint another Chicano to a cabinet post soon.

Somewhat appeased, Valdez conceded a few of Lamm's arguments. He declared that the legislators were not questioning Mrs. Klapper's qualifications and that her appointment was an accepted fact. He placed Lamm's track record into perspective, observing that the Chicano caucus had been "pretty well satisfied" with Lamm and that his record was superior to any previous governor. He did note, however, that the record of his predecessors was "practically zero." Characterizing the incident as the first "real disturbance . . . the first major breech between the Chicano community and Lamm," Valdez concluded that "this was a step backward and we want to move forward."[16]

Bilingual Reemerges

Despite the commotion, the whole episode would have blown over had not more serious issues come to the fore. The Bilingual/Bicultural Education Act, which represented the heart and soul of Chicano legislative aspirations, had been under constant attack by Republicans since the day of its passage. By 1981—midway through his second term—Governor Lamm himself was beginning to harbor private doubts about the program. Although the program was still in its infant stages and some evidence pointed to a reduction in the school dropout rate, research on bilingual education was coming back with mixed reviews.

Lamm was unimpressed with the results. More importantly, he was becoming more concerned with the argument that teaching Spanish in the classroom to Mexican kids was dividing the state into two distinct cultures. By the early 1980s, Lamm's support for bilingual education was based more on the pragmatic necessities of Democratic Party unity than on personal conviction.

Perhaps Arvada's Senator Al Meiklejohn, who had become an institution on the Senate Education Committee, sensed Lamm's vulnerability on the issue. The Republican committee chair fashioned an amendment designed to gut the entire bilingual/bicultural program; then he tacked it onto the general School Financing Bill. The amendment replaced bilingual education with an "English language proficiency program" that stressed English as a second language rather than allowing Spanish to linger in the classroom.[17]

"Dick Lamm could have vetoed that bill," says Senator Paul Sandoval, who, years later, still gets agitated when discussing the subject. "I can remember clearly that we met with Lamm on four occasions and all of us [in the caucus] were there . . . in his office. He guaranteed us in July [the repeal of bilingual] wouldn't happen. He guaranteed us in November it wouldn't happen. He promised us [that he would veto the bill]. I knew in my gut. I kept saying to these guys—to Rich and Federico [Peña]—'he's gonna double-cross us. I can feel it.'"[18]

Paul Sandoval's instinct was right. Governor Lamm did indeed refuse to veto the Republicans' repeal of the Bilingual/Bicultural Act. Lamm said he was faced with an "agonizing, agonizing decision."[19] When asked in a much later interview if he had promised the veto, Lamm replied, "I don't know. It probably was true, yeah. I wouldn't contradict [Sandoval] anyway. I don't remember specifically making a promise but it's the kind of thing I would have done, because I was really trying to hold the Democratic coalition together and particularly for that group [the Chicano Caucus], I wanted them to know that I cared about 'em. But the price just got too heavy.

"If it would have been a separate bill," he explained, "I would have vetoed it. But the problem is that Meiklejohn had added it to a whole bunch of other educational things. . . . As I recall, it had tens of millions of dollars in other compensatory programs that made it very difficult to veto.

"I signed the [original] bilingual education bill. I was all for it. . . . The studies are so mixed that I just don't think bilingual education is an overwhelming solution to the problems of the Hispanic community. But I was all in favor of it as a transition program. It's one of those things it would be easy for a legislator to uphold a veto. But I was the one that would have been blamed for having tens of millions of dollars of other programs go away. I take full responsibility for this. But I was not about to sacrifice all of the other things in that bill for bilingual education."[20]

Sandoval counters: "They could have never overridden that veto. And [as for the rest of the funding] we could have worked that out, too. . . . [Lamm could have] vetoed parts of the legislative Long Bill. I mean there were ways to retaliate even though [we were] a minority party. There were a lot of ways to do it. He backed down on us."[21]

As it turned out, the whole fuss over the bilingual bill had little impact on state policy. A 1981 federal court ruling took the issue out of the hands of the state legislature. Under the ruling, school districts were required to institute bilingual programs under certain circumstances regardless of Al Meiklejohn's or any other lawmaker's desires. The damage to Lamm, however, had already been done. The episode was the turning point that drove the wedge between Dick Lamm and the Chicano community.

The Bilingual/Bicultural Bill was not just any bill.[22] For Chicano legislators, it was a part of their very identity. Facing a Republican legislature, the Hispanic contingent had to fight to deliver the smallest concessions to its constituency. For six years they had clung to the Bilingual Bill as their major accomplishment. For Chicano legislators, bilingual was a litmus test and Dick Lamm had failed the test.

There followed a complete falling out. "I mean," says Sandoval, "we didn't talk to him; we didn't meet him. Nothing. Federico had to because he was minority leader. We told him, 'Look, we know you're minority leader. We know you have to meet with him. . . . Go ahead and do it because of your position. But don't give in to the son of a bitch. And don't ever come to us counting on votes for him. [Peña] would come to us on occasion and say, 'Look, we need this or that,' and we'd say, 'We're flat not doin' it. If we knew that Dick Lamm was behind a bill . . . and [that bill] didn't make shit difference to us, we voted 'no.' Period. En masse. . . . The whole caucus. Except for Federico, because he was minority leader of the House, so he had to maintain party unity. Our perception was, hey, he backstabbed us. He lied to us. The hell with him. . . . If there was a bill that he had vetoed— and if it was a bullshit bill—but it was important to him—en masse we would vote with the Republicans to override the veto. Appointments. Lamm would bring an appointment up in the Senate. Rich'd come over: 'Kill the son of a bitch.' We'd kill it; we would, oh yeah. We were hell on wheels."[23]

It was politics with a personal vendetta that played out for years and had long-term ramifications for Colorado's political history. When Lamm later ran in the Senate primary against then Democratic candidate Ben Nighthorse Campbell, Hispanic leadership turned en masse to Campbell and played a key role in Lamm's defeat. Some Chicano politicos continued to back Campbell in the 1998 Senate race even after Campbell had switched to the Republican Party. The reason: His opponent was Dottie Lamm, wife of the former governor. Mrs. Lamm, more liberal than her husband, had little to do with the governor's past feud with Chicanos, yet she still incurred the wrath of past conflicts and carried the weight of the "sins of the husband."

Lamm's Assessment

Looking back on the wreckage, Governor Lamm surmises that the conflict encompassed far more than just bilingual education or the appointment of a cabinet director. Lamm's reading and his assessment of societal problems in the 1980s were taking him in wholly different directions from those he walked as a young liberal environmentalist in the '70s. One of those directions concerned the nature of culture in relation to education and success. "As I look back on this," said Lamm in an interview at his think-tank office at the University of Denver, "more than language, more than immigration, was the idea, as they interpreted it, that I thought there were flaws in Hispanic culture. I said, 'Look there's flaws in all cultures. There's certainly a lot of flaws in American culture.'

"I think those Hispanic kids there in West Denver are the very key to my kids' futures," continued Lamm. "But everything I tried and everything that [Education Commissioner] Cal Frazier tried—I mean we supported bilingual education, English as a Second Language, special compensation, all these other things—I mean I spent a lot of time on this. Nothin' worked. Nothin' worked. And I got very frustrated. . . .

"I'm sayin' to Rich [and others on the Chicano Caucus] 'Look it! Go down to Del Pueblo [Elementary School in the heart of the West Side]. . . . Here's the record with Hispanic teachers. No better! They're not discriminating against these kids. Tell me what's going on. . . .' I said, 'Look Rich, we've tried everything with these Hispanic kids. The problem is obviously not brains. . . . These are smart kids [but] they're not [succeeding]. . . . Particularly the boys—they get to be about twelve years old and all of a sudden, something happens and you have these amazing dropout rates. . . . I can understand if you got an Anglo teacher that sort of tracks these kids but Hispanic teachers have no greater success rates than Anglo teachers.' I said, 'Rich, come on we, gotta talk about this, because we got a problem. This is a deeper problem than just simply saying we're victims and we don't have anybody on the school board.' It seemed to me when I worked for the Colorado Anti-discrimination Commission that racism was *the* problem. It was soon into my governorship when I thought it was *one* of the problems."[24]

By the early '80s, Lamm's reading had ranged far from any traditional liberal fare. He was picking up books from his shelf like Lawrence Harrison's *Underdevelopment Is a State of Mind* and *Who Prospers?* "I was very influenced by a variety of books on culture," said Lamm. "It seems to me the largest income groups in America are all minorities that have been discriminated against. The highest family income groups in America are Japanese Americans. . . . The Jews. Chinese Americans. Korean Americans. None of 'em had it easy. Are Jews smarter? One has to ask. I don't think so. I think those cultures that stress education and upward advancement and getting ahead. I think the Asian love of learning [allows them to be successful]. So I'm interested in culture as one of the factors that have one group of people succeed disproportionately and other groups fail disproportionately. . . . I think the Hispanics have to address the fact that Hispanic dropout rates, no matter where you go [are high]. It varies from culture to culture; in other words the Cuban dropout rate is different from the Mexican or the Puerto Rican, but there are still some cultural aspects to this and Larry Harrison's book, *Underdevelopment as a State of the Mind* [sic], really helped clarify my thinking on that. I am impressed that the problem of the differential in success rates from various people is much more complicated than just simply saying, 'Well, I've been discriminated against.'"[25]

Castro, and indeed the majority of the Chicano community, perceived this shift as a clear betrayal of the liberal values Lamm championed in his earlier years. "The structure was cracking," said Paul Sandoval as he recalled the rancor of the early '80s. "Dick Lamm was becoming a lot more conservative than he was when he originally went into office."[26] Far worse, his criticisms appeared to them as a frontal assault on Chicano culture at a time when right-wing conservatives were gearing up to roll back the hard-won reforms of the 1970s.

Lamm makes few ideological concessions to these criticisms. He retracts none of those controversial ideas about culture and he maintains that, far from abandoning liberal ideals, he was building the "new liberalism" from the shattered remnants of the old. Nevertheless, a somewhat regretful Lamm shoulders much of the responsibility for the bitterness of the feud.

"I did a poor job," says Lamm, "in trying to articulate my concerns. . . . I'm a blunt guy. . . . And I didn't do that human side. . . . I should have had 'em over for dinner. . . . I was so busy. I had young kids. I was in the mansion. I didn't maintain the human side of this. So whenever we sat down to talk, it would get off either on immigration or language or culture and these people pretty soon thought, well, my god, this guy's a raving racist. I think that Ruben Valdez had some questions about where I was on a lot of issues. But I think that Ruben can evaluate me as a human being much better than some of the other legislators because Ruben—when he was in the cabinet—saw me in so many different [roles]. God, we practically lived together; we went on retreats together, we played poker together, and all these other things. I think that Ruben Valdez saw the full Dick Lamm. Other people just said, 'Who the shit is this guy comin' in who would veto the bilingual education bill and now is criticizing our culture?' I'm in politics. I know enough about the human side of things. I should have . . . reached out to them instead of just having lost contact. I think it was my fault, not theirs."[27]

Relations between Dick Lamm and the Chicano community hit rock bottom in the mid-80s. Lamm had already made several forays onto the national stage with a series of controversial statements calculated to capture headlines. "We've got a duty to die and get out of the way," he once said, in describing his opposition to expensive and usually fruitless treatments for the terminally ill.[28] He had already won the nickname "Governor Gloom" for his apocalyptic prophecies about a society destined to unravel unless it took drastic measures to rope in its excesses. "Charlie Brown says there's no issue too big you can't run away from," he says, "and it's really true. You can see why politicians become nebbishes."[29] Whatever else he was—liberal, conservative, or otherwise—Dick Lamm was no nebbish. He reveled in his bluntness and consciously searched for the right words to maximize shock value. He avoided the "big yawn" at any cost.

The Immigration Time Bomb

In 1985, Lamm made another dramatic entrance into a contentious national debate. This time it was a book, co-authored by Gary Imhoff, that enveloped him in controversy. It was vintage Lamm. *The Immigration Time Bomb* read the title in big red letters, which fairly exploded from the surface of the book's cover. Subtitled *The Fragmenting of America*, the ideas within were complemented by Lamm's appearance before the Congressional Joint Economic Committee on immigration issues.[30] The governor spelled out his themes in typical Lamm fashion: blunt with no holds barred.

"Immigration to the United States," he begins on page one, "is massive and . . . out of control."[31] In the same prophetic language that characterized his style for over a decade, Lamm warned that America must reduce immigration or face economic, social, and cultural catastrophe. Lamm's critique of immigration policy embraced the gamut of contemporary American anxieties: competition for jobs among the working poor, increasing crime rates, expansion of social services. He laid these problems out in straightforward and compelling language. These socio-economic issues may well have been debated with civility within the Chicano community.

The Chicano community had for decades been deeply divided and profoundly ambiguous on this sticky issue. David Gutierrez, the most thoughtful scholar on Mexican immigration, recalls how his grandfather, a second-generation American in East Los Angeles, would harangue against "wetbacks" one moment, then offer one of his many illegal alien friends a small loan or a ride to the store the next.[32] César Chávez agonized before deciding to oppose the influx of cheap undocumented labor coming over the border and threatening, in his view, the fragile gains achieved by his United Farm Workers in California.[33] Castro had seen this ambiguity firsthand in Curtis Park, where significant numbers of Mexican-American citizens looked upon their immigrant cousins with fear and condescension and where gangs in the '70s often squared off along the lines of long-established New Mexico manitos versus Mexican immigrant newcomers.

Lamm attacked so broadly, however, and so indiscriminately that he invited a bitter response.

For one, Lamm denied any two-way relationship—any give and take—between U.S. policy and the Third World population knocking on the American door. "The people of the United States are not responsible for how other governments treat their citizens or for the living standards of other countries," he wrote.[34] This notion was preposterous considering how many immigrants at the time streamed in from Vietnam, Cuba, and Central America. U.S. Cold War policy in these regions had consistently, consciously, and calculatedly spawned destabilization that encouraged mass migration to the United States. In fact, at the very moment Dick Lamm wrote, Oliver North was busy instigating the very type of warfare that caused so many Central Americans to pour over the borders.

What exacerbated Lamm's conflict with Chicano leaders, however, was the issue of culture. In a chapter entitled "The Splintered Society," Lamm placed much of the burden for the nation's disunity on the alleged failure of the Hispanic community to assimilate. "I believe," he wrote, "that America's culture and national identity are threatened by massive levels of legal and illegal immigration."[35] By his count, the proportion of Spanish-speaking immigrants reached 50 percent and this concentration was one of the factors that rendered contemporary immigration more dangerous than that of earlier historical periods. What is more, charged Lamm, the ethnic pride movements—the very movements that had nurtured Castro's early political development—failed to encourage sufficient assimilation into the American mainstream.[36] Another chapter, entitled "Language: The Tie That Binds," expressed a deep-seated fear about the dangers for countries where "two language groups clash."[37] In Lamm's view, what was lurking was a "Hispanic Quebec" in the southwestern United States. He believed an entire region, hostile to American culture, resistant to the English language, and forever threatening secession, would emerge into a separatist nightmare as more immigrants spilled across the border.

Debate at the Radisson

Lamm's words cut at the heart of nearly every Chicano leader in the state, but it was Richard Castro who led the charge against the governor. The most dramatic confrontation occurred in July 1986, during a formal debate between Castro and Lamm in downtown Denver's Radisson Hotel. The debate left emotions raw on both sides.

Governor Lamm, appearing more distinguished than ever with his shock of white hair, nevertheless seemed impatient and defensive. He had absorbed some heavy blows following the previous month's Congressional testimony. Castro had said that Lamm's remarks "played to nativism and racism." Senator Phil Hernandez had called for the governor's resignation. Audrey Alvarado of the Latin American Research and Service Agency said that Lamm's testimony was "reminiscent of the anti-Asian, anti-German, anti-Jewish and anti-Catholic sentiments that were evident in years past."[38] Still, as Governor Lamm stepped up to the podium, he reiterated without compromise the arguments he had presented to Congress. "A country needs a social glue to hold itself together," he said. Then he clicked off the following points:

- "If we do not assimilate, we build into the country's future a deadly disunity. . . .
- "There is a developing pattern of linguistic ghettos, of concentrations of Spanish-speaking immigrants where Spanish is the dominant language and where immigrants are enabled never to learn English. . . . They are served by Spanish-language networks of radio and television. They can live their whole lives in Spanish.
- "Our country does not demand uniformity, but it does demand elemental levels of assimilation. . . . We must make sure the melting pot continues to melt."[39]

Facing a sullen, heavily Chicano audience, the air fraught with tension, Governor Lamm chafed at intimations that his comments were racist. As a former civil rights lawyer, as a governor who claimed credit for bringing 125 Hispanics into state office, Lamm was in no mood to accept "the idea that I have to take on my back all the sins that have been committed over the years to the Hispanic community. . . . The charge of racism," he said, "has much too long been used to prevent us from dealing with some very important problems. . . . I honor the Hispanic community; I honor your contributions, but we got a problem. Hispanic kids are not succeeding in near the numbers that we need them to."[40]

Castro, whose usual inclination was to crack a tension-breaking joke, remained grim-faced as he stepped to the podium for rebuttal. Gone was the usual smile and ready humor. Dick Lamm, he believed, just didn't get it.

He failed to understand neither the unique nature of the Chicano historical experience nor the unique nature of Mexican immigration to the United States. The Mexican-American population in the Southwest did not follow the same path as the classical American immigrant, who crossed the Atlantic from Europe, settled first on the East Coast, and assimilated into the American mainstream within two to three generations. Castro's words recalled his first Chicano studies classes at Metro, the experience of his wife's family, and his own personal search for his family roots in the Hispanic Homeland.

"The first point I would like to make," Castro began, "is that the overwhelming majority of Hispanics in the Southwest are not recent immigrants. A good number are the descendents of early colonialists who were both Spanish and Indian and were settling towns and villages in the Southwest in the early 1600s before the Pilgrims even touched our shores. A good number," he continued, "are the sons and daughters of Mexicans who fled the Mexican Revolution during 1910 and 1920." Castro had to look no farther on this point than his wife's family, who had resided in Colorado for sixty years. "My point is that the Hispanic community is a diverse group of people with diverse levels of assimilation. Yet the Governor would have the public believe we all arrived yesterday.

"After lumping us all together," Castro went on, "he attempts to build a case that Hispanics pose some potential threat to this country's national unity. . . . What are the facts?" he asked. "Hispanics are fiercely loyal and patriotic. Look at the record." Castro then laid out a set of statistics detailing the disproportionate participation of Hispanic soldiers in U.S. war efforts from World War II to Korea to Vietnam. Surely he visualized here the picture of his father in naval uniform during World War II, his uncle in a Japanese POW camp in the Philippines, and his old buddies at Metro who had done stints in Vietnam. "These are clearly not statistics," he concluded, "that would indicate that Hispanics are on the verge of destroying this nation's national unity."

He took issue as well with the subject of language and "linguistic ghettos." One can picture Lamm walking down West Thirty-second Avenue past the Spanish-language movie theater, past the *taquerías* and *panaderías*, shaking his head and feeling that America was coming apart at the seams. Lamm saw the mass use of Spanish on the streets, on cable television's Channel 51, and on KBNO radio as divisive. "Bilingualism for individuals," he stated, "is a blessing. Bilingualism for a society is a curse."

Castro looked at that same situation and saw it not as a curse but as a bridge. "With respect to language," he said, "let me state that Hispanics in the Southwest recognize the need to speak English. That does not mean that Hispanics need to deny their language and culture. . . . John Nesbitt, in his book *Megatrends*, stated that the three languages for the future will be English, Spanish, and computer. We have a national treasure in this country. Those who can speak Spanish can provide the 'cultural bridge' that will be so essential in promoting political, economic and social understanding with our neighbors to the South." Castro saw the mass use of Spanish as an opportunity, not a threat.

At the heart of the debate were two differing approaches to assimilation. Castro accused Lamm of trying clumsily to hammer the unique Hispanic experience in America into the mold of the European immigrant experience. "Historically," said Lamm, "America was a new world, a place where many nationalities and many languages would come together and live in a kind of harmony while they assimilated to the national norm. We accepted people of many cultures but they learned English, the language of the new country and they became a new people, not just merely an extension of the countries of origin. . . . American-born citizens would show tolerance for the newcomers' differences as long as they Americanized. There was a sort of covenant: The new immigrant would learn English and a useful skill in the United States and he would participate in the political system by becoming a citizen, a voter, and if necessary a soldier. In return, he would be accepted as a political equal and he would become an American. . . . That, in fact, is the American experience."

But that was not the experience for Hispanics, argued Castro. "I would suggest," he stated, "that when you focus on the Hispanic community . . . that you ought to talk about this region of the country as it truly evolved and not mix and match immigrant groups like we're all the same." Europeans had come to America voluntarily. Their very presence on North American shores indicated an acceptance of the terms of the "covenant" to which Lamm had referred. They may have yearned for the culture of the Old Country, but with battered suitcases and meager bundles of possessions in hand, they had made a free choice. For most Hispanics, that "covenant" never existed.

"[Lamm's view] takes a totally eastern orientation," said Castro, "and [implies] that we somehow came through Ellis Island. Ladies and gentlemen, the vast majority of the people here in this room didn't come through Ellis Island. We didn't immigrate to this country. We were in the country when the United States immigrated to us."[41] Castro, of course, was referring to the 1848 Mexican War when the United States forcibly annexed the Southwest. The first Mexicans here were not immigrants at all, but constituted, instead, a conquered people who, in some respects, shared the plight of Native Americans. The defeated Mexicans were neither asked to assimilate nor were they allowed to when they so desired. For over a century, they remained "strangers in their own land."

Later, waves of Mexican immigrants frequently remained outside the bounds of the immigrant "covenant." During the Mexican Revolution, which began in 1910, Mexican refugees crossed the border in great numbers and found jobs in the usual places: the copper mines, beet fields, orchards, and railroads. When these jobs dried up during the Depression, however, Mexicans were forcibly deported back to their homeland by the thousands to be replaced by white workers.[42] During and after World War II, Mexicans, under the Bracero Program, came by the hundreds of thousands, encouraged by government and agribusiness to harvest the crops on American farms. One California senator even claimed Mexicans "were more suited for stoop labor because they were built closer to the ground." Although this migrant work force slowly created the roots of many Mexican-American communities, the terms of their contract spelled out their special status: They were temporary, expendable, and—after the harvest was completed—unwelcome.[43] This constituted the Mexican covenant with America.

This complex combination of circumstances stretching over a century from the Texas conquest to the civil rights era of the 1960s and '70s shaped a unique environment for Hispanics in the United States. It was an environment strewn with barriers to assimilation far more formidable than those faced by the European immigrants from Ellis Island, an environment that soured the atmosphere for acceptance and cooperation by later waves of Mexican immigrants.

Castro maintained that vast numbers of loyal Hispanics had tried for decades to enter the American mainstream but had the door slammed in their faces. "Hispanics were assimilated enough to fight in World War II," he said. "Yet tragically, those who died were not good enough to be buried in Anglo cemeteries in Texas. . . . Assimilation is a two-way street, Governor. The history of the Southwest with respect to Hispanics has been one of exclusion by the majority society, yet we have continued to attempt to assimilate despite all odds."[44]

Nationalism and Ethnic Identity

Castro raged over Lamm's attack on the ethnic identity movement and the Hispanic pride movement—the very movements that had nurtured Castro's political development. Unlike Lamm, Castro viewed these organizations as vehicles to a new type of assimilation—an assimilation that would allow Hispanics to participate in the American mainstream without being drowned in it, without losing their culture, without wandering too far from their own inner identities, without losing their sense of who they were.

Lamm glibly labeled this movement a fake. "At this historic moment," he wrote in his book, "Hispanic immigrants to America are inventing an 'Hispanic' ethnic identity. . . . This Hispanic identity is created consciously, purposefully, by those who wish to use the tool of ethnic identity to forge a power base."[45]

Castro responded with barely controlled anger: "The next time I look at my grandmother, my father and mother, my wife and my children, the next time I go to a baptism, a wedding or a funeral, I will remember your theory that the Hispanic ethnic identity is a myth and is only being used as a political tool. I will ask myself who are you trying to scare and why are you so fearful of Hispanic pride and culture."[46]

Among Lamm's more offensive statements was his attack on the National Council of La Raza, of which Castro himself was a member. Lamm first had drawn a distinction in his book between "liberal" and "corporate" pluralism. In the former model, "individual differences are tolerated, accepted and appreciated by society as a whole." Corporate pluralism, wrote Lamm, means that "rights and identity within a society are determined . . . by the ethnic, racial, religious, or other sub-community with which one identifies."[47] Power is bestowed upon some and withheld from others because of their race. Having made this distinction, Lamm then placed the National Council of La Raza among the ultra-nationalists and separatists who advocate for a racially closed society. "There are groups . . . " wrote Lamm, "who do advocate corporate pluralism, even separatism, and we are right to treat them with suspicion. For example, the National Council of La Raza operates today as a mainstream political group, but its *Plan Espiritual de Aztlán* calls for a revolutionary nationalism for Chicanos and assumes that 'social, economic, cultural and political independence is the only road to total liberation from oppression, exploitation and racism.'"[48]

Lamm's scholarship here fell far enough off the mark to invite legal action. Undoubtedly, the governor confused the Council of La Raza with the more radical (and moribund) Raza Unida Party. The *Plan Espiritual de Aztlán* is more accurately associated with the Crusade for Justice, which sponsored the 1969 Chicano Youth Conference from which the plan emerged. Nevertheless, the Raza Unida Party did share with the Crusade the concept of Aztlán—the concept of an independent Chicano homeland in the Southwest. The brand of nationalism espoused by the Crusade was indeed a revolutionary nationalism forged, as it was, in an era when Ho Chi Minh left an anti-imperialist imprint on most of the national movements of the day. The radicals' nationalism, whether that of the Crusade or the less rigidly ideological Raza Unida, was based on the combination of ideas curiously shared by Woodrow Wilson and Vladimir Lenin: If a people shares the same culture, the same language, the same ethnicity, the same history, the same religion, the same geography, it possesses the same right to self-determination as do other nations.[49] Therein lay Corky's rationale for the right to an independent Chicano homeland in the territory of "Aztlán," and therein also lay José Angel Gutiérrez's similar claim from his home base in Texas. That doctrine had played well to a minority of militants in the '70s, but among the millions of Chicanos across the American Southwest, the idea of a separate nation had fallen flat. Few could envision the far-flung archipelago of Chicano population centers stretching from south Texas to northern New Mexico to southern California to the isolated barrios of cities across the entire Southwest as something that comprised a unified nation.

The National Council of La Raza, to which Governor Lamm referred, had indeed formed as an offshoot of Gutiérrez's Raza Unida Party, created to tap into the ample resources of the Ford Foundation. Since 1968, however, the organization had undergone enough splits and mutations that it could no longer be credibly linked to La Raza Unida Party.[50] Standing next to the Crusade and La Raza Unida's bold platforms for self-determination, the ideas of the National Council of la Raza formed a mild alternative. It was, in short, not revolutionary; it was not anti-imperialist; it was not separatist.

The Council, claimed Castro, "works to promote better cross-cultural understanding, educational access, media imaging and social services." Almost disingenuously, given his credentials on the left wing of the Democratic Party, Castro invoked the support of corporate America to cast the most respectable sheen upon its middle-class moderate outlook. "The list of its corporate supporters," said Castro, "reads like a 'Who's Who' in the corporate community: General Motors, Levi Strauss, AT&T, Coors, . . . Coca Cola, McDonald's. . . . What could be more American than working to develop a corporate partnership with these members of the Fortune 500?

"In your rush to paint the National Council of La Raza as a closet revolutionary organization," he told Lamm, "you have defamed and distorted the good name of this prominent Hispanic group. . . . The National Council never published, wrote, or developed the *Plan Espiritual de Aztlán*. I called Raul Yzaguirre, the National Executive Director, yesterday, and he denied having anything to do with the *Plan Espiritual de Aztlán*. He also indicated that he had written to you some time ago pointing out this major flaw in your book. He said he never received a reply."[51]

That same day, State Senator Don Sandoval, with Castro's support, had introduced a resolution to the NCLR's board of directors in Los Angeles seeking a court injunction to stop sales of Lamm's book until he issued a retraction of his portrayal of the organization.[52] This tactic failed and was viewed unsympathetically by both the press and the public as an attempt at censoring Lamm's offensive ideas.

Strategic aspects aside, however, the grievance was a real one. Associating the National Council of La Raza with the revolutionary rhetoric of the *Plan Espiritual de Aztlán* was roughly tantamount to mistaking the moderate NAACP for the Black Panther Party or Louis Farrakhan's Nation of Islam. It lumped together all Hispanic organizations—moderate, revolutionary, militant, or separatist—into one indistinguishable jumble. All those Mexican groups, it implied to the general public, are radical, subversive, and bristling with hostility towards whites.

This was not the first time Anglo politicians, or for that matter Anglo society, had lumped the diverse Latino community of the Southwest into one indistinguishable mass. Historically, mainstream America made no distinctions between native-born Chicanos and recently arrived Mexican immigrants. Those whose American roots could be traced back 400 years were shunned no less than recent arrivals. Whenever the screws were tightened, whether during the deportations of the Depression, the repatriations of Operation Wetback in the '50s, or the Immigration and Naturalization Service crackdown in the '80s, the entire community suffered. Families were torn asunder and jobs withheld from citizen and non-citizen alike. In earlier years middle-class assimilationist organizations such as the League of United Latin American Citizens and the GI Forum, tended to distance themselves fearfully from Mexican nationals, but by the late 1970s those same organizations, including the Council of La Raza, were undergoing a sea change in their orientations toward immigration. Attacks on Mexican immigrants, they concluded, created a climate in which all Hispanics became targets.[53]

Lamm might have defused the situation by issuing an apology for confusing Raza Unida, the Crusade for Justice, and the 1969 Youth Conference with the Council of La Raza. Instead, he dug in deeper by mocking the latter's attempt at a court injunction. "That's the best news I ever heard," he stated upon hearing the council's resolution, "because quite frankly sales were lagging. They needed something like this."[54]

The Immigration Climate

Viewing his overall record, one must conclude that, in his heart, Dick Lamm was no racist. He shunned theories of innate racial superiority, anguished over the festering problems in the barrio, and clearly made contributions as governor to fostering racial equality. But operating in an environment that cried out for diplomacy, the former governor took on, instead, the role of a loose cannon; his comments fueled the growing racial tension of the period.

That tension was far reaching. The same conservative wave that splashed onto American shores during the Reagan era hit international beaches as well. Worldwide, the culture of fast money, conspicuous consumption, and corporate takeover gave rise correspondingly to profound anxiety among the middle and working classes, who felt threatened and mocked, and whose traditionally stable jobs were displaced. In searching for answers, the most conservative elements came up with a time-tested formula: scapegoating the outcast. In France, Jean Marie le Pen's National Front blamed society's ills on the wave of immigrants from North and sub-Saharan Africa. The English National Front focused on immigrants from the Caribbean and Pakistan. German and Austrian right-wingers turned their attention to the Turks in their midst. In America, the wave of southern immigration came from Mexico and the war-torn countries of Central America. However well-intentioned, Governor Lamm's words flowed directly into this perilous stream of ethnic scapegoating.

Other liberals surveying the landscape found the sources of the nation's woes elsewhere: a bloated defense budget, a calculated policy of disinvestment in the nation's core industries, the excesses of mammoth corporations stomping about in a newly deregulated economy, the extravagant consumption of the newly rich. Lamm found that the problems plaguing America during this deeply conservative period sprang disproportionately from the wave of third-world people who tended the gardens, tiled the roofs, stitched the collars, and flame-broiled the burgers so that mainstream Americans could prosper and live well. They were strange words coming from the mouth of a man who was once the state's leading liberal. Castro carefully refrained from labeling Lamm a racist but bristled at his inflammatory language. "It *plays* to racism," said Castro, "and I stand by that."[55]

And so they squared off: the former governor claiming to offer a new direction for liberalism—a liberalism of hard choices; the former legislator claiming that the governor—in wildly misinterpreting the history of his beloved Southwest—had transformed himself in a few short years from liberal to archconservative. Indeed, for all his emphasis on innovation, Lamm served up a rather dusty old paradigm for grappling with the dilemma of ethnic relations: the paradigm of the melting pot, the paradigm of assimilation, pure and simple. Castro's whole life experience—his search for identity in the southern Colorado homeland, his marriage to the daughter of a Mexican immigrant, his quest on the West Side and in the General Assembly for a more just society—had taught him that a cut-and-dried approach to assimilation did not mesh with the unique Chicano experience in America. Assimilation needed to happen, of course, but it needed to be accompanied by a new sense of balance. It needed to allow breathing room for nationalist sentiment; it needed to nurture the quest for bilingualism and the search for an ethnic identity. It required a more humble approach from the mainstream and a recognition of the dialectic, of the interplay between mainstream and minority cultures. In Castro's eyes, this new approach could only strengthen America, rather than tear it apart.

xi

the peña years

The clash with Governor Lamm reflected a new stage in Rich Castro's career. Almost imperceptibly, Castro had emerged by the mid-1980s as the most visible spokesman for Denver's Chicano community. His new stature reflected not as much an unbroken rise to prominence as a more subtle repositioning of the entire constellation of local Chicano leadership.

In earlier years Castro had played a supporting role, working backstage while others occupied the limelight. During the Movement's formative years in the '60s, Corky Gonzales's leadership remained undisputed, if not unchallenged. Playing to a national as well as local audience, Corky's presence towered over Denver's other Movement leaders. On the neighborhood level, Waldo Benavidez had carved out a small kingdom on the West Side and remained Castro's mentor throughout the life of the West Side Coalition.

Entering state politics in the '70s, Castro remained in the shadow of more forceful leaders in the General Assembly. Giant among Hispanic legislators was Speaker of the House Ruben Valdez, followed by the dynamic Polly Baca Barragan, who early on chaired the powerful House Rules Committee, and Paul Sandoval, whose influence stemmed from his position on the Joint Budget Committee. In city government, Sal Carpio had gained considerable clout as the first Chicano city councilman in twenty years.[1]

As the 1980s rolled in with Castro's influence burgeoning among Democrats in the General Assembly, a fast-rising new face eclipsed him once again in the State House: Federico Peña, the man destined to become Denver's mayor, surged rapidly into the leadership role.

By the mid-1980s, however, all of these leaders, with the exception of

Peña, had begun to fade from the spotlight. Corky's Crusade for Justice had run aground on the rocks of sustained police harassment, infighting, and an abrasive, confrontational style which no longer rang true. Health problems following an automobile accident and a stroke further weakened Corky's political voice. Waldo had fled to Albuquerque in the mid-'70s and there led a quiet life in exile for years, opening up a record store before returning to Denver. When he came back to Denver, he retained but a small circle of loyalists. Ruben Valdez ran the Colorado Department of Human Services for three years, made an unsuccessful run for lieutenant governor in 1981, then was appointed to head the state Department of Labor, where he performed commendably but largely outside the arena of public controversy. Eventually, he became one of the most successful lobbyists on Denver's Capitol Hill, where he plied his trade quietly outside the public spotlight. Sal Carpio moved from city council to the federal government, becoming director of Denver's Department of Housing and Urban Development; but he, too, tended to work outside of the public forum. Polly Baca Barragan moved on to a seat in the state senate but received less local press coverage than Castro, in part because her position as vice-chair of the Democratic National Party shifted her focus away from local issues.

Only Peña, Denver's first Hispanic mayor following his election in the spring of 1983, remained in the public eye. As Mayor, Peña became engrossed in citywide issues, however, his public statements tended to reflect less the views of the Chicano community than those of Denver as a whole. Peña's success in mainstream politics increasingly put him out of touch with the community that had spawned him.

In contrast—through a combination of circumstances—Castro found himself in a position to be all over the city, always in the public eye, author of a stream of columns for the Hispanic press, forever pursued by *Denver Post* reporters searching for a quote. When Hispanic issues such as Lamm's attack on immigration policy arose, Castro became the most prominent personality to respond.

Still, Castro owed his rise in influence, as well as his mobility and visibility, to the position he acquired in the Peña administration. From 1983 until his death in 1991, Castro directed the city's Commission on Human Rights and Community Relations.

"I think," said former House speaker Ruben Valdez, "that after he left the legislature . . . he began hitting his stride. In the legislature, he was bound. I mean there's a set agenda that you deal with. . . . I think he felt he had done what he could at the legislature and was kind of confined there. I think ultimately he was ready to go and free himself to do more stuff. With the Human Rights Commission, he wasn't as restricted. It gave him the time to meet with people and design programs. [It] gave him a broader base, a better forum, more visibility, and an opportunity to do what he really wanted to do and that is work with people. . . . He was dealing with community groups; he was in touch with them; he was visiting them; he was sharing ideas with them. He got to be a friend of many, many people and not only the Hispanic community but the Greek community and the Jewish community. He had a real broad base and he was the kind of guy who could work with everybody. I think that's where Rich was really shining; that's where he found his niche."[2]

Peña's Rise

Federico Peña's rise to power is a story in itself. Young, articulate, bold, and visionary, Peña surprised veteran politicians with consecutive upset victories, first over long-term incumbent mayor Bill McNichols, then over popular district attorney Dale Tooley in a June 1983 run-off. That a Chicano won in a city with a minority Hispanic population—18 percent—thrust Peña immediately into the national spotlight.[3] Willie Velasquez, director of the Southwest Voter Registration and Education Project, stated, "His victory makes him a major Hispanic political force in America." Comparing Peña to San Antonio mayor Henry Cisneros, who headed up a city which was 54 percent Hispanic, Velasquez said, "I'm of the opinion that Peña's election is more significant than Henry Cisneros's. When people begin to analyze what he did up there, the real importance of Federico Peña to Hispanic politics and American politics as a whole will be seen."[4] Velasquez was referring to Peña's ability to forge a multi-racial coalition with broad-based voter appeal across the racial spectrum. In his ability to forge a multi-racial coalition, Peña's victory surely represented a milestone.

In building that coalition Peña consciously downplayed ethnic politics. "Reporters from Texas and *Time* and *Newsweek* call," said Peña in an interview with *The Denver Post*, "and it's always the same: 'You're going to become one of the leading Hispanic figures in America.' I tell them, 'No. I am just trying to get elected mayor of Denver, . . . The point it seems to me that everyone is missing, is that this city has gone beyond the question of one's ethnic background. Dynamic growing cities like Denver . . . are willing to elect an individual who is competent whatever his background. That's the really important message that is coming out of this campaign."[5]

Despite these comments, Mexican Americans on the West or North Side looked upon Peña as something of a messiah or at least the culmination of a dream. "I have lived fifty-three years in the state of Colorado," said seventy-one-year-old Peter Torres, "and I never thought I would see this day."[6] Elderly Hispanics saw his success as the payback for decades of political frustration. Younger Chicanos flocked to canvass neighborhoods and encourage their neighbors to vote. In the final days of the campaign,

Peña forces registered 5,000 new Hispanic voters, an achievement that provided the margin of final victory.[7] Father José Lara of Our Lady of Guadalupe Church on the North Side recalled, "I drove people to the polls. Some of the people . . . they hardly could walk, they were so old. But they were willing to go to the polls."[8] The excitement generated by the first Peña campaign brought Chicanos into Denver's mainstream political process like never before.

Early on, Peña and his team sensed a change in the demographics of the city—a change that would favor a different direction for city government. "The city was getting younger and more diverse," says Peña advisor Tom Gougeon. "The heart and soul of the previous [McNichols] administration—a lot of them were pretty great people, but the average age was getting up there into the seventies and beyond. They were almost exclusively white older men. They had a circle of associations in the community and I think a lot of the rest of the community just didn't circulate in the same universe. . . . There's a direct correlation between the fact that there were a hundred and some organized neighborhood groups in Denver and the fact that for the past fifteen or twenty years, those people were told, 'People in power make these decisions; you don't really have a role. [Neighborhood organizers] are just troublemakers.' Essentially these people organized themselves in communities, made themselves important, and became the constituency that unelected Bill and elected Federico. Looking at the pattern of voting, a huge number of people had turned out to vote in Congressional races and gubernatorial races that wouldn't vote in a Denver election. That told us they didn't think [city government] was relevant. Clearly there was a constituency that was isolated enough that it didn't participate. But all that was changing and I don't think Federico made it change. It was overdue. Denver was gonna pick somebody more activist, younger, more open, and more responsive at that moment."[9]

The younger, more open activist that Denver eventually selected came from Texas in the early 1970s while Castro was embroiled in conflict on the West Side. In those times, Peña was a "long-haired radical"—a lawyer who took the most controversial cases while working with MALDEF, the Mexican American Legal Defense and Education Fund. A reader of the Crusade's newspaper, *El Gallo*, could find Peña's name in ads requesting witnesses for police brutality cases. He represented Crusade defendants in cases surrounding the controversial 1973 St. Patrick's Day shootings. He represented a witness in the grand jury convened for the Boulder bombing cases, which had killed Florencio Granado.[10] (Later on, Peña tended to distance himself from the militants, telling the *Rocky Mountain News*, "Somebody reminded me the other day that after the Revolutionary War, John Adams represented British soldiers. People needed help. They had a right to representation.

We were asked to help and we did. Whatever analogy people want to draw from that is up to them.")[11] As staff attorney for the Chicano Education Project, he traveled the Western Slope and San Luis Valley advocating major reforms in school financing and assisting parents in setting up bilingual/bicultural programs.[12] Robin Johnston, then chair of the State Board of Education, remembers fighting "over every comma" in her negotiations with CEP regarding bilingual education. Peña was "aggressive, to say the least," she said.[13]

Peña in the House

Castro's relationship with Peña was a complex one. While the Chicano Caucus in the legislature worked to enact bilingual legislation, Peña pushed it from the outside through CEP. This is where they first crossed paths. "At that time," recalls Peña, "Ruben Valdez was Speaker of the House but Rich was also very active on those issues. I met with a lot of legislators . . . and Rich always came across as someone who did his homework, who worked very hard, who was passionate about his views and was well respected by the community. . . . He was meticulous. When he went to debate an issue, he was well prepared, he knew the issues; he wasn't shooting from the hip, and he felt strongly about things. Those were the skills I looked for in a legislator. I looked to the way Rich conducted himself in the legislature as a model."[14]

When Peña won election to the House from his North Side district in 1979 he gravitated quickly towards Castro whom he described as a mentor.[15] "When I was a freshman, he was assistant minority leader and he helped me learn the ropes; he taught me how the committees worked . . . and he kind of took me under his wing. . . . He was a great teacher."[16]

Nevertheless, Peña stood apart in a number of ways from Castro and his colleagues on the Chicano Caucus. The future mayor was not a Colorado native; he had not been one of that circle of East or North Side boys who had grown up together, watched Denver's Chicano Movement spring up, then successfully entered electoral politics. He had taken no part in the events of that hot summer of 1973, which saw Rich Castro shot and bleeding on the corner of Eleventh and Santa Fe. Peña was a new kid on the block, an outsider, a Tejano, born and raised in Brownsville. There were class differences as well. The others had grown up in working-class homes; they had been the first of their families to go to college if not high school. Peña's dad had graduated from Texas A&M and become a broker for the Gulf Pacific Cotton Company in Brownsville. Peña had consequently been reared in a "classic upper-middle-class Catholic family" (according to schoolmate Antonio Zavaleta) and had graduated from the University of

Texas Law School in Austin.[17]

Other qualities set Federico Peña apart. Peña participated in the Chicano Caucus but he was not one of the boys. Caucus members worked hard, but several—Castro among them—tended to play hard, too. The gregarious Castro could always be found socializing at Nick Frango's Congress Lounge across the street from the capitol building, at the Lancer Lounge, at the Parlor on Broadway, or on weekends at Don Sandoval's southwest Denver bar, the Bull Ring.[18] Peña was a loner; he avoided the hanging out and the hard drinking and often remained aloof. Though engaging less in the camaraderie, he quickly emerged as a leader to be reckoned with in the House of Representatives.

After only two years in the House, the dynamic Peña leapfrogged into a position of leadership, passing Castro in the process. As the 1981 session began, Representative Bob Kirscht (Pueblo) held the influential position of house minority leader—leader of the House Democrats—that he had inherited from Ruben Valdez. In the post-Watergate Democratic heyday of 1975–76, Valdez and Kirscht had run as a team, taking over respectively the offices of speaker of the house and house majority leader. The next term, when Republicans regained control, Valdez became minority leader. Kirscht took over when Valdez ran for lieutenant governor in 1979. By 1981, House Democrats had grown disenchanted with Kirscht's increasingly conservative leadership and staged what Peña described as a coup d'etat.

Representative Wayne Knox, one of the engineers of the coup, recalls, "We were all pretty much agreed we weren't happy with Kirscht, but you don't know that you're gonna be successful. You're taking on the current minority leader who's not gonna be very happy. . . . There could be a little retribution. Not a lot, but he had an impact on committee assignments, where a person's office is, where they sit on the floor."[19]

As assistant minority leader, as a ranking liberal Democrat with six years' seniority, Rich Castro logically appeared next in line for the job. However, during informal strategy sessions when all the support was tallied up, Castro came up several votes short.

As virtually no ideological differences separated Peña from Castro at the time, the decision centered (as is so often the case in the legislature) on the personalities. "Rich was a little bit more laid back," recalls Knox, "a little bit more easygoing; he had a wonderful sense of humor." Furthermore, he had been in an awkward position, having served as assistant minority leader under Kirscht with the understanding that he would not challenge Kirscht's leadership.[20]

Senator Paul Sandoval speculates that Castro's humor worked against him. "Legislators admired Rich," he explains. "They thought a lot about him; they listened to him; he was persuasive. . . . But Richard's sense of humor made people laugh. [That] humor was a tremendous strength, but outside of the Chicano Caucus, it was perceived politically as a weakness by fellow legislators. . . . Federico is very non-humorous . . . but he was perceived as an up-and-comer. He was a lawyer. He presented himself very well. He was very articulate. Good looks. The whole gamut of what it takes to be a politician."[21] What is more, he represented new blood and he enjoyed a smooth working relationship with Governor Lamm. In the Chicano Caucus, Castro held the utmost respect, but across the broad spectrum— among urban, suburban, and rural Democrats from all over the state— Peña had the wider appeal.

Peña oftentimes displayed a hard, uncompromising edge, a quality that may have endeared him to a minority party accustomed to tough legislative infighting on the issues that meant the most to them. Lyle Kyle from the Legislative Council described the Republican reaction to Peña's ascension to Democratic leadership in the House. "When Federico Peña ran for minority leader," he says, "the Republicans had a contest for majority leader. Both contestants—they were young bucks comin' up—stepped aside and they elected Ron Strahle, a Republican from Fort Collins who . . . had been a mover and shaker for ten years and who had been speaker of the house. They were nervous about Federico. Federico was fast on his feet and they wanted somebody that had experience . . . as their spokesman."[22] Considered aloof, mistrustful, and an outsider by many, the new house minority leader was clearly feared and respected by the opposition.

Within two years, the apprentice Peña had surpassed his more senior mentor Rich Castro. The meteoric rise left a bad taste for some in the Chicano Caucus, who thought Castro unjustly upstaged. Representative Knox, however, insists that Peña did not come in "with banners waving. . . . We didn't have anybody jumping up and down saying they'd do it."[23] And Peña is quick to respond to charges of unrestrained ambition. "I did not want to become house minority leader," he says. "Wayne Knox and [Representative] Jerry Koppel came to me and said, 'We want someone to be more forceful and who will represent more of the fundamental Democratic Party values than Mr. Kirscht.' I was shocked because I was basically a freshman. I had conversations with people and asked them, 'What about Rich? What are his views?' I think I even talked to Rich because I was very sensitive; he'd been in the legislature a long, long time. I think what finally happened was Rich did not have the votes . . . because there were different factions, there were people from the out-state area, there were conservative members of the party. As a result, they elected me. But let's start with some real basic facts. This was not my idea. I did not want to become minority leader."[24]

Reluctant or not, Peña's challenge to Bob Kirscht established him as a serious political player and established him also as the type of risk-taker capable of winning bigger races. The new kid on the block in the State House of Representatives in 1981 became the new kid on the block in the mayoral race in 1983.

Peña's Activist Vision

Embedded in Peña's mayoral campaign slogan, "Imagine a Great City," was the idea that city government must actively intervene to shape Denver's direction. Mayoral advisor Tom Gougeon described his view of the differences between the McNichols and the Peña orientation to government.

"If you watched Denver city government over most of the McNichols years, it tended to be pretty laissez faire. All the things that were going on downtown was a good example. It was completely responding to commercial imperatives and there was no focus on the qualitative things that make a good downtown. It had the largest skyscrapers and a huge amount of investment and yet all that investment was making it a less interesting place. You had a bunch of very expensive modern office towers that killed off street life. You had parking garages that deadened some of the blocks. You had the mall—this great new asset to work from—but the city hadn't really driven the mall; it had been Phil Milstein [director of Downtown Denver, Inc.], the Regional Transportation District, and a bunch of other people. Lower Downtown was being demolished. All those historic buildings—we lost half the buildings in Lower Downtown in the ten-year period between the early '70s and the early '80s. The cultural facilities were struggling. Half of them were closing one day a week because they didn't have the resources to operate. There wasn't any coherent response to all this. Making sure downtown succeeded wasn't really an explicit agenda item that I saw on the previous administration. I think the previous administration had tended to leave all that to the business community and to the market. Downtown would be what they determined it to be. Our orientation was, gee, we have a huge stake in what happens here. We need to be out front in saying here's what we want from downtown; here's what we're willing to try. There are things we care about; there are assets that are important to downtown; there's certain stuff we will and won't tolerate. Lower Downtown's historically and commercially important. We're interested in preservation. We were bringing the whole concern for urban design back. [We had the] belief that city government is a viable tool that can do a lot of things. It can be a leader; it can be a productive force; it can be a vehicle for addressing community needs. It's not passive; it doesn't deflect those responsibilities to other people. It was a complete reversal of that sense that other people make those decisions. It was putting the city out in front, sometimes way out in front.

"The Cherry Creek Mall and all that nonsense that was going on about, 'Oh, they want to build a huge mall and the neighborhood's upset.' Previously the city had just sort of stayed out of the way on that but we jumped into the middle of it. It wasn't always the wisest thing to do but it was certainly the character of the Peña administration. All those issues: the convention center, the airport. Rather than just sit back and let 'em muddle along and see what happens and let other people take the lead, Peña's people believed the city had a role to play and sometimes the most significant role to play. It was sort of a culture. The people who were attracted to working in the administration were generally activist people. If they had faults and were guilty of sins and omissions, it was always trying to do too much and getting too far out in front—wanting to take on too much change. It was never people sitting back with their feet up on their desk, saying, 'Let's go slow. Let somebody else do this.' There were equally activist views on neighborhoods. How do you support the rebirth of neighborhoods? How do you make a neighborhood work? This [activism] was the fundamental reason that Federico ran and the fundamental reason that a lot of us got involved in the first place."[25]

Historians Stephen Leonard and Tom Noel compared the Peña administration to the era of mayor Robert Speer, whose vision and government intervention left a tremendous visual imprint on Denver through the turn-of-the-twentieth-century City Beautiful program.[26]

Taking the Reins from Min Yasui

It was in this context of a dynamic, activist administration that Peña appointed Rich Castro, his former mentor in the House of Representatives, to head up Denver's Commission on Human Rights and Community Relations. The commission had first been set up in 1947 under mayor Quigg Newton, who sensed the precariousness of the old order of racial oppression and moved to establish an agency that could at least study the problems of race if not actually address them.[27]

Under McNichols, the commission had operated under the directorship of Minoru Yasui, a Japanese American, who had garnered great respect in the civil rights world by purposely violating a curfew order on Japanese Americans in 1942 in order to initiate a test case to challenge the law. As a young lawyer, Yasui had walked the streets of Portland after the 8:00 P.M. curfew until police finally arrested him. For his trouble, he ended up serving nine months in solitary confinement in the Multnomah County Jail. Yasui was a hard taskmaster, who ran the agency with an iron hand, as well as a hard worker, who regularly put in twelve- and fourteen-hour days. Castro's relation with Yasui had always been laden with paradox.

This, after all, was the same Min Yasui who had conducted the investigation into police brutality when a younger, brasher Castro had suffered a beating at the hands of the Denver Police in Curtis Park. Yasui's investigation cleared the police of any wrongdoing. "The finding was not that there was no police brutality," Yasui stated. "The finding was that no brutality could be proven. . . . We can't prove brutality although there is a doubt in the back of my mind."[28] Castro's painstaking testimony had been disregarded, and Castro's supporters repeatedly labeled the investigation a "whitewash."

More threatening to Yasui, the key Chicano members of his own agency had bitterly taken him to task. George Garcia, consultant to the Commission on Chicano Affairs, was fired in May 1970, shortly after the investigation on police brutality announced its findings. Garcia had written an internal memo to his boss calling the entire investigation "garbage." He claimed Yasui had questioned his professionalism because he had failed to reach out to the Chicano community in an effort to convince them that the brutality investigation was not a whitewash.[29] In Garcia's eyes, Yasui expected him to go out and calm the multitudes with a transparent cover-up. Garcia claimed other reasons as well. His decision to run for lieutenant governor as the La Raza Unida candidate was an additional factor in his dismissal, he asserted. "I was too Chicano," he said. "This is because I took a stand when I joined the commission that my commitment was to the Chicano community and always has been since."[30]

Naturally, Yasui denied any political reprisal and labeled the anti-Chicano bias accusation directed at him as "ridiculous." He cited, instead, "flagrant violations of regulations . . . continued violations of directives set forth by the mayor's office . . . and unsatisfactory performance of his duties."[31] Yasui's protests, however, were not helped by the resignations of two additional Chicano staff members within a week of Garcia's ouster. State senator Roger Cisneros and Armando Atencio resigned their positions on the same day, stating jointly that the Commission on Community Relations "is no longer serving the needs or desires of the Chicano community within the City and County of Denver." Said Cisneros, "I feel that in this day and age of turmoil and disturbances, that it is important for all agencies to review their role and not be reluctant to change and to meet the new demands of the 1970s." In resigning, he could devote his time to organizations that "I feel are looking toward the future, rather than devoting time to an organization that, in my opinion, has outlived its usefulness to the Chicano community."[32]

Through it all, Mayor McNichols stuck by his man. Confronted with Chicano demands to fire Yasui, McNichols replied, "I intend to commend him for the good job he has done."[33] When their lives first intersected in 1970, the relationship between Castro and Yasui was a stormy one.

Nevertheless, within two years, Castro was working for Min Yasui. Earning a meager $14,000 a year as a state representative in the mid-'70s, Castro hired on part-time with the commission as a consultant primarily for the Commission on Youth.[34] Colleagues say he got on well with Yasui, came to respect him, learned a great deal from him. Still, when a budget crunch materialized in the late '70s, Castro lost his job.[35] Senator Paul Sandoval claims that Yasui fired Castro for taking a public position favoring a pay raise for firefighters. "Richard was close to Min Yasui," he said. "It broke Min's heart to do what he had to do."[36]

Castro's convoluted history with the Commission on Human Rights and Community Relations brings into play a basic question: Exactly what is the role of that small agency on West Colfax, which Castro directed for almost the entire eight years of the Peña administration? Certainly, with all the talk of whitewashes, there were many who saw the commission as a token gesture—a public relations facade set up to deflect criticism from liberals, progressives, and radicals directed at the mayor. Set up an agency to advocate for the poor, minorities, and the disenfranchised; feed it a starvation budget that keeps it alive but powerless. Allow the mayor to cover himself on his left, as he runs the real business of the city in alliance with the bankers and brokers on Seventeenth Street.

The Role of Castro's Agency

Though the agency had always lacked political punch, the reality of its presence reveals a much more nuanced and complex picture. As director of human rights and community relations, Castro took charge of some fifteen functions in city government. There were commissions on discrimination, women, aging, youth, disabilities, the hearing impaired, and childcare. Also included were the Mayor's Advisory Task Forces for African Americans, Hispanics, Asians, Native Americans, and the gay and lesbian community. There was an Office of Citizen's Response to handle grievances against police, quarrels between neighbors, complaints concerning public utilities. Describing the various duties of the director, Steve Newman, the man who inherited Castro's job in Mayor Wellington Webb's administration, said, "You had all those commissions, all those advisory task forces, every community group conceivable. You gotta be there. And when the mayor calls and says, 'Look, I can't make this meeting tonight,' you have to do it. The position is like a mini-mayor."[37]

"The Commission acts as a liaison between the mayor's office and community organizations," said *The Denver Post*. "Historically, it has been used as a vehicle to resolve disputes between neighborhoods and city government."[38]

Vickie Calvillo, who worked for the commission under three administrations beginning in 1974, described her job more in terms of intelligence gathering. "We were supposed to be the eyes and ears of the administration," she says. "We were supposed to know our community—I used to have the whole Southwest quadrant under McNichols—know the leaders in the neighborhoods, know the organizations, their purposes, what they were doing, if they were doing a good job or weren't doing a good job, evaluate what the programs were doing, know what we needed, be in a position, if asked, to advise the administration."[39]

All this activity was accomplished with the tiniest of staffs. When Castro took the helm in 1983, the ranks were sorely depleted from the loss of federal funding and the drying up of grant money resulting from the Reagan budget cuts. Castro's staff numbered no more than twenty-eight; his budget hovered around $3 million.[40]

The effects of Reagan's federal budget were multiplied further by the profound recession that hit the Denver economy in the early '80s and plagued the city throughout the years of the Peña administration. National economic woes hit locally all the harder because the Rocky Mountain energy boom of the '70s collapsed miserably as oil prices plunged to new depths. The massive flow of investment in energy projects slowed to a trickle. As geologists and computer programmers lost their jobs, Denver's tax base began to dry up liked a plugged oil well. There were few dollars to be found for a social worker heading a human rights agency.

Reaganomics and recessions aside, the Human Rights Commission had never been awash with money, had never been a major priority. At its height during the Carter years, the staff had topped out at sixty. The director of the commission occupied a position structurally outside of the mayor's inner circle; it was not a cabinet-level position. Looking at a flow chart of the city power structure, the Commission for Human Rights and Community Relations stands off to the side of the nine major departments whose heads, along with a few key aides, constituted the cabinet. The big departments—Safety (which has been compared in scope to a municipal version of the Defense Department), Public Works, Aviation—these were the deliverers of service; they oversaw thousands of employees; they commanded the big budgets.

That Richard Castro, whose roots ran so deep in the Chicano community, should labor in relative obscurity, caused consternation among some of his friends. There are some who claim he was shunted aside because he was late in coming to Federico Peña's first election campaign. "Rich wasn't hot to support Federico," says Paul Sandoval. The cautious Castro harbored doubts about Federico's viability as a candidate and also retained some hopes for city councilman Sal Carpio's entrance into the race. Paul Sandoval claims that he, cousin Don Sandoval, and Ruben Valdez had to meet with Federico at Trader Vic's on the ground floor of the Radisson Hotel shortly after the election to "basically force him to give the position [of commission director] to Rich."[41] Senator Don Sandoval, putting a different spin on the same episode, said that the three had to "beg" him to appoint Castro.[42]

Paul Sandoval further claimed, "Rich was extremely hurt he was not part of the cabinet. It was a question of who Peña listened to. Though Richard was perceived as close, he was not within that circle of being listened to.... He would always vent his frustration that Federico would not listen to him."[43]

Peña remembers things differently. He appointed Castro to the human rights commission, he says, because he was the right man for the job. "We worked together a lot in the legislature," he recalled, "and it seemed to me that one of his great passions as an individual and as a legislator was in the human condition.... If you go back and look at the fights that he would wage on the floor of the House of Representatives, whether it was supporting the Martin Luther King holiday or bilingual education or matters affecting the Jewish community, he was always there raising the controversial human rights issues that frankly nobody else would raise. He was the point person. For that reason, I thought it made enormous sense for him to take that position in the City and County of Denver.... On a professional, philosophical, and intellectual basis, that's why I asked him to take that position. On a personal level, Rich and I were very good friends ... we had a personal affinity and we got along very well.... I thought he would be perfect for the position."[44]

Responding to the charge that Castro did not have the ear of the mayor, that he did not occupy a place in the inner circle, Peña replied, "That's news to me.... I always considered him to be a cabinet member anyway in the [sub-cabinet] position he was in. Certainly he was at most of my regular meetings with the cabinet. He was always present at those meetings that we had at least once a week and so he was fully engaged.... As far as I'm concerned, Rich was close to me, advised me, and had an enormous impact on my policies.... Go back and look at the eight years of the record and you'll see Rich's influence throughout my administration. Many of the things we did were, I think, a reflection of Rich's work and his commitment ... to neighborhoods or to human rights issues or to people with disabilities.... If Rich wanted a cabinet position, he would have come to me and said, 'You know, after so many years, I'd like to be considered for this or that position,' and to my knowledge, I don't recall him ever saying that to me."[45]

"I do think the nature of those agencies," said Tom Gougeon, "where you've got the manager of safety who's got thousands of employees and a couple hundred million dollar budget sitting at the table and you've got Rich who's got twenty employees—that's a reality for anybody who doesn't have the line management responsibility for dollars, bodies, and service delivery obligations. Those people have a disproportionate influence . . . because that's where the action is; they have all the resources. . . . Safety's got helicopters and guns and an army. It's a somewhat different world; they have their own reality. . . . If you're off running one of those big departments, you're buried in the realities of lawsuits and service delivery, contracts, and personnel issues. Those people come to the table saying. 'Here's the dynamic within the cops or within the medical staff.' On the other hand, if you're Rich, you're saying, "Yeah, but the community's really upset about this or that.' In some ways, people like Rich have a better overview. If you aren't managing 10,000 people every day, you've got some time to hear more about what's happening in the community and maybe see some things that the other folks just aren't gonna see. . . . Maybe before you drive off the cliff somewhere, someone like Rich is gonna know that's where you're headed and that's part of his job—even though it might be annoying sometimes—to alert those managers and say, 'I think there's a big problem with where you're going with this.' There are hundreds of those kinds of things in the course of normal business within the city. Rich didn't have a lesser role but a different role."[46]

These differing views of Castro's strategic position grew into a schism between the mayor and some segments of the Chicano community, which surfaced early and began slowly to spread. It was a gap that requires further exploration, but as to Castro's role in city government there can be little doubt. The position as director of the Commission on Human Rights and Community Relations fit Rich Castro like a glove, and that is where he belonged. His gifts were those of an organizer, a talker, a street social worker, not an administrator. To appoint him director of social services or manager of parks and recreation just to provide him with a formal cabinet-level position would have constituted a colossal waste of his talents. He would have withered on the vine.

And so Castro threw his energies into the commission for human rights and devoted himself to its major goals: peacemaking between disparate community elements, advocacy for those shunted aside by mainstream society, public relations for his new boss at the City and County Building, and, perhaps most importantly, opening access to city government to those neglected or shut out by prior administrations.

Directions and Duties

Castro set the tone of accessibility through the manner in which he ran the agency. His door was always open, his management style democratic. It differed markedly from the style of his predecessor, Min Yasui, who, though effective on many levels, ran a top-down operation inside the agency. The significance here was clear: Castro's aim was to open up communication with groups excluded during the McNichols administration, indeed by all previous administrations.

Castro would come in to the office at six in the morning, read the papers, and fire off the FYI memos to the hundreds of people he kept in contact with, directing their attention to a newspaper clipping here or a letter to the editor there. Then the schedule would begin, from seven in the morning often until ten at night, with perhaps a quick break for a beer around five before he'd go back and hit it again.

His life became a bustling swirl of meetings—town hall meetings, neighborhood meetings, crisis intervention, mediation. "What does the Native American community think is important?" said Vickie Calvillo, who currently works with the Police Review Board. "What's important to the Jewish community; what are its priorities? They identified their issues; they identified what they wanted done. Richard's position would be, 'OK, how can I help implement some of these things?'"[47] In a strange sort of way, it resembled the classic community organizing Castro had done with the West Side Coalition years before. Identifying the issues of the community comes right out of the Alinsky school of organizing. This time, however, Castro, the insider, emphasized harmony and cooperation with the powers of the city rather than confrontation.

One quagmire Castro walked into typified the delicate and complex role he occupied in the Peña administration. Curtis Park—that East Side landmark where Castro had worked, organized, and been beaten by Denver's police—had changed little since 1970 despite a few upscale remodeling jobs in the surrounding neighborhood during the energy boom. If anything, the recession of the 1980s brought increased misery to the park and to the residents of the immediate area. Drug dealers openly hawked their wares, while whiskey was brazenly consumed. With these activities came a corresponding rise in the level of violence and robbery. In a 1986 incident, one of two men suspected of drinking pulled a gun and shot the police officer who had stopped him. The wounded officer, Frank Padilla, returned fire and killed his assailant, Orval Gonzales.[48] That same year, dozens of children witnessed another shooting in the park, this one allegedly from a drug deal turned sour. "The kids were so scared," said a pool attendant, "they were screaming and running into the building for protection."[49] Nearby families feared taking their children on picnics or using the playground facilities. The criminals had taken over the park; the residents wanted it back.

Castro attended meetings at the Curtis Park Community Center for months, trying to formulate a plan to rid the neighborhood of problems. Residents discussed sprucing up the swimming pool, closing down restrooms where junkies could be found shooting heroin, and redesigning the park to make it harder for drug users to hide or to stash their wares. They decided to rename the place "Mestizo Park." Castro coordinated activities between Denver Housing Authority, youth agencies, mental health agencies, and the Parks and Recreation Department. He tried to raise money for improvements from corporate donations. He negotiated with police chief Tom Coogan to beef up protection. The city moved to implement the entire plan in the mid-summer of 1986. Castro left one meeting with a warning: "[Adding police patrols] is going to cause some problems. The police won't limit enforcement to dope dealers. They also will enforce bottle laws, curfews and other minor ordinances," which, he said, the community must be ready to accept.[50]

Castro's statement proved prophetic. Within a month some community members were directing their wrath toward the Denver Police, who had begun patrolling the park en masse in the wake of the shooting incident. "Curtis Park Labeled 'Police State'" read the headline in *The Denver Post*.[51] Much of the criticism stemmed from Ana Marie Sandoval, a long-time neighborhood resident, who argued, "Coming in with this many officers is like trying to kill flies with a gun. We feel, under the guise of so-called protection of the community, there is a great deal of harassment of young people; there is a lot of stereotyping of young people and intimidating them by saying they are pushing drugs or being involved in drugs. The fact that this park is empty is an indication that the community is not being allowed to use it through intimidation. Everywhere you look there are policemen. Yesterday there were fourteen motorcycle policemen in this park. They kept people from coming and relaxing by going up and circling them on their motorcycles. Police cars come up and drive on the lawn and create holes. If there is a problem with drugs, it should be dealt with, not only as a police problem, but as a lack of community services in this area. . . . There are very few, if any, private outlets or social services the youths can turn to."[52]

In the days of the movement in 1970, Castro's role in Curtis Park seemed clearer cut. The cops—outsiders by definition—were coming in, nightsticks swinging, and bloodying up the neighborhood kids. Establishing an independent civilian Police Review Board was the overriding issue. Castro never gave up his vision for a review board and remained forever an advocate of such a solution.[53] Never did he gather the clout, however, to see this vision through. In the meantime, he tried quietly in the background to cushion the neighborhood from an overzealous police presence. "He worked very closely," said Mayor Peña, "with Police Chief Zavaras in terms of in-service training and sensitivity."[54]

But as a city government insider in 1986, an older Castro had to view the situation from a good many other perspectives, not the least of which encompassed the majority in the neighborhood who had clamored for a more forceful police presence. Thus, Castro found himself trapped between a suspicious East Side neighborhood desperate for police protection but resentful of the heavy hand, and a nervous police force unwilling to prioritize, unwilling to distinguish between major crime and minor misdemeanors. "Maybe there's a middle ground," said Castro. "The majority of people down here want more police protection."[55] But the search for that elusive middle ground proved difficult. A year later Castro, still searching, told the *Rocky Mountain News*, "I think there's been a turnaround. There have been months of efforts to bring the community residents together." But still, he said, reclaiming the park for family enjoyment "isn't going to happen overnight."[56] Between those lines, one can read the frustration haunting Castro as he served as point man for the administration in one sticky situation after another.

xii

no exceptions

Shortly before his death, Castro found himself again on the front line of another explosive issue. In the fall of 1990, the director of the human rights commission played a crucial role in presenting a new civil rights ordinance before a divided city council. It was his agency—meager though its numbers were—that was slated to enforce the measure.[1]

Denver had never before passed a comprehensive law banning discrimination. The new ordinance outlawed discrimination on the basis of the usual categories: race, color, religion, national origin, gender, age, marital or military status, physical or mental disability. Two additional words, however—"sexual orientation"—turned the debate into an issue destined to rock the whole state and lead eventually to a legal dispute pursued all the way to the United States Supreme Court.

Castro's position as human rights director kept him intimately in touch with the ugly manifestations of hatred that invaded the fringes of public life. In the months prior to the city council vote, Castro noted the numerous incidents that came to his attention. There had been, for instance, a 100-percent increase over the previous year in anti-Semitic vandalism and harassment. The Egg Shell, a popular Jewish-owned breakfast spot in Lower Downtown, had been set afire and vandalized, with four swastikas painted in white on the basement and main floors. The incident, following on the heels of similar activities, prompted Mayor Peña to order a general investigation of racist incidents in Denver. There was the beating of Japanese students at Teikyo University in southwest Denver, when six students were robbed and attacked by youths wielding baseball bats. In a very informal poll by the *Rocky Mountain News*, 60 percent of the twenty Teikyo students selected at random reported harassment by white teenagers ranging from racial taunting to egg throwing to urinating in front of them.[2] There were several occasions when nightclubs denied access to black residents. And there were repeated incidents of beatings and harassment of gays, especially in the area along South Broadway, the location of several gay bars and restaurants. These bordered the Baker neighborhood that, until recently, had been Castro's home turf. "This [legislation] is probably twenty years overdue," Castro told the *News*.[3] Castro viewed these disparate hate crimes as part of a seamless fabric of bigotry. The beating of a gay man at the Compound Bar represented for Castro the same mindset that led to the torching of a Jewish-owned restaurant in LoDo or the denigration of a Mexican immigrant worker. To wean out gays or lesbians from the net of protection would not only encourage harassment of gays but also encourage the harassment of other marginalized groups. To deliberately exclude a historically persecuted group from protected status would result in creating a climate conducive to hatred or discrimination against all persecuted groups.

Of course, in a liberal Democratic city, this stand did not come without political benefit. Early in his first mayoral campaign, Peña successfully sought to bring the gay community into the coalition of discontented forces that eventually brought him victory. Less than a year after his election, the mayor stuck his neck out by announcing his personal boycott of the St. Patrick's Day Parade, whose organizers voted to ban members of the gay community from carrying a banner in the march. Parade chairman Jim Eakins termed Peña's announcement "insulting" and added that parade officials "have seen to it over the years that every minority group is represented. I don't consider [homosexuals] a minority group. We're just not going to shove this down people's throats."[4]

Eakins's response indicated the depth of emotion on this issue smoldering beneath the surface, waiting to explode. Popular as the new ordinance was in some circles, it took little time for a fierce reaction to mobilize. Castro took considerable heat from the culturally conservative sectors of his own Chicano community.[5] Catholic Archbishop J. Francis Stafford added that the "language of the ordinance could lead to legal acceptance of homosexual or bisexual alternatives to heterosexual marriage and further threaten the integrity of the family."[6]

Scarcely had city council given birth to the ordinance when Citizens for Sensible Rights, a conservative Christian-based group, began a petition drive to repeal the language that included "sexual orientation" as a protected status. The group's leader, Dr. Richard Heckmann, labeled homosexuality "abnormal sexual behavior," and used the specter of the AIDS virus to whip up sentiment against gay rights. Added Presbyterian minister Lou Sheldon, who journeyed to Denver for the California-based Traditional Values Coalition, "This nation is in a battle for its soul; America today stands at the crossroads. We live comfortably in our families but a war is waging," he announced. "Homosexuality is a dysfunctional behavioral problem because you do not reproduce; you do not bond. . . . The marriage bed has always been reserved for the male and female since the Judeo-Christian ethic. If you remove the male and female out of the marriage bed and make it a man-boy, woman-girl, two men two women, man-animal and man-daughter or mother-son, then what you have done is you have brought about a total destruction of Western civilization."[7]

Couching the struggle in such monumental terms spurred the gay community into what seemed a fight for survival. They fought like never before; they formed the Equal Protection Ordinance Coalition and appointed Mayor Peña as one of two honorary chairs. The coalition won hands down. In a May 1991 referendum, eight months after the original passage of the Civil Rights Ordinance, Denver voters rejected by a 54- to 46-percent margin the attempt to overturn the gay rights portion of the legislation. In doing so, Denver became the largest city in the nation to endorse gay rights legislation through a popular vote.[8]

The victory, however, merely set the stage for an even more heated battle. Within a year, voters statewide set out to overturn local gay rights legislation by offering Amendment 2 to the state constitution. The language in the amendment banned "protected status" for homosexuals, thereby annulling legislation already in place in Denver and Boulder. Voters passed the amendment following a highly charged campaign in November 1992. Although the U.S. Supreme Court eventually overruled Amendment 2, the episode placed Colorado in the forefront of the "Cultural Wars," those vehement ideological, social, and sometimes even biblical battles waged between the liberal left and the conservative, largely Christian right throughout the 1990s.

By the time these last two referenda came before the voters, Castro had succumbed to a stroke at the tragically early age of forty-four. His role in promoting the Denver city ordinance, however, had already marked him as a local leader in a struggle to broaden the definition of human rights. His credo as director of the human rights commission: "Liberty and justice for all—no exceptions."

Thus, the latter stages of Castro's career can be characterized by an increased recognition that a universal, all-inclusive concept of human rights must necessarily accompany a nationalist perspective. While emerging as the most prominent spokesman for the particular interests of the Chicano community, Castro was simultaneously pushing forward the idea that the innate humanity of everyone must be recognized and respected.

This orientation surfaced repeatedly. Castro was all over town, show-ing up at meetings not only for the Hispanic community but also for every conceivable community organization: neighborhood, African-American, Greek, and Italian groups. He attended Native American powwows at the Coliseum and visited Arizona to educate himself about a land dispute be-tween Hopis and Navajos. He helped form the Jewish-Chicano Dialogue. When the lowest-paid workers in Denver organized Justice for Janitors under the sponsorship of the Service Employees Union, he was there in support. When Denver's poor and transient population faced an undercount in the 1990 Census, Castro headed efforts to ensure their inclusion. The *Rocky Mountain News* took to using the adjective "beloved" to describe his connection to the community, and it was there in those endless meetings where the affable and ever-present Castro earned that description. That he took his share of hits from his own Chicano community is undeniable. Nevertheless, his constant presence earned him a great deal of respect all over Denver.

Stepping up to the Pulpit

From the beginning, Castro used the position of human rights director as a pulpit from which to expound his blend of nationalism, universal human rights, and progressive liberalism. He was forever quoted in the two Den-ver dailies. He penned a stream of letters and guest columns for the *Post* and *News* and a weekly column for *La Voz*. He wrote for the *Colorado States-man*, the periodical for political insiders. He hosted a TV program on Chicano affairs and appeared on radio talk shows. *Time* magazine quoted him, and he wrote guest columns for national publications.

It is true that some of his bursting energy was inspired by political considerations. It is clear, for instance, that he was eyeballing Denver's District One seat in the U.S. House of Representatives, which, since 1974, had remained the private domain of Pat Schroeder. Adored in Denver for her family-oriented politics and her wit, for establishing an early feminist presence in the male-dominated House, and for her ability to wield power through committee chairmanships, the indomitable Schroeder would even-tually have to move on. Several of Castro's colleagues encouraged him to position himself to enter the ensuing battle to succeed her. The more vis-ibility he gained by taking stands on national issues—the more he em-braced the role of point man for liberal perspectives in a liberal city— the more viable his candidacy would be in the upcoming power vacuum.

It was also true that his boss encouraged Castro's ideological campaigns. "I know there were some issues," recalls Peña, "where he would write national columns . . . that were hard hitting. But they needed to be said, and I said, 'Terrific, do it. Another mayor might have said, 'You can't do that; you can't write those kinds of things.' But I gave him lots of flexibility because I think it was the right thing to do. I think that voice needed to be heard, I certainly encouraged him, and he certainly felt free to do it. Governor Lamm: There's an example of where, as mayor, I needed to work with him on certain issues. The governor knew that I disagreed with him on many things he did and said about the Hispanic community. . . . Rich, however, had the flexibility to come at it much more directly. . . . He would understand that as mayor there were certain limitations on things I could say or do and he had a little more flexibility. We would talk about those things and deal with them very strategically."[9]

Practical political considerations or no, Castro, through his columns and public comment, did indeed evolve into a frontline local spokesman for both the liberal left-wing of the Democratic Party and a substantial segment of the Chicano community.

Among the several issues that smoldered and then burned white-hot in the liberal community during the Reagan years was American support for the peculiar variations of fascism that sprang up in the most poverty-stricken countries of Central America. Throughout the decade, El Salvador had been run first by the dictators of a military junta, then by a centrist Christian Democratic president, and then by a right-wing party whose founding father, Roberto D'Aubuisson, had acquired the nickname "Colonel Blow Torch." All the while, real power in this tiny coffee-exporting nation consisted of an assortment of shadowy groups behind the scenes—hit men connected directly or obliquely to the Salvadoran military. It was these "death squads" who destroyed the fragile foundation of democracy by systematically assassinating the political opposition, murdering progressive priests and nuns, and terrorizing peasants in guerrilla-controlled areas.

To the south, Nicaragua experienced the radical Sandinista revolution in 1979, which toppled the regime of Anastasio Somoza, an archetypal Central American dictator whose family had bled the country dry for two generations. Remnants of Somoza's army gathered in Honduras and Costa Rica and organized themselves as "Contras," or counterrevolutionaries, to overthrow the new leftist revolution. Just as Franco had used Morocco as a staging area from which to invade Republican Spain in the 1930s, the Contras used their base camps in neighboring countries to launch raids into the border areas of Nicaragua. Their methods often paralleled those used by the Salvadoran death squads.

The left wing—or what was left of it—in the United States was appalled, indeed apoplectic over the use of taxpayer dollars to finance terrorist activities in their own hemisphere. Nevertheless, driven by the tensions of the Cold War, American dollars were finding their way—covertly or overtly, legally or illegally—into the coffers of both the Salvadoran military and the Contras. Generous quantities of aid, advice, and CIA expertise turned both entities into virtual dependencies of the United States government.

Rich Castro joined the opposition to this policy early on. While his colleagues in Central American–based human rights agencies were busy documenting the grisly murders and mutilated bodies left by the death squads, Castro championed his colleagues' cause locally at public forums and in his newspaper articles. He visited Tucson in support of the new "Underground Railroad"—a collection of religious groups who helped smuggle Salvadoran refugees into the United States.[10] He accused the government of holding a "double standard for refugee status" in which Central Americans were consistently denied asylum status generally granted to refugees from communist countries. To grant equal status, he explained to the *Denver Catholic Register*, would amount to "an admission that [Central Americans] are fleeing due to U.S. policy."[11]

Castro was particularly drawn to the figure of Archbishop Oscar Romero, gunned down by a Salvadoran death squad while celebrating mass in the spring of 1980. Perhaps the martyred priest reminded him of his own childhood aspirations to the priesthood; perhaps the clergyman's evolution from conservative member of the church oligarchy to outspoken opponent of the military reminded him of the myriad transformations of consciousness he witnessed during the days of the Chicano Movement. In a commentary in the *Statesman*, Castro quoted the archbishop's sermon to the army, which he delivered the day before he was murdered. "No soldier is obliged," he said, "to obey an order contrary to the law of God. It is time that you come to your senses and obey your conscience rather than follow sinful commands."[12]

Years later, in another column for *La Voz*, Castro recorded his reaction to viewing the movie *Romero*: "Romero, faced with human suffering, confronts the dilemma that all people of compassion must confront; either become numb to the pain of those around, or begin to take action on their behalf. Ultimately he cannot ignore the poverty and suffering of his people, and finally compassion—not politics or ideology—compels him to choose sides to take a stand on behalf of the poor—effectively signing his death warrant. Romero is transformed from timid scholar to the champion and voice of the poor.

"There are three types of love that impact mankind," Castro added in the same column. "There is the love of self that each of us possess. . . . As humans we also experience romantic love for another. . . . However, there is another type of love that each of us should help cultivate. This is the love of our fellow man. Until there is peace in Central America, none of us in the U.S. are at peace, for it is our tax dollars that contributes to pain and suffering in that region."[13]

Through such columns, Castro sought to bring an international perspective to his work as human rights commissioner; he sought to inform his constituency about persistent global problems as well as local ones.

He sought also to inject that spirit into city policy. When Daniel Ortega, president of Nicaragua and head of the Sandinista Party, visited the United States in July of 1986, conservatives vilified him as an agent of the Evil Empire, an exporter of terrorism and monolithic communism and a threat to American security. Castro's attitude had been best expressed in a single headline addressed to Reagan's secretary of state in the Commentary and Opinion section of the *Statesman*: "Secretary Shultz, Red-Baiting Won't Work." In the subsequent article Castro compared Sandinista accomplishments against the activities of the Contras and concluded, "The Sandinista record . . . appears more consistent with democratic principles."[14]

It is not surprising, therefore, that Castro tried to humanize the face of the "enemy" by urging his boss to meet with Ortega when he came to Denver to address a meeting of the National Bar Association at the Marriott Hotel. "Rich encouraged me to speak to Daniel Ortega, which I did," says Peña.[15] Following the usual pattern, Peña trod a cautious path. "It's a courtesy visit," commented Peña's press secretary, Lauren Casteel. "The mayor meets with heads of state . . . whenever time permits. . . . I think it would be equally controversial if the mayor suddenly excluded Ortega from what has been a consistent pattern."[16] Castro, however, followed a more direct route and helped set up a forum for Ortega at St. Cajetan's Church on the Auraria Campus. "[It's] a great opportunity for Colorado and the nation to hear another viewpoint on what is happening in that Central American country," Castro told the *Rocky Mountain News*.[17] Thus, as the U.S. president tried to bleed the Sandinistas along their own borders, dehumanize them in the media, and isolate them from the American political landscape, Castro and other Denver peace leaders did their best to tweak the nose of the Reagan Administration.

The Language Battle Reemerges

Castro entered another battle closer to home. Once again he grappled with the dilemma of framing a balanced and moderately nationalist perspective, and once again the issue hinged on the sensitive subject of language. In 1983, as Colorado's Chicano Caucus struggled to retain bilingual education, Dr. John Tanton, a Michigan ophthalmologist, with considerable guidance from former U.S. senator S. I. Hayakawa, formed U.S. English, an organization dedicated to the idea that "English is, and ever must remain, the only official language of the people of the United States."[18] Prodigiously, the group grew to a quarter of a million members within six years, touting a board of directors that included such prestigious figures as novelist Saul Bellow, child psychologist Bruno Bettelheim, and former CU-Boulder activist turned conservative commentator Linda Chávez. *Time* characterized the organization as one that "promoted the idea that the influx of Latin immigrants in recent years has threatened the primacy of English."[19] Familiar territory for Castro, it represented a set of controversies that spilled over from Castro's acrimonious debate with Governor Lamm, who counted himself among the members of U.S. English.

This time, however, the battle centered on a series of state initiatives sweeping the country, all of which were designed to legislate English as the official language of those respective states. Republican state representative Barbara Philips (Colorado Springs) tried first in 1987 to enact the law in the General Assembly. Echoing the language of Governor Lamm, Philips pointed to a "movement afoot for non-assimilation. This is very divisive. If the government gives status to other languages and does not protect English as our common language, we are going to be a divided people."[20] "We respect ethnic groups," she stated in another interview. "But we expect them to become part of the mainstream of American life." Philips insisted her bill was not a punitive measure and should be supported by Hispanics. "If they want their children to excel," she said, "they should learn English. It's kind of a minority bill in a way."[21] Castro marked this particular passage in his own copy of the *Rocky Mountain News* story and scribbled in the margin: "Who is she kidding?"[22]

The Legislative Council, the research arm of the State Legislature, suggested that the one-sentence bill carried with it little impact on daily life. A council report likened its effect to the naming of a state bird. Castro, however, looked at the context of the bill and perceived in it something sinister, something that amounted to a frontal assault.[23]

He outlined the sordid history of past practices directed at language minorities: American Indians torn from their families for placement in boarding homes so that "their language and customs could be obliterated";[24] Chinese barred from testifying in court; the German language prohibited as a school subject; and the suppression of Spanish in school systems all over the Southwest.[25] He delineated his fears of a wide array of punitive measures: elimination of bilingual ballots, bilingual education, bilingual health services, court interpreters. Most importantly, however, he again warned against the creation of a climate of fear, distrust, and xenophobia. "While this measure purports to stand for unity, motherhood and apple pie," he wrote, "its hidden agenda is racist, divisive and ethnocentric. Of course all Americans should speak English. But you don't accomplish this . . . by putting a one-line measure into the Constitution. Amendments . . . have traditionally given rights and benefits to our citizens. The English Only Initiative unquestionably will . . . take away rights. . . ."[26] He noted the ironies. For his scrapbook, he clipped out an Ed Stein editorial cartoon from the *Rocky Mountain News*, which featured a map of Colorado. All of the Spanish names sprinkled across the four corners of the state— the Rio Grande, Pueblo, La Junta, Salida—were converted to their English equivalents—Big River, Village, Council, and Exit. Even the state's name was changed; Colorado had become "Red" in order to stay in compliance with Barbara Philips's bill.

Through the Movement years of the '60s and '70s, Rich Castro had witnessed the nation grope its way to a new understanding of the relationship between the American mainstream and its ethnic minorities. Based on respect for ethnic differences, this new perspective was variously labeled "multi-culturalism," "ethnic pluralism," or, more informally, the "salad bowl" approach (rather than the melting pot) to ethnic diversity in American society. Now at the end of a decade of conservative leadership, Castro saw this new awareness coming under systematic attack. In his mind, English-only represented just one more wrecking ball slamming away at the pillars of multicultural understanding. To one advocate of the English-only measure, Castro cautioned that the country "would do well to reinforce the unique American concept of pluralism which makes this country great instead of promoting suspicion of those who look or speak differently."[27]

As it turned out, Philips's bill never made it out of committee. Faced with a veto from Democratic governor Roy Romer, who called the bill "meaningless and symbolically irritating," Republican lawmakers found it expedient to allow the bill to die.[28] This tactical victory, however, merely opened the door for a statewide initiative in November 1988. U.S. English poured $100,000 into the campaign as Castro once again played the lead role in mobilizing forces against it. This time Castro's coalition, Coloradans for Language Freedom, went down, embarrassingly so. By a 64- to 36-percent margin, Colorado's voters approved Philips's initiative, making the state the seventeenth to enact such legislation.

"I'm obviously disappointed that the margin would be that large," said a discouraged Castro. "I regard Colorado voters as very independent voters and I'm very saddened to see that they bought into this."[29] Mayor Peña sought immediately to proscribe damages by signing an executive order barring city officials from discriminating against those who spoke languages other than English. "We have thousands of employees . . . ," stated Peña, "who may be interpreting this on their own. I want to make sure everybody understands what the policy of the city is so we have a consistent policy. I don't want someone over at Denver General to say 'Gee, maybe we can't provide translating services anymore . . . or someone at the department of social services saying, 'Well, perhaps we shouldn't be handing out bilingual material anymore.'"[30]

Equal protection laws for gays, immigration laws, insurgency and counterinsurgency in Central America, English-only initiatives—these were the issues that cut through Colorado's heart, indeed, the heart of America. They enveloped the country in rancor and defined the direction of political debate. In each case, Castro stood at the vortex of controversy, articulating and honing those positions that gave shape to the liberal and progressive thought of the times. Always on the front lines, he did little that was not controversial.

Assessing the Peña Years

In the final analysis, however, Castro cast his fate in his last years with the Peña administration and his impact is necessarily intertwined with Peña's. After all, the guest columns, weekly commentaries, and letters to the editor were signed "Rich Castro, Director, Agency for Human Rights and Community Relations." His views were officially linked to the city; he was an integral member of the Peña team.

The Peña legacy remains a complex mix of success and failure. "I was twenty years ahead of our time," Peña told *Denver Post* columnist Tomás Romero shortly before the end of his term. "A Mexican American Federico Peña should not have become mayor of Denver until the next century."[31] The meteoric rise and acceptance of the Hispanic middle class in the 1980s may more accurately argue that the coming of Federico Peña was right on time. Nonetheless, the pioneering aspects of Peña's terms as mayor will remain among the most important parts of his legacy.

As for the rest, local historians have already begun the debate. Nobody disputes his role as builder, as the guiding hand behind the transformation of Denver's landscape. Denver International Airport above all, but additionally the convention center, the new library, Coors Field, the Cherry Creek Mall, and the emergence of LoDo as the center of night life—these can all be traced back to the activism of the Peña era.

These grand projects represented a calculated choice springing from the political and economic soil of the '80s. The precipitous decline in the price of a barrel of crude oil had brought Denver's economy to its knees. Much of America suffered from recession during the 1980s, but Denver, dependent on energy investments scattered throughout the Rocky Mountain region, proved more vulnerable than most. At the federal level, the Reagan administration was putting its money into missiles to fight the Cold War rather than social services. This double bind clearly limited the options available to the young mayor and directed his focus to those massive projects he believed would bring economic recovery to the city.

"Our main challenge in the early '80s was the economy," recalled Peña. "There's just no question about that. You look at those problems and you say the priority, first of all, is to save the city and make sure it's financially and economically strong and viable."[32]

Castro's heart never pulled him into the center of these giant construction projects, but neither did he question their necessity. Nor did he question the partnerships between government and business that emerged to carry those projects out. "I would like to say," he told a group of Hispanic firefighters in 1987, "that these . . . are particularly difficult times for local elected officials. The federal and state government have both cut back drastically the financial support and assistance the inner cities once enjoyed. Today it is a challenge for mayors and city councils to develop new strategies to maintain a level of service without cutting out needed programs. This is the reason we talk so much about airports and convention centers. For not only do they generate tax revenue for programs, but equally important they help generate jobs."[33]

The mayor's preference for gigantic construction projects was likened by some to the Keynesian economics practiced during the Roosevelt era: Spend your way out of economic hardship. Prime the pump with deficit dollars to stimulate a tottering economy. Mayoral advisor Tom Gougeon, however, maintains that Peña's priorities would have remained the same regardless of the state of the economy. Downtown was in decline even before the recession. Cultural facilities, such as the Denver Center for the Performing Arts and the library, were struggling. The development of Cherry Creek was bogged down. The tax base was eroding as middle-income families fled to the suburbs. "On balance, says Gougeon, "where the city was in the early '80s was fairly precarious. If the economy had gone through the roof or the economy had gone to hell, we would have done all the same things because either way, that was the only scenario that was gonna keep Denver a viable fiscal entity."[34]

Peña's thrust lacked sufficient populist content to merit any comparisons to a localized version of the New Deal. His accomplishments, nevertheless, remain impressive. The tons of concrete and miles of structural steel did lay a foundation and infrastructure from which the city catapulted into the astonishing economic prosperity that marked the 1990s. So, too, it created the framework for the rejuvenation of the downtown area, a renewal that enabled the city to survive the primary threat it faced in the 1980s: the abandonment and decay of the inner core that was robbing the city of its vitality just as the outer layer of suburbs was growing wildly. That this transformation occurred in the midst of an economic downturn made Denver's reversal of fortunes even more impressive.

The Peña administration must likewise be credited with opening up the city to groups of people who never dreamed they would have access to power under the stodgy white establishment that managed the city up through the McNichols administration. Castro himself stated, "We have changed the complexion of the boards and commissions that assist with the running of city government. . . . [We have] dramatically increased the numbers of minorities who are in cabinet and sub-cabinet positions. Manual Martinez, Rich Gonzales, Ruth Rodriguez, David Gonzales. These are Hispanics who are running key agencies. . . . The Peña administration, hopefully, will be remembered as the administration that opened up the process to a broad range of individuals."[35]

State representative Doug Linkhart lauded Peña for instituting town meetings and opening up the political process to neighborhood groups and community organizations.[36] Though critical of some aspects of the mayor's links to the black community, the Rev. James Peters, head of the East Denver Ministerial Alliance, maintained that Peña ripped through the massive barriers merely by being elected. A black mayoral candidate could not have succeeded without Peña's having first broken the color barrier, he said. "I think he proved that a minority can get the job done, can change the city."[37]

A Growing Malaise

As segments of Denver basked in the glow of these changes, however, the very neighborhoods where Castro grew up and practiced his politics, the very neighborhoods that formed the original core of support for Peña were treading water to survive or just plain sinking into despair. The dropout rate for Hispanics at West, North, and Lincoln High Schools persisted stubbornly and unacceptably at 50 percent. Peña and the city could not be held directly responsible for this; that job belonged to the Denver School Board. Nevertheless, the dropout rate reflected the malaise and flagging spirits hovering over the Chicano community. Official poverty statistics demonstrated that the numbers of poor grew steadily during the Peña years. A Piton Foundation study found that the poverty rate among Latinos had grown from almost 24 percent in 1979 to over 30 percent in 1989.[38] It showed, further, that Denver had the third-highest poverty rate in the central core area among eleven large western cities and contained among those same cities the largest poverty gap between city and suburbs.[39]

Most dramatic was the coming of the gangs. They started claiming turf on the East Side at Fuller Park adjacent to Manual High, then spread like a virus into Clayton (where Castro grew up) and Park Hill, into Highlands on the North Side and Ruby Hill on the south. On the same West Side streets where Rich Castro had tried to organize in the movement days rose the Inca Boyz, cultivating, like other gangs, an aura of hardness and a reputation for mercilessness.

The emerging gang culture wreaked havoc on the quality of life in Denver's inner-city neighborhoods. Teenage kids, touting themselves with such labels as "original gangsters," concealed pistols in the pockets of their fashionably baggy pants. The mindless display of a covert gang sign or the color of a baseball cap might be enough to incite violence. Late-night parties turned deadly as revelers stood terrorized by exchanges of gunfire. Homeowners and owners of small businesses who had worked years to keep their places up watched—demoralized—as their property was violated repeatedly with crude, brazen graffiti. The easy money from drug deals on the street mocked the hard work of struggling mothers and fathers. The rash of senseless drive-by shootings instilled youth with gnawing fear and left parents second-guessing whether they could even let their younger kids play tag in the front yard. One former gang member wrote that the killers sought out victims who looked, acted, and felt the most like themselves—a tragic expression of self-hatred.

All this took root on Peña's watch, and Peña himself expressed profound regret for the failure of his administration to stifle the proliferation of gangs. "If I had sought a third term," he said, "my priorities would have been dealing with the educational issues and the human issues."[40] The new airport did not translate into better lives for the poor. Nor did the new convention center or the coming of Nieman Marcus or Lord & Taylor to the new Cherry Creek Mall. As hopes faded in the ghettos and barrios surrounding downtown Denver, so too did the image of Federico Peña in those same neighborhoods.

Some of this descent must be attributed to the ravages of recession, another part to the normal rough-and-tumble nature of city politics over an eight-year period. You cannot please everyone. Expectations during the election of 1983 reached a fever pitch. Advisor Tom Gougeon stated, "The voting patterns were that the Hispanic community . . . didn't participate in Denver municipal elections and then in 1983 they did by huge margins. You've got tens of thousands of people who never paid any attention to city government and suddenly a Hispanic is the mayor. . . . The growth in expectations was so enormous that he was just sort of destined to take the biggest beating from the Hispanic community."[41]

"The extreme disappointment had to happen," agreed Father Jose Lara of the North Side's Our Lady of Guadalupe Church. "We poor people are waiting for somebody to solve all our problems, so when somebody says 'Imagine a great city' and he's Hispanic, we think, 'Hey, rejoice.'"[42]

Expectations filled not only the hearts of ordinary citizens in the Chicano community but those of Hispanic leaders and politicians as well.

This latter group was an intimate community, related often by blood or marriage, often by ties of friendship and godparenting, which stretched back over several generations crisscrossing between Denver and New Mexico, San Luis and Pueblo. Everyone knew everyone. It was politically diverse and contained the usual numbers of competing personalities. Even if the mayor were disposed to shower patronage disproportionately upon the Chicano community (he was not), there were not enough jobs to go around.

When Hispanics were fired, the ripples in this small pond were magnified tenfold. Such was the case, for example, when Anna Flores, a woman entrenched for years in West Side politics, lost her post as director of the Denver Commission on Aging in 1988. It was Castro himself who had to ask an old friend for her resignation. Following, as it did, the firings of two other Hispanics, Flores's treatment elicited outrage from a network that ran deep in the community. "When you have Hispanic people who worked very hard for you and these people are being nipped off one at a time," complained labor leader Joe Maestas, "it becomes very questionable if there's any integrity in the administration. We're not saying he doesn't have the right to appoint people, but he's not showing sensitivity to the ones who put him in office."[43]

Even as he noted the rising discontent, Castro staunchly defended the mayor. "This particular mayor," he said, "has made incredible progress in terms of minorities at all levels. . . . Opportunities exist now that have not existed for many decades."[44]

Contributing to the widening chasm were Peña's choices for four top advisory posts: Tom Nussbaum, Tom Gougeon, Kathy Archuleta, and Sandy Drew, who constituted his inner circle. They were young, brilliant, and hardworking. They held Federico Peña in affectionate esteem, and he, likewise, valued them for their loyalty, talent, and raw intelligence. They were not well regarded, however, by many in the Chicano community. Individually brilliant, yes, but somehow disconnected and unrooted, unscarred by the struggles of the last twenty years, unmoved by the hunger that stemmed from the decades-long political exile of the Chicano community. Paul Sandoval disdained them as "yuppies." Others labeled them (referring to the two men) "the bearded, faceless ones" and still others "the gang of four."[45] Even Archuleta, a former administrator of bilingual programs for Denver Public Schools and the only Hispanic among the four, was not considered part of that activist core that had advanced the Chicano community over the last two decades.

As gatekeepers, the trusted members of the inner circle were overly zealous from the viewpoint of their critics. They were the schedulers and coordinators, the public relations experts who erected walls and moats between Peña and his most passionate constituency. So close to the heart-beat of the West and North Sides as a campaigner, Peña by mid-term stood aloof and isolated from the community. "When Federico was campaign-ing," said Paul Sandoval, "his pitch was, 'If I'm the mayor, the door is open.' That turned out not to be true. . . . People felt they don't have anyone to go to."[46]

To this Peña replied, "It is impossible for me to handle all those day-to-day routine sort of calls that others can competently handle. Most people think they can just pick up the phone and talk to the mayor. My work schedule makes that physically impossible. I am running the city."[47]

Certainly some of Peña's critics had their personal axes to grind. Paul Sandoval failed to get the appointment he aspired to as manager of parks and recreation.[48] Representative Phil Hernandez was Anna Flores's son-in-law.

Allegations and counter-charges aside, however, there is little doubt of Peña's essential focus: Build the airport, build the convention center, build the stadium. It was the big projects that kept the wheels of Denver's teetering economy turning. The physical landmarks—the concrete and steel structures—had always been the kind of things that mayors are remem-bered for, the kind of things that go in the history books. These priorities tended to marginalize the social work–centered politics—the neighborhood issues, the empowerment issues, the social justice issues—which Rich Castro had practiced since the 1960s. In a sense, Castro's issues were left dangling by the new Democratic Party politics, the new liberalism that was shaping up in the 1980s.

Castro learned painfully of his own isolation when he ran for the school board in 1989, a position he naturally gravitated to. He should have been a shoo-in. He ran as an incumbent by virtue of his appointment to the board six months prior to the election in the wake of Paul Sandoval's resignation. He had a slew of endorsements from influential Democrats and city lead-ers. He was the only Chicano running. When the ballots were tallied, how-ever, Castro came up 281 votes short, the first election defeat he'd ever suffered.

In defeat, Castro was humble and gracious, though very much hurt. Several factors caused the setback. Fourteen candidates had vied for three vacant positions in the citywide race and Castro finished a close fourth. The two top vote getters, Sharon Bailey and Martha Johnson, both came from the Park Hill neighborhood of northeast Denver, where voter turnout was especially heavy.[49] Park Hill was directly affected by the vote on the new airport, which appeared on the same ballot. Paul Sandoval claims that the winners' strategy of single-voting—encouraging supporters to vote for only one candidate instead of three, also proved decisive as it deprived

Castro of hundreds of second- or third-choice votes he would normally have received. In the more affluent southeast, where voter turnout was traditionally high, the more conservative Tom Mauro, who courted Republicans early on, defeated Castro, the most liberal of fourteen candidates. Most discouraging was the low turnout in the Castro strongholds: the West Side and northwest Denver. Only 35 percent of voters cast ballots in District 2 on the West Side, and 39 percent in North Denver's District 5. This compared with a 47-percent turnout citywide and 48- to 56-percent turnout in southeast Denver. This gap in voter turnout provided the margin of victory for Mauro.[50] Had West- and Northsiders turned out in the same proportions as the predominantly white South Side, Castro would have skated to victory.

These latter numbers particularly galled *Denver Post* columnist Tomás Romero. In a scathing piece penned right after the election, Romero wrote bitterly: "Nice going, Raza. For those of you who failed to vote in last Tuesday's school board election . . . I have but one word: Good. . . . Taste it, Raza. Taste the bitter pill of self-inflicted political poison. . . ."[51] As it had in so many years past, political apathy reigned in the barrio and once again deprived Hispanics of a piece of political power.

Castro was the best the liberals had to offer the poor. While other Democrats sought solutions in high-tech growth or government/corporate partnerships, Castro stuck close to the roots that inspired his own entry into politics: the Roosevelt New Dealers who had thrown a lifeline to his grandparents and the Kennedy liberals who pushed the War on Poverty to its limits. Castro forever fixed his gaze on the disenfranchised, the marginalized, the stranger, the underdog. But his vision in 1991 — a vision that embraced the overall vision of the Democratic Party — failed to inspire masses of residents on the North Side, the West Side, or the Curtis Park area. Politically they remained sullen, mistrustful, cynical, or unmoved. Castro's campaign failed to get these residents to clear out a few moments from the daily grind — from their jobs, from childcare, from television, from the long-awaited beer after work — to go down to St. Joseph's Church or Skinner Middle School long enough to cast a ballot. In the '60s and '70s, the early Movement had touched the souls of many of these people. The Peña campaign had done likewise in 1983.

But ten years after Ronald Reagan's ascendancy to the White House, Castro had become painfully aware that the political climate in America had undergone radical change. Chicanos could now aspire to govern major cities, and a vital new middle class had risen up in their midst. In the core city, however, for all the hope generated in the Movement years, for all the plans and blueprints formulated by Democratic politicians, frustration and apathy still held a tight grip on the imagination of a struggling populace. America had slid back—rollbacks in social services, self-absorption among the middle class, stagnation in the barrio. Castro himself seemed frustrated as he watched the promise and the memories of the Movement slipping away from those left in his old haunts on the West Side.

xiii

a lifetime of transformation

Nine hundred Denver Yellow Cab taxi drivers pooled enough money in 1979 for a small down payment to a Texas business-man and began running the company for themselves as a co-operative venture. Though punctuated by passionate debates over policy and business strategy, relations among the drivers for the first few years remained nonviolent, if not exactly civil. By the mid-1980s, how-ever, with the arrival of Denver's recession, tensions boiled over. By April 1991, the co-op hovered near bankruptcy and at least one fistfight broke out in a parking lot on Ringsby Court. Some of the tension sadly broke down along racial lines, and a few drivers asked city councilman Hiawatha Davis, who represented northeast Denver, to step in to try to lower the temperature. This type of mediation was bread and butter for the human rights commission, so Davis naturally invited his longtime friend Rich Castro to accompany him.

Arriving at Wyatt's Cafeteria in Aurora, the two received a call inform-ing them that drivers had postponed the meeting. Taking advantage of the unexpected break, they sat down for lunch. Castro took just one bite. His speech began to slur; he sounded to Davis as though he were drugged. "Have you ever had a stroke?" asked Davis. "No," replied Castro. "Do you have high blood pressure?" "Yes." Davis quickly called 911 and Castro remained fully conscious as the ambulance whisked him to nearby Aurora Presbyterian Hospital.[1]

Some of Castro's friends had been concerned about his health for sev-eral years. "I noticed, for one, that he was gaining weight," said high-school friend Ken Maestas. "I could see his skin taking on a certain kind of color, at times blotchy. He admitted to me that he was sleeping only three or four hours a night. . . . He told me he never realized he'd ever go as far as he did in the political world. He was getting national recognition as a political force and I think this made him drive harder. He was leading a pretty fast life towards the end. . . . I used to chastise him; I said, 'Rich, this going from fundraiser to fundraiser and gaining weight is going to be your undoing. When's the last time you had a checkup?' 'I don't know if I ever had a checkup,' he said."[2]

Castro's condition sank swiftly as he lost consciousness in the intensive care unit. Within two days, Representative Tony Hernandez stood up before the state legislature, where he announced to a stunned and tearful crowd that Castro had just received last rites. Rich Castro died much loved and very young. A cerebral hemorrhage—a ruptured blood vessel in the brain—took his life at age forty-four. Mayor Peña ordered city flags lowered to half-mast. Governor Roy Romer issued the same order for flags at state buildings.

The Cathedral of the Immaculate Conception on Colfax and Logan—a place where Castro had demonstrated in the '60s for racial equality within the Church—was packed with 2,000 people on April 17. "They were black, brown, yellow and white," wrote the *Rocky Mountain News*. "They were men, women, children, Republicans and Democrats."[3] All had come to bid farewell and pay final respects to a man who had touched their lives.

Both dailies had paid homage to Castro on their editorial pages the previous day. "Having known this modest but eloquent man so well," wrote *The Denver Post*, "we know that this community's rededication to the goals of equality and justice that Castro pursued so doggedly would mean more to him than any eulogies. And thus we join the many thousands of people he befriended in pledging to continue his fight for liberty and justice for all. *Vaya con Dios, Amigo*."[4] Wrote the *News*: "If friends are the medicine of life, as the Old Testament says, then Richard Castro could have opened a pharmacy."[5]

Post columnist Tomás Romero wrote, "He belonged to everyone. . . . For three days crowded corridors and waiting rooms of the intensive care unit [at Aurora Presbyterian] resembled a gathering of the United Nations. Native Americans, blacks, Jews, Greeks, Asians and other families that make up the American kaleidoscope came. Elders came as did children and people in wheelchairs. Virginia with towering grace insisted that they be allowed to come. Men and women in fine woolen coats sat next to those wearing humble garments. They were there as one community to weep openly, hold each other, share stories and wondrously intermingle grief with laughter."[6]

A misprint on the funeral service brochure listed "Ballbearers" instead of "Pallbearers." His closest friends in the sanctuary hid their chuckles knowing that Castro himself would have loved the joke.[7] Eulogies continued for two and a half hours. "Richard Castro loved people," said future mayor Wellington Webb, "And we all loved him."[8] Federico Peña raised his fist at the conclusion of his eulogy: "*Que viva la justicia,*" he said. "*Que viva la comunidad. Que viva la causa. Que viva Rich Castro.*" When it was over, Peña walked to the casket, wiping tears from his eyes. He tapped it twice gently and said, "I'm going to miss you, Buddy."[9]

If Richard Castro's journey was a short one, it covered a lot of territory. From his innocent years at Annunciation to the frenetic years in the Peña administration, the landscape in Denver—political, psychological, economic—insofar as it concerned race relations, had undergone a transformation of epic proportions. Even the language had changed, even—with the addition of the ñ to Denver newspapers—the alphabet. Castro saw it all.

The change in the life of his family reflected the change in the greater community. In trading his state legislator's job in 1983 for the job of director of the human rights commission, Castro also upped his salary from $14,000 to $40,000. He was still doing "people" things, wrote *Denver Post* reporter Cindy Parmenter, but the pay was better.[10] Castro moved his family to a two-story brick home in West Washington Park, a dozen blocks out of the barrio, far more modest than their neighbors' homes east of the park but, nevertheless, comfortably placed within the great American middle class. Compared to his father's work for eighty-two and a half cents an hour in the tool crib at Eaton Metals, the Castro family had traveled a long way.

On his economic journey, Castro joined thousands of others who followed similar paths. The economic ascent of many families from migrant worker to professional in one generation was even steeper and more dramatic than that of the Castros. Whatever the individual path, the new Chicano middle class, like its black counterpart, which was streaming out of Five Points and north Park Hill into Aurora and southeast Denver, became an abiding reality on the American scene during Castro's short lifetime. In this massive social process, Castro was variously an active player, a shaper of policy, and a struggling, passive voyager carried along by the tide.

"The Chicano Movement," says Cecelia Garcia, "really moved us—meaning young people like myself who are now middle aged—into another socioeconomic level. . . . Our parents came here from New Mexico to either work in the fields or work as housekeepers. I am the fifth generation of what would be considered housekeepers. In order to move out of that type of labor force, we knew we had to have another level of education. It was a different era. Now people just go down to Metro and sign up; it's no big deal. But at that time, people like Richard Castro and Virginia Castro were sacrificing and taking the time to work with children like myself to give them the opportunity to go to college, the opportunity to break away from five generations of housekeeping. They were really the living proof that you could go to school—to college! And they in turn told us that we didn't have a choice, that we had to go to college for a better life."[11]

The 1990 census indicates that approximately 30,000 Hispanic families, a figure that represented something over 27 percent of all Hispanic families spread throughout Colorado, had reached the income level of $35,000 a year. By comparison, 1970 figures show just 4,000 families or 8 percent of the total of Hispanic families had climbed to a level of $15,000 a year.[12] This great thrust upward and outward from the West Side, from Curtis Park and Highlands into the four corners of Denver, into the suburbs of Northglenn, Lakewood, and Littleton, failed to conform to the vision of the revolution. In the eyes of the revolution, the geography of the inner city was not to be abandoned; the kinship ties that lay at the core of community were to be found within the confines of Denver's barrios. To the extent that the community would rise up economically it would be a collective rising—like union members receiving an across-the-board pay raise—not an individual one. However, the vitality of those revolutionary ideas proved insufficient to bottle up the energy of the coming middle-class explosion. Too much talent, too much desire had been too long suppressed. For those with the ability or dedication, the will or the luck, the ambition, the talent, or the shrewdness, America's definition of the good life could not be denied. Not, at least in the last quarter of the twentieth century, as the more blatantly racist structures crumbled and left in their ruins expansive openings of opportunity. Not in the face of America's enormous capacity to absorb the challenges of alternative and revolutionary ideas.

Yet the triumph of the reformers over the revolution left little room for smugness on the part of the victors. Few reformers attempted to deny the impact of the Crusade and other militants on the achievements of the Movement. It was the militants, after all, who shaped the general Movement, who thrust the key issues into the public forum, who often created the very openings through which others followed.

From a distance, for all their differences, the two elements of the Movement—reform and revolutionary—formed a symbiotic relationship, each one flourishing in the presence of the other. The revolution thrived best in the shadow of the two Kennedys and Johnson's Great Society. Only in the openings created by this environment could visions of more sweeping changes be nurtured on a mass level. The ideas of the radicals required a climate characterized by hope, by the belief that change is possible, by the idea that government and civil society have a moral obligation to create a more just social structure. They required a climate that encouraged the ideas of empowerment for those who never possessed power. They required the liberal worldview that in the clash between nature and nurture, environment held the upper hand and people need not be condemned to poverty because of the circumstances of their birth. They required an open society ready to examine fresh ideas. It was in the cynical atmosphere that permeated the late '70s and '80s, as the nation turned increasingly to individual rather than communitarian answers to vexing problems, that the radical alternative dried up.

Every momentous turning point in American history—from the Revolution to the Civil War, from the Progressive Age to the New Deal—was forged within the intricate interplay between radical and moderate forces. The Chicano Revolution failed to grasp the idea that the Castros and Benavidezes, the Kennedys and McGoverns, were not their worst enemies. Instead the two sets of familiar neighbors turned on each other ferociously. For this, the radicals must bear their fair share of the burden; their rhetoric proved too self-righteous, their accusations of selling out too loose.

But if the revolution needed the liberals, the opposite was also true. As the Peña administration focused its energy on the airport, the convention center, major league baseball, and the Cherry Creek Mall, conditions in the inner city spiraled downhill, and the rise of gang culture made things increasingly unlivable. The liberals lost their compass. Castro, on the local level, was the best they had in the way of a conscience, but as an individual in a big system, as a compromiser and a moderating influence by nature, his impact was limited. The compass had to come from beyond the administration. Without a movement from the bottom up to call attention to the glaring realities of barrio and ghetto life, there is little wonder that city leaders and, indeed, American liberalism drifted off into a macro-economic approach not too distant from their conservative rivals—government-corporate partnerships and incentives for high-tech growth to the exclusion of much of the working class. There was no one around to prod them, to call them back home.

Within the barrio itself, the liberals tended to reach out to those who maintained hope for success, to those who retained the confidence or drive to go on to college or a higher-paying job. To those alienated, however, to those beaten down, to those thousands who had lost faith or who never possessed it, to those who dropped out of school, who remained underemployed, who continued to see their sons suffer from police beatings or harassment, the liberals of the '80s and '90s had little to say. Militants and radicals had once reached out and touched the soul of many in this constituency. For those interested in broadening the base of progressive change in America, this was a constituency they could ill afford to overlook.

The experience of Rich Castro on the West Side in the 1970s, the experience of Waldo and Corky, the West Side Coalition, the Inner City Parish, and the Crusade for Justice document dramatically the imperative that all segments of the Movement need to coexist, if not without conflict, at least without threats and bloodshed. That coexistence required the explicit renunciation of violence by all sides. It required that leaders refrain from romanticizing violence, from dehumanizing their opponents, from cheering on the rank and file as they carried guns all over the neighborhood. Anything short of this meant subjecting the movement to suicidal doses of destruction.

As it was, a lot of good people went their separate ways with bad tastes in their mouths about politics, a cynical distaste toward the Movement, and a reluctance to tell the story to the next generation.

Shortly before his death, when Rich Castro saw Corky Gonzales for the last time, the two former adversaries embraced in a gesture that symbolized the melting away of years of rancor, a gesture at long last of reconciliation and forgiveness. Heartfelt as it was, the embrace carried with it an aura of sadness and emptiness. It came fifteen years too late.

A Benign Nationalism

In the burning days of the Movement, Castro's view of the growing nationalist sentiment in the Chicano community had parted significantly from Gonzales's. Corky dreamed about Aztlán; he earnestly contemplated the possibility of an independent homeland for Chicanos in the Southwest. The Crusade's separatism, however, was more than just a geographical vision. Its persistent reluctance to partake of coalition politics, its instinctive self-perception that it represented the vanguard of the Chicano Movement, tended to insulate it and set it apart—psychologically as well as politically—from mainstream society, from the majority of the Chicano populace, even from a great many Chicano militants.

Castro knew well that militant nationalist sentiment is not born in a vacuum. Without exception, twentieth-century national movements among minority populations—whether in Chechnya or Kurdistan, beyond the Russian Pale of Settlement, in Canada or Colorado—all grew in soil saturated by the arrogance of the dominant societies. Among the universal grievances found scattered across the globe in these movements were the very ones Castro had grappled with on the West Side: fear of and disrespect for the native language of conquered peoples; police forces running amok, hounding minorities and beating them bloody; the construction of elaborate, sometimes subtle barriers to limit opportunities for upward mobility; and the gradual erosion of cultural and psychological identities.

It was not the underpinnings of Corky's radical analysis that Castro parted with; it was his conclusions. Castro rejected militant forms of nationalism on both practical and idealistic grounds. Neither his outgoing personality nor his life experience inclined him toward separatism. He viewed America, even during discouraging times, as a dynamic democracy, capable—with considerable prodding—of positive change. As part of the rising, newly prospering Chicano middle class, he had little economic motivation to sever ties with white society. Nor did he find much yearning for a separate society among his less fortunate countrymen. Despite powerful communal ties, despite the oftentimes insulated and self-reliant culture among Spanish-speaking arrivals, the idea of national self-determination just didn't stir many of those struggling for day-to-day existence in Denver's barrios. The feelings towards America—the love and hurt, the hope and resentment—were far too complex to tie up into a neat bundle of nationalist solutions.

Castro was aware, too, that militant nationalism forever teeters on the edge of a moral precipice. However progressive in its inception, however responsive to the sufferings of a subjugated people, it crosses easily over the thin line that separates fighting oppression from becoming the oppressor. Redrawing national maps on paper according to ethnic demographics never reflects the multinational reality of human interaction. Often as not, it leads to new minorities and new forms of oppression. Even as Castro entered his last days, the darkening clouds over the Balkans and former republics of the Soviet Union prepared to reveal to the world once again the malignant side of nationalist dreams.

And so, Rich Castro characteristically searched for middle ground. Rejecting the Dick Lamm version of assimilation as a blunt instrument poised to undermine an undeniably vibrant Hispanic culture, rejecting the nationalism of Corky Gonzales as impossibly separatist, Castro joined many others of his generation who sought to live comfortably and fully in two worlds. Perhaps author and artist José Antonio Burciaga put it most succinctly. "I am the Southwest," he wrote in a book of essays entitled *Drink Cultura*. "I am tortillas and frijoles, but I am also hamburgers and hot dogs."[13] This was the bi-national option, the recognition of new possibilities to participate in, enjoy, and savor the richness of mainstream American culture while at the same time partaking and breathing in the richness of Chicano culture.

It required a softer form of nationalism, and this Castro pursued with relish and vigor. Schooled on the West Side, he did not shy away from ethnic politics. He insisted that the Hispanic community get its share of old-fashioned political power in the electoral arena. He registered the Hispanic voter in the style of Willie Velasquez, who honed voter registration into a political weapon. He fought to redistrict political boundaries advantageous to Hispanic politicians. He forged coalitions and caucuses to further Hispanic interests. He sought to gain a measure of respect for the Spanish language his grandparents had brought from New Mexico.

He never ceased the effort to preserve the heritage of the Indo-Hispanic people and to pass on the oft-hidden stories of Chicano history to the next generation. "*El sueño de Rich Castro*"—Rich Castro's dream—included the documentation of Hispanic contributions to state government and the chronicling of Hispanic life in Colorado through the medium of roadside markers along the state highways. In this quest he was well suited. His own personal history rooted in the coalfields and valleys of southern Colorado, in the mountains and dry plains of northern New Mexico, on the streets and parks of Denver's barrios, and in the chambers of Colorado's General Assembly, represented a living reflection of the Chicano heritage, a great rich slice of Chicano history. In his search for a collective and personal identity, Castro embodied a wellspring of nationalist sentiment.

But other facets of his life pulled him in other directions: the Irish blood of his great grandfather, no particular anomaly in the Chicano experience; the diverse and integrated character of the industrial East Side where he grew up; the all-American innocence of a Catholic high school in the early '60s; a personality drawn to people of all backgrounds; and a belief that standards of justice should apply to everyone—no exceptions. These factors drew Castro naturally and inexorably into the multinational mainstream of American culture. Just as Castro's roots reflected the Chicano experience in the Southwest, so, too, did they temper his sense of nationalism and drive him toward an understanding of a bi-national identity.

Accepted by increasing numbers of Castro's generation, this was an idea born of the complexity and uniqueness of the Chicano experience in America.

Notes

Prologue

1
Gutierrez is not his real name. I heard this story in the winter of 1978 from a customer in my taxicab.

2
Lupe Herrera, interview by the author, tape recording, Denver, CO, 13 March, 1992. The daughter of United Farm Workers' organizers Alfredo and Juanita Herrera, Ms. Herrera grew up in West Denver and attended Baker Middle School and West High School.

3
Richard Castro, "A Survey of Social Welfare Utilization Patterns in the Auraria Community of Denver," Master's thesis, University of Denver, 1972. Available on microfilm.

4
Denver Planning Office, *The West Side Neighborhood: A Tract Analysis*, December 1972.

5
Castro's bust is located on the second floor of the State Capitol. The Richard T. Castro Community Center is at Twelfth and Mariposa. Castro Elementary School is the former Westwood Elementary, 845 South Lowell. Castro is depicted on a mural across the street from Mitchell Elementary School, Thirty-third and Marion. An exhibit in Castro's honor was shown at the Museo de las Americas, 861 Santa Fe. The Human Services municipal building at 1200 Federal also bears the name Richard T. Castro Building.

6
David J. Weber's book, *Foreigners in Their Native Land*, took its title from two quotations written in the 1850s: "A victim to the wickedness of a few men, whose imposture was favored by their origin and recent domination over the country; a foreigner in my native land; could I be expected to endure their outrages and insults?" Juan Nepomuceno, Seguín, Texas, 1858. "It is the conquered who are humbled before the conqueror asking for his protection, while enjoying what little their misfortune has left them. It is those who have been sold like sheep—it is those who were abandoned by Mexico. They do not understand the prevalent language of their native soil. They are foreigners in their own land. . . ." Pablo de la Guerra, speech to the California Senate, 1856, quoted in David J. Weber, ed., *Foreigners in Their Native Land* (Albuquerque: University of New Mexico Press, 1973), vi.

Chapter 1

1
Olga Curtis, "Metro State: Denver's Invisible College," *Empire Magazine, Denver Post*, Feb. 2, 1969, 8-12.

2
Ibid., 8.

3
Rocky Mountain News, Feb. 13, 1967, 42.

4
Archie Castro, interview by the author, tape recording, Denver, CO, 10 June, 1993. The father of Richard granted an interview at his home. Among many other topics, he spoke of his own work and that of his wife, Josephine.

5
Andy Lovato, interview by the author, tape recording, Denver, CO, 13 December, 1992.

233

6
Bobby Federico, interview by the author, tape recording, Denver, CO, 9 December, 1992.

7
Anthony Lopez, interview by the author, tape recording, Denver, CO, 1 February, 1993.

8
Andy Lovato interview.

9
Normando Pacheco, interview by the author, tape recording, Denver, CO, 28 June, 1993.

10
Ralph Guzman, "Mexican American Casualties in Viet Nam," *La Raza*, Nov. 1, 1971, 12. This figure was quoted in Ernesto Vigil, *The Crusade for Justice* (Madison: The University of Wisconsin Press, 1999), 115.

11
Andy Lovato interview.

12
Celina Benavidez, interview by the author, tape recording, Denver, CO, 9 July, 1995.

13
Matthew S. Meier and Feliciano Rivera, *The Chicanos: A History of Mexican Americans* (New York: Hill and Wang, 1972), 258.

14
Maurilio Vigil, *Chicano Politics* (Washington, D.C.: University Press of America, 1978), 34.

15
Christine Marin, *A Spokesman of the Mexican American Movement: Rodolfo "Corky" Gonzales and the Fight for Chicano Liberation* (San Francisco: Robert D. Reed and Adam S. Eterovich, 1977), 2.

16
Vigil, *Chicano Politics*, 105. Vigil pinpoints UCLA as the source of UMAS. Springing up around the same time, according to Vigil, were the Mexican American Student Association (MASA) in southern California, which eventually merged with UMAS, and Mexican American Student Confederation (MASC) in the Bay Area. The Mexican American Youth Organization (MAYO) was already established in Texas.

17
This statement comes from a compilation of newspaper articles and pamphlets published simply under the title *UMAS by Chicanos*, printed by UMAS Publications in December 1970. The quotation comes from an anonymously written essay entitled "UMAS: A Creature of Controversy," 1968, 17.

18
Juan Gómez Quiñones, *Chicano Politics: Reality and Promise, 1940–1990* (Albuquerque: University of New Mexico Press, 1990), 118. The Normando Pacheco interview provides evidence that the same issues undertaken by UMAS nationally were also the same issues confronted by UMAS at Metropolitan State College.

19
Carlos Muñoz, Jr., *Youth, Identity, Power: The Chicano Movement* (London, New York: Verso, 1989), 130-34. This publication discusses the origins of Chicano studies departments in universities throughout the Southwest.

20
Normando Pacheco interview.

21
Normando Pacheco and Anthony Lopez interview.

22
The dual nature of Richard Castro's personality was noted by practically everyone interviewed for this study.

23
Vincent C. de Baca, ed., *La Gente: Hispano History and Life in Colorado* (Denver: Colorado Historical Society, 1998), xv. C. de Baca writes in the introduction: "Hispano farming villages still practice a communal work ethic that extends from regulation grazing rights to cleaning irrigation ditches." In the same volume Richard Louden (editor and annotator) quoted from "Some Memories from My Life, as Written by Elfido Lopez, Sr.," 27: "When the wheat got ripe [in Branson, Colorado, in the years before 1937] the men got together and they would cut one man's first all together. The women would get together and cook for the men." Similarly, Carey McWilliams, *North from Mexico*, 158, describes the communally based irrigation system in the Rio Grande Valley.

24
This theme was underscored in several interviews including those with Celina Benavidez, Virginia Castro, Cecilia Garcia, Andy Lovato, Lupe Herrera, Roger Medina, and Joe Sandoval.

25
Roger Medina, interview by the author, tape recording, Denver, CO, 13 April, 1993.

26
Normando Pacheco interview.

27
Virginia Castro and Normando Pacheco interviews.

28
Charles Carter, "Minority Groups List Grievances at MSC," *Denver Post*, October 21, 1969, 3.

29
Carol McMurrough, "MSC 'Dual Standards' for Hispanos Charged," *Denver Post*, December 4, 1969, 34.

30
Charles Carter, *Denver Post*, October 21, 1969, 3.

31
Ibid.

32
Normando Pacheco interview.

33
Dr. Kenneth Phillips, interview by the author, tape recording, via telephone, 5 October, 1999.

34
Normando Pacheco interview.

35
Ibid.

36
Weber, *Foreigners in Their Native Land*, 2. "Not until 1972," writes Weber, "did trained historians publish a synthesis of the 450 years of Mexican-American past. Before that for nearly a quarter of a century, the only published overview of Mexican American history was *North from Mexico* . . . by Carey McWilliams, a journalist, attorney and civil libertarian." Weber writes that the two historical surveys written in 1972 were Matt S. Meier and Feliciano Rivera, *The Chicanos: A History of Mexican Americans* and Rodolfo F. Acuña, *Occupied America: The Chicano's Struggle Toward Liberation*. Nevertheless, other excellent works had been published on specific regional topics. Chief among them was

the Ernesto Galarza study of migrant labor, *Merchants of Labor.*

37
Muñoz, Jr., *Youth, Identity, Power: The Chicano Movement*, 141.

38
George I. Sanchez, *Forgotten People: A Study of New Mexicans* (Albuquerque: Calvin Horn, Publisher, Inc., 1967), reprinted from the previous 1940 edition, vii. "A Minority Nobody Knows" was written by Helen Rowan for *The Atlantic*, June 1967, 47-52.

39
Daniel T. Valdes y Tapia, *Political History of New Mexico*, unpublished manuscript, 1960, 1. Mimeographed copy available in the Western History Department of the Denver Public Library.

40
Virginia Castro interview.

41
Rowan, "A Minority Nobody Knows," *The Atlantic* June, 1967, 47-52. This work was cited in Weber, *Foreigners in Their Native Land*, 1.

42
George I. Sanchez, *Forgotten People: A Study of New Mexicans* (Albuquerque: Calvin Horn, Publisher, Inc., 1967). Sanchez discusses the nature of the land grants in *Forgotten People*, 5-6. He describes how New Mexicans were overwhelmed by the new system after the Treaty of Guadalupe Hidalgo, concluding, "In the march of imperialism, a people were forgotten, cast aside as the by-product of territorial aggrandizement," 12. He describes the confusing legal battles that constituted an "onslaught" against Hispanic land ownership, 18. Stan Steiner, *La Raza: The Mexican Americans* (New York: Harper Colophon Books, 1969), discusses the loss of land, 57-60.

43
David Sandoval, interview by the author, tape recording, via telephone, 26 June, 1995.

44
Ibid.

45
McWilliams, *North from Mexico*, 37.

46
New Mexico was not the only region of Mexico isolated from the nation's center. The southern tier of states, for instance, is equally isolated both geographically and culturally, yet they have all remained within Mexico. Nevertheless, Valdes and others have maintained that New Mexico's distinct isolation makes the region a unique case.

47
Jorge J. E. Garcia, *Hispanic/Latino Identity: A Philosophical Perspective* (Malden, MA: Blackwell Publishers, 2000), 2.

48
David Sandoval interview.

49
Daniel T. Valdes and Tom Piño, "Majority-Minority Relations," pamphlet printed by University Park News, Denver, CO, 1968, 3, available at Denver Public Library, Western History Dept.

50
Valdes and Piño, "Majority-Minority Relations," 9.

51
Luis Valdez, "The Tale of La Raza," *Bronze*, vol. 1, no. 1, November 25, 1968, quoted in Muñoz, Jr., *Youth, Identity, Power*, 63.

52
McWilliams, *North from Mexico*, 67-8.

53
Richard L. Nostrand, *The Hispano Homeland* (Norman: University of Oklahoma Press, 1992), 14 and 18. Nostrand writes that New Mexicans considered themselves "Spanish" during the Spanish colonial period from 1598 to 1821, but that was a "racial designation that included the mestizo majority," 14. He continues that this "Hispano concept of [Spanish] ethnicity is not easily justified, because although Hispanos are peculiarly Spanish culturally . . . they are, as Arthur L. Campa pointed out, no more Spanish than anyone else, and they are certainly not Spanish in a racial sense," 18.

54
Andy Lovato interview.

55
James Patrick Walsh, *Young and Latino in a Cold War Barrio: Survival, the Search for Identity, and the Formation of Street Gangs in Denver, 1945–1955*; Master's thesis, University of Colorado, Denver, 1996, 28-29.

56
David G. Gutiérrez, *Walls and Mirrors: Mexican Americans, Mexican Immigrants, and the Politics of Ethnicity* (Berkeley: University of California Press), 1995, 2. Although Gutiérrez refers mostly to California, which has experienced dynamics different from Colorado, he writes eloquently of his own family's ambiguity towards Mexican immigrants. This theme recurs throughout the book. See, for example, Gutiérrez's quotes from Mexican sociologist Manuel Gamio, who wrote *Mexican Immigration to the United States* in 1930, 61.

57
Walsh, *Young and Latino in a Cold War Barrio*, 29. Walsh quotes Curtis Park resident Enrique Hank Lopez: "The bitterest race riots I have ever witnessed—and engaged in—were between the look-alike, talk-alike *surumatos* and *manitos* who lived near Curtis Park." Quoted from Enrique Hank Lopez, "Back to Bachimba: A Hyphenated American Discovers That He Can't Go Home Again," *Horizon*, winter 1967, 81.

58
Gómez Quiñones, *Chicano Politics*, 7. Gómez Quiñones writes that *Chicano* is an "abbreviation for Mexicano." He continues that the word "was given political connotations by young activists." Mauricio Vigil, *Chicano Politics*, 31. "'Chicano' . . . manifests the new political awareness and activism . . . of the 1960s and 70s." Alice H. Reich, *The Cultural Construction of Ethnicity: Chicanos in the University* (New York: AMS Press, Inc., 1989), 60-61, discusses other possible derivations of the word *Chicano*, but generally agrees that the self-naming that occurred in the '60s gave the term its current connotation.

59
Ruben Salazar, "Who Is a Chicano?" from the collection of excerpts entitled *UMAS* by Chicanos from the University of Colorado, Boulder, 11.

60
Robert Maize, "HYC, UMAS, CHE Consolidate," *The Paper* (Metro State's student newspaper), vol. 4, no. 2, March 11, 1971, 1. Andy Lovato and Virginia Castro interviews.

61
The word *Latino* was preferred by some over the word *Hispanic*. It had the drawback of inferring European roots. It had the advantage in the eyes of some, however, of having been chosen by the Latino and not the Anglo community. In this view, which is disputed

by others, the word *Hispanic* became the choice of the U.S. Census Bureau in 1980; therefore it was not part of any self-naming process. Castro rarely used this term probably because it was not in popular usage in Colorado before his death in 1991.

62
Roger Medina interview.

Chapter 2

1
Virginia Castro, interview by the author, tape recording, Denver, CO, 23 March, 1992.

2
Normando Pacheco interview.

3
Alfredo and Juanita Herrera, interview by the author, tape recording, Denver, CO, 25 March, 1992.

4
Joan London and Henry Anderson, *So Shall Ye Reap: The Story of César Chávez and the Farmworkers Movement* (New York: Thomas Y. Crowell Co., 1970), 162. Chávez testified that about 80% of farmworkers experience some effects from pesticides every year. See also Samuel Meyer, "Fatal Occupational Injuries to Older Workers in Farming, Bureau of Labor Statistics," excerpt from *Monthly Labor Review Online*, October 2005, vol. 128, no. 10, available from: http//www.bls/0.pub.mir/2005.

5
Juanita Herrera interview.

6
Cecelia Garcia, interview by the author, tape recording, Denver, CO, 7 July, 1995. Garcia is the twin sister of former state representative Celina Benavidez.

7
Virginia Castro interview.

Chapter 3

1
Magdalena Gallegos, "The Forgotten Community," *Colorado Heritage*, Issue 2, 1985 (Denver: Colorado Historical Society), 5-20.

2
Rocky Mountain News, October 28, 1969, 1W. The process was also described in "Site History Stormy," *The Paper*, the Metropolitan State College student weekly, January 12, 1972, Auraria Supplement, 3.

3
Gallegos, "Forgotten Community," 20.

4
Adolfo Gomez, interview by the author, tape recording, Denver, CO, 3 February, 1992.

5
Virginia Castro interview.

6
Gallegos, "The Forgotten Community," 20, describes the role of the Auraria Residents' Organization. Father Garcia and the ARO fought to defeat the bond election, then tried to get compensation for the residents when they lost. The role of the West Side Coalition (which had its roots in El Centro Cultural) was described in interviews by Waldo Benavidez, Adolfo Gomez, and Virginia Castro. This role was also mentioned in "Site History Stormy," *The Paper*, January 12, 1972, 3.

7
Virginia Castro interview.

8
Waldo Benavidez, interview by the author, tape recording, Denver, CO, 12 July, 1995.

9
Waldo Benavidez interview.

10
Jerry Garcia, interview by the author, tape recording, Denver, CO, 22 February, 1996.

11
Waldo Benavidez interview.

12
Frances Fox Piven and Richard A. Cloward, *Poor People's Movements: Why They Succeed, How They Fail* (New York: Vintage Books, 1979), 270.

13
Adolfo Gomez, interview by the author, tape recording, Denver, CO, 3 February, 1992. For discussion of the Jane Addams style of social work, see Walter Trattner, *From Poor Law to Welfare State: A History of Social Welfare in America* (New York: Free Press, 1979), 137, 143.

14
Waldo Benavidez interview.

15
P. David Finks, *The Radical Vision of Saul Alinsky* (New York: Paulist Press, 1984), 13-18.

16
Ibid., 61-66, describes Chávez's relation with the Alinsky organization. Mario Barrera, *Beyond Aztlán: Ethnic Autonomy in Comparative Perspective* (New York: University of Notre Dame Press and Praeger Publishers, 1988), 57, states, "The influence that the Saul Alinsky school of organizing has had on Chicano politics has generally not been recognized, but it is extensive."

17
Waldo Benavidez interview.

18
Rodolfo F. Acuña, *Anything But Mexican: Chicanos in Contemporary Los Angeles* (New York: Verso Publishers, 1996), 20. Acuña puts the displacement of Mexicans from the Chávez Ravine area to make way for Dodgers Stadium in the perspective of other urban renewal projects, e.g., freeways, music centers, and hotels. Mexicans and Mexican Americans are often uprooted to benefit the mainstream community.

19
Waldo Benavidez interview.

20
Quoted in Elizabeth Anne Huttinger, "Citizens Action in Housing Issues: A Case Study," Master's thesis, Colorado State University, November 1973, 50.

21
Waldo Benavidez interview.

22
Adolfo Gomez interview.

23
George Rivera, Aileen F. Lucero, Richard Castro, "Internal Colonialism in Colorado: The West Side Coalition and Barrio Control," in Vincent C. de Baca (editor), *La Gente: Hispano History and Life in Colorado* (Denver: Colorado Historical Society, 1998), 208. Castro and his coauthors discuss the origins of the West Side Coalition in relation to the fears Westsiders had about further encroachment into the neighborhood from the Auraria Higher Education Center.

24
Adolfo Gomez interview.

25
Ibid.

26
Jerry Garcia interview.

27
Waldo Benavidez interview.

28
Ibid.

29
Waldo Benavidez, speech to the University of Denver Graduate School of Social Work, tape recording, May 3, 1972. Tape is part of Virginia Castro's personal collection.

30
Waldo Benavidez interview.

31
Mario Barrera offers this analysis in *Beyond Aztlán*, 58. His quote is from Charles Levine, "Understanding Alinsky: Conservative Wine in Radical Bottles," *American Behavioral Scientist*, vol. 17, no. 2 (November-December 1973), 282.

32
Rivera, Lucero, Castro, "Internal Colonialism in Colorado," 212.

33
Ibid., 211.

34
Ibid., 217-18.

35
Huttinger, "Citizens' Action in Housing Issues," 43-44.

36
Ibid., 69-70.

37
Ibid., 71.

38
Ibid., 73.

39
Ibid., 70-71.

40
Celina Benavidez interview.

41
Ibid.

42
Ibid.

43
Huttinger, "Citizens' Action in Housing Issues," 61. Huttinger cites a survey of 275 people in the West Side neighborhood taken by the West Side Action Center. According to the survey, 85 percent of property owners and 98 percent of renters favored downzoning the area to protect single-family homes from encroachment by commercial property and high-density dwellings.

44
Ibid., 55-6.

45
Ibid., 56.

46
Rivera, Lucero, Castro, "Internal Colonialism in Colorado," 212.

47
Huttinger, "Citizens' Action in Housing Issues," 58.

48
Ibid., 63.

49
Rivera, Lucero, Castro, 214.

50
Vigil, *The Crusade For Justice*, 171-79. Vigil describes two conflicting recall efforts that highlighted the animosity between militants and moderates. Nevertheless, DiManna alienated almost all Chicanos across the political spectrum. Salvatore Carpio eventually replaced him in a recall election.

51
Cecelia Garcia interview.

52
Waldo Benavidez interview.

53
The personality differences were noted in numerous interviews, particularly those with Cecilia Garcia, Lupe Herrera, Don Schierling, and Waldo Benavidez himself.

54
Waldo Benavidez interview.

55
Rivera, Lucero, Castro, 220.

56
Cecelia Garcia interview.

57
Lori and John Helms, interview by the author, tape recording, Denver, CO, 23 March, 1992.

58
Virginia Castro interview.

59
Richard Castro, "A Survey of Social Welfare Utilization Patterns in the Auraria Community of Denver," Master's thesis, University of Denver, 1972. Available on microfilm.

60
Ibid.

61
Andy Lovato interview.

62
Ibid.

63
Eloy Mares, interview by the author, tape recording, Denver, CO, 7 July, 1993. Mares, a neighborhood hero for his football prowess at Annunciation High School, later played football for the University of Denver and then returned to coach at his high school alma mater, where he first met Castro. Mares worked for Juvenile Justice in the late '60s as a probation officer when they reunited through the Youth Services Bureau.

64
Andy Lovato interview.

65
Frantz Fanon, *The Wretched of the Earth: The Handbook for the Black Revolution That Is Changing the Shape of the World* (New York: Grove Press, 1968), 52.

66
Muñoz, Jr., *Youth, Identity, Power*, 85-6.

67
Quoted in Mauricio Vigil, *Chicano Politics*, 174. Vigil cites Rona Fields and Charles Fox, "The Brown Berets," *The Black Politician*, July 1971, 58.

68
Ibid., 174.

69
Vigil, *The Crusade for Justice*, 111. Vigil describes the formation of the East Side Brown Berets under the leadership of Roddy Miera.

70
Eloy Mares interview.

71
Vigil, *The Crusade for Justice*, 111. Vigil writes, "Most members of his [Miera's] gang joined the Berets and the gang ceased to exist."

72
Andy Lovato interview.

73
Andy Lovato interview. This is confirmed by Vigil, *The Crusade for Justice*, 123, who writes, "The Eastside Brown Berets held dances at the Curtis Park Community Center and Annunciation School, using the proceeds to support their activities. They had taken the proceeds from one dance and purchased the entire stock of billy-clubs at a surplus store."

74
Chuck Green, "Police Brutality," *Denver Post*, April 22, 1970, 76. An account describing violence in the disturbance appears in "5 Youths Arrested at Scene of Accident," *Denver Post*, April 15, 1970, 48.

75
James Crawford, "Group Angered over Alleged Police Beatings," *Rocky Mountain News*, April 17, 1970, 8.

76
Ibid., 8.

77
Two stories provide the basis for this discussion. John Morehead, "Brutality Probe Continued," *Denver Post*, April 22, 1970, 3, and Crawford, *Rocky Mountain News*, April 17, 1970, 8.

78
Denver Post, April 22, 1970, 22, and *Rocky Mountain News*, April 17, 1970, 8.

79
Rocky Mountain News, April 17, 1970, 8.

80
"Lawyer Says Castro Passed Lie Test," *Denver Post*, April 29, 1970, 2.

81
Vigil, *Crusade for Justice*, 20.

82
Walsh, *Young and Latino in a Cold War Barrio*, 104-12.

83
Vigil, *Crusade for Justice*, 129.

84
Virginia Castro interview.

85
Rocky Mountain News, April 17, 1970, 8.

86
John Morehead, "Hispanos Jam Council Meeting," *Denver Post*, April 28, 1970, 3.

87
Chuck Green, "Police Brutality," *Denver Post*, April 22, 1970, 76.

88
Denver Post, April 28, 1970, 3.

89
Denver Post, April 28, 1970, 76.

90
"Clarification Asked in Police Probe," *Rocky Mountain News*, May 8, 1970, 17.

91
James Crawford, "Group to Present Demands in Brutality Case," *Rocky Mountain News*, April 23, 1970, 8.

92
Rykken Johnson, "Hispano Group Plans Further Police Probe," *Rocky Mountain News*, May 11, 1970, 8. Also see Chuck Green, *Denver Post*, April 22, 1970, 76.

93
Denver Post, April 28, 1970, 3.

94
Rocky Mountain News, May 11, 1970, 8.

95
George Lane, "Garcia Tells of His Ouster," *Denver Post*, May 24, 1970, 2.

96
John Morehead, "Grand Jury to Hear Charges of Brutality, *Denver Post*, April 27, 1970, 1. Also, "Benavidez Supports Probe by Grand Jury, *Denver Post*, April 27, 1970, 3.

97
"Jury Finds No Brutality Evidence," *Rocky Mountain News*, June 6, 1970, 5.

98
James Crawford, *Rocky Mountain News*, April 17, 1970, 8.

Chapter 4

1
Archie Castro interview.

2
Ibid. Barron Beshoar, *Out of the Depths* (Denver: World Press, 1942). Beshoar's book remains a classic on the subject of the Great Coalfield War and the Ludlow Massacre.

3
Archie Castro interview.

4
George McGovern and Leonard Guttridge, *The Great Coalfield War* (Boston: Houghton Mifflin Company, 1972), 2-3.

5
Sarah Deutsch, *No Separate Refuge* (New York: Oxford University Press, 1987), 88.

6
Everett Chávez, interview by the author, tape recording, Denver, CO, by telephone, 7 August, 1993.

7
Beshoar, *Out of the Depths*, 62.

8
Carl Ubbelohde, "Mine Explosions near Trinidad, 1910," *A Colorado Reader* (Boulder: Pruett Press, 1962), 90.

9
Beshoar, *Out of the Depths*, 80, and McGovern and Guttridge, *The Great Coalfield War*, 126.

10
McGovern and Guttridge, 81.

11
Ibid., 31.

12
Deutsch, *No Separate Refuge,* 104.

13
Ibid., 104.

14
McGovern and Guttridge, 214.

15
Ibid., 228.

16
Quoted from a speech by mayor Wellington Webb at a ceremony honoring Castro at the State Capitol, April 13, 1993. The date marked the second anniversary of Castro's death. The ceremony included the unveiling of a bust of Castro sculpted by his friend Emmanuel Martinez.

17
Virginia Castro and Archie Castro interviews.

18
Virginia Castro interview.

19
Nostrand, *The Hispano Homeland*, 19-21. Nostrand defines the Homeland centered in northern New Mexico north of the Socorro area. By 1900, this Homeland had expanded into the San Luis Valley and as far north as the Arkansas River Valley in southern Colorado. Small pockets of the Homeland extended even into the panhandle areas of Texas and Oklahoma.

20
The idea of the "Borderlands" where Mexican and Anglo cultures intersected has been explored by a great many historians. The American scholar who originally popularized the term is Herbert E. Bolton, *The Spanish Borderlands: A Chronicle of Old Florida and the Southwest*, Chronicles of America Series, vol. 23 (New Haven: Yale University, 1921).

21
Texas had already gained independence from Mexico in 1836.

22
Eileen Bankson, interview by the author, tape recording, La Veta, CO, 20 June, 1993.

23
Ibid.

24
A version of the story of the Taos Rebellion can be found in: Marc Simmons, *New Mexico: A History* (New York: W. Norton & Company, Inc., 1977). Simmons offers a concise explanation of the *encomienda* and the *repartimiento* systems which reduced the Pueblos to near slave status and which spurred on the rebellion, 55-6. The rebellion itself is described on 66. Fray Angelico Chávez, *My Penitente Land* (Albuquerque: University of New Mexico Press, 1974), 182-86, also describes the event and its origins.

25
Chávez, *My Penitente Land*, 186.

26
Fray Angelico Chávez, *Origins of New Mexico Families: A Genealogy of the Spanish Colonial Period* (Albuquerque: Museum of New Mexico Press, 1992), 268-69.

27
Bankson interview. Bankson cited as her source the *Archives of the Archdiocese of Santa Fe* (Santa Fe: Academy of American Franciscan History, 1957).

28
Bankson interview.

29
Lena Starr, interview by the author, tape recording, via telephone, 15 August, 1993.

30
Father Castro's service is traced in the *Archives of the Archdiocese of Santa Fe* for thirty-eight years from 1802 to 1840. They show him appearing in Santa Cruz for seven years and in Santa Clara off and on for fifteen years. He appears also in Picurís, in the pueblo of San Ildefonso, and in the missions at Pecos, Abiquiu, and San Juan, 244. Conditions for the Church in the nineteenth century are described in David J. Weber, *The Mexican Frontier: 1821–1846* (University of New Mexico Press, Albuquerque, 1982). He wrote, "Priests tended to avoid isolation, hardship, danger and low salaries and to gravitate toward more comfortable urban parishes," 72.

31
Bankson interview.

32
Weber, *The Mexican Frontier*, 57.

33
Ibid., 5.

34
John L. Kessell, *Kiva, Cross, and Crown* (Albuquerque: University of New Mexico Press, 1987), 454. Kessell states that Father Castro was present at the baptism for eight-day-old José Manuel Aguilar in 1828, the last recorded baptism of an Indian by a Franciscan at the mission at Pecos. He was still dispensing the sacraments in San Juan shortly before his death in 1840. Records show that Father Castro continued working in his parish all his life. Eileen Bankson believes that Castro's devotion to his family is illustrated in a story related in Ralph Emerson Twitchell, *Leading Facts of New Mexico History* (Cedar Rapids, Iowa: Torch Press, 1911-17), 55. Twitchell writes that in 1827, six years after Mexico gained independence from Spain, tensions between the native Mexican population and the *"gachupines"* or Spanish-born residents of Mexico ran so high that the government decreed that all gachupines must return to Spain. As a Spanish immigrant, Father Castro was ordered back to Spain. However, with another Franciscan colleague, Father Alvino, Castro was able to slip $500 into the hands of the proper territorial official. Thus encouraged to show his mercy and tolerance, the official found reason to exempt both priests from banishment. In speculating what prompted Castro to bribe this man, Bankson asserts that Father Castro simply wanted to stay with his family.

35
Anaya, *Bless Me, Ultima*, 236.

36
Don Sandoval, interview by the author, tape recording, Denver, CO, 6 May, 1994.

37
Isais Castro's link to Father Juan José Castro presents compelling evidence for Eileen Bankson's version of Castro's lineage. Isais Castro's connection to the family is remembered definitively by Lena Starr, Archie Castro's cousin, and by Gaspar Castro, Archie's uncle.

38
Gaspar Castro, interview by the author, tape recording, via telephone, 9 August, 1993.

39
Nostrand, *The Hispano Homeland*, 70.

40
Louis Sporleder, "Growing Up in La Plaza de los Leones," *A Colorado Reader*, Carl Ubbelohde, ed. (Boulder: Pruett Press, 1962), 110.

41
Gaspar Castro interview.

42
Louis Sporleder, *The Romance of the Spanish Peaks* (Denver: O'Brien Printing, 1960), 10.

43
Gaspar Castro interview.

44
Ibid.

45
Deutsch, *No Separate Refuge*, 89.

46
This information was gathered from captions on the photo exhibit at the Walsenburg Mining Museum, PO Box 229, Walsenburg, CO, 81089, located in

the old jail building on 120 West Fifth Street.

47
Archie Castro interview.

48
Ibid.

49
Deutsch, *No Separate Refuge*, 100.

50
Archie Castro interview.

51
Ibid.

52
Ibid.

53
Ibid.

54
Rosanne Sanchez, interview by the author, tape recording, Denver, CO, 19 June, 1993.

55
F. Stanley, *The Mora, New Mexico Story* (Pep, Texas, 1963), 7.

56
Simmons, 140.

57
Ibid., 147.

58
Richard Castro, "Hispanics Play a Key Role in Civil War," *La Voz*, April 4, 1990, 6.

59
Rosanne Sanchez interview.

60
Richard Castro, "Hispanics Play a Key Role in Civil War," 6.

Chapter 5

1
Anthony Lopez interview.

2
Archie Castro interview.

3
Quoted in Stephen J. Leonard and Thomas J. Noel, *Denver: Mining Camp to Metropolis* (Boulder: University Press of Colorado, 1990), 391.

4
Archie Castro interview.

5
David Halberstam, *The Fifties* (New York: Villard Books, 1993), 207.

6
Leonard and Noel, *Denver: Mining Camp to Metropolis*, 391-2.

7
Ibid., 392.

8
Ed Byorick, interview by the author, tape recording, via telephone, 7 July, 1994.

9
Quoted in Leonard and Noel, 367.

10
Richard Gould, "Hard Times on Packinghouse Road," June 1984, unpublished, 68. Information came from an interview with Alfonso Gonzales at his home in North Denver.

11
Archie Castro interview.

12
Ibid.

13
Richard Castro, "And Miles to Go: Mexican Women and Work, 1930-1990," *La Voz*, February 28, 1990, 6. Castro was reviewing Vickie Ruiz's book, *Western Women: Their Land, Their Lives*, for the commentary section. He was placing the work experience of his mother into the context of the experience of other Hispanic women who had historically been exploited.

14
Eloy Mares interview.

15
Ricardo Veladez, interview by the author, tape recording, Denver, CO, 8 March, 1993.

16
Ibid.

17
Ken Maestas, interview by the author, tape recording, Denver, CO, 3 April, 1993.

18
Gould, "Hard Times on Packinghouse Road," 2.

19
Ken Maestas interview.

20
Bobby Federico interview.

21
Bill Jones, "Girl, 13, Admits Bossing Tiger Tot Gang," *Rocky Mountain News*, March 11, 1954, 5.

22
"Father, Uncle of Tiger Tot Gang Member Held," *Rocky Mountain News*, March 13, 1954, 6.

23
Robert L. Chase, "14 Kids Out of Control," *Rocky Mountain News*, March 15, 1954.

24
Normando Pacheco interview.

25
Gang territories on the East Side in the 1950s were described by "Haymoe," an ex-Head interviewed by James Patrick Walsh in December 1995 for "Young and Latino in a Cold War Barrio," 71. These were generally confirmed in my interviews with Ricardo Valadez and state senator Paul Sandoval.

26
Emmanuel Martinez, interview by the author, tape recording, Morrison, CO, 27 June, 1994.

27
Ibid.

28
Ibid.

29
Ricardo Valadez interview.

30
Ibid.

31
Roger Medina interview.

32
Ken Maestas interview.

33
Virginia Castro interview.

34
Roger Medina interview.

35
Paul Sandoval, interview by the author, tape recording, Denver, CO, 25 May, 1994.

36
Roger Medina interview.

37
Andy Lovato interview.

38
Archie Castro interview.

39
Luis Rodriguez, *Always Running* (New York: Touchstone Press, 1994), 41.

40
Roger Medina interview.

41
Bobby Federico interview.

42
Ed Byorick interview.

43
Archie Castro interview.

44
Ibid.

45
Leonard and Noel, 193.

46
Ibid., 193.

47
"Declaration of Protective Covenant, University Hills, Inc.," November 3, 1949, Colorado Historical Society.

48
Stirling Kahn, interview by Stan Oliner, videotape, 24 March, 1994, Colorado Historical Society.

49
Dave Smith, interview by the author, tape recording, Denver, CO, 2 July, 1993.

50
Ibid.

51
Ibid.

52
Ibid.

53
Senator Paul Sandoval interview.

54
Archie Castro interview.

Chapter 6

1
Joe Sandoval, interview by the author, tape recording, Denver, CO, 2 November, 1992.

2
Anthony Lopez interview.

3
Ken Maestas interview.

4
Thomas J. Noel, *Colorado Catholicism* (Boulder: University Press of Colorado, 1989), 24.

5
Ken Maestas interview.

6
Ibid.

7
Andy Lovato interview.

8
Eloy Mares interview.

9
Ken Maestas interview.

10
Ibid.

11
Anthony Lopez interview.

12
Normando Pacheco interview.

13
Roger Medina interview.

14
Andy Lovato interview.

15
Ken Maestas interview.

16
Ibid.

17
Don Sandoval interview.

18
Ken Maestas interview.

19
Ibid.

20
Andy Lovato interview.

21
Eloy Mares interview.

22
Andy Lovato interview.

23
Eloy Mares interview.

24
Archie Castro and Andy Lovato interviews. Both pointed to Father Woodrich as the primary inspiration for Castro's desire for the priesthood.

25
Andy Lovato interview.

26
Ibid.

27
Ibid.

28
Ken Maestas interview.

29
Levi Beall, interview by the author, tape recording, Denver, CO, 2 December, 1992. Beall was Paco Sanchez's partner at radio station KFSC.

30
Robert Perkin, "Study of a Critical Denver Problem," *Rocky Mountain News*, January 31, 1954, 1.

31
Ibid., 11.

32
Levi Beall interview.

33
Ibid.

34
Ibid. The Good Americans Organization still has a building used for dances and community events on the corner of Forty-seventh and Lipan.

35
The formation of the Latin American Education Fund was reported by the *Rocky Mountain News*, February 13, 1954, 33.

36
The League of Latin American Citizens (LULAC) was formed in Texas in 1929, a split-off from the Order of Sons of America. Moving to New Mexico in the 1930s, it had spread to Colorado by the 1940s, according to Mario Barrera, *Beyond Aztlán*, 23.

37
Barrera, in *Beyond Aztlán*, 23-4. Barrera says many considered LULAC the "quintessentially assimilationist" Chicano organization. Like the GAO, it sought acceptance by the mainstream by including in its aims and purposes such wording as "As loyal citizens of the United States of America . . . we accept that it is not only the privilege but also the obligation of every member of this organization to uphold and defend the rights and duties vested in every American Citizen by the letter and the spirit of the law of the land. . . ." Its official language was English and it encouraged all Mexicans to seek naturalization papers. David G. Guttiérrez in *Walls and Mirrors*, 76, writes "they insisted that the best way to advance in American society was to convince other Americans that they too were loyal, upstanding American citizens." Nevertheless, LULAC members and those of other assimilationist groups often professed pride in their heritage and stood in the thick of struggle for civil rights and equality.

38
Richard Castro, "Commentary," *La Voz*, March 7, 1990, 6.

39
Senator Paul Sandoval interview.

40
Ricardo Veladez interview.

41
Ibid.

42
Andy Lovato interview.

43
Richard Castro, *Denver Catholic Register*, October 23, 1985, 1.

44
Ibid., 1.

45
Jack Galvin, interview by the author, tape recording, via telephone, 14 December, 1994.

46
Stewart Miller, interview by the author, tape recording, via telephone, 17 December, 1994.

47
Ibid.

48
Andy Lovato interview.

49
Jack Galvin interview.

50
Ibid.

51
Fray Angelico Chávez, *But Time and Chance: The Story of Padre Martinez* (Santa Fe: Sunstone Press, 1981), 123-27. Father Machebeuf's disdain for and discriminatory treatment of the Hispanic clergy runs as a theme throughout this book.

52
Craig Hart, interview by the author, tape recording, Denver, CO, 10 June, 1993.

53
Ibid.

54
Ibid.

55
Craig Hart and Jack Galvin interviews.

56
Andy Lovato interview.

57
Ibid.

Chapter 7

1
Waldo Benavidez used the "Little Beirut" description in his interview, while Celina Benavidez invoked the comparison to Northern Ireland.

2
Manuel Martinez, interview by the author, tape recording, Denver, CO, 13 June, 1993.

3
Ibid.

4
Quiñones, *Chicano Politics: Reality and Promise, 1940-1990*, 103. Quiñones defines *Chicanismo* as a form of "radically political and ethnic populism." It emerged as a "challenge to the assumptions, politics and principles for established political leaders, organizations, and activity . . . and once again the issue of national identity was in the forefront." It was often "distrustful of known electoral *politicos*" and encompassed "separatist and anti-corporation tendencies."

5
These leaders' ties with the Crusade for Justice were discussed in various interviews with Rubén Valdez, Emmanuel Martinez, Don Sandoval, Waldo Benavidez, and Virginia Castro.

6
Senator Don Sandoval interview.

7
John C. Hammerback, Richard Jensen,

and José Angel Gutierrez, "No Revolutions Without Poets: The Rhetoric of Rodolfo 'Corky' Gonzales," in *A War of Words: Chicano Protest in the 1960s and 1970s* (Westport, CT: Greenwood Press, 1985), 54.

8
Ibid.

9
Ibid.

10
Ibid.

11
Christine Marin, *A Spokesman of the Mexican American Movement: Rodolfo "Corky" Gonzales and the Fight for Chicano Liberation, 1966-1972* (San Francisco: Robert D. Reed and Adam S. Eterovich, 1977), 2.

12
Ibid., 2.

13
Rodolfo Gonzales, *I Am Joaquin: An Epic Poem* (New York: Bantam Books, 1967), 9.

14
Marin, 4.

15
Carlos Larralde, *Mexican American Movements and Leaders* (Los Alimitos, CA: Hwong Publishing Company, 1976), 199.

16
Eloy Mares interview.

17
Ibid.

18
Ibid.

19
Ron Wolf, Doug Vaughn, and Rosemary Cowles, "The Redfearn File," *Straight Creek Journal*, March 24, 1977, 1. This five-part series documents the career of one FBI and Denver Police Department informant, Timothy Redfearn, who infiltrated several dissident organizations in Denver. Although he concentrated on the Socialist Workers' Party, his reports included information on UMAS at Metropolitan State College and the Crusade for Justice. According to this article, "J. Edgar Hoover [set up] a vast network of informers classified into two types: 'racial' and 'security.'"

20
Ernesto Vigil's book, *The Crusade for Justice*, describes repeated attempts by the Denver Police Department to convict Crusade members, generally unsuccessfully. Vigil himself was acquitted on felony assault charges in a jury decision that took thirty seconds, 242. The Crusade formed a committee of lawyers, the Chicano Defense Liberation Committee, that defended Crusade members in numerous cases.

21
Ernesto Vigil, 170-1. Vigil describes an incident in which the Crusade and the Black Panther Party intervened to stop violence between rival black and Chicano gangs at Curtis Park in 1971.

22
Eloy Mares interview.

23
Craig Hart interview.

24
Waldo Benavidez interview.

25
Quiñones, *Chicano Politics*, 128-31.

26
Virginia Castro interview.

27
Richard Castro, speech to the University of Denver Graduate School of Social Work, tape recording, spring 1972, provided by Virginia Castro.

28
Vigil, *The Crusade for Justice*, 184.

29
Waldo Benavidez, speech to the University of Denver Graduate School of Social Work, tape recording, spring 1972, provided by Virginia Castro.

30
Castro helped establish an alternative school on the West Side called Academia del Barrio, which placed considerable emphasis on Chicano culture and heritage. He taught a course in Chicano studies at Metropolitan State College in 1973. Later, he wrote a weekly column in *La Voz* from 1987 to 1991, which was oftentimes devoted to Chicano history.

31
Adolfo Gomez interview.

32
El Gallo, July 1968, 3.

33
Vigil, *The Crusade for Justice*, 165.

34
Rodolfo A. Anaya and Francisco Lomeli, eds., *Aztlán: Essays on the Chicano Homeland* (Albuquerque: Uni-

versity of New Mexico Press, 1989), 1-5.

35
Ibid., 1.

36
Ibid., 2.

37
Rodolfo A. Anaya, "Aztlán: A Homeland Without Boundaries," Anaya and Lomeli, *Aztlán: Essays on the Chicano Homeland*, 236-41. Gómez-Quiñones, *Chicano Politics*, 124, asserts that the plan's "incomplete analysis" allowed later writers to strip the document of its "radical element . . . reducing the concept of Aztlán to a psychological ploy, and limiting advocacy for self-determination to local community control."

38
Waldo Benavidez speech to Univeristy of Denver Graduate School. Juan Haro, *Ultimate Betrayal* (Pittsburgh: Dorrance Publishing Co., 1998), 45. Haro complains that anyone who took a job with the city, county, or state was considered a sell-out by Corky.

39
Quoted in Vigil, *The Crusade for Justice*, 27.

40
Gonzales, *I Am Joaquin*, 9.

41
Alurista, "El Plan Espiritual de Aztlán," Anaya and Lomeli, *Aztlán*, 2.

42
This relationship was described in interviews with Lyle Kyle, Celina Benavidez, and Waldo Benavidez.

43
Quoted in Ron Wolf, "The Benavidez

Case, Part One," *Straight Creek Journal*, July 16, 1974, 1.

44
Jerry Garcia claims that the Crusade took on a role of public leadership in the news media during the protests at West High School in the spring of 1969 known as "The Blow Out." He asserts, however, that this role was tenuous and that the Crusade was still considered a group of outsiders.

45
Jerry Garcia interview.

46
Claim was made by Jerry Garcia.

47
Adolfo Gomez interview.

48
Jerry Garcia, Adolfo Gomez, Juanita Herrera and Virginia Castro interviews.

49
Ron Wolf, "The Benavidez Case, Part One," 1.

50
Ibid.

51
Ibid.

52
Jack Lang y Marquez, interview by the author, tape recording, Denver, CO, 4 February, 1992.

53
Waldo Benavidez interview.

54
Anonymous, interview by the author, tape recording, Denver, CO, 10 March, 1996. Informant was well connected with La Escuela de Aztlán.

55
Ibid.

56
Ron Wolf, *Straight Creek Journal*, July 23, 1974, 1. Also anonymous interview.

57
Jerry Garcia interview.

58
Waldo Benavidez interview.

59
This information represents a compilation of several articles, including George Lane, "Fracas 'Personal Dispute,'" *Denver Post*, July 6, 1973, 2; "Rep. Benavidez held; 2 shot in later fray," *Rocky Mountain News*, July 6, 1973, 10; and Ron Wolf, *Straight Creek Journal*, July 23, 1974, 1. Adolfo Gomez discussed the firing of Juan Archilla and Willie Montoya in his interview.

60
Quoted in Ron Wolf, *Straight Creek Journal*, July 23, 1974, 1.

61
Quoted in *Rocky Mountain News*, July 6, 1973, 10.

62
Denver Post, July 6, 1973, 2; *Rocky Mountain News*, July 6, 1973, 10; *Straight Creek Journal*, July 23, 1974, 1.

63
Straight Creek Journal, July 23, 1974, 1.

64
Rocky Mountain News July 6, 1973, 10; *Straight Creek Journal*, July 23, 1974, 1.

65
Andy Lovato interview. Also the *Straight Creek Journal*, July 23, 1974, 1.

66
Cecelia Garcia interview.

67
Ibid.

68
Ibid.

69
Celina Benavidez interview.

70
Pete Reyes, interview by the author, tape recording, Denver, CO, 22 June, 1994. Reyes was president of the CU Boulder UMAS chapter in the early '70s.

71
Ernesto Vigil, *The Crusade for Justice*, 190.

72
Santiago Valdez, "Este," a poem in Spanish translated by Francisco Sisneros and Anthony Sisneros in the introduction to Anthony Sisneros's "The DiManna Recall," Master's thesis, University of Colorado, Boulder, 1975. Available at Norlin Library, University of Colorado, Boulder.

73
"Granado Trial in Third Day," *Denver Post*, November 13, 1972, 2.

74
Pete Reyes interview. This is confirmed in Ernesto Vigil, *The Crusade for Justice*, 188.

75
Straight Creek Journal, July 23, 1974, 1.

76
Ibid.

77
Ibid.

78
Ibid.

79
Ibid.

80
Rocky Mountain News, July 6, 1973, 1.

81
Celina Benavidez interview.

82
Virginia Castro interview.

83
Celina Benavidez interview.

84
Harry Gessing and Jane Cracraft, "Three Men Killed, 1 Hurt by Second Blast in Boulder," *Denver Post*, May 30, 1974, 1.

85
Twenty years after the bombings, newspaper articles still wrote about the controversies spurred by speculations about the incidents. *La Voz*, for instance, carried an article entitled "Mexican Americans Commemorate Bombings that Claimed 6," May 18, 1994, 3. The *Rocky Mountain News* ran an article, "Old questions pop up on CU bombings," May 5, 1994, 43.

86
El Gallo, July 1973, 4.

87
Jerry Garcia interview.

88
Waldo Benavidez claims in his interview that he went to talk to Corky over dinner in a meeting set up by Father

Torres. Instead of the expected spaghetti dinner, he received a fierce beating from the former professional boxer. Juan Haro described the same incident, to which he was a witness, in his book, *The Ultimate Betrayal*.

Chapter 8

1
Gary Gerhardt, "Coalition Dismantling Considered After Fray," *Rocky Mountain News*, July 7, 1973, 13.

2
Don Schierling and Jerry Garcia interviews.

3
Virginia Castro interview.

4
Waldo Benavidez interview.

5
Jane Earle, "Rep. Benavidez, Family, Flee Home," *Denver Post*, June 20, 1974, 1. See also Jane Earle, "Flight of Benavidezes, Protest Tied to Events," *Denver Post*, June 23, 1974, 34; and interviews with Jerry Garcia, Adolfo Gomez, and Waldo Benavidez.

6
Waldo Benavidez and Adolfo Gomez interviews.

7
Waldo Benavidez interview.

8
Jerry Garcia and Adolfo Gomez interviews.

9
Jerry Garcia interview

10
Waldo Benavidez interview.

11
Ibid.

12
Jane Earle, "Rep. Benavidez, Family, Flee W. Denver Home", *Denver Post*, June 20, 1974, 28.

13
Cecilia Garcia interview.

14
Cecilia Garcia interview.

15
This view was expressed most strongly in the interview with Virginia Castro.

16
Waldo Benavidez interview.

17
Waldo Benavidez interview. See also Ron Wolf, "The Benavidez Case, Part Two," *Straight Creek Journal*, July 23, 1974, 1.

18
Interviews with Adolfo Gomez and Craig Hart. See also *Denver Post*, June 23, 1974, 34, and *Straight Creek Journal*, July 23, 1974, 1

19
Waldo Benavidez interview.

20
Jane Earle, *Denver Post*, June 20, 1974, 1.

21
Ron Wolf, *Straight Creek Journal*, July 23, 1974, 1. See also interviews with Jerry Garcia and Adolfo Gomez.

22
Jerry Garcia interview.

23
Jane Earle, *Denver Post*, June 23, 1974,

34. Also see Ron Wolf, *Straight Creek Journal*, July 23, 1974, 1; and interview with Virginia Castro.

24
Virginia Castro interview.

25
Ron Wolf, "The Benavidez Case, Part One," *Straight Creek Journal*, July 16, 1974, 1.

26
Ron Wolf, *Straight Creek Journal*, July 23, 1974, 1.

27
Adolfo Gomez and Virginia Castro interviews.

28
Ron Wolf, *Straight Creek Journal*, July 23, 1974, 1.

29
Virginia Castro interview.

30
Ron Wolf, *Straight Creek Journal*, July 23, 1974, 1. Also, interviews with Jerry Garcia and Adolfo Gomez.

31
Jerry Garcia interview.

32
Jane Earle, *Denver Post*, June 23, 1974, 34.

33
Rich Castro's estimate in *Straight Creek Journal*, July 23, 1974, 1.

34
Jerry Garcia interview.

35
Virginia Castro interview.

36
Ron Wolf, *Straight Creek Journal*, July

23, 1974, 1.

37
Adolfo Gomez interview.

38
Jane Earle, *Denver Post*, June 20, 1974, 1.

39
Jerry Garcia interview.

40
Jane Earle, *Denver Post*, June 20, 1974, 1.

41
Jerry Garcia interview.

42
Waldo Benavidez interview.

43
Jerry Garcia interview.

44
Ron Wolf, *Straight Creek Journal*, July 16, 1974, 1.

45
Roger Medina interview.

46
Earle, *Denver Post*, June 23, 1974, 34.

47
Manuel Martinez interview.

48
Election Commission, City and County of Denver, Rocky Rushing, Information Management Director.

Chapter 9

1
Lyle Kyle, interview by the author, tape recording, Denver, CO, 5 June, 1992.

2
Lyle Kyle interview.

3
Charles Vigil, *The Hispanic Contributions to the State of Colorado*, quoted in Rich Castro's column, "Early Hispanic Contributions to State Government," *La Voz*, August 1988.

4
Ruben Valdez interview.

5
Lyle Kyle interview.

6
Ibid.

7
Ruben Valdez interview. See also "Valdez Serves His Colleagues Ribbon-Flavored Hot Peppers," *Denver Post*, January 29, 1971, 4.

8
Don Sandoval interview.

9
Richard Castro, "Early Hispanic Contributions to State Government," *La Voz*, August 1988.

10
Lyle Kyle interview.

11
Ruben Valdez interview.

12
Paul Sandoval interview.

13
Ruben Valdez interview.

14
Carl Hilliard, "'Minority' legislator really works at his job," *Denver Post*, undated clipping from Richard Castro's files written just prior to Castro's de-

parture from House of Representatives in 1983.

15
Don Sandoval, Paul Sandoval, and Ruben Valdez interviews.

16
Don Sandoval interview.

17
Richard Castro, "Early Hispanic Contributions to State Government," *La Voz*, August 1988.

18
Rocky Mountain News, January 23, 1995, 4N.

19
Lyle Kyle interview.

20
"Apportionment Plans Are Voided in Colorado and 5 Other States," *Rocky Mountain News*, June 16, 1964, 3. Also, Calvin B. T. Lee, *One Man One Vote: WMCA and the Struggle for Equal Representation* (New York: Charles Scribner's Sons, 1967), 96-8.

21
Lyle Kyle interview.

22
Ibid.

23
Waldo Benavidez interview.

24
Lyle Kyle interview.

25
Andy Lovato interview.

26
Paul Sandoval interview.

27
Don Sandoval interview.

28
Paul Sandoval interview.

29
Roger Medina interview.

30
Jack Lang y Marquez interview.

31
Steiner, *La Raza*, 209.

32
Jeffrey Kobrick, "The Compelling Case for Bilingual Education," Earle J. Ogletree and David Garcia, eds., *Education of the Spanish Speaking Child* (Springfield, IL: Charles C. Thomas Publisher, 1975), 350.

33
Ibid., 354.

34
Herschel T. Manuel, *Spanish-Speaking Children of the Southwest: Their Education and the Public Welfare* (Austin: University of Texas Press, 1965), 119.

35
Kobrick, "The Compelling Case for Bilingual Education," 349.

36
Dr. Diego Castellanos with Pamela Leggio, New Jersey State Department of Education, Trenton, New Jersey, 1983, 66.

37
Ogletree and Garcia, *Education of the Spanish Speaking Child*, 335.

38
Castellanos, 81.

39
Ibid., 83.

40
Denver Post, June 4, 1977, 30. Also, interview with Paul Sandoval.

41
Lau vs. Nichols, 414 US563, 39 L. Ed. 2d 1 (1974).

42
Castellanos, 115-17.

43
Paul Sandoval interview.

44
Ibid.

45
Ibid.

46
Denver Post, March 13, 1977, 3.

47
Lyle Kyle interview.

48
Ruben Valdez interview.

49
Don Sandoval interview.

50
Rocky Mountain News, March 18, 1977, 8.

51
Ibid., 8.

52
Paul Sandoval interview.

53
Denver Post, January 28, 1977, 16.

54
Ibid., 16.

55
Denver Post, January 14, 1977, 2.

56
Denver Post, January 28, 1977, 16.

57
Denver Post, March 23, 1979, 18.

58
"Hispano Legislators in for Major Test of Power," *Denver Post*, March 13, 1977, 3.

59
Jorge Amselle, *Center for Equal Opportunity*, monograph based on conference held by Center for Equal Opportunity, September 18, 1995, on Capitol Hill. Center for Equal Opportunity, 815 15th Street NW, Suite 928, Washington, D.C.

60
Dan Bell, "Hispanos Victims of Discrimination, Report Charges, *Rocky Mountain News*, May 29, 1970, 5.

61
Rocky Mountain News, May 31, 1977, 6. Also see Jane Hulse, "Legislature Loses Ruling in Hiring Flap," *Rocky Mountain News*, May 19, 1982, 52.

62
Rocky Mountain News, May 1, 1982, 52.

63
John Sanko, "Affirmative Action Plan Given Emergency OK," *Rocky Mountain News*, July 29, 1987, 6.

64
Paul Sandoval interview.

65
Ibid.

66
Richard Castro, "Hispanics win Gerry-

mandering Ruling," *Colorado Statesman,* June 29, 1990, 6.

67
Richard Castro, "Reapportionment: The Key Issue for Hispanics in 1991 and Beyond," *La Voz,* December 26, 1990, 5.

68
Pete Reyes interview.

69
Ibid.

70
Charles Roos, "District Map Is Heading for Court Test, *Rocky Mountain News,* March 10, 1982, 8.

71
Sharon Sherman, "Court Requires Explanation on Reapportioning," *Denver Post,* March 9, 1982, 1.

72
Denver Post, undated, from an article in Richard Castro's files.

73
Sharon Sherman, *Denver Post,* March 9, 1982, 1.

74
Richard Castro, *La Voz,* December 26, 1990, 5. See also *Colorado Democrat,* vol. 1, no. 3, and Richard Castro, *Colorado Statesman,* June 29, 1990, 6.

75
Denver Post, May 2, 1989, 1.

76
Colorado Statesman, July 10, 1987, 6.

77
Ibid., 6.

78
Hilliard, "'Minority' legislator really works at his job," *Denver Post.*

79
Wayne Knox, interview by the author, tape recording, Denver, CO, 13 March, 1998.

80
Don Sandoval interview.

81
Nolbert Chávez, speech at the University of Denver, April 13, 1997.

82
Nick Frangos, interview by the author, tape recording, Denver, CO, May 1994.

83
Lyle Kyle interview.

Chapter 10

1
Richard Douglas Lamm, *Current Biography Yearbook 46,* May 1985, 239.

2
Ibid., 240.

3
Charles Roos, "Lamm Carries Plea to Rural Voters," *Denver Post,* September 22, 1974, 53.

4
Joan White, "Lamm Says Chicanos 'Qualified,'" *Denver Post,* November 1, 1974, 19.

5
Ibid.

6
Ibid.

7
Charles Roos, "Lamm Makes Cabinet Selections," *Denver Post*, January 11, 1975, 3.

8
Ibid.

9
Todd Engdahl, "Lamm-Chicano Rift Simmers," *Denver Post*, September 30, 1977, 2.

10
Todd Engdahl, "Group Hits Way Chicano-Held Job Filled," *Denver Post*, September 29, 1977, 2.

11
Rocky Mountain News, September 30, 1977, 4.

12
Ibid.

13
Jonathan Dedmon, "Klapper Appointment Irks Chicanos," *Rocky Mountain News*, September 30, 1977, 5.

14
Ibid.

15
Ibid.

16
Ibid.

17
Denver Magazine, May 1981, 66-8. See also Tim McGovern, "Lamm Has Fellow Dems Fuming," *Rocky Mountain News*, May 11, 1981, 4.

18
Paul Sandoval interview.

19
Tim McGovern, *Rocky Mountain News*, May 11, 1981, 4.

20
Richard Lamm, interview by the author, tape recording, Denver, CO, 14 July, 1997. Since 1987, ex-Governor Lamm had been director of the Center for Public Policy and Contemporary Issues.

21
Paul Sandoval interview.

22
Jody Strogoff, "The Rocky Relationship Between Lamm and Chicanos," *Colorado Statesman*, January 15, 1982, 1.

23
Paul Sandoval interview. See also "Chicano Group Drops Lamm for 82," *Denver Post*, June 1, 1981. Pete Reyes is quoted here: "The only conclusion we can come to is that he abandoned the principles of the Democratic Party."

24
Richard Lamm interview.

25
Ibid.

26
Paul Sandoval interview.

27
Richard Lamm interview

28
James S. Kunen, "Richard Lamm," *People Weekly*, January 20, 1986, 46.

29
Ibid.

30
Joan Lowy, "Lamm Says Hispanic As-

similation Essential to Avert 'Deadly Disunity,'" *Rocky Mountain News*, May 30, 1986, 38.

31
Richard D. Lamm and Gary Imhoff, *Immigration Time Bomb: The Fragmenting of America* (New York: Truman Talley Books, 1985), 1.

32
David Gutierrez, *Walls and Mirrors: Mexican Americans, Mexican Immigrants, and the Politics of Ethnicity* (Berkeley: University of California Press, 1995), 3.

33
Mario T. Garcia, *Memories of Chicano History: The Life and Narrative of Bert Corona* (Berkeley: University of California Press, 1994), 249.

34
Lamm and Imhoff, 29.

35
Ibid., 77.

36
Ibid., 78. Also see 83 and 94.

37
Ibid., 99.

38
"Debate Made into Mockery," *Rocky Mountain News*, June 3, 1986, 32.

39
Videotaped copy of debate between Richard Lamm and Richard Castro at Radisson Hotel, recorded by Mountain Bell Corporate Public Relations, Denver, July 1986, Virginia Castro's personal collection.

40
Ibid.

41
All of the above quotes from both Lamm and Castro were taken from the videotape of the June 1986 debate.

42
Mario T. Garcia, 73. See also Rodolfo Acuña, *A Mexican American Chronicle*, (New York: American Book Company, 1971), 118.

43
Acuña, 127-28.

44
Debate videotape.

45
Lamm and Imhoff, 96.

46
Debate videotape.

47
Lamm and Imhoff, 93.

48
Ibid., 93.

49
E. J. Hobsbawm, *Nations and Nationalism Since 1780* (Cambridge: Cambridge University Press, 1990), 5, 20, and 40. Hobsbawm traces some of these characteristics back to John Stuart Mill in the eighteenth century, but maintains that the twentieth century brand of nationalism was defined by Lenin, Wilson, and even Stalin.

50
Gutierrez, 118 and 274.

51
Debate videotape.

52
Constance Johnson, "Hispanics to Seek

Ban on Lamm Book," *Rocky Mountain News*, July 17, 1986, 8.

53
Gutierrez, 200-202.

54
Constance Johnson, *Rocky Mountain News*, July 17, 1986, 8.

55
Debate videotape.

Chapter 11

1
Leonard and Noel, *Mining Camp to Metropolis*, 403.
2
Ruben Valdez interview.

3
Bill Walker, "Peña: JFK Inspired His Vision of the Future," *Denver Post*, June 12, 1983, 10A.

4
Bill Walker, "Victory Is Called Milestone," *Denver Post*, June 23, 1983, 1A and 12A.

5
Bill Walker, "Peña: JFK Inspired His Vision of Future," *Denver Post*, June 12, 1983, 10A.

6
Denver Post, May 19, 1983, 1B.

7
Dale Tooley, *I'd Rather Be in Denver: Dale Tooley's Own Story* (Denver: Colorado Legal Publishing Co., 1985), 54-5. See also Diana Griego, "Hispanic Fervor for Peña on Wane," *Denver Post*, March 15, 1987, 1B. For a statistical analysis of Peña's dependence on the minority vote, see Rodney E. Hero and

Kathleen M. Beatty, "The Elections for Federico Peña as Mayor of Denver: Analysis and Implications," *Social Science Quarterly*, vol. 70, no. 2, June 1989, University of Texas Press, 301 and 304.

8
Diana Griego, *Denver Post*, March 15, 1983, 1B.

9
Tom Gougeon, interview by the author, tape recording, Denver, CO, 3 June, 1998.

10
Walker, *Denver Post*, June 12, 1983, 10A.

11
Ibid. Peña's quote contains the inaccuracy that John Adams represented British soldiers after the Revolution. He was obviously referring to Adams's role in defending the soldiers in the Boston Massacre that happened five years before the Revolution.

12
Ibid. Paul Sandoval also spoke of Peña's role in this regard in his interview with the author. Also see Jane Earle, "The Story of the Chicano Education Project," *Today's Education*, November/December 1977, 76-7.

13
Rocky Mountain News, June 14, 1983, 16.

14
Federico Peña, interview by the author, tape recording, Denver, CO, 8 August, 1997.

15
When Ruben Valdez ran for Lieutenant Governor in 1979, Peña was elected to replace his vacant seat on the North Side.

16
Peña interview.

17
Rocky Mountain News, June 14, 1983, 16.

18
Interviews with Nick Frangos and Don Sandoval.

19
Wayne Knox interview.

20
Ibid.

21
Paul Sandoval interview.

22
Lyle Kyle interview.

23
Wayne Knox interview.

24
Peña interview. Upon losing his position, Representative Kirscht quit the Democratic Party in disgust and joined the Republicans.

25
Tom Gougeon interview.

26
Leonard and Noel, 478.

27
George V. Kelly, *The Old Gray Mayors* (Boulder: Pruett Publishing Company, 1974), 53. Also see Leonard and Noel, 371.

28
Rykken Johnson, "Hispanic Group Plans Further Police Probe," *Rocky Mountain News*, May 11, 1970, 8.

29
George Lane, "Garcia Tells of His Ouster," *Denver Post*, May 24, 1970, 2.

30
Ibid.

31
Ibid.

32
"Cisneros, Atencio Resign Positions," *Rocky Mountain News*, May 28, 1970, 21.

33
Ibid.

34
Vickie Calvillo, interview by the author, tape recording, Denver, CO, 17 September, 1997.

35
Jack Lang y Marquez and Ruben Valdez interviews.

36
Paul Sandoval interview.

37
Steve Newman, interview by the author, tape recording, Denver, CO, 23 June, 1997.

38
Neil Westergaard, "Peña expected to name Castro as Community Relations Chief," *Denver Post*, September 23, 1983, 1.

39
Vickie Calvillo interview.

40
JJ Albi, "Community Relations Are Castro's Concern," *La Voz*, July 11, 1984, 3.

41
Paul Sandoval interview.

42
Don Sandoval interview.

43
Paul Sandoval interview.

44
Federico Peña interview.

45
Ibid.

46
Tom Gougeon interview.

47
Vickie Calvillo interview.

48
Kevin Flyn, "Neighbors Resolved to Reclaim Curtis Park," *Rocky Mountain News*, May 24, 1987, 10.

49
Paul Hutchinson, "Residents Want Their Park Back," *Denver Post*, June 24, 1986, 1.

50
Ibid.

51
Renate Robey, "Curtis Park Labeled Police State," *Denver Post*, August 19, 1986, 3b.

52
Gary Gerhart, "Curtis Park Group Blasts 'Police State,'" *Rocky Mountain News*, August 19, 1986, 6.

53
See for example Andrew Schlesinger, "Council Strengthens Police Commission Bill," *Rocky Mountain News*, June 27, 1978.

54
Federico Peña interview.

55
Renate Robey, "Curtis Park Labeled Police State," 3b.

56
Kevin Flyn, "Neighbors Resolved to Reclaim Curtis Park," 10.

Chapter 12

1
Bill Briggs, "One Person to Enforce Anti-Bias Law," *Denver Post*, October 21, 1991, 1c.

2
Ann Carnahan, "Students Face Harassment," *Rocky Mountain News*, October 22, 1990, 7.

3
Brian Weber, "Plan Seeks to Ban Gay Bias," *Rocky Mountain News*, September 10, 1991, 11.

4
Suzanne Weiss, "Peña Backs Gays Over Parade," *Rocky Mountain News*, March 10, 1984, 1.

5
See for example, Thaddeus Herrick, "Gay Activists Face Resistance from Blacks and Hispanics," *Rocky Mountain News*, January 25, 1993: "To be perceived as gay is to be going against Mexican culture," said Gary de Herrera, spokesman for La Gente Politica, a Hispanic homosexual rights organization.

6
J. R. Moehringer, "Homosexuals Say Foes Have Politicized Gay Community," *Rocky Mountain News*, May 15, 1991, 30.

7
Ann Carnahan, "This Nation in Battle for its Soul," *Rocky Mountain News*, May 15, 1991, 30.

8
Renate Robey, "Voters Reaffirm Civil Rights for Gays," *Denver Post*, May 22, 1991, 1.

9
Federico Peña interview.

10
Rich Castro, "Archbishop Oscar Romero," *The Statesman*, March 3, 1983, 8.

11
Harv Bishop, "Refugees Are Facing a 'Choice of Evils,'" *Denver Catholic Register*, October 19, 1988, 4.

12
Rich Castro, "Archbishop Oscar Romero," *The Colorado Statesman*, March 3, 1983, 8.

13
Rich Castro, "Romero: Human Rights Champion," *La Voz*, November 8, 1989, 5.

14
Rich Castro, "Secretary Schultz, Red Baiting Won't Work," *The Colorado Statesman*, May 10, 1985, 4.

15
Federico Peña interview.

16
Joseph B. Verrengia, "Leader Under Heavy Scrutiny During Whirlwind Denver Visit," *Rocky Mountain News*, August 1, 1986, 36.

17
John Sanko and Mike Anton, "Ortega's Visit Seen as Image Polishing," *Rocky Mountain News*, July 31, 1986, 30.

18
Quoted in "Say It In English," *Time*, February 20, 1989, 22.

19
Ibid.

20
Karen MacPherson, "Storm Growing Over English Only Bill," *Rocky Mountain News*, February 1, 1987, 12.

21
James G. Wright, "Hispanic Leaders Criticize Language Bill," *Rocky Mountain News*, December 31, 1986, 6.

22
This was part of a Rich Castro scrapbook provided to the author by Virginia Castro.

23
Berny Morson, "English Only Bill Has Sinister Tone, Castro Says," *Rocky Mountain News*, January 10, 1987, 40.

24
Rich Castro, "Supporters of English Only Bill Are Confused," *The Colorado Statesman*, February 27, 1987, 8.

25
Maria Montelibre, "Colorado Hispanics United Against English Only Bill," *La Voz*, January 14, 1987, 1.

26
Rich Castro, "The English Only Initiative is a Chocolate Covered Lemon," *The Colorado Statesman*, November 27, 1987, 5.

27
Rich Castro, "Ethnic Pluralism Is an American Tradition," letter to the editor, *Denver Post*, November 27, 1986.

28
John Sanko, "Governor-Elect Romer

Pledges He'll Veto English-Only Bill, *Rocky Mountain News*, January 8, 1987, 6.

29
Sue Lindsay, "Official-English Battle Back in Courts," *Rocky Mountain News*, November 10, 1988, 28.

30
Jennifer Gavin, "Peña Outlaws Bias Based on Language," *Denver Post*, December 28, 1988, 1.

31
Tomás Romero, "Go Forth into the Sunshine, My Friend," *Denver Post*, June 26, 1991, 9B.

32
Brian Weber, "Looking Back, Peña Sees a Dual Legacy," *Rocky Mountain News*, November 20, 1993, 21.

33
Rich Castro, address to the Second Annual Awards Banquet of FIRE, the organization of Hispanic firefighters, December 4, 1987.

34
Tom Gougeon interview.

35
Rich Castro's address to FIRE, 6-7. Undated internal newsletter of Denver Fire Department. Part of Virginia Castro's personal collection.

36
Doug Linkhart, "Peña's Legacy Bringing People into the Process," *La Voz*, December 5, 1990, 5.

37
Michelle Fulcher: "Peña Legacy: Is the City Greater?" *Denver Post*, June 23, 1991, 1A.

38
Diane Giacomo Peck, ed., *Poverty in Denver: Facing the Facts, Key Findings and Recommendations* (Denver: Piton Foundation, 1994), 6.

39
Ibid., Piton Data Profile, 15.

40
Brian Weber, "Looking Back, Peña Sees a Dual Legacy," *Rocky Mountain News*.

41
Tom Gougeon interview.

42
Diana Griego, "Hispanic Fervor for Peña on the Wane," *Denver Post*, March 15, 1987.

43
James G. Wright, "Firing Infuriates Hispanics," *Rocky Mountain News*, June 18, 1988, 11.

44
Ibid.

45
Paul Sandoval interview. Also see Gary Delsohn, "Four Peña Advisors Are Backbone of Denver's New Administration," *Denver Post*, September 15, 1983, 1A.

46
Diana Griego, "Hispanic Fervor for Peña on the Wane," *Denver Post*, March 15, 1987.

47
Ibid.

48
Federico Peña interview.

49
Janet Bingham, "Three Newcomers

Win Denver School Board Seats, Mauro Edges Castro," *Denver Post*, May 17, 1989, 1A.

50
Janet Bingham, "Vote Low in Castro Bastion," *Denver Post*, May, 1989, 1B.

51
Tomás Romero, "How to Go From Being Deciders to Being Petitioners in One Easy Lesson," *Denver Post*, May 18, 1989.

Chapter 13

1
Robert Jackson, "Davis Numbed by Castro Stroke," *Rocky Mountain News*, April 13, 1991, 8.

2
Ken Maestas interview.

3
Robert Jackson, "2000 Bid Farewell to Rich Castro," *Rocky Mountain News*, April 18, 1991, 6.

4
"Vaya Con Dios, Ricardo," editorial, *Denver Post*, April 16, 1991, 6B.

5
Rocky Mountain News, April 16, 1991, 31.

6
Tomás Romero, "Rich Castro, Singer of Psalms of Peace," *Denver Post*, April 17, 1991, 9B.

7
Don Sandoval interview.

8
Gary Massaro, "Hundreds Mourn Castro's Death," *Rocky Mountain News*, April 15, 1991, 7.

9
Robert Jackson, "2000 Bid Farewell to Rich Castro," *Rocky Mountain News*.

10
Cindy Parmenter, "Still Doing 'People' Things, But the Pay Is Better," *Denver Post*, March 3, 1985.

11
Cecelia Garcia interview.

12
1990 Census of Population, Social and Economic Characteristics, Colorado, "Income in 1989 of Households, Families, and Persons by Race and Hispanic Origin, issued 9/93 by U.S. Department of Commerce Economics and Statistics Administration," 122. Figures for 1970 obtained from *1970 Census of Population, Characteristics of the Population/ Colorado*, v. 1, part 7, issued by U.S. Department of Commerce, "Poverty Status in 1969 of Families by Family Income, Persons of Spanish Language or Spanish Surname," 771.

Bibliography
Primary Sources

Interviews

Bankson, Eileen, interview by the author, 20 June, 1993, La Veta, CO, tape recording.

Beall, Levi, interview by the author, 2 December, 1992, Denver, CO, tape recording.

Benavidez, Celina, interview by the author, 9 July, 1995, Denver, CO, tape recording.

Benavidez, Waldo, interview by the author, 12 July, 1995, Denver, CO, tape recording.

Byorick, Ed, interview by the author, 7 July, 1994, telephone, tape recording.

Calvillo, Vickie, interview by the author, 17 September, 1997, Denver, CO, tape recording.

Castro, Archie, interview by the author, 10 June, 1993, Denver, CO, tape recording.

Castro, Gaspar, interview by the author, 9 August, 1993, tape recording.

Castro, Virginia, interview by the author, 23 March, 1992, Denver, CO, tape recording.

Chávez, Everett, interview by the author, 7 August, 1993, telephone, tape recording.

Federico, Bobby, interview by the author, Denver, CO, 9 December, 1992, tape recording.

Galvin, Jack, interview by the author, 14 December, 1994, telephone, tape recording.

Garcia, Cecilia, interview by the author, Denver, CO, 9 July, 1995, tape recording.

Garcia, Jerry, interview by the author, Denver, CO, 22, February, 1996, tape recording.

Gómez, Adolfo, interview by the author, Denver, CO, 3 February, 1992, tape recording.

Gougeon, Tom, interview by the author, Denver, CO, 3 June, 1998, tape recording.

Hart, Craig, interview by the author, Denver, CO, 10 June, 1993, tape recording.

Herrera, Alfredo and Juanita, interview by the author, Denver, CO, 25 March 25 1992, tape recording.

Herrera, Lupe, interview by the author, Denver, CO, 13 March, 1992, tape recording.

Kyle, Lyle, interview by the author, Denver, CO, 5 June, 1992, tape recording.

Lamm, Richard D., interview by the author, Denver, CO, 14 July, 1997, tape recording.

Lang y Marquez, Jack, interview by the author, Denver, CO, 4 February, 1992, tape recording.

Liebert, Alberta, interview by the author, Denver, CO, 23 March, 1995, tape recording.

Lopez, Anthony, interview by the author, Denver, CO, 1 February, 1993, tape recording.

Lovato, Andy, interview by the author, Golden, CO, 3 December, 1992, tape recording.

Maestas, Ken, interview by the author, Denver, CO, 3 April, 1993, tape recording.

Mares, Eloy, interview by the author, Denver, CO, 7 July, 1993, tape recording.

Martinez, Emmanuel, interview by the author, Morrison, CO, 27 June, 1994, tape recording.

Martinez, Manuel, interview by the author, Denver, CO, 13 June, 1993, tape recording.

Medina, Roger, interview by the author, Denver, CO, 13 April, 1993, tape recording.

Newman, Steve, interview by the author, Denver, CO, 23 June, 1997, tape recording.

Pacheco, Normando, interview by the author, Denver, CO, 28 June, 1993, tape recording.

Peña, Federico, interview by the author, 8 August, 1997, telephone, tape recording.

Phillips, Dr. Kenneth, interview by the author, 5 October, 1999, telephone, tape recording.

Reyes, Pete, interview by the author, Denver, CO, 22 June, 1994, tape recording.

Sanchez, Rose Ann, interview by the author, Denver, CO, 14 June, 1993, tape recording.

Sandoval, Dr. David, interview by the author, Pueblo, CO, 26 June, 1995, tape recording.

Sandoval, Don, interview by the author, Denver, CO, 6 May, 1994, tape recording.

Sandoval, Joe, interview by the author, Denver, CO, 2 November, 1992, tape recording.

Sandoval, Paul, interview by the author, Denver, CO, 12 May, 1994, tape recording.

Schierling, Don, interview by the author, Denver, CO, 10 March, 1992, tape recording.

Smith, Dave, interview by the author, Denver, CO, 2 July, 1993, tape recording.

Starr, Lena, interview by the author, 15 August, 1993, telephone, tape recording.

Toliver, Brenda, interview by the author, Denver, CO, 29 October, 1997, tape recording.

Valdez, Ruben, interview by the author, Denver, CO, 6, June, 1994, tape recording.

Veladez, Ricardo, interview by the author, Denver, CO, 8 March, 1993, tape recording.

Periodicals

Colorado Democrat
Colorado Heritage
The Colorado Statesman
Denver Catholic Register
Denver Magazine

The Denver Post
El Gallo (newspaper of the Crusade for Justice)
The Paper (Metropolitan State College's student newspaper in the 1970s)
Rocky Mountain News
Straight Creek Journal
Today's Education
La Voz

Secondary Sources
Books

Acuña, Rodolfo F. *Anything but Mexican: Chicanos in Contemporary Los Angeles.* New York: Verso, 1996.

Acuña, Rodolfo F. *A Mexican American Chronicle.* New York: American Book Company, 1971.

Acuña, Rodolfo F. *Occupied America: The Chicano's Struggle Toward Liberation.* San Francisco: Canfield Press, 1972.

Amselle, Jorge. *The Failure of Bi-Lingual Education*, Center for Equal Opportunity, Monograph based on conference held by Center for Equal Opportunity, September 18, 1995 on Capitol Hill. Center for Equal Opportunity, 815 Fifteenth Street NW, Suite 928, Washington, DC 20005.

Anaya, Rudolfo. *Bless Me, Ultima.* Berkeley: Tonatiuh-Quinto Sol International Publishers, 1972.

Athearn, Frederic J. *Land of Contrast: A History of Southeast Colorado.* Denver: Bureau of Land Management, 1985.

Beshoar, Barron. *Out of the Depths.* Denver: World Press Inc., 1942.

Burciaga, Jose Antonio. *Drink Cultura.* Santa Barbara: Capra Press, 1993.

Carroll, Peter N. *It Seemed Like Nothing Happened: The Tragedy and Promise of America in the 1970s.* New York: Holt, Rinehart, and Winston, 1982.

Castellanos, Dr. Diego, with Pamela Leggio. *The Best of Two Worlds: Bilingual-Bicultural Education in the States.* Trenton: New Jersey State Department of Education, 1983.

Chávez, Fray Angelico. *But Time and Chance: The Story of Padre Martinez of Taos*. Santa Fe: Sunstone Press, 1981.

Chávez, Fray Angelico. *My Penitente Land*. Albuquerque: University of New Mexico Press, 1974.

Chávez, Fray Angelico. *Origins of New Mexico Families: A Genealogy of the Spanish Colonial Period*. Albuquerque: Museum of New Mexico Press, 1992.

de la Garza, Rodolfo O., Martha Menchaca, and Louis DeSipio, eds. *Barrio Ballots: Latino Politics in the 1990 Elections*. Boulder: Westview Press, 1994.

Deutsch, Sarah. *No Separate Refuge*. New York: Oxford University Press, 1987.

Fanon, Frantz. *The Wretched of the Earth: The Handbook for the Black Revolution That Is Changing the Shape of the World*. New York: Grove Press, 1968.

Fergusson, Erna. *New Mexico: A Pageant of Three Peoples*. New York: Alfred A. Knopf, 1951.

Finks, P. David. *The Radical Vision of Saul Alinsky*. New York: Paulist Press, 1984.

Garcia, Jorge J. E. *Hispanic/Latino Identity: A Philosophical Perspective*. Malden, MA: Blackwell Publishers, 2000.

García, Mario T. *Memories of Chicano History: The Life and Narrative of Bert Corona*. Berkeley: University of California Press, 1994.

Gonzales, Rodolfo. *I Am Joaquin: An Epic Poem*, New York: Bantam Books, 1967.

Gutiérrez, David G. *Walls and Mirrors: Mexican Americans, Mexican Immigrants, and the Politics of Ethnicity*. Berkeley: University of California Press, 1995.

Halberstam, David. *The Fifties*. New York: Villard Books, 1993.

Hammerback, John C., Richard J. Jensen, and Jose Angel Gutierrez. *A War of Words: Chicano Protest in the 1960s and 1970s*. Westport, CT: Greenwood Press, 1985.

Haro, Juan. *The Ultimate Betrayal*. Pittsburgh: Dorrance Publishing Co. Inc., 1998.

Hobsbawm, E. J. *Nations and Nationalism since 1780*. Cambridge: Cambridge University Press, 1990.

Ignatiev, Noel. *How the Irish Became White*. New York: Routledge, 1995.

Imhoff, Gary, ed. *Learning in Two Languages: From Conflict to Consensus in the Reorganization of Schools*. New Brunswick, NJ: Transaction Publishers, 1990.

Kelly, George V. *The Old Gray Mayors of Denver*. Boulder: Pruett Publishing Company, 1974.

Kessell, John L. *Kiva, Cross, and Crown*. Albuquerque, University of New Mexico Press, 1987.

Lamm, Richard D., and Gary Imhoff. *Immigration Time Bomb: The Fragmenting of America*. New York: Truman Talley Books, 1985.

Larralde, Carlos. *Mexican-American Movements and Leaders*. Los Alamitos, CA: Hwong Publishing Co., 1976.

Lee, Calvin B. T. *One Man One Vote, WMCA and the Struggle for Equal Representation*. New York: Charles Scribner's Sons, 1967.

Leonard, Stephen J., and Thomas J. Noel. *Denver: Mining Camp to Metropolis*. Boulder: University Press of Colorado, 1990.

Manuel, Herschel T. *Spanish-Speaking Children of the Southwest: Their Education and the Public Welfare*. Austin: University of Texas Press, 1965.

Marin, Christine. *A Spokesman of the Mexican American Movement: Rodolfo "Corky"Gonzales and the Fight for Chicano Liberation, 1966–1972*. San Francisco: Robert D. Reed and Adam S. Eterovich, 1977.

McGovern, George, and Leonard Guttridge. *The Great Coalfield War*. Boston: Houghton Mifflin Company, 1972.

McWilliams, Carey. *North from Mexico.* New York: Greenwood Press Publishers, 1968.

Meier, Kenneth J., and Joseph Stewart, Jr. *The Politics of Hispanic Education.* Albany: State University of New York Press, 1991.

Meier, Matthew S., and Feliciano Rivera. *The Chicanos: A History of Mexican Americans.* New York: Hill and Wang, 1972.

Meier, Matthew S., and Feliciano Rivera. *Readings on La Raza: The Twentieth Century.* New York: Hill & Wang, 1974.

Muñoz, Carlos. *Youth, Identity, Power, The Chicano Movement.* London, New York: Verso, 1989.

Noel, Thomas J. *Colorado Catholicism.* Boulder: University Press of Colorado, 1989.

Noel, Thomas J. *Denver's Larimer Street.* Denver: Historic Denver, Inc., 1981.

Nostrand, Richard L. *The Hispano Homeland.* Norman: University of Oklahoma Press, 1992.

Ogletree, Earle J., and David Garcia, eds. *Education of the Spanish-Speaking Urban Child.* Springfield, IL: Charles C. Thomas Publisher, 1975.

Piven, Frances Fox, and Richard A. Cloward. *Poor People's Movements: Why They Succeed, How They Fail.* New York: Vintage Books, 1979.

Quiñones, Juan Gomez. *Chicano Politics: Reality and Promise, 1940–1990.* Albuquerque: University of New Mexico Press, 1990.

Reich, Alice H. *The Cultural Construction of Ethnicity: Chicanos in the University.* New York: AMS Press, Inc, 1989.

Rodriguez, Luis. *Always Running,* New York: Touchstone Press, 1994.

Sanchez, George I. *Forgotten People: A Study of New Mexicans.* Albuquerque: Calvin Horn Publishing, Inc., 1967.

Simmons, Marc. *New Mexico: A History.* New York: W. W. Norton & Co., Inc., 1977.

Sporleder Sr., Louis B. *The Romance of the Spanish Peaks.* Denver: O'Brien Printing, 1960.

Stanley, F. *The Mora, New Mexico Story.* Pep, TX, 1963.

Stanley, F. *The Roy Story.* Nazareth, TX: SFL Crocchiola, 1972.

Steiner, Stan. *La Raza: The Mexican Americans.* New York: Harper and Row Publishers, 1969.

Tooley, Dale. *I'd Rather Be in Denver.* Denver: Colorado Legal Publishing Company, Inc., 1985.

Trattner,Walter. *From Poor Law to Welfare State: A History of Social Welfare in America.* New York: Free Press, 1979.

Twitchell, Ralph Emerson, *Leading Facts of New Mexico History.* Cedar Rapids, IA: Torch Press, 1911–17.

Ubbelohde, Carl. *A Colorado Reader.* Boulder: Pruett Press, 1962.

Valdes y Tapia, Daniel T. *Political History of New Mexico.* unpublished, 1960, available in the Western History Department of the Denver Public Library.

Vigil, Ernesto. *The Crusade for Justice.* Madison: University of Wisconsin Press, 1999.

Vigil, Maurilio. *Chicano Politics.* Washington D.C.: University Press of America, 1978.

Weber, David J. *The Mexican Frontier, 1821–1846.* Albuquerque: University of New Mexico Press, 1982.

Theses and Documents

1970 Census of Population, Characteristics of the Population/Colorado, V 1, Part 7, U.S. Dept. of Commerce, "Poverty Status in 1969 of Families by Family Income, Persons of Spanish Language or Spanish Surname."

1990 Census of Population, Social and Economic Characteristics, Colorado, "Income in 1989 of Households, Families and Persons by Race and

Hispanic Origin," issued 1993 by U.S. Dept. of Commerce, Economics and Statistics Administration.

Castro, Richard. "A Survey of Social Welfare Utilization Patterns in the Auraria Community of Denver," Master's thesis, University of Denver, 1972.

"Declaration of Protective Covenant, University Hills, Inc.," November 3, 1949. Colorado Historical Society.

Denver Planning Office. *The West Side Neighborhood: A Tract Analysis*. December 1972.

Huttinger, Elizabeth Anne. *Citizens' Action in Housing Issues: A Case Study*. Master's thesis. Colorado State University, November 1973.

Peck, Diane Giacomo, ed. *Poverty in Denver: Facing the Facts, Key Findings and Recommendations*. Denver: Piton Foundation, April 1984.

Sisneros, Anthony. "The DiManna Recall." Master's thesis. University of Colorado, 1975.

Walsh, James Patrick. "Young and Latino in a Cold War Barrio: Survival, the Search for Identity and the Formation of Street Gangs in Denver, 1945–1955." Master's thesis, University of Colorado at Denver, 1996.

UMAS by Chicanos. Boulder: UMAS Publications, December, 1970. Loaned to author by Virginia Castro.

Valdes, Daniel T., and Tom Piño. "Majority-Minority Relations." Pamphlet printed by University Park News, Denver, Colorado, 1968. Available at Western History Department, Denver Public Library.

Index

ABOUT THE AUTHOR

Richard Gould has lived in Denver since 1960. Twenty years of teaching high school social studies and sixteen years of driving a Yellow Cab have nurtured in him a fascination for local events and local history. Gould's abiding interest in Hispanic culture first arose when he was trying to learn Spanish in an Arizona federal prison, where he served time for draft resistance during the Vietnam War. Working in a trailer factory near the old Packinghouse district and driving a taxi through the streets of North and West Denver made him acutely aware of the rich ethnic mix that pervades the city of Denver. In the 1990s, Hispanic students at the Alternative High School in Englewood urged Gould to teach courses on Chicano history, which he did for over a decade. Gould currently resides in South Denver with his wife, Susan, and two rowdy high school–aged kids, Sam and Sarah.

COLORADO HISTORICAL SOCIETY